THE SOVIET STATE

A Study of Bolshevik Rule

THE SOVIET STATE

A STUDY OF
BOLSHEVIK RULE

By

BERTRAM W. MAXWELL, Ph. D.

Professor of History and Political Science
Washburn College

Author of "Contemporary Municipal
Government of Germany"

STEVES & WAYBURN
Publishers
TOPEKA, KANSAS

Printed in the United States of America
by F. M. Steves & Sons
Topeka, Kansas

To

M. L. M.

PREFACE

This study is an attempt to describe the structure of the Bolshevik Government and to portray the relationship of the citizen to the state in the Soviet Union. It is based on observation and on an extensive study of laws and decrees. Since the author realizes that the laws of the Soviet Union are frequently divergent from the actual state of affairs, he has been careful in drawing conclusions. Legal provisions, however, are apt to prove a snare in other countries besides the Soviet State.

Although this treatise deals largely with legal relationships, yet the realistic point of view has been followed consistently, without, it is hoped, falling into the all-too-common error of creating a purely impressionistic picture. It is said that any study of Soviet Russia is likely to result either in an extremely favorable attitude or in a violent opposition on the part of the student. The writer flatters himself that he has approached this study objectively, has divested himself of ideological bias, and has produced as a whole, an impartial representation of political, social, and legal conditions in Soviet Russia today.

The writer wishes to express his gratitude to the Social Science Research Council for a Grant-in-Aid to finish this study. Thanks are also due to Professors S. N. Harper and Leanard D. White of the University of Chicago for reading most of the book and offering valuable criticism and suggestions. I am under obligation to Miss Margaret Wright for faithful and painstaking secretarial work in connection with the preparation of the manuscript. Needless to say that many persons not mentioned here have been helpful to the writer; however, the author alone is responsible for any mistakes in this study.

The chapters on Municipal Government and Civil Service and the Judiciary are based in part on the writer's articles in the *National Municipal Review* and *The American Political Science Review*.

Bertram W. Maxwell.

Washburn College
January, 1934

CONTENTS

PART I

THE ORGANS OF GOVERNMENT OF THE SOVIET STATE

CHAPTER I

CHAPTER II

CHAPTER III

CHAPTER IV

CHAPTER V

CONTENTS

CHAPTER VI

CONTENTS

CHAPTER IX

PART II

THE CITIZEN AND THE STATE

CHAPTER X

CHAPTER XI

CHAPTER XII

CHAPTER XIII

CHAPTER XIV

CHAPTER XV

CONTENTS

PART I

THE ORGANS OF GOVERNMENT OF
THE SOVIET STATE

THE SOVIET STATE

PART I

THE ORGANS OF GOVERNMENT OF THE SOVIET STATE

CHAPTER I

INTRODUCTION

RUSSIA BEFORE THE REVOLUTION OF 1917

THE CENTRAL GOVERNMENT

Before the Revolution of October 1905, Russia was an absolute monarchy. The year 1905 brought Russia a nominal constitutional monarchy wrested from the tsar by a series of revolutions and riots. The Manifesto of October 30, 1905, granted the people "the immutable foundations of civil liberty, based on real inviolability of person, freedom of conscience, speech, meetings, and associations." It enlarged the franchise of the masses for the election of the State Duma (parliament), an institution established grudgingly after the disastrous outcome of the Russo-Japanese War, in August 1905. But this action by no means abolished the autocracy. Legally and practically the autocracy lasted until 1917, when it collapsed of its own rottenness. The Fundamental Laws promulgated on April 23, 1906, served as underlying principles of Russian constitutional law. In accordance with these principles the tsar headed the empire, nominally a constitutional monarchy, practically an autocracy, as can be seen in studying the powers of the emperor. All executive authority of this vast land was concentrated in him. The appointment, dismissal, and responsibility of ministers was entirely lodged in him. There was not a fraction of political responsibility of the ministry to parliament, and in fact, any such

1

practice would have been contrary to the Fundamental Laws. In their conduct of political business, the ministers were solely responsible to the emperor. To be sure the State Duma under certain limited conditions could interpellate a minister, provided it was in regard to some illegal act on his part, but whatever the outcome of the interpellation, the Duma had no influence upon the conduct of the government or on appointment or dismissal of members thereof, individually or collectively. Furthermore, the tsar had an absolute veto of all legislation passed by parliament. The Fundamental Laws of 1906, which were merely a revision of the old Fundamental Laws of the Russian autocracy, served as the constitution of Russia. These laws were not subject to amendatory action on the part of the Duma; the tsar alone had authority to initiate revision. In order to dissipate any illusion as to the powers of the Duma, it may be pointed out that the emperor had the right to convoke, prorogue, adjourn, suspend, or dissolve the Duma. There was only one restriction upon the will of the emperor; namely, that both houses of the Duma "are convoked every year by the emperor."[1] Otherwise the fate of parliament was, not as a matter of legal fiction but literally, in the hands of the emperor, for the Fundamental Law provided that "the duration of the annual sessions of the State Duma and State Council, and the length of the recesses in the course of the year are prescribed by edict of the tsar."[2]

The history of the Russian parliament tells its own story as to the ample use the emperor made of this power. In addition to the authority of the sovereign, granted to himself by himself, he had a tremendous influence in the upper house, since one-half of the members of the State Council (upper house) were appointed by him. The presiding officer of the State Council was also appointed by imperial order.

In administrative matters the authority of the tsar was supreme, since the Fundamental Law provided that "the power of administration, in its entirety, belongs to the emperor throughout the Russian State", and "the emperor by virtue of his supreme administrative authority issues in accordance with the laws, decrees for the establishment and operation of the various branches of the state administration, as well as the orders necessary for the execution of the laws",[3] but since no law was effective without his confirmation, the power of the tsar was great indeed.

The entire administration of the land was under the direct jurisdiction of the sovereign. He appointed all important officials, he granted titles and distinctions, and limited the power and civil rights of government officials. All persons employed in state offices were the servants of the tsar. The field of international relations, foreign policy of the government, declaration of war and peace, negotiation and conclusion of treaties were in absolute and exclusive jurisdiction of the sovereign. The vicious and cruel practice, so well remembered from the history of the years 1905-1914, of proclaiming martial law and "state of emergency" was a tremendous weapon in the exclusive jurisdiction of the emperor for the suppression of any opposition on the part of the people, and for almost twenty-five years most of the cities and provinces of the empire were living more or less continuously under such rule. This is the more striking when it is remembered that such powers are used by civilized governments only in extreme situations.

In addition to all the powers enumerated above, the tsar had the authority granted to him by Article 87 of the Fundamental Laws to promulgate exceptional decrees having the power of law. To be sure, these laws were considered temporary, but in practice many of them assumed a permanent nature without legislative sanction.

THE RUSSIAN PARLIAMENT (Duma)

The Russian parliament was bicameral in structure. The lower house, known as the State Duma, was elective; the upper house, known as the State Council, consisted of a membership half of which was appointed by the tsar and half elective by a complicated and highly restricted franchise.

The electoral law of Russia on the eve of the war was the mutilated version of the act of December 11, 1905. Although the original law was very conservative, yet at least it gave a limited opportunity for a relative expression of public opinion. Under this law the first and second Duma were elected, but by an imperial decree of June 3, 1907, the entire franchise system was changed so as to give the highest representation to the reactionary landed nobility, and as a result the third Duma was slavishly subservient to the autocracy. In addition to being unfair, the new election law was perhaps the most stupid and complicated electoral procedure in the history of suffrage. The law of June 3, 1907,[4] provided for the election of the members of the Duma for five years by voters who were at least twenty-five years of age, male Russian subjects, not attending an educational institution or in the service of the armed forces. This requirement was in addition to property qualifications, and the voters were divided into four classes: (1) landowners, (2) burghers, (3) peasants, (4) industrial workers. The first class was divided into two sections, large and small landowners; and the city voters were also divided into two groups, first and second class. These groups voted separately for an electoral college. The electoral college in turn assembled in the government seat of each province to elect the deputies.

The new electoral law was so constructed as to give a majority to the landowners, and thus the State Duma became an echo of the autocratic government. In the five big cities, St. Petersburg, Moscow, Kiev, Odessa, and Riga, representatives were elected by direct vote, the voters balloting in separate groups, which on the order of the minister of the interior could be split into even smaller divisions resulting in gerrymandering *par-excellence*. In general it may be safely stated that the electoral law of 1907 made the election procedure a pliable weapon in the hands of the autocracy. The masses remained unrepresented until the revolution of 1917.

The State Council (upper house) consisted of two groups: (1) the State Council proper; (2) various divisions and committees of the Council.

The State Council in the parliamentary sense (the upper chamber) was composed of two classes of members: elected members and appointed members. The first class was chosen by five different electoral groups: namely, the clergy, the provincial zemstvo assemblies, the nobility, the Academy of Sciences, universities, wealthy merchants, and manufacturers. The members were chosen for nine years with the exception of those elected by the provincial assemblies, the latter being elected for only three years. The qualification for voting was extremely high, hence only a very small class had the franchise. The appointive members designated by the emperor were persons whose views were agreeable to the government. Frequently the appointed members fell from grace and were not included in the annual New Year list of appointment, thus being delegated to the non-active list. The work of the Duma was so hampered by all kinds of machinery emanating from the autocratic will that it became a parliament in name only, until it broke over the traces on the eve of the Revolution. The whole administration was conducted by the council of ministers, solely and only responsible to the emperor, appointed and dismissed by him.

Needless to say that, under such organization as briefly described above, the words of the famous Manifesto of 1905, "To grant the people the immutable foundations of civil liberty, based on real inviolability of person, freedom of conscience, speech, meetings, and associations", remained empty words. The *nagaika, knout,* machine guns, repression, and virtual political slavery were the portion of the people until they rose as a mighty wave and swept away the bloodiest and most stupid autocracy of modern times.

CIVIL SERVICE

Peter the Great, among other attempts to westernize Russia, introduced in 1722 a "table of ranks" consisting of fourteen classes of civil officials (chinovniki) ranging from mere filing clerks to privy councillors.[5] Advancement in civil service also brought with it advancement in social status, but few persons of plebeian origin could reach the higher ranks. Officials attaining the rank of "actual state councillor" automatically became hereditary nobles. The old nobility resented this "corruption of blood"; but with the growth of the empire, the nobles alone were not sufficiently numerous to render all the civil service necessary for the administration of the state. The admission of non-nobles into civil service was, however, rigidly restricted, not so much by educational qualifications as by stipulations that sons of officials, military officers, orthodox clergy, merchants of the first class, and members of the learned professions should be given preference. Others were admitted provided they were graduated from middle and higher educational institutions with honor (gold

medal). Jews were in general excluded, exceptions being made
in the case of the medical service. Women were excluded up to
about ten years before the collapse of the autocracy, and then
they were admitted to minor offices only.

The civil officials of noble birth were considered a privileged
class and were promoted more rapidly than their colleagues of
low birth. Only in exceptional cases did the latter advance to
the higher ranks of service. Those lacking financial means and
influence were doomed to stay in the lowest ranks. The revolution of 1905 theoretically ended this discrimination in favor of
the nobility and the wealthy, but in reality the old practice continued, the new rule remaining a dead letter. In general, the
life of the civil official was circumscribed in every way, and at
the least suspicion of harboring liberal ideas he was dismissed.
Every official was his brother's keeper, the superiors watching
the behavior, especially political behavior, of their inferiors. No
civil servant could enter matrimony without permission of the
higher authorities. After thirty-five years of faithful service,
the civil officials were pensioned, receiving full pay; after twenty-
five years, they could be retired on half pay.

Liability for Unlawful Acts of Officials

State liability for illegal official actions was limited. The
fundamental laws theoretically recognized liability; in practice,
however, royal ordinances were exempt from the usual legal
responsibilities. The tsar possessed broad discretionary powers,
which were decisive in all matters of administration. This
exemption applied not only to imperial ordinances but to a great
number of regulations of subordinate administrative agencies
which were not subject to appeal for review (as for instance,
orders in regard to administrative exile). Russian administrative
jurisprudence was interpreted in that department of the Senate
which was not touched by the judicial reforms of 1864.[6] "The
first department", as this division was called, examined the most
important of controversial administrative matters. The personnel
of this body consisted of ultra-conservative groups, such as
governors and directors of the department of police. The
imperial ministers not only easily escaped the supervisory power
of the Senate but could actually bring pressure upon the Senate

and the senators. This may be said more especially of the minister of justice, since by his recommendations senators were appointed or transferred from one department to another, and it was that official who decided upon the salaries of senators. Senators could be relieved of their positions against their will at any time. The first department of the Senate was theoretically under the management of the senators but in practice administered by solicitors who were subject to the authority of the minister of justice. These solicitors supervised the activities of the various departments and passed on the correctness of judicial decisions. Upon them depended the approval of resolutions of the Senate, the working out of "consenting propositions", etc. Besides the minister of justice other ministers also had influence in the matter of decisions by the Senate. Certain matters before being decided upon by this body had to be sent to the interested ministers, who returned them after a period of many months and sometimes kept them for several years. Furthermore, ministers and their assistants took part personally in the deliberations of the departments when certain matters in which they were interested were discussed, and they had a deciding vote. If a minister was not in agreement with the resolution of the majority of the Senate, he could refuse to sign the resolution, and the matter had to be forwarded to a higher instance (such as plenary session); finally, appeal could be made to the emperor through the "first department" of the imperial council. In some cases decades passed by before a final decision was made. Furthermore, the procedure of the Senate was characterized by extremely archaic rules. In a plenary session votes were counted not only of those present but also of senators who were already dead, on the assumption that if the dead members had lived they would have decided thus. Frequently the ministers who took part in the sessions of the Senate were the judges of their own affairs, but private persons who were interested parties could not even be present when the appeal was taken up in that exalted body.

The responsibility of officials in pre-revolutionary Russia was entirely dependent upon the discretion of the authorities. Disciplinary punishment was imposed by the order of the immediate superior and frequently by that superior upon whom depended

the appointment of the guilty official. This authority had a right
to fine subordinates to the amount of one-third of their annual
salary, transfer officials to an inferior position, dismiss them from
the service, and put them under arrest for seven days.

Private persons could enter suits for damages against officials
in civil courts without permission of the superior of the officials
concerned, but the decision in these matters was not made by the
ordinary courts but in a special session composed of the
governor, vice-governor, and other officials of the local administration. The state treasury was responsible for the acts of an
official only when the latter acted as agent of the treasury in its
business transactions. For any other damage done by officials
the treasury was not responsible. For compulsory requisition of
real estate, however, a just and proper compensation was made
by the government.

The Judicial System

The Judicial System of Russia on the eve of the Revolution of
1917 was based on the Statute of November 20, 1864, (Sudebni
Ustav) and on subsequent statutes passed in 1878 and 1889. The
judicial functions were separated from administrative functions;
the independence of the judges was recognized, although by the
law of May 20, 1885, the principle of irremovability was curtailed; the trials were public and a jury was used in the more
serious criminal cases.

The judiciary consisted of (1) justices of the peace in the two
capitals and the six most important cities of the empire. These
courts had jurisdiction of a variety of civil cases and of numerous
offenses. In civil cases involving less than thirty rubles and
criminal cases punishable by arrest of no more than three days,
the judgment of the justice of the peace was final. In more
serious cases the decision of the justice court could be appealed
to an assembly of justices of the peace (mirovoi syezd) composed
of at least three justices of the peace. In some cases a final appeal
could be made on points of law to the Senate, which could order
a retrial by an assembly of justices of the peace in another
district. (2) Zemski and urban courts which existed in all parts
of the empire, and served the purposes of the justices of the peace.
The zemski courts were to be found in rural districts and the

urban courts in the towns. The jurisdiction of these courts was similar to that of the justices of the peace. A district assembly consisted of the district marshal of nobility, the district member of the circuit court, the judges of the town courts, and the sectional zemski chiefs (the official who had charge of the zemski court and supervision of peasant institutions in a given section of the district). These assemblies received appeals from decisions of town and zemski courts. (3) Circuit courts, which had an extensive jurisdiction over a territory embracing several districts. The circuit courts had a president and large number of judges. These courts were divided into small divisions presided over by vice-presidents. The individual sessions of the court consisted of at least three judges. The circuit courts had jurisdiction over all important civil and criminal cases. In very serious criminal cases a jury could be used. The judges of the circuit courts were appointed by the tsar upon the recommendation of the minister of justice. Attached to the circuit courts were judicial inquisitors, who were appointed by the chief presidents of the courts of appeals. The duties of the inquisitors consisted in preliminary investigations of criminal cases. (4) Judicial palata or court of appeals to which cases from the circuit courts could be appealed. The jurisdiction of the palata embraced in some cases several provinces. The palata was divided into civil, criminal, and other departments presided over by a chairman and several judges. A chief president presided over an assembly of all the judges of the departments. The judges of the palata were appointed in the same manner as the judges of the circuit courts. The palata could also take jurisdiction of original cases of a grave character in which the government was involved. While there was no trial by jury in the palata, in some serious offenses against the government, representatives of the various civil strata were called in to participate in the trial on equality with the judges. The decision could not be appealed but was subject to review by way of cassation. (5) The Court of Cassation. Within the Governing Senate there was provided by the statute of 1864 a Supreme Court of Cassation which was divided into criminal and civil departments. Each department was subdivided into sessions of the entire department and sessions of separate divisions of the department. The full session consisted of at least seven senators (judges) and three judges made up the sessions of the separate divisions. The senators were appointed directly by the tsar. All cases which could not be appealed to lower courts came under the jurisdiction of this Court by way of cassation. The Court of Cassation also had the exclusive authority to interpret the laws of the empire and these interpretations became binding on all courts.

The Procuracy (Prosecution)

The procuracy was headed by a chief procurator who served under the supervision of the minister of justice and was known as the procurator-general. The various judicial divisions had procurators and assistants. The procurators attached to the various courts were appointed by the tsar on the recommendation of the minister of justice. The assistant procurators of the circuit courts were appointed by the minister of justice on the recommendation of the procurator of the judicial palata.[7]

Secret Police as the Guardians of the State

One of the integral and important parts of the tsarist administration was the so-called "secret police" which was originally organized as the third section by Nicholas I, ostensibly for the purpose of keeping the emperor informed of abuses and irregularities. In practice it developed into a terrorist organization, its chief purpose of existence being the suppression of liberal political activity. Its members were arbitrary, corrupt, and ignorant; its procedure was summary and secret, and meted out punishment to thousands, frequently in the form of exile by administrative order. Ostensibly suppressed by Alexander II, in theory and practice it was reorganized into the Ochrana and created into a separate department of the ministry of the interior, granted enormous funds for secret activities, and eventually dominated the entire ministry. The corps of gendarmes, whose existence was anterior to the third section, was incorporated into it; and the entire organization was placed under the jurisdiction of the under-secretary of the interior, who became the head of all the police with the title of under-secretary for the administration of the police.

The secret police carried out the various extraordinary measures for the safety of the state. These measures were based on a decree dated August 14, 1881, consisting of a collection of old enactments in regard to extraordinary rights of the ruling powers, which contained multiple forms of measures of public control and coercion carried out through the agency of the secret police. The decree of August 14 provided for extraordinary measures for safety called "reinforced and extraordinary guard." The people living in a territory "under extraordinary guard" were at the mercy of military and police officials and their co-workers. The various decrees issued by the authorities provided for arrests and fines in punishment for acts of sedition on the part of the population. In reality the repressions were frequently applied to innocent acts in no way connected with the safety of state. Thus the people were prohibited to express too enthusiastic approval in theaters by applause or curtain calls. To be sure the intent of the decree of 1881 was that the extraordinary measures were to be introduced for a short time in individual localities; in practice, however, whole provinces were for years under "extraordinary rule", with the result that it was almost impossible to find even a single district which was not affected in some degree by extraordinary regulations. In 1905 even official circles admitted that an entire generation had grown up which had never lived under a normal enforcement of law. Under the abnormal conditions, local police and gendarmerie received wide powers in regard to arrest, search, and exile. They had a right to forbid all kinds of public, social, and even private meetings, and they could close commercial and industrial organizations, printing presses, and similar enterprises. The governors - general and governors received extensive powers to close periodicals, cancel and dissolve called meetings of professional, rural, and urban organizations, close educational institutions, sequester real estate, seal up movable property and stop income from it. They could also expel from service officials of all ranks, especially those of the three lower categories.[8] This disciplinary authority was extended to embrace rural, urban, and professional elective officials. The governors-general could, under these provisions, withdraw from the jurisdiction of ordinary courts all kinds of cases and transfer them to courts martial or decide upon them in administrative manner. When the above mentioned measures did not prove satisfactory to the authorities, martial law and state of siege could be declared under which the commander-in-chief of the armed forces of the district was given dictatorial powers. These arbitrary actions were justified by the excuse that the safety of state necessitated all kinds of excesses, although they had no foundation at law.[9]

Provincial Administration

Russia, before the Revolution, was divided for purposes of administration into seventy-eight governments (guberniya), twenty-one regions (oblast), and one circuit (okrug). At the head of each government was a governor, whose administrative competence was limited, since the management of numerous institutions was reserved for the central government, and therefore the governor was in a measure simply the local administrative organ of the ministry of the interior. The governors were appointed and dismissed by the tsar on the recommendation of the minister of the interior. In general the governor had supervision of the police of the entire government excepting the gendarmerie; he furthermore, safeguarded the rights of the church, nobility, and other classes. In addition, public health and general welfare of the territory were in his jurisdiction. In some governments there were to be found governors-general who were appointed directly by the tsar to administer one or more governments and who had more extensive powers, which included the command of troops within the territory entrusted to them. The two capitals, Moscow and St. Petersburg, and some of the more important cities were separated from the general government administration and were ruled over by a municipal governor, appointed by the emperor.

County Administration (Uyezd)

The governments were divided into 756 districts (uyezd); at the head of each was a chief of police (ispravnik), who was appointed by the governor. Under the jurisdiction of the chief of police were to be found in the principal localities, deputies (stanovoi pristav) who were generally illiterate and ignorant of any legal provision, yet endowed with extensive and practically undefined powers. Because of their unreasonableness, oppression, and cruelty they were universally feared and hated by the rural population. Under these officials served a corps of mounted rural police (uryadniki), who were given authority to arrest all suspected persons on the spot. These officials soon became the terror of the rural communities. In the urban communities in every house there was to be found a combination of detective and porter called *dvornik,* a position unknown in any other country. One of the duties of this person was to report to the police authorities suspicious characters or any matter which would be of interest to the police. The bulk of his reporting was in the field of political heresy.

Local Administration

The Canton (Volost)

The canton (volost) consisted of a number of communes and had an assembly composed of members elected by the village communes. The delegates to the assembly elected an elder (starshina).

The lowest rural administrative unit was the village commune, which had an assembly consisting of all the peasant householders of the commune, who elected a head man (starosta). To the casual reader this description may give the impression of considerable local self-government, but in reality the actual power was in the hands of police officials and bureaus of the province and district.

The Zemstvos

In addition to the institutions of provincial and district government described above, there were to be found on the eve of the World War in forty-three governments of European Russia, zemstvo institutions.[10] These zemstvos were elected by provincial and district assemblies instituted by Alexander II in 1864. They consisted of a representative council (zemskoye sobraniye) and of an executive board (zemskaya uprava) which was elected by the council. The membership of the executive board was divided into five classes: (1) large landowners of the nobility who really represented no one but themselves; (2) delegates elected by the small landowners and clergy; (3) delegates of the wealthy burghers; (4) delegates of the middle urban class; (5) delegates of the peasants elected by the volost (canton).

The zemstvos originally had extensive powers in the field of taxation, education, public health, roads, etc., but the central government continually hindered the work of this institution. In 1890, Alexander III curtailed the activities of the zemstvos to such an extent that almost every endeavor on their part had to be submitted to higher authorities and bureaucratic red tape. Not until after the revolution 1905 did the iron fist of autocracy relax its grip on this struggling and extremely limited institution of local self-government. The autocracy was jealous of every indication of self-government and to its very end fought maliciously against the popular will. Yet in spite of all obstacles, in the years between 1905 and 1917, the zemstvos had entered into many different phases of economic and cultural life of the country.[11]

MUNICIPAL GOVERNMENT

THE CITY IN THE PRE-REVOLUTIONARY PERIOD

The Russian city was not given legal status until comparatively recent times. In 1758 Catherine II granted a charter bestowing upon the cities the rights of individuals before the law, and the privilege of taking part in the conduct of municipal affairs was extended to nearly the entire adult male civil population. Since this legislation was too far in advance of the general political and social conditions then prevailing in the Russian Empire, it was never carried out and soon became obsolete. In the years between 1862-1870 a series of ordinances were issued to reorganize municipal government with a view to granting the cities some degree of self-government.

Finally, in 1870 the so-called Municipal Act, modeled after the Prussian municipal ordinances, was promulgated. Under that act all citizens paying local taxes were granted the right to vote and to serve on municipal boards. The electorate was divided into three classes in accordance with taxes paid by them. A municipal council was created, the membership of which was elected by indirect vote. Theoretically the city government was supreme within the limits of its jurisdiction; practically, the control of municipal affairs was vested in a royally appointed governor who was assisted by a special board of municipal affairs.

In the years between 1870 and 1917 the central government tightened its grip on civic governments. In 1892 a municipal decree was issued which materially curtailed the jurisdiction of municipalities. The suffrage was henceforth confined to owners of real property; as a result, only about one per cent of the city population was qualified to take part in municipal elections. The mayors and members of municipal boards became objects of govermental scrutiny and were classified as imperial officials, subject to the jurisdiction of civil service courts. In striking contrast the powers of the appointed governor were increased; he received authority to suspend municipal ordinances which he deemed contrary to law or outside the jurisdiction of the city. Eventually the governor was placed in a position to exercise an absolute veto on municipal activity. In addition, the imperial minister of the interior could at anytime suspend city ordinances which met with his disapproval. Such was the trend of all municipal legislation and attitude on the part of the central government up to the time of the overthrow of the autocratic régime in 1917. The short-lived Provisional Government issued a decree on June 9, 1917, which introduced democratic municipal practices based on universal suffrage, but since eight months after its inception the Kerensky régime was overthrown by the Bolsheviks, the new municipal system was destroyed after an existence of only five months.[12]

CHAPTER II

THE COMING OF THE SOVIETS

The Creation of the Soviet State

The creation of the Soviet state cannot be ascribed merely to the miseries which followed the World War. The Soviets are a result of centuries of oppression and ignorance which unfortunately cannot be described here. It is the intention of this brief introduction to indicate events which led to the formation of the present régime. When war was declared in 1914 against Germany, old animosities were forgotten, and the people rushed to arms with great enthusiasm. It appeared that a victorious war would restore the prestige of the tsar, but early in the war even the more intelligent, conservative elements realized that they were dancing on a volcano. The most moderate suggestions for reform in the Duma were answered by the adjournment of that body. By 1916 because of corruption, peculation, and graft on the part of the government, starvation and famine stalked the streets of cities. The situation was so critical that even the members of the imperial court, who were far removed from the people, could see the danger ahead and became frightened and frantically implored the tsar to establish a responsible government. Instead the emperor, under the influence of his consort, prorogued the Duma; but the fat was in the fire, the days of unquestioning obedience were over, and the parliament refused to obey the imperial command. In the meantime, the mighty force of popular resentment broke out. There were bread riots on the streets of the large cities. The parliamentary leaders were, however, cautious in their actions and constituting themselves into a "Provisional Committee of the Duma" oscillated between joining the people and making a last appeal to the tsar; but the governmental structure was rotten to the core and even at the slight impact of an unorganized popular riot, it collapsed. The Provisional Committee was forced by popular pressure to transform

16

itself into a provisional government even before the tsar was
asked to abdicate. Within five historic days of 1917 all vestige
of the edifice built by centuries of oppression and bloodshed disappeared. The Provisional Government consisted mostly of conservative liberal elements and one moderate socialist, Kerensky,
but the tendency was to the left and gradually the more conservative elements dropped out and Kerensky became the man
of the hour. His efforts, however, were unequal to the demands
of the time. The eight months interlude between the overthrow
of the autocracy in March and the seizure of the government by
the Bolsheviks in November is illustrative of a vain endeavor of
a liberal government, devoid of popular support, to stem the tide
of revolution. Frantically Kerensky attempted to muster an
armed force to support his government, but the army had dis-
integrated; no officer's life was safe at the front or in garrison.
Moreover the peasantry, seeing an opportunity to avenge ancient
wrongs, seized the landlords' lands, and drove the owners from
their estates with much cruelty and bloodshed. The urban
proletariat was becoming increasingly radical and listened with
avidity to the propaganda of the Bolsheviks, who were waiting
for the opportune moment to seize the government. The ranks
of the Red Guard, a revolutionary fighting unit, were thronged
with workers who demanded complete control over industry, dis-
possessing owners and driving managers from factories and
plants. The non-Russian elements of the empire made use of
the chaos and set up states of their own. In the midst of this
bedlam and indecision there was only one political group who
knew how to appeal to the war weary and starved millions, and
that was the Bolshevik minority. Its program pledged immediate
peace, transfer of all political power to the Soviets,[1] transfer of
all lands of the landlords to the peasants, and factories to the
workers, freedom to the non-Russian elements, and bread. These
pledges promised to satisfy the confused longing of millions who
yearned for reparation for woes and wretchedness imposed by a
cruel despotism, and, therefore, multitudes were deserting the
Provisional Government and flocking to the banner of the Bolsheviks. Between July and September there were two abortive
attempts to overthrow the Provisional Government. In July 1917,
the Bolsheviks in response to a demand for action were involved

against their better judgment in an unorganized uprising in Petrograd, which was easily suppressed by the weak Provisional Government; in September of the same year General Kornilov, the Commander in Chief of the Army, permitted himself to be persuaded by some reactionary members of the Duma to attempt the establishment of a military dictatorship; this undertaking, however, ended disastrously. The attempted coup, moreover, incited an increasing number of the common people to forsake the Provisional Government and join the extreme left. The Soviets, who before the Kornilov affair were under the leadership of the more moderate wing of the Socialist party, fell completely under the influence of the Bolsheviks.

As the power of the Provisional Government waned, the Bolsheviks in turn waxed, gathering strength in numbers and influence. Finally on October 23, the Central Committee of the Bolshevik party resolved under the urging of Lenin, who was then in hiding, to rise in armed rebellion. Accordingly on the fateful days of November 6 and 7, the Bolsheviks, supported by armed workers, sailors, and sympathizing elements in the Petrograd garrison, overthrew the Provisional Government and confronted the Congress of Soviets then meeting in Petrograd and since by that time the Bolsheviks had a majority in that body, the victorious Communists were readily accepted. Urban centers throughout Russia followed the example of Petrograd. The Bolshevik leaders, now the new government, designated themselves as the Council of People's Commissars and proceeded at once to issue three decrees: (1) proposing immediate peace to all belligerent countries, (2) declaring landlord property in land abolished forever, and declaring all land the property of the state to be used by peasants on a basis of personal labor, (3) establishing workers' committees in all industrial plants.

The Bolsheviks, having seized the power in the memorable November days of 1917, proceeded to establish a dictatorship of the proletariat based upon their theories which they had formulated during the many years of exile, incarceration, and underground existence. While the structure of government was not fully worked out at that time, the fundamental idea was that any government which is to express the will of the masses must be a dictatorship of the working class. In fact the Bolsheviks have never denied that their system of government is a dictatorship. The details of the Bolshevik régime were rounded out in the stress and strain of a tremendous upheaval, civil war, and invasion. It is also important to remember that it was not the intention of the Bolsheviks to establish an isolated, socialistic state in Russia, but they were expecting that the Russian revolution would be a forerunner of world revolution, and that eventually the entire world would follow their example. However, having met with failure as far as world revolution was concerned, they had to modify a good many of their theories and adjust them to a situation of an isolated socialist state surrounded by capitalistic governments.

Theoretically the rule of Soviet Russia is vested in the proletariat, that is, in the manual industrial workers. Practically, however, it is vested in the All-Union Communist Party which expresses, according to the Bolsheviks, the will of the working class, and constitutes "the vanguard of the proletariat", which will eventually lead the masses of the world into the camp of Communism. Although the Communist Party is a highly centralized organization, it is too unwieldy to actually exercise rule, and therefore it is controlled by a Central Committee consisting of sixty-nine members; this committee, however, is subject to the will of the Political Bureau (Polit-bureau) composed of ten members, the best known of whom is Stalin, who are also members of the Polit-bureau. As in any other large organization, the rank and file of the party members have little influence in the formulation of Party policies; it is merely their duty to carry out implicitly the orders of the leaders who represent the Party. Obedience is probably the most important duty of any member of the Communist Party, and it is because of this iron discipline that the Communist Party was able to overcome the opposition, not only of its internal enemies but that of the world. The outstanding figure in Soviet Russia up to 1924 was Lenin. It was he who by his surprising moderation and mature counsel carried the Party through a terrific period of civil war, intervention, and famine. His prestige was of such magnitude and his unselfish character was so well known that his decisions were seldom, if ever, questioned. At his death in 1924 there was a great danger of a split in the Party, which would have caused the fall of the

Bolshevik régime in Russia. The controversy between Stalin, secretary general of the Party, and Trotsky, and other members of the opposition is too well known to necessitate description here. Suffice it to say, that Stalin emerged victorious from this dangerous controversy, and has assumed the authority of Lenin.

In taking up the discussion of the structure of the Soviet government one must make clear that it is the Party that formulates policies, and the governmental apparatus installed for purposes of administration of the country is merely the instrument through which the Party, or rather the leadership of the Party, expresses its will. To be sure the party organs frequently perform acts of a purely governmental nature; but generally speaking, the will of the Party is expressed through a highly complicated structure of organically connected organizations which were created by the Party and are subordinate to it. These various organizations are headed by the Soviet government, followed by the Labor Unions, Communist Union of Youth, etc.

The Soviet government, which is, no doubt, the most important instrument through which the Party expresses its will (and which will be described in detail later), was established, as was mentioned before, following the collapse of the Provisional Government. The new government designated itself as the Council of the People's Commissars and distributed the various offices among the outstanding leaders of the Party. Lenin took over the presidency of the Council of People's Commissars, and Trotsky became the first foreign minister, to be transferred later, when Russia was facing a critical situation, to the post of the commissar of war. While at first the Bolsheviks were inclined to come to an understanding with various other revolutionary groups, eventually members of the Communist Party were given the most important governmental positions, and the members of the other revolutionary factions were removed. In the first years of Bolshevik rule it was hardly possible to distinguish between the apparatus of the state and that of the Communist Party. In the course of time, however, there developed a dualism, consisting of the Party on the one hand, and the Soviet government on the other; but it was the Party apparatus which served as an instrument for the determination of Bolshevik policies, and the state apparatus became the administrative medium by means of which the policies determined upon by the Party leaders were carried out. Until recently the governmental and party agencies were kept superficially separate, but lately there have been occasional lapses to earlier practices of using the Party apparatus, not only for purposes of formulating policies but also of carrying out policies. There are instances in which the higher organs of the Party have issued orders to subordinate organs of the state without going through the formality of using the channels of superior state organs. In general, however, these cases are the exception rather than the rule.

It is only fair to state that this subordination of government organization to the will of the Party is not at all shocking to the people of Russia, and there appears to be a general acceptance of this principle. The public is reminded by political text-books, newspaper articles, and party leaders time and time again of the necessity of absolute control of the Party over the entire network of state apparatus and state administrative agencies. Although there is universal suffrage in Russia and the majority of the people are eligible to hold office, yet it is inevitable in a country where only one party has a legal existence, that state officials of any importance would in the very nature of things belong to the Party. In the first place the party membership consists of a cohesive group composed largely of a determined class-conscious faction which is capable to exercise a strong influence on the minds of the voters; in the second place the voters themselves know well enough that it would not be in their interest to elect officials who do not belong to the Party, since they would be excluded from the Party councils. Moreover the very nature of the Soviet governmental structure (as will be shown later) is such that the most important offices are not filled by direct popular vote but indirectly by congresses of Soviets outside the influence of the rank and file of the voters. It must be remembered that Party leaders, such as Lenin and others, have retained their positions until they were removed by death or had committed the unforgivable sin of questioning decisions of the Party. Occasionally some leaders hold no governmental position at all. Stalin, the most influential leader in the Union, after his rise to power held no office; he has accepted membership in some important agencies of the government only in recent years.[2] It is therefore highly important in discussing the Soviet government to keep in mind that the Party is the paramount factor in the Soviet administration, and that the Soviet government is there to carry out the will of the Party.

Origin and Development of the Soviet Constitution

Upon assuming power and creating a temporary executive in the form of a collegium called the Council of People's Commissars, the Bolsheviks proceeded to create the necessary governmental organs. The third Congress of Soviets then in session was declared the legislative organ of the new régime.

The Constituent Assembly, which was called by Kerensky for the purpose of deciding on a form of government, was convened after the Bolshevik *coup d'état*. The new authorities dispersed it on the charge that it did not represent the "will of the masses." The Congress then passed two resolutions entitled "the Declaration of the Rights of the Laboring and Exploited Masses" and the "Declaration of the Rights of the Peoples of Russia." These declarations laid down the fundamental principles upon which the Russian Soviet Constitution is based. In November 1917 the Congress of Soviets created a Central Executive Committee which was to serve as a centralizing agency and be responsible to the Congress.

Many projects and proposals for a constitution for Russia were suggested and submitted between November 1917 and April 1918. Finally a commission for the drafting of a constitution was appointed by the Central Executive Committee, which met in its first session on April 8, 1918. After many meetings in which several projects were discussed, a final draft was submitted to the fifth Congress of Soviets meeting in July 1918, and was ratified by that body on July 10, 1918. In accordance with the constitution "Russia is declared a republic of Soviets of workers', soldiers', and peasants' deputies. All central and local authority is vested in these Soviets. The Russian Soviet Republic is established on the basis of a free union of free nations, as a federation of national Soviet republics."[3]

The constitution proceeds further to declare as a fundamental principle the "abolition of exploitation of men by men, the entire abolition of the division of the people into classes, the suppression of exploiters, the establishment of a socialist society, and the victory of socialism in all lands"; . . . . then reiterates the resolution of the third Congress of Soviets in regard to nationalization of land and natural resources and transfer of factories, mills, mines, railways, etc., to the control of workmen under the centralized agency of the Council of National Economy. It further affirms the cancellation of the external debts of the former governments and the transfer of all financial institutions to the Soviet government. In following chapters the constitution repudiates all secret treaties and urges the conclusion of a "general democratic peace without annexation and indemnities", and condemns imperialism and the exploitation of weaker peoples. In section 2, the constitution provides for the political principles upon which the federation is to be founded, enumerates the governmental agencies through which the government is to function, incorporates a "bill of rights" for the "toiling masses", and provides for protection and naturalization of foreigners belonging to the "toiling masses."

After the adoption of the constitution the new government was faced by most difficult problems. The old empire crumbled, and new states were set up within the limits of the empire. The new régime was harassed both by allied intervention and by civil war, and separatist movements were encouraged by former allies and enemies. Neighboring states attempted and succeeded in annexing Russian territory. The outlook was dark and for a while the Soviets exercised authority only over a small part of the former empire comprising the provinces of Petrograd and Moscow. By 1920, however, White Russia and the Ukraina gave up the attempt to set up independent states and entered into a military and economic union with the Russian Socialist Federated Soviet Republic (R. S. F. S. R.). Georgia, Armenia, and Azerbaidjan entered into agreement with Russia and in 1922 organized themselves into the Transcaucasian Soviet Federated Socialist Republic. By energetic activity the Soviets gradually recovered the various territories of the Near East and Far East, and soon the Soviets were ready to organize the Union for mutual protection and united policy. When the tenth All-Russian Congress of Soviets met in 1922, Stalin proposed the formation

of a Union of Soviet Socialist Republics, and this recommend-
ation was adopted by the Congress together with a declaration
and treaty of Union. The declaration was to serve as a constitution for the Union, and was adopted by the All-Union Congress
of Soviets on December 6, 1922, and promulgated July 6, 1923.
The Union according to the constitution was composed of the
Russian Socialist Federated Soviet Republic, White Russian
Socialist Soviet Republic, Ukrainian Socialist Soviet Republic,
Transcaucasian Socialist Federative Soviet Republic, Uzbek
Socialist Soviet Republic, Turkmen Socialist Soviet Republic,
and Tadjik Socialist Soviet Republic.

The treaty of the Union delegated to the Union government
the conduct of foreign affairs including the conduct of diplomatic
relations, negotiation of treaties, declaration of war and the conclusion of peace, foreign loans, regulation of domestic and
foreign trade, transport, posts and telegraphs, national defense,
administration of the Union budget, "the establishment of a
monetary, fiduciary and credit system", and the creation of a
system "of general taxation and of taxes appropriate for each of
the republics, and local taxes." "The establishment of a single
system of credit" formulates general plans for national economy
and general principles for the development and use of land and
mineral deposits, forests, and water ways throughout the Union.
The constitution also authorizes the Union to establish general
principles of education, pass legislation for the regulation of
immigration, and formulate a basis for judicial institutions and
legal procedure for the administration of criminal and civil
justice. The Union is furthermore empowered to establish
general measures for the protection of public health, and regulate
weights and measures. Citizenship and rights of foreigners in
the Union, general amnesty, repeals of decrees of various
political subdivision of member republics which are contrary to
the federal constitution, and confirmation and alteration of
fundamental principles of the federal constitution are within the
jurisdiction of the Union. While the constitution provides for
the withdrawal of the individual republics, in practice this stipulation is of no significance as no individual republic would dare
to attempt such a measure. Citizens of the individual republics
are also citizens of the Union.[4]

THE FEDERAL AND NATIONAL PRINCIPLE OF THE SOVIET STATE

As it was stated before, the R. S. F. S. R. as well as the U. S. S. R. is built upon the federal principle and upon the idea of national cultural autonomy, a fact important for the understanding of present day Russia since the Soviet Union is composed of many nationalities. The dominant Russian element embraces only forty-three per cent of the population. In order to induce the various alien peoples to join the union "The Declaration of the Rights of the Peoples of Russia" promised the equality and sovereignty of the peoples of Russia, the right of peoples of Russia to free self-determination inclusive of forming independent states, the repeal of all and sundry national and national-religious privileges and limitations, and the free development of national minorities and ethnic groups inhabiting Russia. Naturally not all of the promises were kept. However, no fair minded observer would deny that cultural autonomy is one of the outstanding features of the Soviet Union. As it will be remembered in the "Declaration of Rights of the Toiling and Exploited people", it was stated that the "Soviet Russian Republic is based upon the principle of a union of free peoples forming a federation of Soviet national republics." To carry out this idea, the Bolsheviks upon assuming power created a special state agency headed by Stalin. In April 1918 Stalin in the name of this organization issued an appeal to the people of the independent bourgeois national states, which were formed in the Eastern part of the former empire, to overthrow their government and to replace them by Soviet autonomous groups. But even before this time, namely on March 22, 1918, a decree in regard to the formation of "Tartar-Bashkir Soviet Republic" was issued, which inaugurated formation of other autonomous groups of national minorities under the supervision of the Soviets. It was, however, only after the country was cleared of the counter-revolutionary forces, and after the German armies had left Ukraina and White Russia, that the Soviets actually began to develop their national policies. At the time of this writing there are to be found in the Soviet Union, seven Union republics; namely, R. S. F. S. R., Ukraina, White Russia, the Transcaucasian Federation, the Republic of Uzbek, Turkmen, and Tadjik. These republics are constituent parts of the Soviet Union. The next in importance are the so called autonomous republics, which are a part of a given constituent republic and are a part of the Union through the medium of that republic of which they are constituent members. Although there are in the Soviet Union fifteen autonomous republics distributed among the constituent republics, the R. S. F. S. R. includes eleven autonomous republics; namely, the Bashkir, Burat-Mongol, Dagestan, Cosack, Karelia, Kirgiz, Crimea, Volga-German, Tartar, Chuvash, Yakut; in the Ukraina is the autonomous republic of Moldavia; and Transcaucasia claims the autonomous republics of Nakhichevan, Abchazan, and Adzhar.

The Bolsheviks in their attempt to grant cultural independence to minorities have even gone a step farther; they have organized eighteen so called autonomous regions in the Soviet Union. These regions are politically backward communities of native Asiatic population, who according to Bolshevik authorities will be given a higher political status when they are ready for it. The lower steps in the ladder of Soviet national political organization are the ten national circuits; 147 national raions; and about 3,200 national soviets. These units represent small national groups in the midst of larger units, that are permitted to develop their own national cultural life. In fairness to the Soviets , it must be said that the national minorities are given every opportunity to develop their cultural interests.

CHAPTER III

CITIZENSHIP, ELECTIONS, AND THE COMMUNIST PARTY

CITIZENSHIP

With the formation of the Union in 1922, all citizens of the constituent republics became at the same time citizens of the Union.[1] Citizens of the Union are also citizens of the constituent republics in which they habitually reside; if, however, by nationality or descent a citizen considers himself attached to another constituent republic, he may choose the citizenship of that republic. Every person in the territory of the U. S. S. R. is considered a Soviet citizen if it is not proved that he is a citizen of a foreign state. Foreigners who have been received into the citizenship of the U. S. S. R cannot claim the rights of their former allegiance. Citizens of the Soviet Union have all the rights and assume all the obligations established for citizens by the constitution and legislation of the U. S. S. R., and the republics in which they live. Foreigners of the workers and peasant class living within the territorial limits of the Soviet Union who are usefully occupied enjoy all the political rights of citizenship. Persons are considered native citizens if one or both of their parents were, at the time of their birth, citizens of the U. S. S. R. When a Soviet citizen marries an alien, each of them retains his original citizenship; provisions, however, are made for change of citizenship as will be seen later. When both parents who are foreigners become naturalized citizens or *vice versa,* when they divest themselves of the citizenship of the U. S. S. R., their children under fourteen years of age follow their parents' allegiance. Children over fourteen years of age may decide for themselves whether they want to follow their parents or retain their original citizenship. Children under fourteen of mixed marriages, who upon separation of their parents remain with the parent who is a foreigner, may retain that citizenship, provided

27

however, the parent who was a Soviet citizen dies or has lost all contact with his children. When one of the parents divests himself of the Soviet citizenship and the other parent dies or has lost all contact with the children, then by application of the parent who has divested himself of the Soviet citizenship, the children up to fourteen years of age staying with him follow him in his citizenship. Children of citizens adopted by foreigners keep their original citizenship.

Foreigners living in the territory of the Soviet Union are admitted to the citizenship of one of the constituent republics and, at the same time, to the citizenship of the Union by the order of the presidium of the Union Central Committee or the presidium of the central executive committee of that constituent republic in which they reside. The refusal on the part of an executive committee of a constituent republic to admit an alien to citizenship may be appealed by the interested person to the presidium of the Central Executive Committee. Foreigners who make application for admittance to citizenship must indicate in that application the constituent republic into which they desire to be admitted.

Foreigners living abroad may be admitted to citizenship of the Soviet Union and one of the constituent republics by the order of the presidium of the Central Executive Committee. In case, however, the application was made to the presidium of the central executive committee of a constituent republic, the order must come from that republic.

In order to divest himself of Soviet citizenship, a person living in the U. S. S. R., must obtain permission of the presidium of the Central Executive Committee of the Union or the presidium of the central executive committee of the appropriate republic. Refusal may be appealed to the presidium of the Central Executive Committee of the Union. A person living abroad must obtain the permission of the presidium of the Union Executive Committee.

Persons who have lost their citizenship can be reinstated by the order of the presidium of the Central Executive Committee of the Union, or by the order of the presidium of the central executive committee of that constituent republic of which he was a citizen. Persons who were deprived of the citizenship of the

U. S. S. R. and of a given republic may be reinstated by the order of the presidium of the Union Central Executive Committee, or by the order of the presidium of the central executive committee of the constituent republic of which they were citizens.

A petition for naturalization or for expatriation must be made to the executive committee of a region, an autonomous republic, or an autonomous region, if the applicant resides within the territory of the Soviet Union. If the applicant lives abroad, application must be made to an accredited representative of the U. S. S. R.

In exceptional cases designated urban centers, which have been given the status of independent administrative economic units, may receive applications for admission or renunciation of citizenship, provided, however, that the persons applying live in the U. S. S. R. This simplified procedure is confined to privileged classes such as foreigners who are workers or peasants who live within the territory of the Union and who are engaged in useful toil. Foreigners who have fled to the U. S. S. R. as a consequence of prosecution for revolutionary activities in their own country or foreigners who have married Soviet citizens may also avail themselves of this privilege.

This ruling is not binding on the local authorities, and they may refuse the request and suggest that the interested parties apply for citizenship in the usual way.[2]

ELECTIONS

While the elections are conducted under the jurisdiction of the several constituent republics, the Union government issues from time to time instructions upon which the electoral machinery is based. These instructions emanate from the Central Electoral Commission organized in connection with the Union Central Executive Committee. In accordance with these directions every constituent republic organizes a central electoral commission attached to its executive committee. Various subordinate electoral commissions are formed in republics, autonomous republics, autonomous regions, villages, and cities. Central commissions in each respective republic exercise a general supervision. The composition of the central commissions, as well as those of the lower units, consists of members selected from workers directly connected with production, farm hands, members of collectives, poor peasants, middle peasants, women's organizations, national minorities, Komsomol, Red Army, and respective executive committees. The regulations stipulate that electoral commissions in republics, autonomous republics, and autonomous regions must be composed of from fifteen to twenty-one members representing various groups. The chairman of these commissions must be appointed in Russia proper by the Central Executive Committee on the recommendation of the All-Russian Central Electoral Commission. As a check on local organs, the law requires that the membership of these commissions must be confirmed by the higher authorities. The duties of all electoral commissions, with the exception of those in villages and cities, are as follows:

(1) Preparing for the election of soviets and congresses of soviets.
(2) Supervising legal conduct at election time.
(3) Designating the period of duration of lower electoral commissions.
(4) Conducting the work of the lower commissions.
(5) Giving information to the appropriate executive committees in regard to the disbandment of electoral commissions and the dismissal of independent members.
(6) Receiving reports from lower electoral commissions in regard to their work.
(7) Giving information to higher electoral commissions and executive committees on the course of election and supplying the necessary materials and reports on the election.
(8) Appointing to lower electoral commissions, of representatives who are to familiarize themselves with the work and course of electoral campaigns.
(9) Investigating protests and complaints concerning the action of the lower electoral commissions and, in case of necessity, the reversal of their decisions.

Raion electoral commissions consist of from eleven to fifteen persons, depending on the size and importance of the particular raion representing the aforementioned groups. In cities and villages, electoral commissions consist of eleven members, but in large and economically important urban centers, the membership may be increased to fifteen persons. In villages it may be reduced to seven members by appropriate authorities. Village and city electoral commissions exercise only the functions as enumerated in points one, two, and seven, but they perform in addition the following duties:

(1) Make out, verify, and publish lists of persons who have been deprived of their franchise.

(2) Send the voters notices of election and take other measures to inform them of the time and place of election.

(3) Divide the territory into electoral precincts.

(4) Organize electoral meetings.

(5) Appoint representatives for the purpose of presiding over electoral meetings and directing their work.

Rural settlements attached to cities send representatives to take part in the work of the urban electoral commission. Large cities which have raion soviets may, by decision of the city soviets, form joint city-raion electoral commissions.

Sub-commissions may be appointed in single large undertakings. In those localities which lack any of the designated elements which are to compose the electoral commission, the appropriate executive committee and soviets may substitute representatives of other public organizations.

The electoral commissions are appointed for the duration of the electoral campaign, covering a definite period decided upon by the higher electoral commissions, and are dissolved after the campaign is finished.

SUFFRAGE

In recent years practically the entire population of the Soviet Union has been permitted to vote; thus in the 1931 election, only three and nine-tenths per cent of adults over eighteen years were deprived of the franchise. In general, all citizens who are over eighteen years of age of both sexes are entitled to vote, provided they are occupied by socially useful work, including housekeeping, or are members of the Red Army and Navy, or are disabled workers. The law extends this privilege to foreigners who are permanent residents in the country and who belong to the working class, and to alien peasants who do not employ outside labor.

Foreigners of "the white-collar" category may be granted the right to vote by appropriate authority, provided their loyalty to the Soviets is beyond doubt. The vote is withheld from persons who have employed and are employing labor, those who have an unearned income, those who are engaged in trade, and those who belong to a class which has been deprived of the franchise in accordance with a provision in the constitution of R. S. F. S. R.

A detailed enumeration of groups who are granted and those who are deprived of the vote shows that practically the entire population is included within the electorate. The following classes have the franchise: fishermen and peasants who sell the products of their toil on the open market; owners of all kinds of undertakings such as dairies, etc., who do not employ outside labor or distribute work to individual households; mechanics who do not employ outside labor or who employ only two apprentices and one journeyman and sell the product of their own toil only on the open market; persons who live on the winnings of state lotteries, or interest on state bonds, or savings which are deposited in state savings banks; persons who receive aid from friends and relatives abroad or insurance benefits from abroad; invalids of toil and war who are conducting small businesses, janitors, bell-ringers and similar employees of churches and, strange as it may seem, members of parish councils; members of the free professions who perform public useful labor; and children of those who have been disfranchised but who have come of age since 1925, who may have been as minors dependent on their parents but who are now performing useful work, although they still may be living with their parents.

Local organs may not deprive persons of the franchise unless they come under the classification of Article 69 of the constitution and other legislation.

The following groups are disfranchised: farmers, stock raisers, and mechanics who employ labor to an extent that enlarges their business beyond that of a toiler; agriculturists and stock raisers who also have trade and industrial establishments such as mills or shops with motor equipment, or those who manage them with permanent or seasonal outside help; persons who rent out complicated farm machinery and motor equipment; owners of large fishing vessels who rent them out; persons who loan money on security of stock, machinery, etc.; persons who charge a land rent which is considered by raion tax commissions as exorbitant; persons who rent orchards or vineyards for purposes of exploitation; (Exceptions may be made when the tax commission does not consider the rents high enough to impose the unified, individual, and agricultural tax.) owners and renters of under-takings who distribute work to individuals to be done at home, or lease or sub-lease these undertakings to a second party; private traders, jobbers and middle men, renters and owners of under-takings of factory-plant dimensions; former officers and officials of the White Armies and leaders of counter-revolutionary bands; all employees and agents of the tsarist police, especially of the corps of gendarmes, and all persons who were directly or indirectly connected with the former police; ministers and officials of the old régime; members of the imperial family; former members of the prison staffs, leaders of the nobility, members of the prosecuting staffs, and those who have held commanding positions in disciplinary battalions; former and present employees of religious cults; persons who have been exiled in an administrative manner for the duration of exile, and those who have been deprived of the franchise by judicial process, and persons in penal institutions. In some instances the members of the families of those who are deprived of the franchise are granted the right to vote. Employers who find it necessary to be absent at harvest time or other seasonal periods may employ outside help without losing their vote.

The village soviets in rural districts and city soviets in urban centers keep lists of those deprived of the franchise for which special forms are provided. The lists are made up at the time of preparation for election by village and city electoral commissions and are confirmed in rural districts by the raion executive committee and in urban centers by city and raion soviets, respectively, in accordance with documentary evidence. All information, oral or written, must be verified.

The electoral commissions, not later than twenty days before election, publish in the press or post in a public place the names of all those who are disfranchised. Persons excluded from voting may enter a complaint to the election commission. This body must forward, within three days, the complaint accompanied by its opinion and documentary evidence to the raion executive committee or the city or raion soviet which confirmed the list. The village electoral commission directs the complaints to the raion electoral commission and the raion electoral commission, to the raion executive committee. The presidium of the raion executive committee or of the raion and city soviet must investigate the complaint within three days, and communicate this decision to the petitioner and the appropriate electoral commission. The complainant may appeal the decision to higher authorities. The entire matter must be decided upon within seven days.

Persons who were deprived of electoral rights in accordance with constitutional provisions may be reinstated in their rights, if they have been engaged during a period of no less than five years in productive labor and have proved their loyalty to the Soviet power. If these persons belong to a professional union, they may upon the request of the union be reinstated sooner.

Other categories of disfranchised persons, with exception of the lower technical personnel of the former police and prison employees, may be reinstated in individual cases by special decrees of the presidium of the Central Executive Committee, provided that these persons can show that they are engaged in productive and socially useful labor and have demonstrated their loyalty to the Soviet power.

Persons who were deprived of their franchise as the consequence of administrative exile or judicial process may be reinstated without further action as soon as they have served their sentence, provided they have not lost their franchise for some other reason. Persons who have been reinstated in their personal rights by higher authorities may not be deprived of their rights by lower organs. Persons whose petitions have been turned down by the presidium of the Central Executive Committee cannot petition again before the expiration of a year, unless new circumstances have arisen or the petition is made by professional or public organizations.

ELECTION ASSEMBLIES

The Soviet voter knows nothing of ballots and ballot boxes. The voting is done *viva voce* in electoral assemblies which are called by the electoral commission or its representative. The voters are informed not less than five days before the election by individual communications as to place and time of the convening of the electoral assembly. The voting for members of city soviets is carried out in assemblies at factories, plants, or professional unions. In larger industrial centers, assemblies may be held at various shifts and departments, or in connection with professional unions, or in precinct assemblies.

The election to village soviets comprising several settlements is carried out in their respective places provided individual settlements have enough voters to elect one member; otherwise a general meeting of all settlements within a reasonable distance is held. Large settlements are divided into electoral precincts; compact national groups may be segregated into special precincts for that purpose. The electoral precincts in rural districts must not exceed five hundred inhabitants. The collective farmers vote with the rest of the population of the village. Isolated settlers vote in the election precinct of the nearest village of the same raion. Workers and employees of Soviet farms, factories, and plants which are situated outside of city limits and have no soviets of their own and workers in motor tractor stations take part in the election of the nearest village or organize an independent precinct. Only persons who have the franchise are permitted to be present at election meetings. At all election meetings a record is kept of all who have come to vote. Forty per cent of the voters present at the electoral meeting at a given precinct constitutes a legal election; otherwise another election must be held. The electoral meeting is opened and presided over by a representative of the electoral commission, who announces the list of candidates and also the names of individual candidates who have come out for election at that time. The chairman also announces the number of places to be filled. The number of candidates to be elected in each precinct is decided upon by the local electoral commission in accordance with current enactments. The voting is done for lists of candidates or for individual candidates, depending upon the decision of the electoral assembly. The electoral commission has no authority to advocate lists of candidates or individual candidates. Lists of candidates sponsored by public, party, and professional organizations and individual candidates may be announced previous to the election in the press or by a poster. The voting for lists does not exclude the voting against an individual candidate on the list. Since, however, the voting is open and oral, it is not wise for the voter to oppose candidates or lists of candidates favored by the party group. The candidates receiving the majority of votes of all electors present are declared elected. The electoral assembly also elects "candidates" (alternates) to the extent of one-third of the number of positions to be filled; the voting for candidates is carried out separately.

In rural districts the voters elect village revisionary commissions composed of five members and two "candidates." Complaints against the conduct of the election must be made within seven days to the electoral commission which has conducted the election, and it must forward the complaints to the higher electoral commission within three days. If the complaint is justified, a partially or wholly new election may be ordered.

In the election of 1931, 70.4 per cent of the rural and 79.6 per cent of the urban electorate voted. Bolshevik writers frequently point out that soviet elections are free, since the non-party element in the soviet elective assemblies is higher than the communist element. Thus in the rural soviets 78.8 per cent of the membership was non-party; however, 59 per cent of the important positions, such as chairmanships of rural soviets, were won by communists. In city soviets almost half of the membership, 49.5 per cent, went to the party and 95.5 per cent of the chairmanships went to the Communists. In the higher units of government, however, the communist led; thus in the All-Union Congress, 73.1 per cent were communists, and in the Central Executive Committee of the Union 79.9 per cent belonged to the Communist party.[3]

ELECTION TO CONGRESSES OF SOVIETS

Only the members of the village and city soviets are elected by direct vote; all other legislative organs are chosen indirectly by soviets. The elections of delegates to congresses of soviets are for the most part carried out indirectly. Delegates to raion congresses are elected at the plenum of city and village soviets, to the number of one delegate for each 300 unit of population; and from state farms, factories, and plants, situated outside of urban settlements, at electoral assemblies to the number of one delegate for each sixty voters. The election to the regional congresses in cities that are subject directly to regional executive committees takes place at the plenum of city soviets at the rate of one member for each 2,500 voters. To represent all other settlements in the raion, the raion congress of soviets elects one delegate for each 12,500 inhabitants.

The All-Russian Congress of Soviets is elected by city soviets at the ratio of one delegate for each 25,000 voters and in regional congresses[4] at the ratio of one delegate for each unit of 125,000 inhabitants. The All-Union Congress is elected by city soviets at the ratio of one delegate for each 25,000 voters and by congresses of soviets at the ratio of one representative per 125,000 inhabitants. Soviet Russia proper sends delegates at the rate indicated from regional, autonomous republican, and autonomous regional congresses. Those constituent republics which have no regional divisions send delegates to the Union Congress elected by the republican congresses. An executive committee is elected by each congress, but the old committee remains in authority until the first session of the new committee is called.

Elections of delegates to soviets may be cancelled wholly or in part. A total cancellation takes place if more than a half of the deputies were elected in violation of the Union or republican constitutions and the instructions of the presidium of the Union Central Executive Committee. The election may be cancelled in part when violations are found in one or several electoral precincts. The voiding of an entire election must be by authority of the higher executive committees in coöperation with the political unit affected. When a new election is called because of violations, the entire election staff is changed; if it is only a partial re-election, a few new members are appointed on the electoral commission.

SPECIAL ELECTIONS

In case of recall, death, loss of franchise, and other disabilities of deputies or in the absence of "candidates", new members are appointed until a special election can be called. The raion election committee appoints representatives for the special election in the village; in cities and raions, representatives are appointed by appropriate city or raion soviets. All voters may take part in special elections.[5]

The Communist Party[6]

There is only one legal political party in the Soviet Union and that is the Communist (Bolshevik) Party. Since this entire study concerns itself with the theory and practice of Bolshevism, it is not necessary to go into detail as to theoretical doctrines of the Bolshevik régime in this connection. Suffice it to say that the Communist "articles of faith" are based on the teachings of Karl Marx as interpreted by Lenin and adapted to the ever varied contingencies of Russian life. The ultimate ideal of the Communist is the creation of a classless society; in the transitional period, however, there must be a dictatorship of the proletariat. This dictatorship of the proletariat, under the control of the Communists, is at present governing most of the former Russian empire. The class struggle, in spite of abolition of capitalism, has by no means abated; new classes, in fact, have come into being. On the one side are ranged the proletariat (workers); poor peasants, who are considered as possible members of the proletariat class but are not as yet entirely won over; and employees and professional men, who are the survivors of the old intelligentsia and considered a doubtful element; and on the other hand, a class which is popularly called the "former people" (Byvshiye Luidi), for whom there is no way out but eventual "destruction." This group is composed of former "exploiters", the nobility, former middle class, private traders, the clergy, and rich peasants (kulaks). Needless to say these elements are disfranchised. The factory workers and farm laborers compose the ruling class and possess a privileged status in regard to food, shelter, medical care, amusements, and education. The various technical experts, who are members of the former ruling classes, are called in to do the work which the Bolsheviks hope a new generation of technicians from the proletariat group will perform in the future.

The lot of these experts until recent times was not a pleasant one; they were distrusted and accused of disloyalty and frequently prosecuted for counter-revolutionary designs, in some cases justly. By 1931, however, a reaction against the baiting of technical experts set in. Stalin himself stated that "it would be stupid and senseless to look upon practically every engineer of the old school as if he were a potential criminal or wrecker."

Conditions have improved for the technical experts, and in some instances their standard of living is superior to that of the workers, but as yet no equality with the proletariat in the full sense of the term has been awarded them.

The Communists believe as the older generation dies out, the class struggle will have ceased, and by the end of the second Five Year Plan, that is 1937, it will have ended.

COMPOSITION OF THE PARTY

The constitution of the Communist Party states that "everyone who subscribes to the party program, works in one of its organizations, submits to party decisions, and pays membership dues is considered a party member." This is not to be understood that anyone who desires to become a member of the Party can do so; in fact, the conditions of admission are very rigid, since the constitution provides that only three categories of persons may be admitted: namely, (1) workers and Red Army soldiers who come from the workers and peasant class; (2) peasants (other than soldiers), hand craftsmen *(kustari)* who are not exploiting another's labor; (3) all others (office employees, and so forth). The first category is divided into two groups, industrial workers who are permanently engaged in physical hired labor; and non-industrial workers, soldiers from the workers and peasant classes, and farm hands. Applicants for admission to the Party belonging to the first groups of the first category must present recommendations of two party members of one year's standing; persons belonging to the second group of the first category must obtain recommendations of two members of two years' standing. Both groups remain on probation for no less than six months. For the admission of members belonging to the second category, recommendations of three members of three years' standing are required and a probationary period of no less than a year; for admission of persons of the third category, recommendations of five party members of five years' standing and a probation period of no less than two years is required. In exceptional cases persons who have been members of some other party may be admitted into the ranks of the Communist Party, but in general the Bolsheviks at present are not anxious to receive the older generation; rather they look forward to the filling of gaps by the communist youth, who have been reared in the Soviet atmosphere and have known no other state of affairs. All recommendations are carefully ratified by a local party committee. The applicants are discussed first by the party cell, and later on are considered in a general meeting of the party, and finally are decided upon by a district party committee. Young people under twenty, with exception of Red Army soldiers, are admitted only through the Komsomol (Young Communist Organization). It is a serious matter for any party member to propose candidates, since the sponsors are responsible for their recommendation and may be subject to severe discipline, even expulsion from the party, should the applicants prove unworthy. Since the industrial workers are favored, their number has increased over against other groups, and in 1930 constituted nearly sixty-nine per cent of the party membership, while the peasant constituted only about nineteen per cent. The rest were distributed among other groups.[7]

While there are some privileges attached to party membership, yet in general, party members are exposed to a very rigid disciplinary régime. They must undergo continuous training in the Marxist doctrine, participate in a variety of civil, social, and party organizations and activities, live up to certain standard of personal behavior, and conduct themselves in such a manner in regard to all kinds of indulgences as to serve as good examples to the people in general. The Party has fixed a "party maximum" for compensation of members, which must not be departed from without special permission. The Communist Party in the Soviet Union is admitted to be a thoroughly disciplined group, which has been carrying out willingly the mandates of the Party for the creation of the Communist economic order. The constitution of the Bolshevik Party emphasizes "complete freedom of discussion regarding controversial matters." Bolsheviks also proclaim that the Party organization is "democratic centralism", but once the Party has come to a decision, it is absolutely essential for every party member, unit, and organization to carry out implicitly the decision of the Party. Dissenters are investigated by the Control Commissions and are subject to punishment, which may take the form of censure or expulsion from the Party depending on extenuating circumstances. The membership of the Party is estimated at nearly three million men and women.

THE KOMSOMOL (The Young Communists)

The Bolsheviks, in their endeavor to retain the power in the Soviet state, leave nothing to chance. They have been carrying on extensive propaganda among the youth of the country by forming organizations for the young. The Young Communists (Komsomol) is an association of young people of both sexes between the ages of fourteen and twenty-three and has an estimated membership of nearly five million boys and girls. The qualifications of membership in this organization are similar to those of the Communist Party and are as rigidly enforced. Young workers and peasants may join the organization without special recommendations, nor do they need to serve a probationary period. Other groups must present recommendations from two Komsomol members of two years' standing and serve one year as probationers. The older Bolsheviks never tire of reminding the members of the Komsomol that upon their shoulders will fall all the burdens and tasks of the proletarian dictatorship after the older generation has disappeared. They are told that they constitute the vanguard of the young generation and are urged to become acquainted with the doctrines of Communism and develop thmselves physically and culturally. They must be active in social and civic work. These young people, trained as they are in an atmosphere of communism, constitute the most enthusiastic element in the Soviet state. The Komsomol is particularly active in the conduct of work among children. Two children's organizations that are the most important in connection with this study are the Pioneers, composed of children between ten and sixteen, which has an estimated membership of nearly three and one-half millions, and the Octobrists,[8] composed of children between the ages of eight to ten. The older organizations are supposed to be the guiding elements in the children's organizations, who thus very early in life receive a thorough training in Bolshevik ideology.[9]

THE PARTY MACHINERY

The lowest unit and the base of organization of the Party is the cell (yacheika) which is usually organized in villages, factories, undertakings, and institutions. This unit must have at least three party members. The cell is the fundamental unit of the Party and has for its purpose the carrying out of the party policies and the recruiting and training of new members. It is supposed to be the backbone of local party and governmental organization. The cells are called upon to assist in propaganda among the masses and take an active part in the political and economic life of the locality and the country at large. As the city and village are the primary units of the governmental structure, so the party cell is the unit in connection with the party organization. The cells elect delegates to the higher party divisions such as that of the raion and oblast. The election of delegates to the highest party organization is, however, carried out by party oblast congresses, which elect delegates to republican and All-Union party congresses. The All-Union Congress meets every year and constitutes the highest organ of party authority. The All-Republican and All - Union Congresses elect central committees which carry out the work of the Congress between meetings of the Party. In addition, every year the Party holds an All-Union Party Conference, which is composed not of delegates elected by various party units, but of officials. The Central Committee of the Union has a membership of seventy-two and is divided into three sections: (1) a Secretariat, which performs the current work of organization and execution; (2) an Organization Bureau (Org-bureau), which concerns itself with the general organization of the Party, sets forth conditions of party membership, supervises the spread of propaganda into the communities, and has the authority to promote and demote party members; (3) the Political Bureau (Polit-bureau), composed of nine members. This is perhaps the most important organ since it formulates the policies of the Party. In theory the Political Bureau is appointed by the Central Committee; in reality the Secretary General of the Party, if he is powerful enough, makes the selection. This is the case at present, since Stalin is the Secretary General.

The Polit-bureau does not hold open meetings, nor is it governed by any definite rules, but it is a well known fact that no important measures are undertaken without permisson of this powerful bureau. To be sure, the formal decisions are as a rule issued as decrees, are countersigned by high Soviet officials, and are published in the press. These decisions are in theory ratified by the Central Committee and eventually by the All-Union Party Congress. In recent years, however, since Stalin has succeeded in vanquishing his opponents such as Trotsky and less dangerous enemies, no decision of importance has been turned down by either organization. In addition to the above enumerated party agencies, there is a central revision commission, composed of party members of at least ten years' standing. This commission serves as an auditing organ in checking up "the speed and proper procedure of handling matters in the central party organs and the proper organization of the Secretariat of the Central Committee of the Party." It supervises the treasury and undertakings of the Central Committee of the Party. The constitution of the Party also makes provisions for a Central Control Commission, which is to be elected at the Congress "preferably from peasants and workers who have had the necessary party, soviet, economic, and industrial experience."

The members of the Central Control Commission who are to work in the central organ of the Central Control Commission or in the Workman-Peasant Inspection must have at least ten years' party standing; members of the Commission who are to be employed in local organs must have at least seven years' party standing; industrial workers and peasants must have at least five years' party standing. The organization of this Central Commission goes back to the early days, when the Soviet Government was largely dependent for the carrying out of its work of administration upon the old officials, who were found to be carrying over the tsarist bureaucratic tendencies in their administrative activities. In order to remedy the situation a decree was issued on January 23, 1918, instituting commissions of control, and on March 8 of the same year, elective control collegia were placed at the head of the entire control apparatus, which later on developed into workers' and peasants' inspection discussed at length in another connection. In 1923, when the twelfth Congress of the Party convened, Lenin suggested the extension of the activities of the party commission for central control and its amalgamation with the Workman - Peasant Inspection. The Congress, in accordance with this proposal, adopted a resolution which among other things states "the chief duty of the Central Control Commission shall be to cultivate a party tendency in all

Soviet organs . . . . The presidium of the Commission is elected at the plenary session thereof and is composed of nine comrades of high standing, *i. e.* members of the central committee."[10]   It further provided that "some members of the presidium of the Central Control Commission enter into the composition of the collegium of the people's commissariats."[11]   The resolution also stipulated that "at least one-half of the remaining members of the control commission were to be appointed in agreement with the Workman-Peasant Inspection, and in carrying out Soviet orders were to be under the supervision of the Workman-Peasant Inspection, and in accordance with special provisions worked out for that purpose." The resolution provided for plenary sessions of the Central Control Commission to meet every two months, immediately preceding the plenary sessions of the Central Committee.   The Central Committee had the authority to send delegates, to whom were extended the right of a consulting vote, to plenary sessions of the Control Commission.   The Party constitution of 1925 provided for plenary sessions every three months and a presidium of twenty-one members with nine alternates, and a secretariat.   At the plenary session a collegium is selected which has the important authority of reviewing "matters concerned with the violation of party ethics, the constitution, and the program of the All-Union Communist Party."[12]

The presidium of the Central Control Commission "delegates three members and three alternates to take part in deliberations of the Political Bureau, and five members and five alternates to take part in the work of the Organization Bureau and of the Secretariat of the Central Committee, with the right of a consulting voice."[13]   Illustrative of the power of the Central Control Commission is the provision that it has "the right to assign tasks within the limits of its jurisdiction to all members of the party organizations."[14]   In order to give the members an opportunity of disinterested action, the constitution provides that members of the Central Control Commission may not at the same time be members of the Party Central Committee and occupy administrative or economic positions.[15]

The constitution makes provisions for control commissions in republican and lower political units, but for the sake of control by the central body, it stipulates that there must be representation of the Central Committee in the lower party organizations. In important and large regions this representation is freed from all work except that of the Party.

PARTY FINANCES

The membership dues of party members and applicants are divided into four categories depending on the size of income: the first category pays one-half of one per cent; the second, one per cent; the third, two per cent; and the fourth, three per cent. Persons who are temporarily unemployed and persons receiving pensions are freed from payment of dues. Persons whose income is undetermined, such as peasants, pay at a rate determined by local committees. Every applicant on probation must pay an entrance fee of three per cent of his monthly wage. Non payment of dues for three months without a good reason is considered as a resignation from the Party.

PARTY FACTIONS IN NON-PARTY ORGANIZATIONS

The Party constitution provides that party factions be organized in all non-party organizations such as professional unions, soviets, coöperatives, etc., which have in their ranks three Communists.

The party faction exercises a strong influence in all organizations out of proportion to its numerical strength. These party groups are, of course, subordinate to party organizations and carry out their principles. In fact the party factions put forward candidates for all important offices within a given organization, and as the members of the faction frequently constitute the most articulate element within a given enterprise or organization, they practically formulate public opinion, both by force of argument and implied intimidation.

THE THIRD INTERNATIONAL
(Comintern)

The organization of the First International can be traced to an association of workingmen formed in London in 1864 and is generally referred to as the "International." The composition consisted of workers from a number of countries and in the course of time acquired influence, especially after it became the proponent of the teachings of Marx. In 1876, because of internal trouble, it was dissolved, but in 1889 the Second International was organized, led by intellectuals subscribing to the doctrines of Marx. Soon, however, because of the development of nationalism, it could not pursue its international policies, and while theorists maintained their international outlook, the rank and file succumbed to the spirit of nationalism. The work of the various component national groups and their leaders consisted of an endeavor to better economic conditions of working men and bring about by evolution a gradual change from capitalism to socialism. When the World War broke out, the majority of the socialists became the supporters of their respective governments, while only a small group maintained the international outlook that labor had nothing to gain from nationalistic aims and should, instead of joining in the imperialistic struggle of their respective governments, make a concerted attempt to overthrow international capitalism. In 1915 the minority met at Zimmerwald, Switzerland, and at a later gathering in 1916, created the foundation for the Third International. When the Russian Revolution broke out in 1917, it became possible for the Russian faction of the minority group to materialize their plans formulated in previous conferences. The Third International (Comintern) was formally established in 1919 at Moscow. The Russian Communist Party (All-Union now) is merely one of some fifty-eight communist parties making up the Third International. The purpose of this organization is to struggle for the overthrow, by violence if necessary, of capitalism and the eventual establishment of proletarian rule all over the world. It undertakes to support established soviet republics in all parts of the world. The sixth Congress of the Third International, meeting in 1928, proclaimed that communistic aims can be realized only by a violent overthrow of the present existing social order.[16]

Needless to say, a good deal of what the various congresses say and resolve is merely "rhetoric" for home consumption. Soviet Russia at this time has neither the time nor money to go on an "international crusade." One must be careful not to mistake emotional outpourings for actuality. The Bolshevik loves dramatics and indulges in them freely. It is probably the only emotional outlet the hard pressed and harassed leaders have at the present time. The World Congress is the highest organ of the Third International and meets at intervals. The Congress elects an executive committee composed of fifty-nine members. This committee has extensive powers, and its decisions are mandatory on all collective and individual members of the Third International. The Third International is not as well disciplined a body as the All-Union Communist Party; internal conflicts, such as the antagonism between Trotsky and Stalin, had its reverberations in "individual" parties all over the world. The present leadership of Soviet Russia is too realistic to wager too much on world revolution, and is concentrating on a domestic policy of socialism; however, the fiery speeches of some individual members of the Third International have succeeded in creating an image of fear in the mind of the world, which explains in part at least the attitude toward the Soviet Union. At this writing responsible Soviet government leaders are preaching coöperation with other nations. Fiery speeches there will be in the future, but realistic necessity is ever before the eyes of the responsible rulers of the Soviet land; therefore, nations might well consider that the famous Third International is not as dangerous as some of the speeches indicate.

CHAPTER IV

MUNICIPAL GOVERNMENT

INTRODUCTION

Before proceeding to discuss the larger units of government one must take into consideration the status of the city. The Soviet power is based on the urban industrial class, and as Lenin expressed it, "the actual and the only foundation . . . for the creation of a socialist society is predominately the large industry." Furthermore, the political nucleus of the Soviet system is to be found in the city. Here is the base of the pyramid, the foundation of the rather involved structure of the Soviet government. On March 1, 1930, there were in the Soviet Union 709 municipalities and 485 workers' and urban settlements. The population of the Soviet Union cities in accordance with the census of 1926 was 24,900,000. The estimated urban population in 1929 was 28,300,000. In Russia proper, there were 485 cities and 316 workers' settlements and settlements of an urban type. Some cities in the Soviet Union and especially in Russia proper, because of an influx of population from the country, had a considerable increase in population, aggregating a total of 32 per cent in the years between 1926 and 1931. The following figures may serve as an illustration:[1]

	1926	1931
Moscow. .	2,124,500	2,781,300
Leningrad. .	1,614,008	2,228,300
Baku. .	452,808	575,200
Kiev. .	513,789	539,500
Kharkov. .	417,342	521,500
Odessa. .	420,788	475,500
Rostov-on-Don. .	308,284	457,100
Tashkent. .	323,613	421,800
Nizhni-Novgorod. .	220,815	350,300
Tiflis. .	292,973	347,900
Dniepropetrovsk. .	233,001	322,800
Stalingrad. .	148,370	294,500
Saratov. .	215,276	277,500
Sverdlovsk .	131,535	223,300
Samara. .	175,662	220,400

The Soviet System of City Government

Bolshevik writers trace the Soviet system in general and city rule in particular to the Revolution of 1905. In the month of May of that year a revolutionary soviet (council) of workers' delegates, finding the authorities of Ivanovo-Voznesenka demoralized and helpless, took over the task of guarding public safety. In October of the same year, the workers of St. Petersburg rose in revolt and organized a soviet, but it proved to be of short duration since the government succeeded in crushing the uprising. When the Revolution of March 1917 overthrew the imperial government, the Soviet of Petrograd was revived, and having drawn into its membership the soldiers, became not only the ruling authority of the city but practically the *de facto* government of the entire land, until the Provisional Government gathered enough strength to assert itself.[2]

Times were, however, too stirring and revolutionary; enthusiasm was running too high for the soviet to pay much attention to the rather prosaic task of city administration and for a time left the details of administration to the old city councils.[3] Soon, however, the Bolshevik war cry, "All power to the Soviets", inspired the soviets to take over all possible authority, but it was after the feeble and much harassed Provisional Government collapsed on October 25, 1917 (old style), that the soviets found themselves completely in possession of all power in every branch of government.

Now that they had the authority the task proved gigantic, and since the revolutionary spirit ran at even whiter heat than in March, the soviets did not seem to find time to settle down to the tedious task of constructive work. Hence the influence of the soviets in the administration of local affairs was negligible. The new government was inclined to leave municipal machinery intact, reserving to the soviet, however, the controlling power. Accordingly, in November 1917, the Petrograd city duma (municipal council) was dissolved, and a new election was held. The middle and liberal classes abstained from voting in protest and thus permitted the Bolsheviks and the "left" Social-Revolutionaries to obtain a large majority in the city duma. The local authorities, in those cities which submitted to the controlling influence of the soviets, were soon confronted with constant interference and meddling on the part of some members of the local soviets. Resistance was useless, and appeals could be directed only to the local soviets. Frequently to end friction and misunderstanding the soviets simply dispersed the local authorities and took over the administration themselves. Unfortunately the soviets at that time had very little administrative experience; their traditions were not those of a governing class, but rather those of a national revolutionary organization, and as a result misrule and inefficiency were rife, often reacting disastrously upon city welfare. There was pronounced resentment on the part of the urban population to the new authority, and it often expressed itself in passive opposition. As the fever of the revolution subsided, the soviets settled down to constructive work, the opposition died down, and eventually the soviets were accepted as the actual municipal authority. Yet up to the last part of 1917, there was considerable agitation in favor of organizing democratic municipal organs.

Before the promulgation of the new Soviet constitution in July 1918, no uniform system of municipal government was to be found in Soviet Russia. The organization and function of municipal organs differed in the various cities of the land. To be sure, the people's commissar of the interior issued from time to time decrees for the purpose of bringing about some standardization in municipal affairs, but not until the adoption of the constitution were those orders taken seriously. Every local soviet considered itself to be the highest authority in a given territory, levying taxes and contributions, and independently organizing its system of administration. Some of these groups went so far as to order execution of opponents, without consulting the central authorities.[4]

CHANGES BROUGHT ABOUT BY THE SOVIET CONSTITUTION

With the adoption of the Soviet constitution in July 1918, a more orderly procedure in municipal administration was established. The fundamental law stipulated that the membership of the city soviet was to be composed of one delegate for each one thousand inhabitants, provided that there were no less than fifty and no more than one thousand delegates in a soviet.[5] The term

of service of the individual delegate was fixed at three months.
For the purpose of actual administration the city soviets were to
elect an executive committee to be composed of one member for
each fifty delegates; this committee, however, was not to be under
three nor in excess of fifteen members.[6] The executive committee was responsible solely to the city soviet of delegates.
A meeting of the soviet could be convoked upon the initiative
of the executive committee or upon the demand of one-half of the
members of the soviet. It was mandatory, in any case, to hold
at least one meeting a week. Within the limits of its jurisdiction
the city soviet was supreme in a given territory.[7] The designated
general scope of work of the city soviets was as follows:

(1) To take all possible measures to carry out the decrees of
the constituted authorities.

(2) To encourage the development of cultural and economic
life in the community.

(3) To give decisions in affairs of a purely local character.

(4) To unify all soviet activities in a single territory.[8]

The city soviets were to organize various departments for the
carrying out of administrative tasks, but there was no provision
as to number or kind of departments the city soviets were to
establish. Indeed these provisions were too vague and general,
and left undecided the questions of competence and organization
of city organs.

Soon after the promulgation of the constitution, civil war
broke out, bringing with it confusion and still further limiting
and hindering the inexperienced local agencies in their attempt
to build up orderly administrative machinery. Military authority
was supreme, and very little attention was paid to constitutional
and legal provisions. It was a period of terrific struggle, famine,
and wretchedness. The entire land, and especially the city, was
hungry and cold and thought very little of self-government.

While theoretically city soviets were to be organized in all
municipalities, in practice a great number of towns neglected to
organize soviets. The revolutionary element, having dispersed
the old city councils and district administrations, assembled
district congresses of soviets and elected district executive committees, which were authorized to administer both the city and the
district. In some instances there were no district bodies and the

provincial authorities ruled the city. In general municipal government as such ceased to exist, and the city was governed by various governmental agencies, mostly by representatives from the center. One of the contributory factors to the demoralization of city government was the absence of competent persons who could take the place of the old intelligentsia. The best elements of the Bolshevik faction were at the front or heading expeditions into the country to commandeer agricultural products for the starving urban centers. In those days of communistic fervor, it was not considered necessary to pay communal workers; a few pounds of bread per month were considered sufficient compensation for city employees, especially since currency at that time lost its purchasing value. In general it was chaos and disorder, and such control as existed came from the center. Obviously no new system of city government could be developed under such circumstances. The earlier rallying cry of "all power to the localities" was transformed into "all power to the center."

From time to time, however, the central authorities endeavored to re-establish or re-vitalize the city soviets. Thus as far back as 1919, the seventh All-Russian Congress of Soviets took measures to re-vitalize the urban soviets, issuing various instructions to that end, but no attention was paid to them. The eighth All-Russian Congress of Soviets, meeting in 1920, recommended that city soviets be organized in all urban settlements for the purpose of local administration, but these instructions were clearly inapplicable in those abnormal times and were not obeyed. In fact years were to elapse before some order could be established. To be sure an ordinance was passed in 1922 by the All-Russian Central Executive Committee for the establishment of city soviets, but it accomplished little.[9] The year 1922 marked the receding of the wave of militant and heroic communism, and the central authorities attempted to draw a line between local and central agencies. The task, however, of bringing about order out of chaos created by civil war and of laying the foundation for municipal traditions was, to say the least, extremely difficult.

It was not until 1925 that the work of developing city organs began seriously. Soviet Russia was facing a tremendous and tedious task of resurrecting civic life and at the same time building municipal institutions based on revolutionary ideals.

Before this could be accomplished, however, it was necessary to clear away the débris of revolution and civil war; damaged streets and buildings had to be repaired, and new buildings and public playgrounds erected. Municipal enterprises of all kinds were encouraged and developed by city authorities. An attempt had to be made to interest the broad masses in actual city administration. Indeed, the places in municipal governmental agencies previously occupied by the well-born were to be filled by men and women of the working class, and a city life created under conditions hitherto unknown in the history of the world.

The Decree of 1925

The Municipal Decree of 1925,[10] which created the present structure of soviet city government, designates the city soviet as the governing body of cities. Like the other soviets, such as those of the county and province, the city soviet is based on Lenin's teachings in regard to control of governmental agencies, namely, "centralized supervision and decentralized activity." The activity, however, is strictly regulated. In common with the city councils of Western Europe, the city soviet is a subordinate organ, but subject to far more supervision by superior authorities.

The Size of the City Soviet

The size of the city soviet depends upon the population of the community. In comparison with city councils of Western Europe and the United States, the city soviets are of enormous proportions. Some of the larger cities in the Soviet Union have urban soviets of over one thousand members. The ratio of representation is so arranged as to draw into the local soviets of the smaller urban centers a large part of the population. Thus municipalities of one thousand inhabitants elect one deputy for every fifteen voters; towns of 1,000 to 3,000, one deputy for every twenty voters. In the larger cities of 50,000 to 100,000, one deputy represents 150 voters; in cities of over 100,000, one deputy represents 200 voters.[11] Every conceivable economic and social group, provided it does not belong to the disfranchised element, is given representation in the city soviet. All men and women of the "toiling" classes who are citizens of the Soviet Union[12] are entitled to vote. This also applies to the former bourgeois elements who are not engaged in "socially useful labor" or are soviet employees. In fact, since the "failure" of the election in 1924 because of abstention from voting, the suffrage has been widened to such an extent as to exclude only an insignificant number of the adult population. The classes which are still denied the vote are private traders, merchants, middlemen (nepmen), clergymen of all denominations, former agents of the imperial police, former high governmental officials, and officers of the white armies.[13] In contrast to the usages in other countries, the soviet election system is organized on the principle of vocational groups and not of territorial divisions. Shops, factories, institutions, and army organizations serve as units for electoral purposes. Smaller groups of the same category are combined to form a constituency. Only in the case of unorganized elements such as housewives, independent artisans, etc., is the territorial scheme used, but frequently these are joined with some organized groups of voters.[14]

CONDUCT OF ELECTIONS

Elections are conducted by an electoral commission of from eleven to fifteen members appointed by the city soviets, the number depending on size and importance of the city,[15] who represent the city soviet, the professional unions, the Red Army, the *Komsomol* (Communist Union of Youth), workers directly connected with production, and the local congress of delegates of women workers. A chairman is appointed by the executive committee of the next higher soviet. The voting takes place annually in election meetings called by the electoral commission. Notice must be given to the voters at least five days before the election. Since 1926 the electoral commission has been forbidden by law to sponsor or propose candidates. Candidates are usually suggested by the Communist group in the electoral meetings and also by the professional unions. Individual voters may announce their candidacy by coming forward in the electoral meetings and presenting themselves for that purpose.[16] The elections are open, and preferences are shown by acclamation or raising of hands.[17] Within seven days after election a protest may be entered in regard to its regularity to the electoral commission of the next higher soviet. The latter may either confirm the election or order a new election, which is conducted by a newly appointed electoral commission. Members of the city soviets may be recalled by their respective constituencies, in which event a special election is arranged.

Duties and Privileges of City Soviet Members

The various instructions governing the conduct of soviet members repeatedly emphasize the seriousness of the work of the deputies. They are warned that all deputies are obligated to take an active interest in the general work of the urban soviet, its committees and commissions. Not only must they attend to their official duties, but it is urged upon them to interest themselves in the various civic organizations. It is impressed upon them that as deputies they are in duty bound to attend all meetings of the municipal assembly, plenary sessions as well as sittings of committees and commissions of which they are members, and to carry out faithfully all their instructions. In no case must they absent themselves from such meetings without previously having given notice to presiding officers. They must familiarize themselves with details of the work assigned to them to such an extent as to be able to make helpful suggestions for the improvement of its execution. Above all, they must keep in close contact with their constituencies, report to them on the activities of the city soviet and its committees no less frequently than every three months, and furthermore take part, if possible, in all meetings or discussions of their constituencies and other organized and unorganized groups of working men and women.

In turn the members of the local soviet may, on the request of the city soviet or its presidium, be excused from their rural work in shops or institutions for the time necessary to carry on their duties as deputies, without the loss of the wage they would have earned during that time. Deputies who are not employed as wage earners, such as housewives and independent artisans, are to be reimbursed for the time spent in exercising their official duties, at the rate decided on by the presidium of the soviet.

Deputies, upon show of credentials, are to have free access to all municipal institutions, undertakings, and officials. They are entitled to demand information and explanations, except that when information is of a confidential nature, the request must come from the presidium of the soviet.[18]

MEETINGS OF THE CITY SOVIET

The first plenary meeting of the newly elected urban soviet is called by the electoral commission and presided over by the president of the previous soviet. At this meeting a new president, presidium, and credentials committee are elected. The report of the electoral commission is also heard at this time. Thereafter the city soviet meets at least once a month. Special sessions may be called by the presidium or on the request of one-third of the members. A three-day notice must be given to the deputies, indicating the exact time and place of meeting.[19] Private citizens are allowed to attend the meetings, but only members may vote.

Since in the larger cities the size of the city soviet precludes debate or discussion, the plenary session merely passes on reports and proposals of the presidium and committees. The plenary session, however, must pass on the municipal budget, loans, accounts, the number of committees, election of delegates for congresses of soviets, and plans of work for the plenary session and committees. One-half of the membership constitutes a quorum for all business.[20]

POWERS OF THE CITY SOVIET

The city soviet under present legal provisions exercises a fusion of legislative, executive, and administrative functions. Although its powers are nominally extensive, it is not by any manner of means autonomous. There is a rigid supervision of all its activities, and nothing can be undertaken unless expressly permitted by higher soviets or their executive committees. While the city soviet is authorized to issue regulations, they must be based on provisions of higher agencies. Before issuing an ordinance the local soviet must ascertain whether or not it would conflict with enactments passed for that purpose from above. In all cases of doubt, higher soviets must be consulted. A provision of a higher soviet on a given subject automatically voids the regulations of the lower on the same subject. Within these limitations the city soviet may pass regulations for the purpose of carrying out administrative tasks delegated to it by higher soviet authorities, and for the maintenance of "revolutionary" law and order in the territory under its jurisdiction.

In the field of general administration the city soviet is authorized to appoint electoral commissions, to direct the activity of ward soviets, to transfer to religious organizations buildings and properties necessary to their ritualistic usages, to supervise the activities of their religious groups, and to make sure that the law in regard to separation of church and state is being strictly observed. It further takes measures for the prevention of disasters such as floods, fires, etc., and renders assistance to the victims of such occurrences, forwards complaints by citizens against the rulings of city organs and city employees to appropriate authorities, and in some instances may institute hearings on the same. The city soviet directs the suppression of crime,[21] keeps records of vital statistics, is the custodian of municipal funds, recalls municipal judges and prosecutors,[22] and renders legal aid to the toiling population.

The financial and taxing jurisdiction of the city soviet extends to the making of estimates and planning, confirming, and administering the budget. It supervises the collection of taxes and assessments levied by the state and sees to it that the funds reach the proper authorities. For the needs of the community the city soviet is permitted to levy and to collect municipal taxes, surtaxes, and assessments as authorized by law, and to petition higher authorities for subsidies and additional revenue. It may engage in the organization of credit and savings institutions, negotiate loans with state, coöperative, and private banks and with persons in the Soviet Union or abroad, and issue bonds and certificates of indebtedness.

In the field of economic-commercial enterprise the city soviet is authorized to manage existing enterprises and organize new undertakings (it may also transfer its establishments to lessees), and in general encourage the development of industry and trade by assisting all coöperative organizations. In addition the city soviet may organize and operate passenger and freight transportation and may manage power houses, water works, disposal plants, and other public services; it may build communal dwelling places and distribute living space in accordance with provisions of the law.

The city soviet is charged with protection of labor, for which purpose it may compel private and public enterprises to observe the laws in regard to payment of wages and fulfillment of collective and individual contracts, and relieve unemployment by establishing, in agreement with labor organizations, employment agencies, public works, and eating places. It sees to the installation by various industries of safety devices and technical improvements for the betterment of labor conditions. It also enforces the law in regard to social insurance.

In matters of public health the jurisdiction of the city soviet covers a wide and varied field of activity. It establishes and operates clinics and prophylactic stations and organizes campaigns for the eradication of social and vocational diseases. To that end it is enjoined to coöperate with health institutions established by higher soviets. It also provides recreation grounds for the encouragement of sports and in general supports any movement which would serve for physical betterment of the community. The city soviet carries on sanitary inspection of dwelling places, laundries, court yards, basements, streets, and other public places. For purposes of general welfare it may regulate the illumination of stairs and house numbers; order repair or demolition of buildings or parts thereof and removal of snow from roofs. It is also responsible for the conditions of sidewalks, parks, playgrounds, water mains and sewers, cisterns and wells, and issues traffic regulations for tramways and busses. From time to time the central authorities suggest to city soviets to clean up all public establishments such as eating places, medical institutions, streets, squares, market places, parks, etc., within a designated time. It frequently orders city soviets to see that apartment houses employ janitors (dvorniki) if none are there. The janitors, among other duties, must supervise the collection of garbage and clean the public privies. The central government may order city soviets to designate particular grounds for the dumping of garbage. The cities of late have been urged to protect parks, promenades, and public greens. The central government is especially emphatic in connection with the protection of city water supply, the establishment of sewerage disposal plants, and the keeping of these services in good condition. The central authorities in recent years have also urged and frequently ordered the betterment of public baths and laundry facilities.[23]

The authority of the city soviet extends also to the regulation of amusement places, moving pictures, restaurants, clubs, tea rooms, saloons and the business hours of shops and stores. It distributes space at markets, fairs, and other places designated for trading. The city soviet, among other tasks, is also charged with the rendering of assistance to needy families of the Red Guards who have been killed in battle or in line of duty. It passes regulations for the protection of motherhood and infancy, and organizes institutions for care of the aged, the disabled, and homeless children.

The city soviet is instructed to make attempts to raise the cultural and educational level of the community. To that end it may organize and maintain general and special educational institutions, clubs, reading rooms, libraries, theatres, and lecture courses on political and general cultural subjects. It passes ordinances for the protection of historical landmarks, monuments, antiquities, and objects of art.[24]

The city soviet, if called upon, must provide quarters for troops and supply them with communal services in accordance with legal provisions. The law authorizes the city soviet to punish violation of its regulations by a fine of not more than one hundred rubles or by a sentence to forced labor for not over one month.[25]

Executive and Administrative Organs

The constitution of 1918 provided that for purposes of actual administration the city soviet was to elect an executive committee which was solely responsible to the city soviet of deputies, but during the civil war and famine, local self-government practically disappeared and was not revived until 1922,[26] when a municipal decree was passed. Under this legislation the independent executive and administrative organs of the city soviet were abolished, and the machinery of the executive committee of the county and provincial soviets was substituted to serve the needs of the municipalities. Furthermore, the presidia of the higher soviets were at the same time considered the executive and the administrative organs of city soviets.[27] This paralyzing legislation had

a discouraging effect on city activity which the central agencies
were anxious to revive, so after three years of fruitless effort on
the part of the central authorities to overcome the dormant condition of the cities, a new decree was passed in 1925, under which
the actual conduct of city administration was delegated to a president and presidium of eleven members, elected by the city soviet
out of its own membership. The presidium serves as a collegial
city executive and constitutes between sessions of the urban soviet
the superior organ of the municipality. It executes all ordinances
in the name of the city soviet.[28] This does not mean that cities
have been freed from administrative tutelage of the higher
soviets, for the law authorizes the city to organize only one
municipal department,. and that is a department for direct
management of communal property.[29] For the administration of
all technical tasks, however, the executive committee of the next
higher soviet designates certain sections of its departments, and
details staffs of technical workers for the municipal activities. To
be sure, these sub-divisions of departments of the executive committee of the higher soviet singled out for this purpose are to be
separated entirely from the rest of the departments, with separate
organization, accounting, and records; they are to have a purely
municipal budgetary account in no way connected with the higher
soviet. In order to modify this rather cumbersome and complicated arrangement, the law provides that the city soviet, in
agreement with the executive committee of the next higher
soviet, may appoint directors to take charge of the subdivisions
of departments assigned to city work.[30]

When the circuits (okrug) were abolished in October 1930,
it was decided by the central government that in cities having a
population up to 50,000 the soviets are to come under the jurisdiction of the appropriate raion executive committees. Cities of
over 50,000, which are industrially important and are culturally
and politically ready, are to be singled out into independent
administrative-economic units. The city soviets of these urban
centers are to come under the immediate jurisdiction of the
presidia of the central executive committees of the appropriate
union or autonomous republic, or the appropriate regional committee. A provision was made that this regulation be applied to

cities of less than 50,000 population if they are economically, politically, and culturally important.

To the cities which have been singled out as independent administrative-economic units are to be attached rural settlements within one raion only. These rural settlements are to organize village soviets in accordance with legislation in this respect. These communities are to take part in the election of the city soviets in accordance with established regulations in this matter. The order in which rural settlements are attached to cities is regulated by the central executive committee of the respective union republics. The city soviets are ordered to organize sections for the purpose of supervising the affairs of the rural settlements.

Committees and Commissions

The decree of 1925 and subsequent legislation[31] provided for the appointment by the city soviet of six permanent committees; namely, communal economy, financial-budgetary business, education, public health, coöperative trade, and Workman - Peasant Inspection. Other committees may be appointed by local soviets in accordance with their needs. In most city soviets there are ten or more additional committees and they are known as administrative, cultural, sanitary, judicial, trade, social security, etc. Deputies may select the committee they prefer to join, but under some conditions they may be appointed to committees not of their choice. Every deputy, however, must be a member of at least one committee, and that one theoretically is in the line of work in which he is most interested or adapted by training and experience. In addition to deputies, private citizens, such as representatives of professional unions, shop committees, and other organizations, may be drawn into committee work. The technical director of that department of city work which comes under jurisdiction of a particular committee must always be included in its membership. Experts and technicians may be invited to single sessions and may have a consulting voice in the deliberations and discussions. This is an indication that the expert and technician are being recognized to some extent in city administration of the Soviet Union.

All committees elect bureaus of at least three members, with a chairman, deputy chairman, and secretary. The bureaus supervise and guide in detail the activity of the committees. The work of the committees in general consists in preparing and examining projects to be reported to the presidium or city soviet. They may also inspect public institutions and enterprises, and report on their condition to appropriate authorities. Committees may appoint permanent commissions (sub-committees) to study in more detail particular departments and administrative branches within the jurisdiction of a given committee. They may also appoint temporary commissions for the purpose of preparing a particular project.[32]

Only a few years have elapsed since Soviet Russia has emerged from civil war and general chaos. The present system of municipal government is still too much under the influence of militant bolshevism and is motivated by fear of a counter-revolution. The cities as yet have not been permitted to develop adequate administrative machinery. Too much stress is laid upon the idea that the city soviets are merely the "cells" of the Soviet state apparatus, that is, organs of proletarian dictatorship.

The movement of particularism of the early years of the soviet régime when there was a tendency to form independent soviet communities gave place to the reaction of excessive centralism. The Bolshevik teachings of "democratic centralism" frequently are converted into bureaucratic centralism. Lenin's insistence on "centralized direction and decentralized activity" for local governments has often degenerated into rule from above to such an extent as to stifle all local initiative. In addition the infiltration of national issues into the activities of municipal governments has created such heavy burdens as to paralize the not too efficient civic authorities. This policy becomes especially obnoxious when it is considered that after all, no matter what decision local soviets may take in regard to general policies, the last word is reserved to the central organs of the Communist Party. But already, even among the faithful communists, doubts are arising as to the advisability of linking city business with the complexities of state policies, and there is a growing demand for more city independence as far as purely local affairs are concerned, and a quiet yet persistent opposition to excessive meddling and supervision from above.

The Proposed New Municipal Decree

In answer to this dissatisfaction a project for a new decree is being considered. The Institute of Soviet Construction and Law worked out the project and submitted it to the Council of People's Commissars of the R. S. F. S. R., which confirmed the draft after making considerable changes, and it now awaits final ratification by the All-Russian Central Executive Committee. The original project had attempted to give the cities large powers by avoiding the detailed enumeration of powers and merely mentioning the fundamental problems of city soviet activity, and thus opened a large field of action which would have meant eventually a departure from the extreme centralization to that of a decentralized and almost autonomous existence of municipalities. This provision translated into practice might have developed along the lines that existed in Germany before the War; namely, that whatever power is not expressly withheld from the city is permitted to it. This heresy, however, was immediately expunged by the Council of People's Commissars when it proceeded to revise the project, and as a result in the official draft of the project there is a rigid enumeration of powers of cities. Although the original project confined itself to municipal affairs only, the official Bolshevik mind could not tolerate even an assumption that the city might be better off in confining itself to purely municipal activities and leaving the conduct of affairs of state to the higher organs of government. The official project incorporates, in the usual Bolshevik manner, functions which are beyond the limits of city activities in other countries. The project of this new decree will no doubt undergo many changes before it is promulgated as law.

CHAPTER V

MUNICIPAL FINANCE AND CITY PLANNING

Municipal Finance

The present municipal financial system of Soviet Russia dates back to 1925. Previous to that time the financial affairs of the city soviets were entirely merged with those of the higher soviets. In 1923, however, a financial decree was promulgated which extended to municipal organs the right to coöperate in the preparation of the budget, but since the cities had no administrative machinery of their own, this grant of authority had but slight practical significance.

THE FINANCIAL DECREE OF 1925

Early in 1925 the Union Central Executive Committee issued a financial decree which laid down general principles governing the field of local finance and taxation, leaving, however, the working out of the details to the constituent republics. Soon after, the Central Executive Committee of R. S. F. S. R. issued a financial decree based on the Federal Enabling Act, which regulated in detail the entire matter of municipal finance. But these provisions were such as to reduce considerably the scope of municipal administration of finances defined by the Municipal Act of 1925, which authorized the city soviets to frame and confirm their budgets.

In contrast to the latter provision, the financial decree makes it mandatory upon the city soviets to present their budgets to the executive committees of the higher soviets for examination, review, audit, and final decision. Indeed, the higher soviets are given a wide range of authority, so that the examination of municipal budgets is by no means a mere formal compliance with the law, for the higher soviets may rigidly curtail the income of municipalities by denying them the right to certain taxes, surtaxes, and other sources of revenue. Furthermore, the law authorizes the executive committees to use their own discretion in making or recommending changes in city estimates, especially if those changes are deemed necessary for the purpose of equalizing income and expenditures.[1]

The authority of the higher soviets over city soviets is further augmented by the provision of the law giving them the right to decide whether certain properties are to be assessed for city or raion taxation, and also delegating to them a general supervisory authority in the matter of tax collection.[2]

In addition, from time to time, the central government makes assessments for special purposes. In 1931 and again in 1932 the Central Executive Committee and Council of People's Commissars have ordered single assessments for cultural and housing needs of urban centers. All persons living in urban centers are subject to these assessments. For the purpose of collecting these taxes the urban population was divided into five categories: (1) workers and employees, persons who receive an income from literary and scientific pursuits, those who are engaged in the arts or receive an income from authors' copyrights or from inventions, coöperative craftsmen and mechanics; (2) non-coöperative craftsmen and mechanics who do not employ paid labor; (3) non-coöperative craftsmen and mechanics who employ no more than three workers, other persons who pay the industrial trade tax at fixed rates (with the exception of those in category two), and other persons who receive income from personal labor but are not in anyone's employment; (4) owners of buildings; (5) owners of business and trade establishments, and persons who have unearned incomes. In cases in which persons received income from several sources the tax is raised in accordance with the rate of income.

The following exemptions are made:

1. Persons who belong to the first two categories if their income does not exceed seventy-five rubles per month.

2. Persons in the military service both of the rank and commanding personnel (with exception of those on indefinite leave); military persons in the commanding staffs who are in the reserve; persons employed in police work and militarized guard duty (inclusive of military fire fighting brigades).

3. Persons decorated with one or more orders of the Union or with honorary revolutionary arms and "heroes of labor."

4. Pensioners who receive pensions from state organs or public organizations and have no other income.

5. Students who receive stipends from the state, if they do not exceed 175 rubles per month.

The tax ranged from 18 to 140 rubles for the first category, if the income was between 75 and 500 rubles per month. In the second category, from 27 to 210 rubles, if their incomes were between 75 and 500 rubles per month. In the third category 36 to 280 rubles, if the income was between 75 and 500 rubles. In the fourth category, 36 to 420 rubles, if the income was 75 to 500 rubles. In the fifth category, 60 to 700 rubles, if the income was 75 to 500 rubles.

Those whose income exceed 500 rubles paid the following rate:

First Category .... 35% of monthly income
Second Category .... 53% ”　　”　　　”
Third Category .... 70% ”　　”　　　”
Fourth Category .... 105% ”　　”　　　”
Fifth Category .... 165% ”　　”　　　”

The first three categories paid the tax in sixteen instalments (every two weeks) beginning with the first part of February and ending the second part of September. The other categories paid three instalments; on the tenth day of March, May, and June.[3]

SOURCES OF REVENUE

Within these limitations cities are assigned the following sources of revenue:

I. *Taxes,* subdivided as follows:
 1. Tax on business buildings.
 2. Tax on dwelling places.
 3. Tax on transportation.
 4. Tax on amusements.
 5. Tax on live stock and raw animal products.

II. *Surtaxes:*
 1. Surtaxes on state business and trade taxes.
 2. Surtaxes on state income tax.
 3. Surtaxes on state tax levied on agricultural lands within city jurisdiction to an extent of not less than 40 per cent.

III. *Surcharges:*

1. Surcharges on fees paid to the state for licenses to sell alcoholic beverages and tobacco within city limits.
2. Surcharges on state notarial fees.
3. Surcharges on municipal court fees.

IV. *Other sources of revenue:*

1. Rents from dwelling places, business buildings, market places, and other establishments.
2. Earnings from city lands, parks, and other similar property.
3. Rents received for trading space on public squares, markets, streets, promenades, beaches, etc.
4. Earnings from municipalized economic - commercial enterprises.
5. Rents from municipal real estate.
6. Revenue from enterprises and undertakings especially assigned to municipalities for that purpose.
7. Parts of profits from state insurance, especially designated by law.
8. Interest on municipal funds.
9. Sale of superfluous city property.
10. Surpluses remaining from the previous year.
11. Back taxes.
12. Profits from stocks in banking institutions and other corporations.
13. Regular and special grants and aids from state funds.
14. Income from special funds and endowments, and stated contributions from institutions and organizations.
15. Loans.[4]

SUBSIDIES

Subsidies and aids are generally granted by the state for the support of educational, medical, and agricultural personnel in schools, hospitals, etc. The subsidies are increased or decreased in accordance with the financial condition of a given municipality. The ultimate decision as to the grant and the amount of the subsidies lies with the executive committees of the higher political units in which the cities are located. In exceptional cases municipalities may receive donations from the state to balance their budgets, provided they are entirely unable to raise funds themselves. Municipalities also have access to special funds and endowments of coöperative building associations and the fund in the name of V. I. Lenin, which is especially designated for the care of homeless children. Finally, there are two types of emergency funds, *viz.,* federal and local. The federal emergency fund is made of surtaxes to federal taxes and of stated sums subtracted from provincial and municipal income and are under the jurisdiction of the executive committees. Both emergency funds are to be used only in cases in which municipalities have given absolute proof of being unable to balance their budgets. This aid, however, is very seldom granted, and the municipalities applying for it are subject to a most rigid inspection.[5]

EXPENDITURES OF CITIES

Expenditures of cities may be sub-divided into the following general items:

1. The support of city soviets, their presidia, and subdivisions of departments of the higher soviets designated for municipal work, municipal courts, prosecutors, and juries.

2. Payment of salaries of city militsia (police). Expenses in connection with criminal investigation, the upkeep of city jails, detention homes, communal buildings, properties, undertakings, welfare agencies, and fire departments.

3. Organization, equipment, and upkeep of lower professional technical schools for the city population; short technical courses for adults, elementary schools, children's homes; kindergartens, schools for adolescents, and institutions for civic training; libraries, clubs, schools for adolescent and adult illiterates, and persons who are about to be called for military service; schools of political grammar;[6] city hospitals, clinics, first-aid centers, etc.

4. Expenses in connection with museums, art galleries, theatres, expositions, archives, and the organization of excursions for cultural educational purposes.

5. Support of various municipal sanitary organizations and undertakings, prophylactic measures against social and contagious diseases, and activities for the suppression of prostitution and pauperism.

6. Expenses in connection with measures to safeguard motherhood, infancy, and children's health in cities.

7. Support of homes and training for the disabled.

8. Grants and subsidies to various local organizations for mutual help and expenses in connection with payment of pensions

to war veterans, their families, and the dependents of those killed in battle.[7]

9. Support of veterinary organizations and measures for the eradication of contagious diseases among domestic animals.[8]

The following municipal expenditures are paid from raion funds:

1. Expenses in connection with soviet elections.[9]

2. Organization, equipment, and support of institutions for mothers and infants, maternity hospitals, and hospitals for social diseases.

3. Disbursements in connection with the operation of agricultural and horticultural experiment stations.

The provincial funds finance the following undertakings:

1. The support of intermediary-technical schools which are not financed by the state.

2. Teachers' training schools and conferences.

3. The organization, equipment, and support of psychopathic hospitals, surgical and ophthalmological institutions, health resorts, convalescent homes, sanatoria, bacteriological institutes and laboratories, meteorological stations, various hydro-therapeutic sanatoria, agricultural and agronomic expositions and courses, dormitories and feeding stations for unemployed, and quarters for troops.

MISCELLANEOUS EXPENDITURES

The city soviets must make the following provisions: the payment of loans and interest on indebtedness, sums designated for special funds, the meeting of unpaid bills of the previous year, capital to be used in the organization of local banking institutions and corporations, and the necessary legal reserve constituting the emergency fund and medical care of insured persons.[10]   The law permits the city soviets to include in the budget items for unforeseen expenditures, which must not, however, exceed three per cent of all disbursements.   The city funds are administered by the financial agencies of the executive committee,[11] and must be deposited with sub-treasuries of the commissioner of finances.

Municipal finance, like all other phases of city administration in Soviet Russia, is still in the experimental stage.   No doubt in time the central government will learn by experience that detailed control of all local activities tends to destroy initiative and eventually reacts disastrously upon city welfare. However, it is fair to state that times are not ripe as yet in Soviet Russia to permit urban communes an existence unfettered by strict supervision and frequently even petty interference from above. No doubt as the years go by Russian cities will demand and obtain governmental status commensurate with their responsibilities.

CITY PLANNING

The Russian cities of modern times have never known the self-government status of Western European and American municipalities. The history of the Russian city is a struggle for at least a vestige of the self-rule it has never succeeded in attaining. On the eve of the Revolution of 1917 the municipalities of Russia were in the iron grip of the autocratic central government. The short-lived and pathetic Provisional Government attempted to introduce Western European municipal practices, which were nipped in the bud by the onrushing storm of the Bolshevik revolution. It would be out of place to recount here the struggle and tragedy of the Russian city in the intervening years between 1917-1925, years of invasion, anarchy, starvation. But like the phoenix, the Russian city has risen from the ashes. Municipal life is still under the rule of the central authority, to be sure, but an authority radically different from the old one, and exercised under conditions which challenge the imagination — mass rule manipulated by a determined minority.

Before the revolution city planning in Russia was given little attention. Since the revolution a vast amount of work has been done in the field of systematized city planning. City planning in Soviet Russia, which is tied up with the general scheme of socializing economic and civic life, can be traced to the promulgation in the uncertain days of 1922 of a Land Code, which theoretically nationalized all land and provided for the distribution of land. Subsequent legislation modified the original provisions of the Code, and the law, as it stands now, recognizes only three types of land users: (1) individual or union tillers of soil; (2) the urban population; (3) state institutions and undertakings. All the rest of the land held by any other class comes automatically under the jurisdiction of the commissariat of agriculture, which may use its own discretion as to the grant of land to the authorized classes and categories of land users in accordance with legal provisions. Hence, the land on which cities are located is designated urban land, and the title is vested in the city population and may be granted for use by it to persons and organizations in accordance with legal provisions.[12]

CITY TERRITORY

The Land law defines urban territory as one unbroken area, separated from adjacent neighboring territory by the city boundary lines. It adds, however, that in city territory, may also be included all lands adjacent to the urban boundary, occupied or vacant, which were under the jurisdiction of the city soviet (municipal administration) as of August 1, 1922.[13]

Furthermore, all lands adjacent to, but outside, the city boundary lines, provided they are not in actual use by tillers of the soil or workers' organizations, may be attached to city territory. All these specified lands then make up the city domain, without regard to present use or previous ownership, save for the exceptions noted. On the other hand, scattered plots, which in the past were claimed by municipal corporations, may not be annexed by the city in question; conversely, separate plots adjacent to city boundary lines, provided they are not in actual tillage by peasants or in use by workers' organizations, may be taken over by the municipality. This does not, however, apply to that part of state land which has been reserved to the jurisdiction of the commissariat of agriculture or its tenants, and was not considered urban territory prior to the promulgation of the Code.

The above mentioned law also provides that certain rural settlements are to be included in city territory provided (1) that they were a part of the city domain prior to 1917 and that city authorities deem it necessary to retain them under their jurisdiction; (2) that they have ceased to be a part of the volost (cantonal) soviets by reason of city annexation as of August, 1922.[14]

THE CHANGE OF BOUNDARIES

The Land Code, the various instructions and decrees of central authorities, and the city planning project worked out by the State Planning Commission (Gosplan) provide for the change of city boundary lines in order to extend the territory of cities under the following conditions: (1) in cases in which the increase of population demands an extension of urban territory to satisfy the need for additional building of dwelling places; (2) for the purpose of city welfare by means of extension of playgrounds, parks, water supply, lighting, sewerage, and other services of public welfare; (3) in cases in which the movement of population has extended beyond the city limits to form a suburb in fact, if not at law. But under no circumstances may annexation take place for the purpose of increasing city revenue by renting lands for agricultural purposes. The legal provisions stipulated that lands outside of city limits in the use of city dwellers for agricultural purposes may be retained by them in that use, if the users organize themselves in land coöperatives, but the lands of these coöperatives and the organizations themselves are subject to the jurisdiction of cantonal authorities; the members, however, retain the right to take part in city elections and are excluded from exercising the cantonal franchise. The consequence of these provisions is that parts of utilized agricultural lands remain under the jurisdiction of the city and parts under the authority of cantonal organs, and the coöperatives are subject at the same time to city and cantonal authority.

CONTROL OUTSIDE CITY LIMITS

The law permits cities under certain circumstances, independently of change of boundaries, to formulate rules and plans for building on lands outside the city limits in order to prevent sporadic construction which might be in time annexed to city territory. From the date of passing and publication of these rules and plans, settlers are forbidden to erect new buildings contrary to these specifications and rules, except temporary and summer structures and additions to buildings already erected. Furthermore, the law grants city soviets considerable authority by the provision that "all lands within the city limits, with forests and greens, city natural resources, beaches and waterfronts within those limits, in whatsoever use they may be, with the exception of lands exempt(which will be named directly) are under the direct jurisdiction of executive committees through the agency of the organs of local administration."[15] A provision of the same law stipulates that exemptions of new subdivisions (excepting land already exempted) from city authority may only be granted in case of state necessity by the authority of special provision of the All-Russian Central Executive Committee and Council of People's Commissars.

The following categories of properties are withdrawn from the jurisdiction of municipal organs and transferred to the various appropriate people's commissars:[16]

1. Sites which are occupied by railway right of ways, stations, terminals, sheds, warehouses, shops, barracks, etc.
2. Territories of commercial ports, docks, wharves, light-houses, etc.
3. Docks and wharves for river traffic which are directly under the jurisdiction of the Union commissar of communication.
4. Real estate used for building of canals, dams, levees, and other hydro-technical works.
5. Lands used in connection with development of state natural resources under the jurisdiction of central mining authorities.
6. Military and naval reservations under the control of the federal government.
7. Sites used for national and local sanatoria.[17]

SUBDIVISION OF URBAN LAND

All city land is divided into three categories: residential sites, land for public use, and sites for industrial districts.

Residential sites are divided into lots in accordance with accepted projects of city planning. If, however, the amount of land assigned to residential districts exceeds by half the extent of territory provided for in the instructions of the commissariat of the interior for such purposes, the remainder of the land may be requisitioned by the city. In the distribution of territory for various subdivisions the concentration of population in a given district, the economic character of the population, the character and type of local buildings, topographical peculiarities, and the sanitary and other conditions of the entire city in general and separate districts in particular must be considered.

The planning and widening of streets and squares and other places of public use, and laying out of new streets are executed in accordance with planning projects. The city soviets are empowered to correct and alter lines of built-up sections and thoroughfares when the lines are broken, uneven, or present other inconveniences from the standpoint of planning or sanitary utility, provided this reconstruction involves no more than ten per cent of the district and does not necessitate the tearing down or transfer of buildings. All misunderstandings are settled by the provincial executive committee. The technical rules for planning, mode of execution, and the norms for the distribution of residential districts are regulated by special rules of the State Planning Commission (Gosplan). In the case of cities which previously did not have definite planning regulations, or whose plans have been disregarded, an exact survey of city territory becomes necessary, to be followed by the formulation of an exact plan of city building.[18]

Vacant lots in built-up districts must be left to the use of those persons and institutions which occupy the adjacent buildings. The transfer of those lots to other persons or institutions may take place only by sublease, after a previous agreement with the city authorities in accordance with established rules. With the transfer of buildings, however, also goes the land. In case of fire or other catastrophes the tenants of the destroyed buildings retain the use of the land on condition that they rebuild within a period of three years.

Thoroughfares, such as squares, roads, boulevards, parks and gardens, which are used for rest, amusement, and educational purposes by the city population; cemeteries;[19] dumping places for snow and garbage; and streams, lakes, and bathing beaches within city limits are considered public places to be used by the entire population. The use of this public territory may be free or on a fee basis. Parts of public squares may be rented out for trade; the law, however, limits such leases to a short period of time and on condition that they do not interfere with the use of the necessary space by the general public.[20]

All other lands under the jurisdiction of the city, such as forests, quarries, and lands of agricultural character including fields, meadows, pastures, truck gardens, and orchards are considered city domain and may be managed directly by the city authorities or leased to private individuals or organizations, or may be given for use free of charge in accordance with the regulation of city soviets.   The development of natural resources within city domain is permitted in accordance with rules passed for this purpose by the central mining authorities.   Without the permission of the central authorities, the city soviets may extract from the soil only building materials, such as rock, sand, lime; for the development of mineral resources is retained by the nation at large.

The development of agricultural lands under the jurisdiction of the city may be undertaken subject to the following conditions: the division of lands into sections the size of which to depend upon the character of the soil and the crops to be raised; the distribution of water necessary for irrigation; the type of agriculture which would serve best the purpose of a given city; and other special needs and peculiarities of the city and its agricultural lands. The redivision of the land already under tillage by private persons or institutions is carried out in accordance with the survey of city domain with due regard to past irregular divisions, improvement of thoroughfares, and general betterment of city territory.   This, however, does not apply to lands which are directly managed or leased by city soviets.

HOUSING

From the very first days of its existence the Soviet government attempted to ameliorate the unspeakable living conditions of the lower classes and proceeded in its own way to carry out its idea by way of nationalization and municipalization of private property.   By 1929, the total value of municipalized property amounted to 8,660,000,000 rubles in which is included expropriated property and additional building since the Revolution. The above sum constitutes 60 per cent of the value of all city property in the Soviet Union, which is estimated at 13,700,000,000 rubles.   Not all private property, however, was confiscated, since up to 1929 considerable numbers of persons were renting out dwellings from which they derived an income.   But in a decree issued in 1929 the right of private persons to rent dwellings was still further limited, and the government expects to liquidate the entire matter of renting by private persons at the end of the Five Year Plan. The rents in cities of over 50,000 have been estimated to run from thirty-five to forty-one kopeks a month for one square meter. The average rent of a working man in Soviet Russia constitutes 9.7 per cent of his income. The minimum living space for one person as decided upon by the commissar of health is to consist of 8.25 square meters.

The terrifically overcrowded conditions of the Soviet Union are well known to all who have ever visited that country. In fairness to the Soviet government, however, it must be said that desperate efforts are being made to overcome this condition.

Model apartments for working men are being erected in cities all over Russia, especially in the so-called new industrial cities such as Bolshoe Zaporozhye. The plans, if carried out on an extensive scale, would require large amounts of expenditures which the government is not able to advance. Hence, to meet the general housing shortage in cities and large towns, a decree was issued by the central government in 1927 providing for the erection by individual workers of houses which cannot be used for profit through sale or lease. Funds have been set aside in municipal banks distributed by housing coöperatives, and building materials may be obtained by workers through central or local housing coöperative associations. The builder has to make an initial investment of 30 per cent of the total cost of the building and comply with certain minimum standards established by the State Planning Commission. Loans were not to extend over a period of ten years. The land upon which the houses were to be erected was leased for a period of fifty to sixty-five years. The building of apartments for groups of four to five families was also encouraged. The time limit for which land might be leased was set, in order not to interfere with the future expansion of the city and carrying out of plans which may call for the use of the occupied land.

In 1928, the All-Russian Executive Committee and the Council of People's Commissars recommended local soviets and executive committees to give their attention to the task of increasing dwelling places and of razing broken down structures and replacing them by new buildings. It was recommended that municipalized and nationalized structures be used for housing purposes. The central government recommended unification of plans for the building of dwellings with due allowance for territorial peculiarities. The various territorial units were informed that their plans for building of dwellings must contain (a) financial estimates with due consideration of local and central sources, (b) estimation of working power and materials, and (c) the rational division of living space in a satisfactory manner to all concerned. For this purpose the R. S. F. S. R. budget set aside in the fiscal year of 1928-29 one million rubles with a promise to increase the grant from year to year. The Central Bank of Communal Economy and Housing was instructed to issue long term credit for the purpose of developing such undertakings and to guarantee their being carried out.

In addition workers and employees were urged to build on a collective basis. It was recommended to the Building Commission of the Economic Council of the R. S. F. S. R. that they work out plans for dwelling places for various districts and create standards for building. The health department was to supervise the sanitary arrangement of these undertakings. In general, attempts were to be made to create better housing conditions from a legal, sanitary, and financial standpoint.

On October 18, 1928, the organization of a Central Union of Housing Coöperatives was confirmed by the Economic Council of the R. S. F. S. R. (Centrozhilsoyuz). The purpose of this organization is to unite unions of housing coöperatives and large house building organizations for mutual activity of its members, and give directions in the development and strengthening of the housing coöperative affairs in the R. S. F. S. R. for the purpose of serving their economic needs.[21]

THE NEW PROJECT FOR CITY PLANNING, BUILDING, AND EQUIPMENT

In June 1930 the commissariat of interior submitted a new project for planning and building of residential districts. According to the project, there is to be a reconstruction of the existing residential districts upon socialist principles. The plan provides among other things that any suburb or subdivision must be considered as one unit in which all elements of production, power, transport, administration, education, and culture are to be united. Dwelling places are to be united into groups of houses and provisions made for (1) children's playgrounds and recreation grounds for adults, (2) children's creches and parks, (3) special rooms for laundry purposes, (4) common dining rooms to be served by one kitchen or by special kitchens within the limits of the buildings or groups of buildings. The project also makes provisions for the organization of communal homes; this, however, is still in the experimental stage. Generally speaking the entire project is planned with a view to collectivization of human existence.

STREET PAVING

Russia in general is probably the most backward country in Europe as far as public services are concerned. Thus, in the beginning of 1928-29 only 20 per cent of the streets, squares, and thoroughfares in the 425 cities of Soviet Russia proper were paved, and these mostly with cobblestones. It is estimated that the paving of streets in all cities of the Union would cost 5,632,000,000 rubles. In accordance with the Five Year Plan only 557,400 rubles were appropriated for the paving of streets, which means that unless most of the Russian cities undertake this task for themselves, the smaller cities in Russia will remain unpaved for a great many years to come. Since most of the transportation in Russia is yet by animal power, it will probably be a long time before any advance is made in the direction of street paving, but if the Five Year Plan for the motorization of street traffic is carried out, the government may awaken to the necessity of street paving to prevent enormous losses in damaged machinery on account of impassable public thoroughfares.

STREET LIGHTING

Street lighting in Russia is still in a primitive condition; in 1929 only 340 cities in Soviet Russia had street illumination, and 85 cities had no street lighting at all. The normal illumination in Western Europe is twenty to twenty-five lights to each square mile. The average number of street lights in the cities of Soviet Russia is two lights for one square mile. It is estimated that several billion dollars would be needed for Russia to emerge from the medieval darkness. The Five Year Plan, however, allots to the entire Union forty to forty-two million rubles, an increase of 30 per cent in street lighting in the R. S. F. S. R. and 123 per cent in the cities of the Ukraina.

PARKS

In 1930 there were only 392 public parks and 394 promenades and greens in the 842 towns of the Union, but as far back as 1925 instructions were issued for the increase of parks and greens. The Five Year Plan has appropriated for that purpose in Russia proper twenty to twenty-two million rubles and for the Ukraina five and one-half million rubles, an increase in the number of parks of 33 per cent.

WATER SUPPLY

Only 328 towns in the entire Soviet Union have modern water supply plants, but even then in some cities only a part of the population is being served. In the most densely populated cities of Russia proper only 179 cities have water plants, and in these cities only 11.5 per cent of the dwelling places are connected with the water works. Between 1902 and 1907 only seventy water plants were built in Russian cities which accounts in some measure for the backwardness of the present time. In accordance with the Five Year Plan four hundred million rubles are to be appropriated for this purpose, which will make it possible to introduce modern water plants into 117 cities and to expand those already in existence. This money will be used for the erection of water mains, although the connection of dwelling places with the water mains will have to be done at the expense of the individual housing administrations.

DRAINAGE AND GARBAGE

The sewerage system in the Soviet Union is still in a primitive condition. In Russia proper there are only twenty-two cities that have sewage disposal plants and only 9.2 per cent of the houses in Russia proper have sewer connections. The sanitary situation then in Soviet Russia is in an abominable condition. In 506 cities of Soviet Russia there accumulates every year about sixty million barrels of solid sewage, only five million barrels of which are taken care of by regular sewerage canals.

The rest of it has to be disposed of by sanitary brigades, but only in 172 cities are such brigades to be found; that is, only 22 per cent of the accumulation of sewage is being disposed of in a more or less sanitary manner. According to the data available only 117 cities have communal brigades for the disposal of garbage, and it is estimated that only 8.7 per cent of accumulated garbage can actually be disposed of. It would take three billion rubles to erect sewage disposal plants in all cities of Russia, but only 150 million rubles were apportioned for this purpose by the Five Year Plan.

CITY TRANSPORTATION

The electric tramway is still the predominate means of transportation in the large cities of Russia. In 1929, thirty-eight had such service. In accordance with the Five Year Plan fifteen additional cities in Soviet Russia and four in the Ukraina are to build tramways. There are only 1,100 mechanized busses in eighty-two cities in Soviet Russia. Busses are more advantageous and cheaper, yet because of the conditions of city streets, they cannot be made use of. The Five Year Plan set aside 245 million rubles for that purpose in Russia proper and in the Ukraina fifty-two million, and is is expected at the end of the Five Year Plan that all cities having a population of 20,000 people will have such means of transport.

PUBLIC BATHS AND LAUNDRIES

The majority of the Russian homes have no running water and hence there is an absence of bath tubs and showers. For this reason the public baths are an absolute necessity. Nevertheless 40 per cent of the Russian cities have no such establishments. For every thousand inhabitants in the cities there are only nine or ten public baths. In the cities of the Ural region there are only five bathing places per thousand people. There is a constant increase of such establishments however, and in 1931 the expenditure for this purpose was raised to thirty-two million dollars. Mechanical laundries are still in the stage of experimentation in Russia. They are to be found only in such large cities as Moscow and Leningrad. Even there they serve only institutions, hospitals, hotels, and the army. Efforts are being made to increase the number of such laundries.

ELECTRICITY

In the last few years electricity has displaced all other means of street illumination in the large cities. In Soviet Russia proper without the autonomous republics, 311 cities have electricity, that is, 73.3 per cent of the cities are using this power. If some of the suburbs are counted in the percentage, the total is increased to about 82.1 per cent. It is well known that one of the fundamental policies of the Soviet régime is the electrification of the country, an ideal, however, still far short of fulfillment.

Soviet Cities Slowly Progressing

As indicated above, city government, as well as government generally in Russia, is still recuperating from the misery of autocracy, civil war, intervention, and anarchy. It can readily be seen by any observer that Russia is groping her way to democracy, a democracy radically different, to be sure, from the accepted Western conception. The central government is still laboring under the psychosis of counter-revolution and intervention; hence, the fear of permitting local self-government, which results in constant interference and regulation of details of local economy that could far better be left to the municipalities themselves. It is, nevertheless, only fair to state that the Russian cities are awakening and planning a brighter future for their inhabitants. Modern improvements are being installed in workers' quarters, and greens and playgrounds are provided for sports and games. New cities are being built where there were only waste and desert. Since 1923, hundreds of millions of rubles have been expended in reëstablishing public services destroyed in revolution and civil war, and new public service systems have been established in thirty cities. Before the revolution only 15 per cent of even the important cities in Russia had public lighting systems, and only ten per cent had electric illumination, the remainder using kerosene or gas; to date, however, 90 per cent of the larger cities in Russia have installed electric lights. The fire-fighting apparatus in the more important municipalities has been motorized. The telephone and the municipal transportation have been improved and extended, and the construction of a subway in Moscow, the first in Russia, is under way. Without seeming unduly optimistic, no fair-minded observer can deny that every attempt is being made in Russia to overcome great difficulties and that in many instances the struggle is successful, in spite of the unwieldy and top-heavy Soviet administrative apparatus.

CHAPTER VI

RURAL GOVERNMENT

The Village

The tragedy of the Russian peasant, his struggles and suffering, was touched upon elsewhere. It is well, however, to remember that the underlying causes for the miseries of the Russian agricultural population were the lack of land, heavy taxation, and the utter neglect on the part of the autocracy to remedy these evils. In addition, the cultural level of the peasant was even lower than that of the urban masses, since the government provided almost no facilities for education and cultural development. Whatever intellectual forces existed were under the control of the Orthodox church, led by an extremely ignorant and superstituous clergy, who resented any attempt at enlightenment of the peasant. As a result nearly 85 per cent of the Russian peasantry before the Revolution was illiterate and was probably the most backward agricultural class in the Western world. From time to time idealistic young men and women of the intelligentsia "went to the people", as they called it, and preached to them, "freedom and land." This propaganda and the extreme misery in which the peasant lived frequently resulted in periodic brutal outbreaks of the peasantry against their masters, which in turn were suppressed in a bloody manner by punitive expeditions led by the universally hated and feared Cossacks. The coming of the Revolution in March 1917 gave the peasant an opportunity not only to avenge century-long wrongs but also to take over the estates of the noble landowners. The peasants, having driven out or murdered the landowners, proceeded to divide the land among themselves. In this struggle not only the poor peasant but also the well-to-do element, commonly called kulaks, took part. These latter frequently became the dominant class in the village.

The much harrassed Kerensky government had no time to pay much attention either to the governmental or economic problems of the village and urged the peasantry to await the decision of the Constituent Assembly. In the meantime very little change was made in the governmental structure of the village. The Bolsheviks, however, when they came into power eight months later, did not hesitate to sweep away the institutions of the past and establish village soviets similar to those existing in the higher territorial divisions. Furthermore, the new authorities were not at all in favor of permitting the wealthier elements to take the leadership; hence committees of poor peasants were organized (Kombedy), consisting of returned soldiers and unemployed factory workers, who had received some experience in Soviet organizations either at the front or in the urban centers. Although originally organized as relief committees for the purpose of expropriating surplus grain and farm machinery from the rich peasants, these committees eventually took over the authority and dominated the Soviet machinery administration in the country side. This resulted in a great many difficulties, and in order to eliminate friction, a mixed system of soviets was organized composed of "rich" and poor peasants respectively. When the All-Russian Executive Committee issued in November 1918 a decree for a new election of village soviets, the elections were in charge of the committees of poor peasants, who were supported by the middle peasants and encouraged by the higher authorities. The outcome was a victory for the poor elements. Since the elected village soviets were now composed of the poor and middle peasants, the committees of poor peasants were abolished, and the soviets became the main organ of administration in the villages, although in the more remote settlements the old system of government remained intact for years. This is not to be understood as meaning that the villages were governed in an orderly manner. Bitter and frequently bloody contests were waged between factions and groups, and at one time the conditions in the villages approximated chaos. The central government, fighting a desperate battle for existence, could not allot very much time to village affairs, and the local elements, consisting mostly of peasants entirely devoid of experience in self-government, were not able to carry on an orderly administration. Finally after several years of disorder, the All-Russian Central Executive Committee issued a decree on October 16, 1924,[1] laying down instructions for the formation of village soviets consisting of elective bodies from three to fifty members and a presiding officer, who is to take charge of all affairs necessary for the carrying out of the decision of the assembly and higher organs of government in between meetings of the village soviet. The president is required to make a report of all his actions at the next meeting of the soviet. Nearly all village soviets have a secretary or clerk, who is supposed to manage the entire apparatus of village administration under the supervision of the president; but because of the absence of qualified men, the village business is wretchedly conducted. In addition to the soviets, the rural communities may also hold mass meetings for the purpose of discussing village affairs and general matters of the districts, provinces, and state.[2]

These mass meetings are differentiated from the meetings of the land associations, which were formed after the Bolshevik Revolution and frequently transcended the administrative limits of a given community. In accordance with the Land Code, the competence of these land associations is in the field of agricultural activity, such as division of unused land plots, the making of rules in regard to the use of communal services, etc. The decree issued on March 14, 1927, provided for a strict separation of the competence of general village mass meetings and the land association. In practice, however, both mass meetings are one and the same. This of course is contrary to legal provision which stipulated that the mass meetings of the land association should consist of all users of agricultural land not less than eighteen years of age, while admission to the general mass meeting is limited to those persons who were enjoying the franchise under the Soviet constitution.[3]

The general mass meeting is called by the local soviet at least once every two months during the winter months, and no less than once every three months in the summer period. In the larger settlements the meetings may be divided into districts and sections, and in cases in which the business to come before the meetings concerns more than one village, a joint meeting of all the villages of a particular territory can be convened. One-fifth of all eligible citizens may demand the call of a meeting, or it may be called on demand of the auditing commission of the village soviets. The presence of 25 per cent of all citizens who have the franchise constitutes a quorum.

The meeting is opened by a person designated by the village soviet, and a presidium of three members and a secretary are elected by the meeting. The village soviet presents the various business projects before the meeting. Individual members may present their own projects. The voting is done *viva voce* and a majority of votes is necessary for a decision. Persons dissatisfied with the majority decision can forward their dissenting opinion to the village soviet. The village soviet executes the decisions of the communal meeting. In case the village soviet finds the decisions of the communal meetings *ultra vires,* or contrary to public weal, the entire matter is referred to the next superior executive committee. Later attempts were made to encourage representations of the professional class, such as the physician, teacher, agricultural expert, etc., to take part in the meetings with a consulting voice. In order to induce as many members as possible of the rural commune to share in the work of the administration, permanent committees were organized to have charge of various phases of communal, economic, and cultural life. In accordance with a regulation issued on March 21, 1927, all members (and candidates) of the appropriate executive committees and village soviets were to become members of at least one permanent committee. These committees, however, are rigidly limited in their work. They meet at least once every three months to report on the work carried out, to the village soviet or to the appropriate superior executive committee.

The competence of the village soviets up to 1930 was very limited. Theoretically the village soviet is an organ of authority which had for its task the development of the rural economy, the struggle with ignorance, disease, and other ills of the commune, and the executing of principles of peasant proletarian government. Since, however, the management of the lands and services of the commune were under the jurisdiction of land associations and not the village soviet, the latter had attempted to work harmoniously with land associations. Nevertheless conflicts were

created between agents of the administration and those who
formulated land policies. In addition the village soviets were
hampered by red tape and centralization and their own ignorance,
which did not permit a rational development of local self
government.

The New Decree in Regard to Village Soviets

From time to time after 1924 the central government issued
supplementary legislation in regard to village soviets, but for the
last few years it has been felt that this make-shift regulation did
not meet the new problems arising in connection with collectivization of agriculture. In addition the central authorities thought
that the village soviets as such were far from taking the leadership in the matter so dear to the heart of the Bolsheviks —
collectivization — and accused them of standing aside from the
movement. Hence after several years of discussion, a new village
soviet decree was issued on February 7, 1930, which makes clear
in emphatic language that the paramount and fundamental duty
of the village soviet is to originate productive plans for collectivization and to carry them out faithfully. They must make a
strenuous effort to "liquidate" the kulaks as a class and organize
the activities of farm hands (batraki), poor (bedniaki), and
middle (seredniaki) peasants for the purpose of "further raising
of agriculture and its socialistic reconstruction." The new decree
emphasizes work among the masses of poor peasants and farm
hands, since the authorities admit that the village at present is
far from being Bolshevik in its composition. In fact, two thirds
of the village soviets in the Union lack immediate party leadership and there are only 25,000 party cells in the 75,000 village
soviets of the country. In order to facilitate the execution of the
above mentioned tasks, the presidium of the Central Executive
Committee of the U. S. S. R. issued the new decree directing the
central executive committees of the constituent republics to organize the village soviets in accordance with prescribed fundamental
principles. When on January 1, 1931, the R. S. F. S. R. and
other constituent republics issued village soviet decrees, the principles of the union decree were naturally incorporated in them.

ORGANIZATION OF VILLAGE SOVIETS

In accordance with the Union decree village soviets are to be formed in all villages except in small settlements which can be united into one village soviet without damaging thereby the economic, political, and cultural life of the small communities. In regions of complete collectivization where several villages are united into one collective farm, the structure of the village soviet in principle coincides with the primary organization of the respective collective farms. At the same time, however, village soviets are to be maintained in all villages as heretofore. In determining the limits of village soviets, the density of the population, nationality, as well as the condition of roads and the means of communication must be taken into consideration. The decree provides for the election of members of village soviets by voters of various groups of the toiling population in accordance with norms established by the Soviet constitutions. In Soviet Russia proper, one deputy is elected for each 100 population; the autonomous republics, executive committees of autonomous regions, and regional executive committees may change this ratio, but this action must be communicated to the All-Russian Central Executive Committee. Under no circumstances, however, can there be less than three members in a village soviet in Russia proper. On the other hand, the old limitation that there may not be more than fifty deputies in a village soviet has been repealed. In addition, rural settlements which are not seats of village soviets may elect representatives to village soviets from the membership of the respective village soviet, or from the voters residing in the community. The decree leaves the decision in regard to the order of election for village soviets and the terms for which they are to be elected to the central executive committees of the constituent republics, provided that decisions are in accordance with the fundamental regulations in regard to elections as determined by the Central Executive Committee of the U. S. S. R. In Soviet Russia proper, members of village soviets are elected for one year. The new decree makes provision for a recall of individual members who have not justified the confidence of their voters at any time and the election of new members in special elections. The village soviet elects from among its members a president and a secretary who serve as executives and are in charge of current activities.[4] In the larger communities a presidium may be elected; in Russia proper no presidium can be elected unless the membership of the soviet consists of no less than fifteen persons. For the purpose of supervision of the financial, economic, and other activities, a revision commission is elected at the time when the membership of the soviet is voted for. This commission exercises control uninterruptedly, maintaining close contact with the voters, and in case of necessity, informing the voters of the shortcomings in the work of the village soviet.

Rights and Duties of the Village Soviet

The village soviet is the highest governmental organ within a given territorial limit. As mentioned before, the Communist party leadership is far from satisfied with the political and economic orthodoxy of the composition of village soviets. Therefore the new decree emphasizes that the village soviets must organize the toiling masses for active participation in the administration and in general socialistic, economic, and cultural work.

It is within the competence of village soviets to decide all questions of local (village) importance, but in the usual Bolshevik manner the new decree insisted that the local soviets must discuss affairs of raion, regional, republican, and state importance. In practice it was found that the average village soviet is not only incapable, through lack of experience and information, to discuss general questions of state craft but the work of local significance is frequently so heavy that there is no time left for the wider work. This, the Bolshevik Party deprecates and bemoans. In accordance with the new decree the local soviets have control within the limits of their territory of the execution by all citizens and officials of the laws and instructions of the Soviet government. They must extirpate all attempts to interfere with the execution of measures taken by the central government and stop all violations of the proletarian class policy in carrying out of laws and measures. This especially is true in regard to the liquidation of the kulak element and the attempts of this class to counteract the policy which is destroying it. The village soviets have the authority to issue obligatory ordinances within their competence as established by law and impose administrative penalties and fines for their non-fulfillment. In addition the village soviets have been given the authority to establish village courts, which are to have jurisdiction over matters affecting settlement of property, labor conflicts, and minor criminal cases. It is interesting to note that the new decree provides that village soviets must support organizations which have for their purpose the militarization of the population, the spreading of propaganda and knowledge of military matters, the organization of military training for youth and territorial units of reserves, and they must see that no improper person is admitted into the ranks of the Red Army.

ECONOMIC AND CULTURAL ACTIVITIES OF VILLAGE SOVIETS

The decree orders the village soviets to take over the direction of the socialistic reconstruction of agriculture by the organization of collective farms and other coöperative enterprises, and to be responsible for the highest possible increase in the yield of fields and sown areas, as well as the development and socialization of cattle breeding both in collective farms and in individual household farms. They must support the soviet farms (sovchozy) and their socialistic state enterprises. In order to enable the village soviets to direct efficiently the organization and work of collective farms, they are ordered to demand periodical reports concerning the activity of all institutions and enterprises participating in the organization of collective farms as well as the collective farms in the territory of the village soviets; to examine and confirm the plans of collective farms and of other coöperative organizations, and in case of their non-compliance with general state plans and production tasks, to give direction for changes; to pass resolutions and ratify requests of collective farms for credit, inventory, etc.; to direct the building work of the collective farms such as dwellings, various buildings for economic purposes, clubhouses, hospitals, etc.

In communities of territories which have not been wholly collectivized, the village soviets must take charge of the maximal raising of individual poor and middle farms by organizing primary coöperative associations, by introducing necessary agricultural improvements, and by increasing the sown area with a view to preparing the individual farms for quickest possible collectivization. They must also explain the tasks of collectivization and prepare the way for its realization. The village soviet must organize the masses of farm hands, and the poor and middle peasants for the struggle against the kulaks. In addition they are to limit, as far as possible, the exploiting tendencies of the kulaks. In the non-collectivized regions the village soviets must endeavor to eliminate the kulak element and bring about total collectivization. The village soviet controls and supervises the correct and reasonable utilization of land by collective and individual farms. It has the right to open litigation for the confiscation of land in charge of organizations and persons who are violating the laws in regard to the nationalization of land and are not fulfilling the production plans, imposed tasks, and obligations to the government. The village soviets supervise and direct the entire work of agricultural societies and their respective territories and have authority to cancel, change, and confirm the resolutions of land societies. In regions of complete collectivization, the land societies are to be entirely liquidated and all their rights and duties to be transferred to the village soviet. The village soviet, furthermore, must supervise the timely fulfillment of all obligations to the government by the collective farms and peasant farms not as yet collectivized in the matter of the collection of the agricultural tax, repayment of debts, delivery to the government of marketable products, fulfillment of contract and production plans, and tasks in connection with the grain procurement and sowing campaigns. The soviets supervise the correct and reasonable utilization of inventory in accordance with the tasks of the socialistic reconstruction of the village. They have control of the correct utilization of labor of the agricultural-technical personnel and the organization and raising of labor discipline in collective and Soviet farms. They must see that the laws and regulations concerning the protection of labor, wages, and collective and labor contracts, and other measures introduced by the Soviet government with regard to the reorganization and protection of labor by state and public organizations and by individual persons are carried out. The village soviets are responsible for the enforcement of labor laws and for holding to account persons guilty of violations. The village soviets also have a right to direct the organization of work of various cultural establishments such as libraries, clubhouses for collective farmers, schools, clubs, nursing homes, public dining rooms, hospitals and other sanitary establishments, etc.; to organize the public services of the village, such as water supply, roads, communication, etc.; to improve the living conditions of the toiling population, to raise the level of social education, and to reconstruct the cultural life on socialistic principles. The village soviets have control over the practical execution of the laws concerning social security of the peasants and administer various privileges granted by law to Red Army soldiers, sailors, former Red Army soldiers, former members of the Red Guard, Red partisans, and their families. The village soviets are to take measures to support and accelerate the collectivization of the farms of the toiling peasants belonging to the above enumerated categories.

The Village Executive

By the decree of 1924, an auxiliary organ for protection of property and public peace was created in the office of village executive. These officers were appointed by the village soviets in rotation, from villagers having the franchise who were eighteen to fifty years of age in case of men, and from eighteen to forty-five years of age in case of women. Persons who did not possess the right of suffrage were taxed for the purpose of covering the expenses of the village soviets in connection with this office. The village executives were appointed for two months and were designated for each group of twenty-five households. Theoretically these village executives were subject only to the village soviets; in practice, however, these guardians of public peace were subject also to the chief of the cantonal (volost) police.[5]

Reorganization of the Office
of Village Executive

On May 10, 1932, the All-Russian Central Executive Committee passed legislation in regard to the reorganization of the office of village executive. In accordance with this legislation the village executives are subordinate to village soviets and are responsible to them. In the territories of complete collectivization there is to be appointed one executive for each seventy-five families; in territories of partial collectivization one executive for each fifty households is designated.

QUALIFICATIONS

The old qualifications were retained, but with the modification that persons who are disfranchised or disqualified by a court from holding positions in state institutions, exiles by administrative and judicial order, and persons awaiting trial by court or still under investigation are disqualified from holding the office of executive. Under the new law the executives are appointed in rotation by village soviets for a period ranging from two to three months. Persons who are holding responsible positions in collectives are exempt from this service, but all those who are disqualified from holding positions still pay a tax in lieu of serving.

THE DUTIES OF EXECUTIVES

The law imposed certain responsibilities on the executives, such as duties assigned to them in connection with electoral campaigns; announcing the general decisions of authorities to the public; keeping order and helping to restore order; supervision in connection with keeping the village in sanitary condition and roads passable; supervision of observation of anti-fire rules; protection of state and public property; serving as escorts for persons who have been held by police and other authorities on their way to report to village soviets; keeping order in crowded places; seeing that obligatory ordinances are kept, and reporting violations; communicating to the village soviet or police all violations of law, and holding all violators, and safeguarding the clues of crime intact; reporting to the authorities the places where liquor is being manufactured illegally, and all persons who are engaged in the illegal sale of liquor; and executing the decisions of the village courts.

Additional duties may be imposed upon executives by special orders of the raion executive committees. Village executives in the exercise of their duties are considered official persons and are responsible for their acts in line of duty.

Sections in the Village Soviets

The Soviet government never tires of admonishing the village soviets that one of their important tasks is to induce the broad masses of the toiling class in the village to partake directly in the administration. They are reminded that it is their duty to organize the farm hands, the poor (bedniaki) and middle peasants (seredniaki) of the village for the purpose of further improvement and socialistic reconstruction of agriculture. The new decree provides that various sections are to be formed for the purpose of inducing the broad masses as well as the members of the village soviets to take part in the every day work of the village soviet. The number and name of the sections are to be determined by legislation of the constituent republics, but they must be constituted in such a manner as to comprise the most important parts of the work of the village soviets. In Russia proper the law provides for the obligatory organization of the following sections: agricultural, general as well as special work of women, cultural, educational, financial, trade-coöperative, and general communal life. Other sections may be organized depending upon the local conditions. In villages which are not the seats of village soviets, settlement sections are formed. In territories where collective farms or production divisions of large collectives or important industrial undertakings are located, groups of deputies must be organized. The work of the agricultural section in a village soviet is similar in its structure to the production conferences. The principal tasks of this section are the organization and work of collective farms, the organization of labor, standard of life, and cultural-educational work. The village soviets are urged in the new decree to induce farm hands and the poor peasants to take a special interest in the agricultural sections. Special groups of poor farmers are to be formed in all village soviets, and it is impressed on the village soviets that they must encourage the work of the poor groups, since they are the main support of the local authorities in the execution of their tasks. In fact no important problem must be solved without first having been submitted for discussion to these groups. It is recommended to the village soviets that they introduce measures for raising the political and cultural standards of the toiling population, and particularly must they pay attention to the work among women of the farm hand class, the poor peasant, and middle group. The central government has never ceased to complain of the backwardness of women in the general work of the soviets, and therefore the village soviets are urged to develop the cultural-educational and political work among women, and use every means to induce them to take part in the work of the soviet and other activities. The soviets are furthermore urged to organize public dining rooms, laundries, nursing homes, children's corners, which would enable the further liberation from domestic serfdom of the toiling women and give them leisure to take part in public affairs.

It has been frequently complained that members of the village soviets are indifferent about public affairs. The new decree states that members of the soviets, being representative of the toiling masses, must take the most active part in the current work of the soviets and serve as a vanguard in the socialistic reconstruction of agriculture. Members of the village soviets are to keep in close touch with their voters, reporting to them periodically concerning their work, on their own initiative as well as by demand of their voters. In addition the members of the soviets must make a report by order of the village soviet to the electorate, in which they explain to the masses all measures undertaken by the soviet government, and they must organize the successful carrying out of these measures. In case of inactivity or indifference of the village soviet expressing itself in the violation of the proletarian class policy, poor direction of the socialistic reconstruction, neglect in the liquidation of the kulaks, etc., a re-election of the village soviet must take place before the expiration of the time for which the members were elected. In the R. S. F. S. R., in case of individual negligence on the part of a member, 40 per cent of the electors may order a recall. The constituent republics are to pass detailed legislation in this matter. The village soviets must render accounts to their voters at least three times a year. In addition, the village soviet must call regular general meetings of the voters preparing in advance the program of these meetings. The resolutions of the general meetings must be carried out by the village soviets. Persons deprived of electoral rights are not permitted to take part in the general meetings convoked by the village soviets. The village soviets are authorized to convoke extended, plenary sittings of the village soviets for the discussion of matters of special public importance. The farm hands, poor and middle peasants, especially those belonging to collective farms, are to take an active part.

VILLAGE FINANCE

The village up to 1932 did not have an independent budget; the village finances were included in the cantonal (volost) budget. This practice was not conducive to independent cultural development, and the new decree therefore proposed to introduce village budgets in all communities. The working out of detailed plans is left to the constituent republics, but in regions of complete collectivization independent budgets must be introduced not later than in the fiscal year of 1931-32. The budget of the village soviet must make allowances for administrative, economic, social, and cultural tasks of local importance and must make arrangements for the maintenance of the village soviets, local education, sanitary establishments, pensions, roads, communications, communal work, and the settlements and expenses in connection with the development of agriculture and maintenance of property and establishments under the jurisdiction of the village soviets.

In the R. S. F. S. R. the law specifies that the village soviets must support the village soviet itself, communal properties and undertakings, village welfare and fire fighting establishments; support, pay rent, heat, and keep in repair buildings and rooms of schools, popular centers, and other village educational centers; equip and support medical and obstetrical consultation centers, nursing homes, and children's playgrounds. In addition the village soviets are financially responsible for equipment and support of smithies and workshops for the repair of agricultural machinery, and similar establishments. They must build and keep in condition roads, bridges, fords, and other transportation and communication facilities of local significance. They must develop and protect communal lands and other properties. The village soviets are furthermore financially responsible for the support and development of communal and other trade and industrial establishments under their management.

The revenue for village expenditures is to be derived from the following sources: (1) incomes from property and enterprises of local importance in the territory of the village soviet, including revenues turned over by the agricultural societies and other organizations to the village soviets, according to Article 52 of the "Fundamental Regulations Concerning Land Distribution and Utilization"; (2) local taxes and dues collected in the territory of the village soviet; (3) contributions to local funds from the consolidated agricultural tax, collected in the territory of the village soviet according to norms established by the legislation of the constituent republics, which must not be less than 30 per cent of the total amount of unified agricultural tax collected in the territory of the village soviet; (4) contributions to local funds from government revenues, according to the legislation of the constituent republics; (5) contributions to local funds from state loans placed in the territory of the village soviet, according to norms established for each separate loan at the time of their issue; (6) funds created by collective farms for the improvement of cultural and educational institutions; (7) contributions and revenues for special purposes, transferred to the budget of the village soviet by resolutions of collective farms; and (8) revenues from self-assessments. These revenues must be spent by the village soviets only for purposes indicated in the resolutions of the general meetings of citizens. In accordance with legislation this assessment in Soviet Russia proper may be made only with the consent of a general meeting at which 50 per cent of the inhabitants having the franchise must be present. A majority is sufficient for this decision. If by lack of attendance a second meeting has to be called, the presence of one-third of the voters is sufficient. The assessments are usually made for cultural and economic purposes of a public character, such as the building and upkeep of cultural, educational, and health institutions and organizations for social security; agricultural establishments, such as agronomical and veterinary institutions, etc.; building of roads; fire protection; public services, such as public baths, wells, ponds, cemeteries, etc.; employment of watchmen.

These assessments are levied on individual and collective economies and on citizens residing in the village who are not occupied by agriculture. The tax may be paid in money, or in

kind, or in labor. In no case must this special assessment be used
for the payment of salaries of local officials, police, village executives, etc. Furthermore the items in local budgets designated for
cultural, social, and economic needs of the population may not be
decreased with expectation that the self-assessment tax will
supply the deficiency. The amounts, however, obtained by self-
assessment may be incorporated in the general fund of the village
soviet, but in making out the budget, provisions must be made
for the operating expenses in connection with undertakings which
have been built by funds raised by self-assessment. In the R. S.
F. S. R. the law assigns to the village budgets the incomes from
all state properties and undertakings of local significance which
are within the territory of a given village soviet and which serve
predominantly the local population. Under this heading come
communalized dwelling places, and business and industrial structures. The village soviets are also entitled to incomes from com-
munal-commercial undertakings such as mills, smithies, workshops, etc.; from land, meadows, pastures, and vegetable gardens,
market places and similar places leased for trading purposes; and
from fishing rights, sand pits, stone quarries, and other similar,
profitable ventures. In addition the village soviet is entitled to
the rents from public reserve lands leased to agricultural associations in accordance with legal provisions.[6]

The village soviet receives 100 per cent of the tax on all
notarial transactions within the village territory, the tax on
land registration, and 30 per cent of taxes paid by private
enterprises located within the village territory. The village
soviets also receive the tax imposed on persons disqualified to
serve as village executives; the special property tax on large
manufacturing plants employing at least thirty-one workers and
using motor power equipment, and on plants employing no less
than fifty-one workers without motorized equipment; and no less
than 60 per cent of the consolidated agricultural tax.[7]

In addition, from time to time the central government of its
own accord levies assessments for special village purposes such
as housing and cultural welfare. Thus in 1931 and again in 1932
the government assessed the rural population in the following
manner:

Incomes in rubles	Workers, employed in cooperative crafts and mechanics, in rubles	Non-cooperative crafts and mechanics, in rubles
Above 40 to 75	8	12
Above 75 to 125	15	25
Above 125 to 175	25	45
Above 175 to 225	40	70
225 and upward	76	130

The village soviets register the purpose of assessment, collect the taxes and dues, and perform all other work in connection with taxation in accordance with legislation of the constituent republics. The village soviets furthermore organize the placing of state loans and explain to the electorate the importance of these loans. They assist the holders of bonds in the fulfillment of loan operations as provided by law.

In general, in recent years the village soviets have received wider powers in the matter of local finance; thus they are permitted to use their own discretion in the matter of transferring funds from one item of the budget to another, as for example— money appropriated for reading huts may be in case of necessity applied to the support of village schools. In a limited way village soviets have some authority over the budget of institutions which are not under their jurisdiction but happen to be located in their territory. The village soviets are warned to avoid deficits, and urged that the funds collected be turned over daily to the State Savings Bank.[8]

CHAPTER VII

PROVINCIAL GOVERNMENT

REORGANIZATION OF PROVINCIAL GOVERNMENT

When the Bolsheviks came into power, they found the tsarist administrative organization consisting of the guberniya (province), uyezd (district), volost (canton), and selo (village), but from the very earliest time of their accession to power they attempted to reorganize the political division of the country in accordance with economic needs. They claimed that the old administrative division was used by the autocracy merely for imposing its will upon the masses through the instrumentality of bureaucracy, but because of the magnitude of the task and precarious internal conditions, the old order was to a great extent retained. As far back as 1919, however, the All-Russian Central Executive Committee appointed a commission for the purpose of formulating a basic plan for the administrative-economic reorganization of the country. The commission brought in a plan upon which was based the work of reorganization begun in 1923 and completed in 1929. In accordance with the original plan every administrative division was to be a homogeneous unit, both from an economic and a natural standpoint, and it had to be a complete unit different from the surrounding divisions. Within this unit there were to be formed in accordance with the same principle, sub-regions or circuits (okrug) which were to embrace a territory considerably smaller than the old guberniya (province). In addition there were to be formed raions which were to cover a territory slightly smaller than the old uyezd (district). Between the years 1923-1929 the Soviet government proceeded to reorganize some parts of the country where the old division was abolished and the new order introduced. In other sections the old order was left intact. Hence before 1930 there were the following territorial formations in the Soviet Union: regions or territories (oblast, krai), provinces (guberniya), circuits (okrug), districts (uyezd), raions, and cantons (volost).

In 1930 after several years of experimenting, the sixteenth Congress of the Communist Party definitely decided to put into operation a new division of provincial government, and the old triple division of guberniya, uyezd, and volost was replaced by a new tri-membered division of oblast, okrug, and raion (four counting the republic). This new division decreased the provincial units in comparison with the year 1917 from 14,592 to 3,860 and in Russia proper in comparison with the year 1922 from 13,051 to 2,451. This reorganization, however, proved to be unwieldy and the sixteenth Party Conference therefore decided to create several experimental territories in various parts of the country where a scheme was tried out which eliminated the okrug (circuit). When the sixteenth Party Congress met in June 1930, a decision was passed to eliminate the okrug and establish the following administrative-economic divisions of the Union: republic, oblast, (or krai), and raion. In those republics which had no oblast division (as in Ukraina) only the republic and raion were retained. At this writing there are all together eleven oblasts in the Union.

The Organization of the Raion Structure

The raion, which was to take the place of the volost and uyezd, is considerably larger in extent that the former lower divisions. The highest organ of authority within the territory of the raion is the raion congress of soviets composed of delegates of all soviets within the territory of that division. The village soviets in the R. S. F. S. R. and Ukraina elect one delegate for each 300 units of population; urban centers and manufacturing plants and factories outside of the city limits elect one delegate for each unit of sixty voters. In other constituent republics the ratio varies, although in every instance the urban population is given perference. While in some instances there are considerable numbers of non-party members in the raion congress, all responsible positions are held by Party members. Between meetings of the raion congress, an executive committee, which is elected by the congress, exercises the superior authority. This committee is composed at the highest of forty-five members, and provision is also made to elect deputies (candidates) to equal one-third of the total membership. In practice the presidium, composed of no more than nine members and four deputies elected by the executive committee, is in charge of the conduct of raion administrative affairs. Since the raion congress meets at intervals of several months, the executive committee exercises the functions which are by law assigned to the congress. Some matters, however, are expressly reserved for the exclusive jurisdiction of the congress; namely, (1) confirmation of plans worked out by higher authorities in the field of economic, social, and cultural affairs; (2) the confirmation of the raion budget and the digest of all local budgets within the raion territory; (3) confirmation of reports of execution of planned projects and proposed projects; (4) the confirmation of assessments and approval of assignments of incomes and expenditures among the raion, villages, and urban soviets, and also the distribution of property among the various units of the raion; (5) the examination of reports on the work of the raion executive committee; (6) the election of the raion executive committee; (7) the election of delegates to superior congresses of soviets. Yet in spite of the legal provisions, with exception of fiscal affairs and the election of executive committees and delegates to higher soviets, it is the executive committee that exercises all aforementioned functions and not the congress itself.

The law prescribes that every raion executive committee must have the following sections: (1) soviet construction and control of execution; (2) industry, labor, and supplies; (3) agriculture; (4) fiscal-budgeting; (5) public education; (6) health. These sections consist mostly of the "toiling" population outside of the membership of the congress. The ultimate purpose of this arrangement is the inducement of the broad masses to enter into the work of the raion administration. The technical staff of the raion administration is centered in departments attached to the executive committee which are designated as (1) general, (2) agricultural, (3) planning-statistical, (4) raion workers and peasant inspection, (5) police and criminal investigation. The law furthermore provides that especially trained officials are to be employed in connection with the administration of the following affairs: (1) local economy and road building, (2) supplies, (3) public education, (4) health, (5) labor, (6) social security, (7) military affairs, (8) physical culture.[1] It is recommended that every raion form a section for the betterment of labor and well-being of women workers, both agricultural and industrial.[2]

The raion administrative machinery is at present operating under difficulties. The chief obstacle in this government division as well as in others is the lack of trained workers. In a recent survey of 900 employees serving as secretaries and technical advisers in connection with raion executive committees, it was found that the majority consisted of young people who have entered the Party between 1926 and 1931. Almost one-third of them have had no practical experience in administrative work. In the lower units of government, such as the villages, the situation is still worse. The superior authorities are uneasy and are advocating campaigns for the training of administrative workers, especially since the raion apparatus was intended to serve as a coördinating agency between the city and the village, and its workers were to serve as trail blazers and guides in the activities of administration. There is still considerable confusion in the administration of raion affairs; in fact it frequently happens that nineteen or twenty inspectors, who are visiting village soviets over a period of two or three months, instead of improving the work of the lower soviets, create disorder and often actually upset the not over efficient village workers.[3]

It is interesting to note that even in such advanced localities as the Moscow region, a state of affairs may be found which is not at all encouraging. The following is a description taken from a Soviet publication and may serve as an illustration. "The Raion administrative division occupies in Zuevo (the raion seat) a little house numbered 1064. A peasant coming from the country will have difficulties in locating it since there has been no sign on the outside for the last eight months. As he enters he finds himself in a room blue with smoke as in an old tsarist pub, crowded and filthy. One can see here amazing things. To the right is the room of the agent, which measures one-half by one-half arshine. Near the table there is always someone sleeping. Above the table hang parts of bedding, scattered boots. At the table the agent questions a citizen, and two persons eat and drink tea. Noise and profanity. In a bookcase in which documents are filed may be seen a balalaika. A short distance away is located a general office where there can be seen a bookcase and a few tables. There is no place to turn around. A narrow passageway is left open leading to the chief's office. In the general office there is also laughter, noise, and loud talk. The office force does not have to work. From the general office room leads a door to the inner office where sits the chief and his assistant by a partly open window; they are used to noise and profanity."[4]

In order to remedy the sad state of affairs, some raions hold regular monthly conferences of soviet workers, and in connection with them schools of instruction are conducted for village soviet workers. Each worker receives at the conclusion of the instruction period a summary of the lectures and suggestions for further practical work.

In some raions the work has been so arranged that raion officials who are to serve in advisory capacity to the lower soviets are compelled to stay in the field for at least five months.

The Oblast or Krai (Region)

After the abolition of the old province (guberniya) and the establishment of oblasts, many undertakings and institutions previously under the authority of the provinces were transferred to the jurisdiction and management of the new divisions. In these are included not only purely oblast enterprises, but also establishments of republican and nation-wide significance. The oblasts coöperate in the organization of new enterprises, the execution of measures in the rationalization of production, and the decrease of cost of production. They give opinions on planned programs, accounts, balances, etc., and distribute profits of state commercial undertakings. In the field of agriculture the oblast organs take measures to regulate the development and collectivization of agriculture, direct all agricultural corporations under their jurisdiction, and take measures for the strengthening and development of state farms, collective farms, and all types of agricultural coöperatives. In addition, to the oblast are delegated some very important functions in connection with transportation, state credit, cultural construction, public safety, communal economy, and other matters of state activity.

Oblast Organs of Authority

The highest organ of authority within the limits of the oblast is the oblast congress of soviets. This body passes decisions on all questions of oblast importance and considers matters of general state significance. The congress hears and discusses reports in regard to the activities of state institutions and undertakings located within its territory. To the congress is reserved the exclusive authority to examine and approve reports of the work of the executive committee. To the congress also is reserved the right to elect the executive committee and the delegates who represent it at the superior congresses.

In accordance with instructions of the All-Russian Executive Committee of September 20, 1930, the membership of the congress is composed of delegates from city soviets, factories, plants, and coöperative farms situated outside of city limits at the rate of one delegate for each 2,500 voters. Raion soviets send to the oblast congress one delegate for each 12,500 inhabitants. Autonomous republics and autonomous regions elect delegates to the oblast congress in their respective congresses at the rate of one delegate for each 2,000 voters from urban centers, and one delegate for each 10,000 inhabitants from rural settlements.

In between sessions of the congress, the highest organ of authority in the oblast is the executive committee, which is elected by the congress. This committee has identical jurisdiction with the congress, except in matters which are reserved for the exclusive jurisdiction of the congress; namely, the approval of the election of executive committees, the approval of the report of the executive committee, and the election of delegates to superior congresses. In its activity, the executive committee is subordinate and responsible to the oblast congress and also to the republican central executive committee and presidium of the republic within whose territory it is located.

For the purpose of administration the executive committee is divided into departments which are designated as (1) the regional council of people's economy, (2) agriculture, (3) trade, (4) finance, (5) communal department, (6) labor, (7) popular education, (8) public health, (9) social welfare, (10) workman-peasant inspection, (11) administration, (12) military, (13) political, (14) the bureau of archives. The current work of administration is in practice carried out by a presidium, elected by the executive committee and divided into four departments; namely, (a) secretariat, (b) organization department, (c) planning commission (obplan), (d) commission of execution.

Administration of justice in the oblast is carried out by the oblast courts and department of justice (prokuratura). For the purpose of coördinating the work of the oblast with that of the Union, the central government is represented in the oblast by officials from the commissariats of transportation, posts, and telegraphs, and the division for the administration of affairs of national minorities.[5]

THE AUTHORITY OF LOWER ORGANS TO ISSUE OBLIGATORY DECREES

In the early days of the soviet régime there was considerable confusion as to the right of lower organs to issue obligatory decrees. Attempts made by the central government to bring about uniformity were nullified by general chaotic conditions of the country. It was not until March 11, 1921, that some definite norms were established. Since that time various regulations have been passed defining the competence of the various units of government to issue obligatory decrees.[6]

On March 30, 1931, legislation was passed regulating that the authority to issue obligatory decrees belongs to executive committees and their presidia, and to city soviets and their presidia.[7]

Departments of executive committees and other local institutions were prohibited to encroach upon this activity. It was provided, however, that should it be necessary for these departments to issue ordinances, they must petition the appropriate executive committees and city soviets. The right to issue obligatory decrees may not be delegated. Between 1927 and 1931 raion executive committees have been given the right to issue obligatory ordinances in regard to the safeguarding of order and the suppression of rowdyism, and also the protection of state and public property. In addition, raion executive committees were given the authority to issue obligatory decrees and rules in all matters concerning the conduct of business, fairs, markets, and places assigned for purposes of trade. Urban soviets, in centers other than governmental seats, which had a population up to 5,000, were placed on equality with those of raion executive committees in this matter. Governmental seats and other urban settlements which had a population of above 5,000 had the same rights as raion executive committees. The most important cities, as far as passing decrees was concerned, were given the legal status of superior executive committees.

Obligatory decrees may be issued for no longer than two years' duration. After that period they automatically become void unless they are newly confirmed and republished for an additional period of time by the appropriate organs. To every obligatory ordinance there must be attached a provision for fines or punishment for its violation, both in administrative and judicial order, in accordance with the provisions of the Criminal Code.

The law prescribes the manner according to which obligatory decrees may be issued. The project of the decree must be discussed at a meeting of the appropriate section of the soviet or executive committee at general meetings of workers and farm collectives. Exceptions to this rule may be made under the pressure of extraordinary circumstances. The obligatory ordinances must be signed by the chairman of the executive committee or the city soviet. It must be given publicity; every obligatory decree must specify the territory in which the ordinance is to be in force and when it is to come into effect. The decree must be announced two weeks before it goes into operation; exceptions may be made in emergencies. Obligatory decrees need no confirmation of the superior authorities in order to become legally operative, provided that they do not violate regulations already in operation. Theoretically then, the lower organs are given some degree of independence from the supervision of the superior authorities. Practically the higher authorities retain control, since the law provides that, in order to secure for the superior organs the opportunity to examine the decrees, every obligatory decree must be sent to the next higher executive committee. Furthermore, the obligatory decrees which are issued by regional executive committees must be sent to the appropriate central authorities of the R. S. F. S.R. or to appropriate autonomous republics.[8]

CHAPTER VIII

ORGANIZATION OF THE CENTRAL GOVERNMENT

INTRODUCTION

The stormy period following the October Revolution brought with it a desire for extreme decentralization. The accumulated wrongs inflicted on the people by the autocratic bureaucracy expressed itself in a desire to sweep away all superior control. The revolutionary Bolshevik battle cry "all power to the Soviets" was soon transformed in certain territories to "all power to localities." A considerable number of independent republics were organized which did not recognize any kind of central control. It was a period of wild disorder, the pendulum swinging from extreme centralization under the autocracy to extreme separatism. By 1918, however, this tendency for local independence practically disappeared, and a period of iron rule from above followed. Civil war brought in its wake excessive centralization, with some of the evils of the old bureaucracy with its red tape and hair splitting pedantry. By the time the seventh All-Russian Congress of Soviets met, which happened soon after the Bolsheviks defeated General Denikin, the local soviets recovered enough to protest decidedly against excessive centralization.[1]

The seventh Congress passed several resolutions which determined the relationship of the local soviets to the central government. The eighth All-Russian Congress of Soviets meeting in 1920 passed decrees which further regulated the relationship of local units to the central government. These regulations were incorporated into the R. S. F. S. R. constitution and have remained practically unchanged up to the present, outside of detailed amendments which are discussed elsewhere. The decrees, among other things, provided that executive committees of the soviets were under the jurisdiction of the superior executive committees, the All-Russian Central Executive Committee, and the Soviet of People's Commissars of the R. S. F. S. R.   The departments of the executive committees were under the jurisdiction of the executive committees and their presidia and were obliged to carry out all the orders of the latter, and also the appropriate departments of the superior executive committees, namely, the departments of the regional and provincial executive committees.   Executive committees had to carry out the directions of the appropriate people's commissariats of R. S. F. S. R.[2]

The regulations of the local congresses of soviets could be changed only by the superior congresses and their executive committees; the regulations of the executive committees and their presidia could be changed only by their elected congresses and superior congresses, executive committees and their presidia, the All-Russian Central Executive Committee and its presidium, and the Soviet of the People's Commissars of R. S. F. S. R.   Thus the decentralization was checked and central organs assumed supreme authority.   With the formation of the Union in 1922 the highest authority was transferred to the Union government.

LEGISLATION

A brief discussion of the Bolshevik fundamental conception of governmental functions as expressed in executive, legislative, and judicial activity should precede a description of the republican and union structure of government.

The Bolsheviks do not accept the time-honored division of governmental function into legislative, executive, and judicial. They claim that, in contrast to Western practices, there is no difference between legislative and executive organs in the Soviet state.   The legislative and administrative competence is interchangeable among various organs.   Soviet public law postulates that the creation of norms is inseparable from administration, and that legislation is linked with government, and, therefore, there can be no differentiation between an act of a legislature and an order which emanates from a governmental organ, as is the case in capitalistic countries.   Authority, it is argued, belongs in the various republics of the Union to soviets, and congresses of soviets, and their executive committees, ranging from executive committees of local soviets to the central executive committees of the several republics of the Union.   Since all the republics of the Union are in their governmental structure identical with the Russian Socialist Federated Soviet Republic, whatever is said of the functions of its apparatus is generally also true of the rest of the republics. Thus the All-Russian Central Executive Committee is in theory the highest legislative, administrative, and controlling organ of Russia proper. In practice, however, the Council of People's Commissars issues all decrees and regulations which are obligatory for the entire territory of R. S. F. S. R. This Council also exercises general administrative functions throughout the territory of Russia proper.[3] The Union Central Executive Committee is nominally the highest legislative authority, but actually it is the Union Council of People's Commissars which issues decrees to be enforced throughout the entire territory of the Union. In harmony with the above reasoning an obligatory decree, issued by an executive committee of a local soviet, is in no way different in the nature of its organic origin or juridical function from a decree or statute issued by a central organ of general competence, and is as binding on the population of a given territory. The fundamental difference between a normative act issued by central executive committees of the Union or of constituent republics and that issued by local soviets is merely that the local authorities issue regulations which are applicable only to a given territory and limited numbers of people, but in its juridical nature this local regulation is local law.

Soviet publicists further declare that in accordance with its juridical function, an obligatory decree is a general normative act and not a concrete order issued for the purpose of regulating the conduct of one or another citizen. There is, however, a difference between obligatory ordinances, which are issued by local organs of Soviet power, such as the appropriate executive committees and soviets within their competence as determined by law, and obligatory decrees, which are normative acts of soviet organs having a special competence, such as people's commissariats. These two types of decrees in their juridical nature differ from one another in that obligatory decrees of the first category concern the general population and designate the duties of citizens; obligatory decrees of the second category are issued as instructions and circulars, namely normative acts directed to state organs for the guidance of their officials. The fundamental difference then between an obligatory decree creating norms and directed to citizens and normative acts addressed to state institutions and officials is rather negative; namely, the violation of an obligatory decree is punished either in the administrative order which may be followed by imposition of administrative fines or is subject to general criminal prosecution by judicial process. Conversely, the non-execution by an official of instructions and circulars may bring with it either disciplinary punishment or special criminal prosecution for service violations, in accordance with provisions of the Criminal Code.[4]

The Governmental Structure of the R. S. F. S. R.

THE CENTRAL ORGANS OF THE R. S. F. S. R.

Since the structures of government of the Union and the various constituent republics are modeled with some variations after the Russian Socialist Federated Soviet Republic, a description of the governmental machinery of the R. S. F. S. R. should precede a discussion of the organs of the government of the Union.

Nominally the highest organ of power in the R. S. F. S. R. is the All-Russian Congress of Soviets. Between meetings of this body, the All-Russian Central Executive Committee exercises its authority.[5] The Congress is composed of representatives of city soviets at the ratio of one delegate for every 25,000 voters, and representatives of regions at the ratio of one delegate for each 125,000 population. It is interesting to note the discrepancy in the representation between urban and rural population. Bolshevik leaders and publicists claim, however, that this disparity is quite fair since the government is admittedly a proletarian dictatorship, the workers being the directing element; therefore, in order to safeguard the predominance of the working class in the state, it must be given the advantage in representation. Within the competence of the Congress come all questions of legislation and administration of the R. S. F. S. R. as a federated republic which are not delegated to the organs of the Union (U. S. S. R.) The Congress, however, has exclusive competence in the matter of amendment and changes in the constitution of the R. S. F. S. R., and the final confirmation of changes and amendments in the constitutions of the autonomous republics which are a part of the R. S. F. S. R.[6] Another function of the Congress is the election of the members of the Central Executive Committee. Since the All-Russian Congress is convened only once every two years, it is merely an assenting body, and its large membership makes it unwieldy to enter into the real business of legislation, which is left to other organs as will be shown presently.

The constitution, however, provides that on the initiative of the Central Executive Committee and at the request of soviets and congresses of soviets, provided it includes no less than one-third of the population of the Republic, an extra session of the All-Russian Congress may be called. The time of meeting of the All-Russian Congress may be changed by the All-Union Congress of Soviets and its Central Executive Committee. Its session may be suspended by the presidium of the Central Executive Committee of the Union. In between sessions of the Congress the highest legislative, executive, and controlling organ of the R. S. F. S. R. is the All-Russian Central Executive Committee. This approximates, to some degree, a legislative chamber, and in practice exercises all functions of a legislature with the exception of matters expressly reserved to the competence of the Congress.[7] All legal codes and decrees which establish general norms for political and economic life and all regulations which inaugurate fundamental changes into the operation of state organs must be confirmed by the All-Russian Central Executive Committee.[8]

In addition, the Central Executive Committee has the authority to confirm decrees affecting autonomous regions. The Central Executive Committee meets in regular and special sessions. Special sessions may be called by the presidium of the Central Executive Committee at the suggestion of the Council of People's Commissars when requested by the central executive committees of six autonomous republics or six executive committees of regions, or at the request of one-third of the members of the Central Executive Committee itself. Theoretically the Central Executive Committee is responsible for all its activity to the All-Russian Congress, which may repeal and change any of the decrees passed by the Committee. Finally, the Union Central

Executive Committee has the authority to change decisions of the Russian Central Executive Committee and its presidium.

The Central Executive Committee elects a presidium presided over by a chairman which constitutes the permanent legislative-administrative power of Russia proper between sessions of the All-Russian Central Executive Committee. This presidium exercises the entire competence of the Central Executive Committee except final confirmation. The presidium, among other powers, has the authority to declare amnesties, issue pardons, change the regulations of regional organs of power, and bestow decorations. In all its activities, however, the presidium is accountable to the Central Executive Committee. The decisions of the presidium may be appealed and changed by the Central Executive Committee and by the presidium of the Central Executive Committee of the Union. The members of the All-Russian Central Executive Committee possess certain privileges, such as the right to take part in meetings of all Soviet institutions with a consulting vote, and the access to the records in all Soviet offices, provided they are not of a confidential nature. They may not be tried by a court of justice without special permission of the presidium of the Central Executive Committee and are not subject to search, arrest, or detention without the consent of the chairman of the Central Executive Committee.

THE COUNCIL OF PEOPLE'S COMMISSARS (Sovnarkom)
The Composition of the Council

The Council of People's Commissars is appointed by the All-Russian Central Executive Committee for the general administration of the country,[9] but it is not only an administrative body but also a legislative organ. In addition to the right to issue decrees and regulations, the Council takes part in the legislative activity of the All-Russian Central Executive Committee and its presidium. The chairman of the Council of People's Commissars is appointed and dismissed by the Central Executive Committee, and the individual commissars are appointed and dismissed by the presidium of the All-Russian Central Executive Committee. In 1925, in order to coördinate the constitution of Russia proper[10] with that of the Union constitution, the commissariats were divided into three classes, non-unified, unified, and all-union. The first two will be enumerated here; the third will be described in connection with the Union government.

The non-unified commissariats consist of social welfare, health, justice, education, and communal economy recently organized. These commissariats are purely republican organs and are responsible to the authorities of the Russian Republic only.

Of special interest is the recently established commissariat of communal economy (Narkomchoz).[11] The duties of this commissariat are, in general, the development of urban dwellings and communal economy, and the building of a socialistic order in existing and newly established urban settlements in harmony with the rapid development of industrialization and the increase of urban population. The commissariat is to strive to induce the Soviet public to take part in the administration of communal economy and to control the activities of communal organs. The new commissariat in relation to the republic is to serve as a directive organ and guide the work of regional departments of communal economy. Some of the detailed duties of the commissariat cover (1) the preparation of plans for urban development, (2) inspection of prepared plans, (3) the working out of rules and regulations, (4) the issuing of standards and rules in regard to planning, (5) the control of activities of all organizations directly connected with the execution of communal and building projects, (6) the coöperation with the commissariat of health in regard to sanitary improvements and services in urban centers, (7) the formulation of financial plans in connection with the central communal bank for the issuing of credit for public service undertakings, and (8) the control of finances appropriated for such purposes. It issues directions for the technical work of municipal administration, such as water supply, sewage, heat, electrification, gas, and transport, and the building and upkeep of sidewalks and streets, parks, baths, laundries, urban lands, and forests. It also supervises the building of schools, administrative buildings, clubs, and places of amusement, independent of any authority which has undertaken these projects. It audits funds for communal and housing purposes and creates price schedules for the use of communal services, buildings, and dwelling places. It controls and regulates housing coöperatives and their development, and assists in the working out of typical projects for non-business buildings. It seeks to reduce the cost of construction and development of standards, works out plans to satisfy the demands of housing communal economy, creates standards of fire prevention, and encourages the development of fire fighting organizations. It organizes institutions for the training of communal workers of all kinds, and assigns to positions technicians who are graduates of educational institutions under the jurisdiction of the commissariat.[12]

On December 15, 1930, the republican commissariat of interior was abolished, and its duties were distributed among the commissariat of communal economy, the presidium of the All-Russian Central Executive Committee, ecclesiastical commissions, administrative commissions, the commissariat of justice, and the commissariat of labor. The presidium of the All-Russian Central Executive Committee took over the general direction of organs of registration of civil acts (marriages, divorces, etc., naturalization of foreigners, the issuance of passports, activities of voluntary organizations, and the records of disfranchised persons). The ecclesiastical commissions took charge of all matters pertaining to cults and religious organizations.

Tasks in connection with territorial division and population statistics were transferred to administrative divisions. The commissariat of justice takes charge of the direction of corrective (penal) labor policies and administers all legislation appertaining thereto. It designates and manages places of exile for persons who are under sentence of compulsory labor but permitted to live at liberty although under conditions of compulsory labor. It supervises the general policy of aid to those who are discharged from penal institutions, and directs the study of crime and methods of opposing it. The commissariat of labor and its local organs direct the work of labor reserves and carry out provisions of compulsory labor laws.

Finally the militsia (police), which was under the supervision of the department of interior, has been organized under the direction of the Council of Commissars into a Chief Administration of Militsia and Criminal Investigation.[13]

The unified commissariats are in charge of finance, labor, supplies, agriculture, and the Workman - Peasant Inspection. To this category also belong the commissariats of heavy industry, light industry, and lumber, recently organized to take the place of the Supreme Economic Council and Grain and Livestock State Farms. The commissariats of this group have a dual status, since they are not only organs of Russia proper and responsible to the Russian Central Executive Committee and the Council of Commissars, but they are obliged to carry out directions of the commissariats of the same name which are to be found in the Union Council of Commissars. In addition to the above mentioned commissariats, there are attached to the Council of Commissars special organs and commissions, such as the representatives of the Union Council of Labor and Defense (S. T. O.), Gosplan (State Planning Commission), and several arbitration commissions.

The Organs of Power of The Union of the Soviet Socialist Republics

When the Union of Socialist Soviet Republics was organized, the structure of the federal government was modeled after that of the R. S. F. S. R.; hence the highest organ of the federation is the All-Union Congress of the Soviets, which consists of delegates from soviets of cities and urban settlements, at the rate of one delegate for each 25,000 voters, and representatives from congresses of soviets at the rate of one delegate for each 125,000 unit of population. In addition, the R. S. F. S. R. is entitled to send delegates from congresses of regions, autonomous republics, and autonomous regions. Those constituent republics which have not reorganized their territories into regions elect delegates at republican congresses. The All-Union Congress is convened no less than once every two years and may meet in an extra session on its own initiative, or on the demand of the Council of the Union or the Council of Nationalities, or at the request of any two constituent republics.

The competence of this Congress covers all matters of legislation and administration of the Union. It has special competence in regard to questions of ratification of changes in the constitution of the Union, the admission of new member republics or the secession of republics, and the election and the confirmation of members of the Council of Nationalities. In between sessions of the Congress, the highest authority is vested in the

Central Executive Committee of the Union, which is divided into two bodies, the Council of the Union and the Council of Nationalities. The Union Council is elected by the Congress of U. S. S. R. from among the representatives of all constituent republics in accordance with the population, and is at present composed of 414 members. The Council of Nationalities is composed of five delegates from each of the constituent and autonomous republics and one delegate from each autonomous region. The membership of the Council of Nationalities is subject to confirmation of the Congress of the U. S. S. R. Each council elects its own presidium composed of nine persons; the two councils jointly compose the Central Executive Committee of the Union. Soviet publicists emphasize that this is not in imitation of the bi-cameral system of capitalistic countries, since the two councils are co-equal in their function and their decisions are considered as actions of the Central Executive Committee, provided both of them have given assent to a given measure though voting separately. In case of disagreement between the two councils, a joint commission is formed for the purpose of compromise, and if this body cannot come to an agreement, the matter is taken up in a later session of the two bodies, and if no decision is reached, then the question is referred to the nearest session of the Congress of the Union. The meetings of the Central Executive Committee are divided into regular and special sessions. Special sessions may be called at the initiative of the presidium of the Central Executive Committee, or at the request of the presidium of the Council of the Union, or the Council of Nationalities, or at the request of the central executive committee of one of the constituent republics. All legal codes and all decrees, which establish general standards for economic and political life affecting the fundamental practices of state institutions, must come for consideration before the Central Executive Committee. The Central Executive Committee of the Union has the authority to repeal or suspend all the regulations of the presidium of the Central Executive Committee and the Council of People's Commissars of the U. S. S. R., as well as the regulations of all governmental organs of the constituent republics.

In between sessions of the Central Executive Committee the presidium of that agency takes over the supreme authority. This body consists of twenty-seven members, in which are included the entire presidia of the Council of the Union and the Council of Nationalities (nine persons from each), and nine additional members elected in a joint session of the two divisions of the Central Executive Committee (the Council of the Union and Council of Nationalities), though the balloting at the joint session is carried out separately by the two councils.

The presidium of the Central Executive Committee elects out of its own members several chairmen to coincide with the number of the constituent republics composing the Union. The chairmen exercise their functions in rotation.

The presidium has the authority to suspend or to repeal decisions of the Council of Commissars or of its individual members and of the central executive committees and councils of commissars of constituent republics. It also has the power to suspend decisions of congresses of constituent republics, subject to examination and ratification of the Union Central Executive Committee. The presidium has authority to pass decrees, regulations, and ordinances; examine, draft, and ratify decrees and resolutions presented by the Council of Commissars, by various departments of the U. S. S. R., and by executive committees and presidia of constituent republics and all other governmental organs. In deference to the polyglot composition of the Soviet Union, the constitution provides that decisions of the Executive Committee and other central organs must be printed in the various languages of the several constituent republics. In addition to the powers mentioned above, the presidium has the authority to determine the relationship between the Council of Commissars and its individual members, and the central executive committees of the constituent republics and their presidia. The presidium is responsible in all its actions to the Union Central Executive Committee.[14] The Supreme Court of the Union, which will be discussed in connection with this judiciary, is attached to the Central Executive Committee.

THE COUNCIL OF PEOPLE'S COMMISSARS OF THE U. S. S. R.
(Sovnarkom)

The Council of People's Commissars serves approximately the same purpose in the Soviet Union as the cabinets in Western

Europe. While the legislative work of the Central Executive Committee is for the most part performed by the presidium, the administration and execution of its decrees are carried out by the Council. The president of the Council is appointed and dismissed by the Central Executive Committee, but the individual commissars are appointed by the presidium. While the Council of Commissars executes all measures passed for the general administration of the Union, and examines all legislative projects to be submitted to the presidium, the Central Executive Committee prepares the unified state budget, and passes on projects for increased taxation and introduction of new taxes. The Council of Commissars has the authority to issue decrees subject to ratification of the Central Executive Committee, and takes part in the legislative work of the Executive Committee and its presidium. In practice the Council exercises a very strong influence in the legislative chambers, since the members of the Council are at the same time prominent members of the Communist Party. The Council of Commissars is divided into two groups, all-union and unified. The all-union commissariats have no counterparts in the constituent republics. The unified commissariats, which are also referred to as directive, are duplicated in every constituent republic.

The all-union commissariats at this writing are foreign affairs, foreign trade, internal supply, army and navy, water ways, transportation, posts and telegraph (communications).

The Organization of the Individual All-Union Commissariats

COMMISSARIAT FOR FOREIGN AFFAIRS

Before the formation of the Union all of the so-called independent republics had their own foreign offices, but since 1922 the foreign affairs of all constituent republics have been conducted by the foreign offices of the R. S. F. S. R. With the formation of the Union all activity in connection with foreign relations has been united into a federal commissariat, and is headed by a people's commissar and a collegium divided into the secretariat, the administrative division, the division of Western affairs, the division of Eastern affairs, the economic - legal division, and the division of the press.

In the staff of the foreign office are also included the Soviet representatives abroad, consulates, and the plenipotentiaries of the foreign office accredited to the various constituent republics, and all other representatives of the commissariat for foreign affairs throughout the territory of the Union.

The general duties of the commissariats are not unlike those of any other foreign office. In detail the duties of the secretariat include the keeping of the minutes of the collegium, the general supervision over execution of decisions, the receiving and filing of correspondence of the members of the collegium, the administration of the organization and upkeep of archives, the supervision of secret documents and codes, and the management of the department of protocols.

The administrative division distributes correspondence of non-secret character, manages the telegraph, telephone, and courier communication, issues visas and passports to certain categories of foreigners and diplomatic passports to Soviet representatives abroad, endorses documents to be sent abroad, and supervises the entire personnel of the foreign office. It organizes the organs of the department, looks after the accounts, buildings, and inventory of the foreign office throughout the Union, provides transportation for members of the department and foreign representatives, protects all foreign representatives in the Union, and supervises the activities of travel bureaus.

The division of Western affairs is subdivided into departments of Central Europe, the Balkans, Scandinavia, Baltikum, Anglo-Latin countries, and America. In general the division has charge of the diplomatic relations of the enumerated countries, studies their political and economic conditions, and attends to the various dealings of these countries with other organs of the Soviet Union. It also supervises the relationship with representatives of these states stationed in the Soviet Union and is charged with coöperation in that relationship.

The division of Eastern affairs exercises the same duties as the Western in reference to the states of Asia and Africa.

The economic - legal division prepares, in agreement with departments concerned, materials for all kinds of treaties and agreements with foreign states. It drafts the projects for these agreements and renders opinions in the course of negotiations with foreign states, supervises the execution of these treaties and coöperates with Soviet organs in this respect, and assists in all legal questions which may arise in the course of international relations. This division also supervises the affairs of Soviet consulates abroad and foreign consulates in the Union. Finally it decides on the status, rights, and duties of Soviet citizens abroad and foreigners in the U. S. S. R. Because of the nature of the work of this division, it employs a large staff of experts in the line of administrative, private, international, and commercial law and admiralty.

The division of the press has varied duties in connection with the collection of materials and compilation of indexes of information concerning political and economic status of foreign states and of the activity of the foreign office and its organs, issues information to representatives of the Union abroad in regard to economic and political development in the Soviet Union, edits the publication of the foreign office, supervises the relationship of the foreign office with the Soviet and the foreign press, and supervises editorial work and libraries and informative work of representatives abroad.

The commissariat for foreign affairs has representatives attached to the council of commissars of the several constituent republics of the Union. In addition, agents of the commissariat, appointed by the representative of the central commissariat in the various republics, may be stationed in the more important centers of the Union. Plenipotentiaries to foreign countries are appointed and recalled by the Union Central Executive Committee; representatives below the rank of plenipotentiaries are appointed and recalled by the Union Council of People's Commissars; the lower ranks of diplomatic officials are appointed by the commissar for foreign affairs. The constituent republics in some instances are consulted as to the appointment of councilors and secretaries to embassies in which they may have a particular interest.[15]

THE COMMISSARIAT OF ARMY AND NAVY

The structure of the commissariat of army and navy is complicated. Although headed by a people's commissar (and collegium), the authority for policy forming is lodged with the Revolutionary-Military Council of the Union, which is composed of the commissar, his deputy, a designated number of members appointed by the Council of People's Commissars, and a bureau of inspection composed of members of the General Staff.[16]

The department consists of two divisions, operative and administrative. There are six subdivisions in charge of detailed duties commonly found in war and navy offices, and they are responsible to specially designated high officers of the service. All divisions and commanding personnel are ultimately responsible to the Revolutionary-Military Council.

The commissariat of army and navy has plenipotentiaries stationed in the various councils of commissars of the constituent republics. The functions of this commissariat are highly centralized and concentrated in the hands of the Revolutionary-Military Council.[17]

THE COMMISSARIAT FOR FOREIGN TRADE

When the various all-union commissariats were organized on November 12, 1923, the decree provided for the formation of an all-union commissariat for foreign trade, and for a unified commissariat of domestic trade to carry out the duties of the abolished commissariat for food; but by a decree issued in 1925, the commissariats for foreign and domestic trade were combined. In 1930, however, because of difficulties in domestic food distribution, this commissariat was divided into two separate all-union commissariats of foreign trade and supply. Foreign trade in the Soviet Union is a state monopoly; hence the duties of this commissariat are very important and extensive. The general duties of the commissariat of foreign trade include the planning and execution of trade relationship of the Union with foreign states. This commissariat, as all others, is headed by a people's commissar and a collegium, and is divided into eight departments—namely, the secretariat, the division of general administration of affairs, the administration of trade undertaking and organs, and the administration of regulation. Attached to it is the planning commission of foreign trade (Vneshtorgplan), the economic-legal division, the financial-accounting division, the transport division, and the chief administration of customs.

In connection with the commissariat of foreign trade, there is to be found the customs- tariff committee, and the central committee for the suppression of contraband, which operates in accordance with special regulations issued by the Union Council of People's Commissars.

The secretariat is in charge of communication of the commissariat with the higher organs of the Union, and supervises the execution by the various divisions of the tasks imposed upon them by the commissariat and superior organs of the Union. The secretariat in addition organizes the secretarial part of various conferences of the commissariat and manages the secret correspondence of the commissariat.

The division of general administration of affairs is in charge of all matters which are not assigned to other divisions, keeps a list of the personnel of the commissariat and its agents throughout the country, carries out duties in connection with inspection and organization of local organs of the commissariat, supplies the economic needs of the department, and is in charge of publications in the field of foreign trade.

The administration of trade undertakings and organs carries out in general the import and export operations of the Union, manages the operation of all organizations of the foreign trade commissariat using state capital, disposes of all funds appropriated to the commissariat for commercial enterprises, and controls profits derived from business transactions of the commissariat.

The administration of regulation issues instructions to the various organs of the commissariat in regard to policies and projects and import-export plans for the consideration of the Council of Labor and Defense through the channels of the State Planning Commission (Gosplan). It establishes, in connection with the appropriate authorities, standards for goods to be imported and exported, presents for confirmation to the Council of Labor and Defense the kind of goods to be imported and exported, issues permits and licenses for export and import of goods, and receives complaints on action of licensed agencies. In general it supervises the activities of all institutions and persons engaged in export and import operations, holding them responsible for provisions of the law governing state monopoly of foreign trade. Finally, it organizes the participation of the

Union in international expositions and fairs, and is responsible for all legal phases in connection with trade.

The financial-accounting division is charged with all matters pertaining to financial policy, bookkeeping, accounting, and the supervision of the activities of all central and local organs of the commissariat in the field of finance and accounting.

The transport division is in charge of all land, water, and air transport in connection with foreign trade and commercial ports within the jurisdiction of the commissariat. The economic-legal division oversees all matters connected with working out of inter-national-commercial agreements, studies foreign markets, tariff policies, and concessions in separate departments of foreign trade, gathers statistics on foreign trade, supplies information and economic advice, compiles periodical accounts, and conducts pre-liminary negotiations in regard to concession in foreign trade. It renders opinions whether or not given foreign firms are to be permitted to trade within the territory of the Union. This division also manages the important work of negotiating for international transport agreements and conventions.

The chief administration of customs is in charge of custom houses, the drafting of international agreements in regard to custom duties and tariffs, the suppression of smuggling beyond the zones assigned to the G. P. U. (State Political Organization), the carrying out of all laws in regard to customs, and the compilation of custom statistics.

The commissariat of foreign trade has authority to station plenipotentiaries at the councils of commissars of the constituent republics, sends trade representatives abroad, and assigns agents to designated customs districts of the Union in agreement with councils of commissars of the appropriate constituent republics.[18]

THE COMMISSARIATS OF TRANSPORTATION (Railways and Roads)
AND WATER WAYS

At the time of the creation of the original union commissariats, a commissariat of communication was created which was in charge of railways and waterways. In recent years, however, when transportation proved insufficient for the rapidly develop-ing industry and agriculture, the department was divided into two separate commissariats, namely, that of transportation and of waterways. As in the case of other commissariats, they are headed by commissars and divided into a number of departments which are in charge of special functions. The commissariat of transportation has charge in general of carrying out the policies of the government in regard to communication, and promotes the "socialist" development of transportation economy, not only from a civil standpoint but also from that of defense of the Union. In general, the commissariat supervises the railroads of the country, organizes them into corporations and exercises a general supervision of the accounting of profit and loss; drafts plans and compiles statistics for the government; suggests projects for reconstruction and rationalization of railroad communication; and organizes new lines and re-inforces old ones, takes charge of operating plants, directs the supply of technical materials, organizes labor on railroads, directs training of employees, and establishes rates. It furthermore takes charge of the entire system of telephone, telegraph, and radio communication on the railroads, coöperates with the commissariat of war and navy in the preparation of railroads for the defense of the Union, and provides for the organization of fire prevention agencies on railroads. Under certain circumstances the commissariat may enter into agreements with foreign railroads. It is given authority to issue obligatory ordinances enforceable on the railroads, and impose penalties for their violation. This commissariat, as other all-union commissariats, is represented by plenipotentiaries at the councils of people's commissars of the various constituent republics and by agents in autonomous republics, regional executive committees, and foreign countries.[19]

The commissariat for waterways has similar duties and functions in connection with water transportation.

THE COMMISSARIATS FOR POSTS AND TELEGRAPH
(Communication)

The scope of competence of this commissariat is not unlike that of the other all-union commissariats and has duties similar to those of a Western European ministry in charge of that branch of state administration. It carries out the duties of organization and administration and is in charge of all means of communication by telegraph, telephone, wireless, and mails. The department is headed by the usual commissar (and collegium) and is divided into five departments designated as general, financial, economical, technical inspection, and central administration of telephone communication. Attached to the commissariat are a planning commission, a technical commission, and a technical council. As is true of all other all-union commissariats, the above commissariat has plenipotentiaries stationed in the various republics of the Union.[20]

THE UNIFIED COMMISSARIATS

It has already been stated that in addition to the all-union commissariats, the Union Council of Commissars consists also of a second group which has its counterpart in the councils of commissars of the various republics and included, until a short time ago, the Superior Economic Council. This latter has recently been divided into three commissariats — heavy industry, light industry, and lumber. This was done on account of the demands on these industries necessitating more specific supervision than the Superior Economic Council could give them.

The commissariat of finance is headed by a commissar whose general duties are the directing of the compilation of the unified state budget, the general supervision of the activities of the republican commissariats of finances, the organization and regulation of the system of circulation of money, and the drafting of tax laws. The commissariat is divided into twelve departments in which are included the following divisions: general budgetary, currency, taxes, state incomes, the financial-economic bureau, the financial-control department, the administration of local finance, the chief administration of state savings banks, chief administration of state insurance, state banks, and the administration of laws in regard to manufacturing state emblems.

While the financial administration of the Soviet Union is a phase of the general planning policy of the government, yet the commissariat of finance, after consultation with other commissariats and representatives of the S. T. O. (Council of Labor and Defense), Gosplan (State Planning Administration), and the appropriate organs of the several republics, prepares every year a unified budget containing estimates of revenue and expenditures. Revenue is derived from taxation and from incomes from state enterprises and undertakings. The taxes in general consist of business turnover tax, agricultural tax, custom duties, and general income and excess profit taxes. Soviet industry, trade, and agriculture are financed through the agencies of four banks: the State Bank, which serves as a bank of issue and regulates the circulation of currency and provides most of the short term credit and agricultural loans in the Soviet Union; the Long-term Credit Bank, which provides credits for industry; the Bank for Foreign Trade, which finances foreign trade transactions; and the Central Municipal and Housing Bank, which provides credit for housing projects.

THE COMMISSARIAT OF LABOR

Before the adoption of the Union constitution in 1923, labor in most of the republics of the Russian Federation was within the competence of the individual republics. With the formation of the Union, the commissariat of labor has become a unified or directive commissariat. The duties of the department of labor include a general supervision of the activities of the various commissariats of the same name in the several republics; the drafting of fundamental laws for the regulation of conditions of work; the direction of the labor market with the coöperation of the labor departments of the several republics; the drafting of projects for social insurance and the control of the All-Union Insurance Fund with the coöperation of the several republics. It also manages the drafting of instructions for arbitration of conflicts between employees and employer; the regulation of wages; and the establishment of uniform labor statistics. It is responsible for the uniform application of all labor laws, and conducts research on all questions pertaining to organization of labor. The commissariat is headed by a commissar (and collegium) and is divided into six departments: general administration, the department of labor market, the department for the safeguarding of labor, the wage-conflict department, statistical department, and the Central Administration for Social Insurance.

The above mentioned departments are self-explanatory with the exception of the wage conflict. This division is charged with such duties as the creation of standards for wages, arbitration in labor disputes of a federal character, and also the drafting of rules in connection with the application of the Labor Code.[21]

THE COMMISSARIAT OF WORKMAN-PEASANT INSPECTION (R. K. I.)

The detailed functions of the Workman-Peasant Inspection (R. K. I.) were discussed elsewhere; in this connection the general administration of departments will be given. In main the duties of the R. K. I. are connected with the improvement of the state apparatus and carry out all measures with this aim in view, so that the apparatus will be adjusted to the ultimate purpose of socialist construction.

The commissariat is headed by a commissar and collegium and consists of four central departments and three independent departments. The four central departments are (1) the operative division, subdivided into nine inspection bureaus—industry and trade, agriculture, finance, transport and communication, army and marine, administrative, culture and education, labor, health and social welfare; (2) the division for the improvement of the state apparatus, subdivided into sections of labor and production, and administrative technique; (3) the division of accounting, subdivided into sections of bookkeeping and accounting; and (4) the general division, subdivided into general offices and secretariat, bureaus of organization and instruction, and economic and financial affairs. The three independent departments are subdivided into branches of information and the press, the judicial division, and the central bureau of complaints and application.[22]

IMPORTANT COMMISSIONS AND DEPARTMENTS OF THE UNION COUNCIL OF COMMISSARS

Attached to the Union Council of Commissars may be found a number of independent departments and commissions, the most important of which are the Council of Labor and Defense (S. T. O.),[23] the State Planning Commission (Gosplan), the State Political Administration[24] (G. P. U.), which is discussed elsewhere, and the commission of education.

The State Council of Labor and Defense was formed for the purpose for formulating economic and financial plans of the Union in harmony with economic and political necessities. The membership of this body is determined by the Council of Commissars. This body has authority to supervise the activities of various commissariates in the field of economic and defense measures. Some of the more important duties of this agency are in connection with the examination and execution of the Union economic, financial, and defense plans. It has authority to examine the conditions of all branches of public economy in the field of finance, industry, trade, and transport, and to take measures for their development. In addition, the S. T.O. has the direct supervision over all economic conferences of the several republics, the State Planning and other permanent commissions of the S. T. O. It ratifies statutes of trusts of nation-wide importance, confirms the statutes of joint stock companies operating throughout the Union, and decides questions in connection with distribution of property among individual state organs and republics which are a part of the Union. The S. T. O. has authority to issue decrees, ordinances, and instructions within its competence, which must be obeyed by all central and local organs of the Union. Its decisions, however, must be forwarded to the Council of Commissars, which may suspend or repeal them. The S. T. O. is given authority to form within itself commissions for the consideration of special problems.[25]

THE STATE PLANNING COMMISSION (Gosplan)

While the S. T. O. is an executive body, the actual planning is carried out by the Gosplan, which also serves as a coördinating body for the planning commissions of the various republics. The Gosplan, as it is now constituted, was created in 1923, yet the idea dates back to the days when Lenin proposed the electrification of the largely agricultural Russia as the first step in the process of transforming it into an industrial nation. The Gosplan has, in general, charge of drafting of "a common All-Union perspective plan" of public economy.[26] It examines the draft of the Union budget and reports on it to the Union Council of Commissars, and examines questions in regard to monetary circulation, credit, banking, and administrative division of the U. S. S. R. It coördinates the plans of Union commissariats in regard to internal trade and decides on the manner of the execution of these plans. It attempts to unify and coördinate the work of various departments in the field of standardization of manufacturing, and in general regulates the activities of all republican organs engaged in research work in connection with the execution of the general plan of Union public economy. In this connection, it regulates the activities of the planning commissions of the various republics. Furthermore, this commission has authority to make decisions in all important matters in connection with economic and social planning. The Gosplan has access to all state institutions of the U. S. S. R., and may require of them all necessary data. It may be also mentioned that the Gosplan was in charge of drafting the first Five Year Plan, completed on December 31, 1932, and is performing the same task relative to the second Five Year Plan and a series of subsequent five year plans in every branch of industry, agriculture, finance, transportation, education, etc.

Finally the very important Commission of Execution should be mentioned which regulates the execution by all governmental and public organizations of the decrees and regulations of the Government and Party. The chairman of the commission is the president of the Council of Commissars, and its membership includes the secretary of the Central Committee of the Communist Party, the commissar of the R. K. I., the presidents of the All-Union Central Council of Professional Unions, the All-Union Coöperative Association *(Centrosoyuz),* and the All-Union Association of Collectives *(Kolchozcenter).* The distinguished status of this membership guarantees the closest relations between its activities and those of governmental, party, and public organizations.

CHAPTER IX

CIVIL SERVICE AND JUDICIARY

CIVIL SERVICE

INTRODUCTION

After the overthrow of the autocracy in 1917, a great number of the old civil servants remained in the service of the Provisional Government. When the Soviets displaced the Kerensky régime, most of the old officials and those who entered the service after the March Revolution left the service, and hence the new authorities were compelled to employ an entirely new and inexperienced personnel without the necessary qualifications. The new government struggled along under this handicap, but gradually succeeded in sifting out the inefficient and creating a new civil service in accordance with Communist ideas.

The Bolsheviks attempted to make the position of civil servants under the Soviet régime different from that in most capitalistic countries by not granting them a privileged status, and by classifying them simply as employees of the state, having the same rights as other persons working for wages. Although to this day there is no special code regulating their status and rights, in recent years it has been found necessary to adopt special rules relating to the employees in governmental institutions and undertakings, whether national, state, or local. It has also been found necessary, from time to time, to divide Soviet civil employees into categories, and accordingly the Council of People's Commissars of the Union, after consultation with the central committees of the various professional unions, decided on a schedule of typical positions, which was later accepted by all national, state, and local institutions.

During the period of military communism, the personnel of state employees reached enormous proportions, but with the coming of the new economic policy and the necessity of cutting down

132

expenditures, the number of civil servants was considerably reduced. In accordance with a decree issued on July 12, 1921, by the Council of People's Commissars, the personnel as found on June 1 of the same year was to be reduced by 50 per cent. A special commission was appointed to work out a plan for this reorganization, and the following decisions were reached: a mechanical reduction of grades and personnel by the end of 1922 and a planned reduction of grades in connection with the reorganization of the bureaus, in which the latter themselves took part. In March 1924, the special commission was abolished; its work was transferred to the Workman-Peasant Inspection[1] and henceforth was merged into the work of general improvement of the state apparatus.

THE REORGANIZED CIVIL SERVICE

On May 1, 1921, the national budget listed 5,674,279 units of civil servants. Six years later, *i.e.* on January 1, 1927, the budget listed a total number of civil servants in all branches of governmental activity as 2,187,955, or an average of one civil servant for each sixty-seven inhabitants of the U. S. S. R.[2]

The reduction of civil service employees from January 1, 1921, to January 1, 1927, amounted to some 3,500,000 persons. Of the total number listed, 565,428 persons were in the service of state institutions and establishments of the U. S. S. R., while 1,064,126 persons were employed by various units of local government. The purely administrative branch of the central government employed 29,455 civil servants, that is 1.3 per cent of the entire civil service personnel; the educational-cultural work, 655,285 (about 30 per cent); the service of public safety, 152,035 (6.4 per cent); and the postal telegraph, telephone, and radio services, 94,145 (4.3 per cent).[3]

The investigation of the Workman-Peasant Inspection showed that the personnel in the administrative branches increased at a sacrifice of such classes of civil workers as teachers, physicians, agricultural experts, etc. In consequence, the Council of People's Commissars issued a decree on September 20, 1927, making it compulsory for the various financial agencies to reduce the allowance for administrative services for the fiscal years 1927-28 no less than 20 per cent. This dismissal of superfluous civil workers made it possible to introduce well defined groups of civil servants and fix a schedule of salaries for workers in the various categories in the national and local administration. The regulation for the creation of classes of employees and grades of compensation is now under the authority of the People's Commissariat of Workman-Peasant Inspection of the U. S. S. R. and federated republics and the appropriate local organs of that commissariat. Appropriate professional unions and interested institutions are coöperating in this matter. The classification of employees in federal institutions is decided on by the appropriate people's commissariat; the classification of civil employees lists in local government budgets is regulated by the councils of people's commissars of the autonomous republics and territorial and provincial executive committees, respectively.[4] Since 1927, an official record has been kept of every civil service employee. Employees have a right to inspect their personal records, to object to them, and to appeal to higher authorities.[5]

GENERAL QUALIFICATIONS FOR CIVIL SERVICE
UNDER THE SOVIETS

Men and women are treated alike in the civil service. Although there is no regulation as to age, the general Labor Code is applied, which forbids employment under the age of sixteen. Foreigners who reside in Russia and belong to the "toiling" masses are given the same consideration as citizens of the Soviet Union. Persons disqualified by judicial process are not permitted to enter or stay in the service. Near relatives are not allowed to serve in the same bureau if one member is under the jurisdiction of another. Exceptions are made in subordinate and elective positions.[6]

The holding of office by the same person in several state bureaus at the same time is permitted only with approval of the directors of the respective departments. Filling of office in a state and private institution by the same person is prohibited. Furthermore, holding of several offices in one or more bureaus is forbidden, if the positions or institutions are in administrative or economic dependence. Exceptions are being made in cases of representatives of the government in Soviet administrative and inspection organs, and of stock associations and other coöperatives receiving governmental subsidies. Members of the militsia (police) and criminal investigation staffs, inspectors and advisers of the Workman-Peasant Inspection and other official inspection staffs, inspectors and agents of the commissariat of finance who perform duties in connection with collection of direct and indirect taxes, public prosecuting staffs, and workers in G. P. U. (State Political Administration) may interchange offices in their respective departments only by special permission of heads of divisions in each particular case.[7]

Persons employed in government service are forbidden to take part, directly or indirectly, in any kind of private trade, enter into contracts for supply and delivery of goods, receive dividends from business enterprises, enter into commercial relationships with state institutions and undertakings, or act as attorneys for third parties in the affairs of institutions and undertakings in which they are employed.

In order to raise the educational qualification of civil service employees, a decree was passed in 1925 providing for employment of graduates of higher institutions *(vuzy)* of the years 1925-26 in all vacant positions and in those vacated by the dismissal of unqualified employees. Beginning with January 1, 1927, all undertakings and institutions, state, coöperative, public and private, are obliged to employ for definite service graduates of universities, institutes, and technical schools to the number of 2.5 per cent of all employees in government institutions and economic undertakings. Other institutions, such as postal, telegraph, and telephone services, are to employ 1.4 per cent of all workers and employees on the pay roll.[8]

The appointment and promotion of employees are regulated in accordance with the provisions of the Labor Code and various special regulations. In practice, examination commissions have the authority to hire and promote employees. Previous experience of the candidates which may have fitted them for higher offices is investigated by departmental examining commissions.

DISCIPLINE, TENURE, AND COMPENSATION

In a decree issued on August 28, 1926, by the Council of People's Commissars of R. S. F. S. R., all state institutions are required to take energetic measures to enforce a rigid service discipline and increase the efficiency of employees. For this purpose, regulations were passed in regard to the duration of the working day and the time for reporting to work and leaving the office. A definite amount of work is given to each employee for which he is to be personally responsible. The enforcement of discipline was delegated to the directors of the state institutions. Tenure, compensation, working hours, and social insurance are regulated, as in the case of other wage-earners, by the general stipulations of the Labor Code. A civil service employee may be ordered for special tasks to a locality other than his usual place of work, for a period not to exceed two months, excepting the time necessary to reach the destination of appointment. The time for this kind of service may be increased for no more than one additional month. Civil servants employed by state and local institutions must be released from their duties by the appropriate authorities of the institutions to which they are attached before being sent to new positions. Civil servants sent to out-of-the-way places may receive additional compensation, expenses, allowances, lump sum subsidies, or bonuses. In order to be entitled to these privileges, the place of appointment must be over 1,000 kilometers on the railroad, or 500 kilometers by other means of transportation, from the original place of residence. The out-of-the-way appointments are divided into two classes: those which are to places difficult to reach from central points and have unfavorable climate or low cultural standards, and all other distant appointments. Compensation of the civil servant depends on the character of the station to which he is attached.

Specially qualified employees who have worked in distant places for over three years receive a leave of three months (exclusive of the time spent on the way) every three or five years of service. Their children have the same privileges in entering educational institutions as manual workers' children.[9]

Professors in institutions of higher learning are selected from candidates competing in national qualifying examinations. Professors and instructors are subject to reappointment at certain intervals. The age limit for technical-scientific workers is sixty-five years. They are entitled to a leave of absence of no less than two months every year, and may receive a leave of from three to six months for every three years of service. Professors and instructors having served twenty-five years receive a pension equivalent to full pay. Upon their death, their dependents also receive a pension. A consort unable to work (man or wife) receives half pay; all the other members of the family unable to work receive one-fourth pay, but in no case may the sum exceed the entire pension.[10]

As in other branches of Soviet service, the responsible positions are held by party members; yet in spite of this, very soon after its inception the Soviet government had to wage a fight against bureaucratism. It seemed that under the Soviet régime, no less than under tsarist rule, the "Chinovnik" soul came to the top. To combat this tendency toward bureaucracy, the control commission of the Party, in its network of branches, is frequently holding "purging" (chistka) sessions, disciplining and removing party members from responsible positions, and frequently expelling them from party membership. In fairness to the Soviet régime, it must be said that the government, through its control commission, in coöperation with the Workman-Peasant Inspection, is waging a fight against bureaucracy, which is so easily developed in any form of government. In conclusion, it may be said also that this constant vigilance is producing a class of civil workers far superior to that under the old régime.[11]

THE JUDICIARY
THE JUDICIAL SYSTEM[12]

When the Bolsheviks came to power in November 1917, they completely destroyed the tsarist judicial system. In erecting a new judiciary the Bolsheviks started out with the thesis of a class philosophy that the fundamental tasks of the courts are to be the safeguarding of the conquest of the proletarian Revolution and the workers' and peasants' rule, the guarding of the rights of the toilers and their unions, the strengthening of social-labor discipline and solidarity of the toilers through hastening their legal education, and the putting into practice of revolutionary legality of the personal and property relations of citizens. They held that the courts are organs of state administration and as such they are not differentiated from other state organs; consequently, the idea of separation of powers is to be rejected. The proletarian court, they claimed, is the organ of the ruling class, and it cannot be separated from that class and its policies. Every judge is to be conversant with all problems of state policy, and all his decisions are to be formulated in harmony with the policies of the ruling class, but in doing this the judge is not in his decisions to forget himself to an extent of being partial to the proletarian elements under all circumstances, even when the toilers are breaking the established Soviet laws.[13] Although there was opposition on the part of some Communists to such a declaration, the Soviet authorities nevertheless in formulating their principles upon which *Soviet Justice* was to be founded, were guided by the above ideology. To be sure, as in many other phases of Soviet policy, there is also here a wide divergence between theory and practice. The courts have not always followed the letter of the law, yet it is worthwhile to bear in mind this theory as the discussion of courts proceeds. The first period in the development of the judicial system of Soviet Russia, that is between 1917 and 1922, was a time of groping and experimentation. In the heat of revolutionary fervor, offenses which were in any way connected with opposition to the new government were dealt with severely by extraordinary or revolutionary tribunals; ordinary cases and offenses were under the jurisdiction of courts which were called ordinary and normal courts. Eventually at the end of 1922, the revolutionary tribunals were abolished and by the Judiciary Act of 1922, the entire judicial system was reorganized.

Between 1922 and 1929 there were many changes and modifications in the administration of justice. In 1926 a Judiciary Act was passed which went into effect in 1927. Under the act of 1926 the judicial system of the Soviet republics consisted of a highly centralized hierarchy of courts and was divided (with some exceptions) into three branches: the people's court, the provincial court, and the supreme court. This rather simple division was complicated by the administrative reorganization of the country where the region (oblast) had replaced the province, the circuit had been abolished, and new units had been introduced called raions. The courts, therefore, had to reorganize in order to adjust themselves to the administrative structure. Hence in 1929 a Union law was promulgated which regulated the organization of the courts to suit the new administrative division. While the new law does not establish federal courts, it lays down general provisions for the organization of the judiciary in various republics of the Union. Under this enactment the courts in the republics of the Soviet Union consist of *people's courts, regional courts,* and *supreme courts.*[14] Inter-raional courts may be organized in accordance with Union and republican legislation. There must be organized a permanent people's court in every raion although sessions may be held in various parts of the raion by itinerant justices. The extent of the district within which a particular people's court operates is decided upon by the regional executive committee on the recommendation of the regional court; the final authority in this matter, however, is lodged with the commissar of justice of the appropriate republic.

The people's court is presided over by one judge and is assisted by two co-judges (judge-jurors). The jurisdiction of the people's court extends to all criminal and civil cases in a given district unless they have been assigned by law to other courts. The people's judges are elected annually by the regional executive committee, but in important centers, such as governmental seats of superior political divisions, the city soviets may exercise this function. Judges are eligible for re-election and may be recalled by the decision of organs which elected them, at the suggestion of the commissar of justice. Before a people's judge is recalled by the regional executive committee, this body must communicate with the commissariat of justice stating all the reasons for the proposed action; the position of the people's judge is furthermore safeguarded by the provision of the law that a people's judge may be removed only by a court verdict or as a result of disciplinary proceedings.

In the early part of the Bolshevik régime, the qualifications of judges were based merely on revolutionary zeal. In recent years considerable attention is being paid to the practical experience of the candidates for judicial offices. Thus, to the usual provision that persons to be eligible for positions of judges must possess the franchise, is the added stipulation that they also must have held responsible positions in a governmental institution or in some other public organization for no less than two years, or must have served in the Soviet Judiciary for three years in no lower capacity than that of an investigating magistrate.

THE SOVIET JURY

The jury, as found in courts of the English speaking world and of some Western European countries, is lacking in Soviet courts. The Soviet law provides for two co-judges (juror-judges) who though temporarily attached to the court, possess, nevertheless, identical judicial rights and duties of the permanent judges. It is interesting to note that, although these laymen decide not only questions of fact but also of law, no specific qualifications are set forth in the law for them. Any citizen who has the right to vote is eligible for the position of co-judge. A person becomes disqualified for three years in case of expulsion from a social or professional organization on account of objectionable conduct.

In accordance with the Judiciary Act of 1926, the lists of the co-judges are prepared by a special commission in each raion. This commission is composed of a member of the raion executive committee who acts as chairman, the assistant procurator, and the people's judge of the district. The co-judges are appointed in accordance with occupational principles; thus 50 per cent come from the workers' class, 35 per cent from the agricultural population, and 15 per cent from the local military units. The commission informs factories and subordinate executive committees of the number of co-judges to which their particular unit is entitled. These groups then proceed to elect the number of co-judges at mass meetings, and the names of those elected are sent to the people's court, which in turn forwards the names to the commission for approval. If necessary, however, the people's judge may make use of the co-judges before confirmation by the commission. The commission apportions the number of co-judges which are to serve in the people's court and the regional court. Generally the co-judges are not required to serve longer than six days in succession in one year. Exceptions are made in cases which cannot be completed within six days. The decision of the people's court may be appealed to the division of cassation of the regional court.

THE REGIONAL COURT

The regional courts are tribunals of original and appellate jurisdiction. They have original jurisdiction in cases of counterrevolutionary offenses, and are in charge of cases of malfeasance and misfeasance in office and of all other crimes assigned to them by the legal enactments of the Union and the constituent republics. They serve as courts of appeals and revision by way of cassation of cases tried in the people's courts. The judicial personnel of the court consists of a president, two deputies in charge of the criminal and civil division respectively, and a number of permanent judges determined by law in each particular court. Generally when trying an original case, the regional court consists of one permanent judge and two co-judges, but when it sits in cassational-supervisory capacity, three permanent judges occupy the bench. The permanent judges are elected by the regional executive committee annually and are eligible for re-election. The election is subject to confirmation of the commissariat of justice. As in the case of the people's judges, the regional judges may be recalled before the expiration of their term, but not without approval of the commissariat of justice, unless the removal is made by court decision by way of disciplinary action. The requirements for office of permanent regional judgeship are not high; the law provides that in addition to the qualification of a people's judge, the candidates for the regional bench must have had three years of judicial experience in a position no lower than that of the people's judge to qualify as presidents and deputies, and two years for the ordinary judicial position on the regional bench. This provision, however, may be waived by permission of the commissar of justice.

THE CO-JUDGES

As is the case in the people's court, co-judges are used in the regional court, but whereas in the lower courts the qualifications for this group are broad enough to include almost all enfranchised citizens, in the regional court the co-judges must have had at least two years' experience in connection with state and other public and social organizations. The lists of co-judges are made out by a special commission of two regional judges appointed by the president, one member of the regional prosecuting magistracy (procuracy), and three members of the regional council of professional unions and is presided over by a chairman elected by the regional executive committee out of its own members. The names of co-judges must be approved by the regional executive committee, and the latter has the authority to remove from the lists any name which does not meet with its approval.

The Supreme Court in the R. S. F. S. R.[15]

The Supreme Court acts as the guiding element of the entire judicial system of Russia proper and serves as the supervisory organ of all judicial institutions of the Republic. While the Supreme Court has original jurisdiction in cases of great importance to the state, it is primarily a court of appeals (cassation) from the superior courts of the Republic.

The judges of the Supreme Court are appointed by the presidium of the All-Russian Central Executive Committee upon the recommendation of the commissar of justice in agreement with the president of the Supreme Court. The president, his deputy, and the chairmen of the various divisions are appointed directly by the presidium of the All-Russian Central Executive Committee, and can be removed or recalled from office only by the presidium of the Central Executive Committee. The qualifications for the candidacy to the supreme bench are the same as those of the permanent judges of the regional court.

The Supreme Court consists of a plenum and presidium and is divided into three chambers: judicial (civil and criminal), cassational (civil and criminal), and disciplinary.

The plenum comprises all judges of the Court. The law provides that at least half of the entire bench must take part in any session and that the prosecutor (procurator) for the Republic or his deputy must be present. The plenum constitutes the highest judicial authority of the Republic, and to it are referred all matters in regard to interpretation of law and procedure by litigants, departments, procuracy, and other courts. The decisions of the Supreme Court are final throughout the territory of the Russian Republic. In addition, in the plenum of the Supreme Court is lodged the authority of review, with the power of reversing, modifying, or annulling decisions, not only of all the departments of the Supreme Court itself but also of the chief courts of autonomous republics and all other courts of the Russian Federation. The plenum is furthermore empowered to approve all instructions emanating from the presidium and directed to lower courts, and designates the judges for the disciplinary section of the Supreme Court.

THE PRESIDIUM

The presidium consists of the president of the Supreme Court, his deputy, and the presidents of the cassational and judicial divisions. The duties of the presidium are both administrative and supervisory and cover such tasks as designation of judges for various divisions of the Court, appointment of deputy presidents to head the divisions, and examination and approval of reports on the activities of the various divisions. The presidium may conduct special investigations and inspections of the divisions of the Supreme Court and all other superior courts of the Republic. The presidium may, in coöperation with the procurator of the Republic, recommend to the commissar of justice plans for conduct of court inspections and make suggestions for changes in their staffs. The presidium is also authorized to draft proposed legislation in the field connected with its work and submit it for consideration of the commissariat of justice. In the presidium is lodged the authority to institute disciplinary actions against the judicial personnel of the Supreme Court, chief courts of autonomous republics, and intermediate courts throughout the Republic. The presidium, in addition to the duties indicated above, performs certain perfunctory tasks, such as convoking sessions of the plenum and preparing data for the consideration of the plenum.

THE JUDICIAL DIVISION

The judicial division, which is divided into civil and criminal tribunals, is the highest court of original jurisdiction in Russia proper. Not unlike the people's court, this division is presided over by one permanent judge and two co-judges elected from a list of forty-eight candidates, previously approved by the All-Russian Central Executive Committee, who serve for a period of one year. The extent of the original jurisdiction of the division is indefinite, but from the general provision of the Code of Criminal Procedure, it can be deduced that only cases of highest importance to the state are to be tried by this department.[16]

THE DIVISION OF CASSATION

This division of cassation is divided into two tribunals, criminal and civil. Six judges are assigned to each. As a rule not more than three judges occupy the bench and act under the immediate supervision of the Supreme Court. The decisions rendered by the cassational division are final, but upon the protest of the president of the Court or the procurator, the matter may be brought up before the plenum; however, any judge dissenting may submit a written opinion to the president of the Court, who has the authority to uphold the majority opinion or refer the matter to the plenum.[17]

THE DISCIPLINARY DIVISION

The disciplinary division has both original and cassational jurisdiction and consists of three judges of the Supreme Court. A member of the presidium presides over it. Disciplinary proceedings may be initiated by both private and judicial persons. In accordance with the provisions of the law, presidents of courts may institute disciplinary proceedings against judicial workers of their own court or of courts subject to their supervision. The president of a given court cannot, however, institute disciplinary proceedings against the prosecutors attached to his own court. The prosecutor has the same authority in instituting proceedings, except in the case of presiding officers of the court to which he is attached. In the original jurisdiction of the division are included all members of the judiciary above the people's court, important officials of the commissariat of justice, and members of prosecuting staffs. The categories of persons enumerated above may be tried in the disciplinary manner for all official and unofficial acts which are not in accord with the "dignity and position" of judicial employees. Judges who have rendered decisions which have been reversed by the Supreme Court as contrary to the spirit of Soviet law and the "interest of the toiling masses" are also subject to this jurisdiction.

The penalties which may be imposed by disciplinary courts are confined to such punishment as rebukes, transfer to other positions, and in more serious cases, demotion or removal from official position for a period of two years. In its cassational capacity, the disciplinary division reviews decisions by discipli-

nary collegia of the chief courts of autonomous republics and all other judicial tribunals above people's courts. The complaints may be filed either by defendant, complainant, or prosecutor.

THE PROCURACY (Attorney-General)

When the Bolsheviks assumed control in 1917, the organs of prosecution of the tsarist régime were abolished and for three years there was practically no organized prosecution; private persons and collegia of advocates were called upon to perform the duties of prosecutors. It was not until 1920 that provincial departments of justice were instructed to organize sub-departments of prosecution, to which were attached officials who represented the state in criminal cases; but by 1922, when the entire judiciary was being centralized, a Procuracy Act was passed, which is the foundation for the present apparatus of the procuracy. At present the procuracy of Russia proper is headed by the deputy commissar of justice, who is also known as the procurator of the R. S. F. S. R. A number of regular assistants are appointed by the presidium of the All-Russian Central Executive Committee. The procurator of the Republic appoints procurators for the lower political subdivisions of the country, who are responsible to him. In general the procuracy is not only charged with prosecution, but has authority to investigate the "legality of acts of governmental organs, economic institutions, public and private organizations, and of private persons"; it may object to any decision or enactment which is contrary to law, and suggest to the appropriate authorities the suspension or repeal of such legislation, or it may institute "criminal, disciplinary, or administrative proceedings against the violators."[18]

The procuracy also is charged with supervision of proper execution of sentences, it must see that no one is illegally detained, and it has the supervision of the general conditions of institutions of penal confinement or detention. The procuracy also represents the state in civil cases.[19]

In addition to the procuracy there is to be found in connection with the Supreme Court and procuracy an inquisition for important cases, whose functions are carried out by inquisitors who are stationed in districts and a senior inquisitor attached to the regional court. The duties of these officials consist in conducting preliminary inquiries of offenses specifically provided for by the Criminal Code. In their inquiry the inquisitors are to attempt to ascertain either the guilt or the innocence of the accused. They may examine witnesses and summon experts and conduct searches for the seizure of material evidence. The inquisitors' decisions, however, are subject to the final ruling of the procurator or the court. It is within the scope of authority of the inquisitors to discharge the accused or hold him for trial, and in this connection it is their duty to compile a bill of accusation, together with a complete record of the case, to be forwarded to the procurator.[20]

THE SUPREME COURT OF THE U. S. S. R.

The Union constitution provides for only one court — a Supreme Court to be attached to the Union Central Executive Committee. There is no independent federal judiciary, and all cases concerning the Union are tried in the courts of the constituent republics. While the Union constitution merely outlines the jurisdiction of the Court and its relation to the other organs of the Union government and the several republics, subsequent legislation has provided in detail for the organization and authority of the Court. The Supreme Court is composed of a president, deputy president, and thirty judges and operates through the president, plenum, the civil and criminal departments, special sessions for criminal cases, and a military division. The judges are appointed by the presidium of the Union Central Executive Committee and enjoy certain privileges, such as not being subject to search and arrest or being liable for trial by any tribunal without permission of the presidium of the Union Central Executive Committee. Unlike the Supreme Court of the R. S. F. S. R., the Union Court has no presidium, and therefore its president possesses extensive powers in the matter of supervision of departments and their functions. He participates in the sessions of the Central Executive Committee and the Council of Commissars where he has an advisory vote. The president represents the Supreme Court in cases which have been transferred from the jurisdiction of the Supreme Court to the presidium of the Central Executive Committee.

The plenum of the Supreme Court is composed of sixteen judges and a representative of the G. P. U., and the membership is limited to the president, his deputy, three presidents of the departments of the Court, four judges designated by the presidium of the Central Executive Committee, and the presidents of the supreme courts of the seven constituent republics. The plenum is convened in regular bi-monthly sessions by the president, but special sessions may be called by request of the procurator of the Union, the procurator of a constituent republic, or at the initiative of three members of the plenum. Three-fifths of the membership constitutes a quorum, which must include three presidents of courts of the constituent republics. Under some circumstances seven judges may constitute a quorum, provided two presidents of the courts of constituent republics are present. All decisions are made by a majority vote; if the vote results in a tie, the matter must be transferred for final action to the presidium of the Central Executive Committee. The primary function of the plenum is to see that the constitution and the laws of the Union are correctly interpreted and administered. For this purpose the plenum issues instructions and explanations in regard to federal legislation to the supreme courts of the several republics, either at the latter's request, or on the initiative of the procurator of the Union or the procurators of the republics, or on a request of the presidium of the Central Executive Committee and the Union Council of Commissars, or on its own volition. The plenum has the authority of final review and interpretation of decision of its own departments, unless its rulings are reversed by the presidium of the Central Executive Committee.

The Supreme Court may, on request of the Union Central Executive Committee, review and render opinions in regard to constitutionality of decrees passed by the Council of Labor and Defense, the Union Council of People's Commissars, and the central executive committees of the constituent republics and, with permission of the presidium of the Union Central Executive Committee, render opinions on debated enactments of central executive committees of constituent republics. The Supreme Court may furthermore review decisions of supreme courts of constituent republics which are appealed to it on the basis of being contrary to federal legislation or of reacting injuriously on other constituent republics. In such a case the Court may decide on the annulment of the law and recommend this action to the presidium. The Supreme Court is finally charged with the duty of explanation and interpretation of federal laws to the superior authorities of the Union and to the supreme courts of the several republics, and unless objected to by the procurator of the Union, they are considered final.[21] The criminal department is organized by the plenum of the Supreme Court and consists of a president, one permanent judge appointed by the Union Central Executive Committee, and three temporary judges appointed for one year by the plenum of the Supreme Court out of its own numbers. The civil department consists of a president and three judges. The bench of the criminal department at its session as a trial court consists of the president and two judges, one of whom may be a co-judge appointed by the presidium of the Central Executive Committee from a special rostrum of twenty-nine judges, fourteen of whom are chosen from candidates suggested by the presidia of the central executive committees of the constituent republics and fifteen selected from a list of names submitted by the Supreme Court of the Union. The original jurisdiction of the criminal department covers cases of legal, political, and economic offenses committed by members of the Union Central Executive Committee and cases involving either the interests of the Union or two or more constituent republics. This department has been granted by the Supreme Court Act of 1929 the authority to parole prisoners sentenced by this department or by the special session for criminal cases.

In addition to the regular session of the criminal and civil department for trial of original cases, a special session of the Supreme Court may be convened for special cases which involve important officials and members of the Central Executive Committee and which are of importance to one or more constituent republics.[22] The special session consists of a president and two judges from the membership of the Supreme Court.[23]

The military division of the Supreme Court consists of six judges appointed by the president of the Central Executive Committee of the Union and operates under the supervision of the Supreme Court. This department has both original and appellate jurisdiction. Its original jurisdiction extends over certain cases of great importance and offenses involving important members of the military establishments, which have been assigned to it by the presidium of the Central Executive Committee or the plenum of the Supreme Court. In its cassational jurisdiction it takes charge of appeals from lower military tribunals. The cassational chamber of the military division consists of a president and two judges, one of whom must be a member of the supreme court of that constituent republic in which the offense has been committed.[24]

THE PROCURATOR (Attorney-General)

The Union constitution provides for the appointment of a procurator and a deputy by the presidium of the Union Central Executive Committee. The duties of the procurator consist in rendering opinions on questions "subject to the decisions of the Supreme Court of the Union." He also conducts the prosecution at the Supreme Court. He may appeal decisions of the Supreme Court to the presidium of the Union Central Executive Committee. Since 1929 the plenum of the Supreme Court is obliged to give reasons for refusing to follow opinions of the procurator. In addition to the prosecuting duties, the procuracy has extensive authority in connection with judicial review and annulment of legislation contrary to the provisions of the federal constitution or harmful to the interests of the constituent republics. At every Supreme Court session there must be present a representative of the procuracy.

One of the assistant procurators is detailed to supervise the legal activities of the G. P. U., and two assistants are designated to supervise the military division of the Supreme Court, the military prosecuting staffs, and judicial activities in general.[25]

PART II

THE CITIZEN AND THE STATE

PART II

THE CITIZEN AND THE STATE

CHAPTER X

ADMINISTRATIVE COERCION

PENALTIES AND FINES

In discussing the relationship of the citizen and the state in the Soviet Union one meets with an unprecedented situation, and it is necessary to bear in mind that the present government was built upon the ruins not only of a former government, but of a generally accepted system of political philosophy. The new state and new government came out of a cataclysmic upheaval that changed old Russia into a new world, unfamiliar, untried, and bewildering to the Western mind, and the reader must be warned to divest himself of all notions of administrative coercion as expressed in legal norms of the Western world.

Furthermore in the critical period of the Soviet régime, when the very existence of the new government was at stake, there was considerable confusion of authority, especially in the field of administration. The new rulers, in their desire to retain power, frequently crushed unmercifully all opponents, real or suspected. The organs having the right to impose fines and punishment were many and varied and were often unregulated by law, acting on their own responsibility without granting the right of appeal. The Bolshevik leaders, realizing the dangerous consequences of such methods, took alarm, and thus when the fourth All-Russian Congress of directors of administrative divisions of provincial executive committees met in 1920, the consensus of opinion of this body was that it was imperative to regulate the rights of administrative organs in their imposition of administrative penalties and fines. It advocated the passing of rigid regulations for definite norms of penalties and fines. The Congress also recommended a classification of law infractions and violations which were to be punished by administrative order, and proposed that the authority in these matters be exercised only by the presidia of the executive committees and departments of administration.

Eventually, by a decree issued on June 23, 1921, by the All-Russian Central Executive Committee and the Council of People's Commissars, the order of imposition of administrative penalties was strictly regulated whereby administrative penalties as measures of administrative action were connected with the infraction of obligatory decrees.[1]

The decree of June 23 mentioned above authorized district (uyezd) executive committees and collegia of the provincial departments of administration to impose administrative penalties in the form of imprisonment not to exceed two weeks, forced labor without deprivation of liberty not to exceed one month, and a specified fine. In case of refusal to pay the fine and submit to forced labor, the fine was to be five times the wage received for a corresponding task performed as free labor. In 1922 the authorities were permitted in lieu of an unpaid fine to substitute a sentence of imprisonment not to exceed one month.[2]

From 1922 onward legislation was enacted which regulated the issuance of obligatory decrees by the local division of government, and in 1927 and again in 1929 the various divisions of local government were given the right to impose administrative penalties, which hitherto were permitted only to provincial and district executive committees.[3] It must be added, however, that the village authorities could impose administrative penalties only at the discretion of cantonal (volost) and raion executive committees, and then only when the obligatory decrees under which the penalty was imposed were issued by themselves and not by higher executive committees. In the serious problems which confronted village life, such as the struggle against banditry, safeguarding of public property, fire peril, natural catastrophies, pests, etc., the village had to depend and still depends upon the regulations of superior authorities, as the authority of the village soviet is limited. For the violation of obligatory decrees of the local soviets the authorities could issue at first a warning, followed by a fine or forced labor without deprivation of liberty.

Deprivation of liberty was placed outside of the scope of administrative punishment. The maximum fines in villages varied from three to ten rubles; in cities, from fifty to one hundred rubles, depending on the population. Forced labor was imposed for a period not to exceed five days in rural communities; at the request of the violator, forced labor could be substituted for a fine. In imposing a fine the authorities were instructed to take into consideration the economic status, political awareness, and the character of the violator. In the past the authorities who had the right to impose administrative punishment and fines were (1) the heads of the administrative divisions and their deputies; (2) the presidia of city soviets; (3) the heads of the division of the militsia (police) in cities; (4) the heads of raion administrative divisions with the confirmation of executive committees; (5) the cantonal (volost) executive committees;[4] and (6) the village soviets.

The heads of administrative divisions imposed penalties for the violation of obligatory decrees issued by the executive committee of the appropriate administrative-territorial unit, and the presidia of city soviets had the same rights within the limits of towns (outside of governmental seats) and settlements having a population of over 5,000 people.[5] The administrative divisions of the raion, with permission of the raion executive committee, could impose penalties for such offenses as (1) the infraction of obligatory decrees of the raion executive committees and, (2) the infraction of ordinances of the superior executive committees (provided this right had been delegated to the above committees).

The penalty could not exceed one week of forced labor if the violated ordinance had been issued by the raion executive committee; and a fine could not exceed ten rubles and forced labor, two weeks, if issued by other authorities. The village soviets, when the raion executive committees had granted them the authority to impose penalties for violation of their ordinances, could issue a warning followed by fines not to exceed one ruble or forced labor not to exceed two days.

The law prescribed in detail the order in which administrative punishment was to be imposed. A complaint had to be made out by the police or by other authorities as the case might be (such as sanitary inspection bureaus, technical, trade, and fire supervision, forest service, etc.). In rural settlements a complaint could also be made out by members of village soviets and village administrators. The complaint was first presented to the accused person to be signed by him and witnesses, if such be found, and by the person making the complaint. The accused could refuse to sign the complaint, but this refusal did not stop prosecution. The complaint was forwarded to the appropriate administrative division, which could dismiss the case, or impose a penalty, or order a judicial trial. A decision had to be made by the lower authorities within two weeks after the violation; higher organs could extend the time to one month. The central authorities could extend the time of the lower organs to one month, but after the elapse of this period the complaint was cancelled. No person could be punished for the same violation both by administrative and judicial process.[6]

The decision as to punishment had to be made in writing and delivered to the accused within two months; failure to do so voided the decision. The entire period from the day of violation to the actual imposition of penalty was limited to six months. The police executed the administrative orders in municipalities, while in rural districts the village soviets carried out the orders through the police and village administrators.[7]

Forced labor was generally performed at the place of residence and in no case farther than ten *versts* from residence. The offender reported to a special "bureau of forced labor" or its agent and, in localities where there are no such bureaus, to the directors of public works. Village offenders reported to the village soviet.[8]

Fines for violation of city ordinances, such as traffic regulations on streets and public places, had to be collected at the time of violation by the policeman in charge of enforcing the particular regulation. The fine for such offenses in the chief cities was not to exceed one ruble; in other municipalities, fifty kopeks. Upon refusal to pay at once the fine could be tripled. The action could be appealed to higher authorities within three days in cities, and five days in rural settlements.[9] Bolshevik writers admit that local authorities looked upon fines as items of state income and hence frequently imposed excessive fines for minor offenses.[10]

The central authorities, in order to remedy this evil, issued a decree on January 4, 1928, limiting the power of local authorities to levy administrative fines. The federated republics were instructed to pass regulations prohibiting the local authorities from issuing obligatory ordinances and imposing administrative fines in matters upon which the higher authorities had already promulgated their own ordinances.

The federal regulation of January 4, 1928, limits the imposition of fines, (1) when they were actually designated by law; (2) when they were for violations expressly designated by instructions and obligatory ordinances of the authorities of the U. S. S. R. and the several republics; and (3) when they were designated by obligatory ordinances of local soviets based upon and defined by law.

The following fines could be imposed by various authorities if not otherwise provided by law: (1) the authorities of the U. S. S. R. and federal republics, for violation of official regulations and obligatory ordinances, not over one hundred rubles; (2) executive committees of territorial, provincial, and circuit units and city soviets, for violation of obligatory ordinances, not to exceed one hundred rubles; (3) district executive committees, soviets in district seats, and other towns having a population of over five thousand people, not to exceed fifty rubles and in municipalities of less than five thousand, not above ten rubles; (4) rural districts and executive committees of raions, for the infraction of their obligatory ordinances, not to exceed three and five rubles, respectively. The superior executive committees could impose a fine in rural districts up to ten rubles. The law does not permit the garnisheeing of wages of workers and employees for non-payment of administrative fines.

In order to reduce the evils in connection with administrative penalties to a minimum, a law was passed on March 30, 1931, providing for appointment of commissions to investigate violations and decide upon imposition of penalties.[11] In the raions the commissions are formed in connection with the raion executive committees, and in municipalities these commissions are attached to either city or ward soviets, depending on the size of the urban commune.

The personnel of the commission is to consist of the chief (or his deputy) of the appropriate police administration, who serves as chairman, and the members of the judicial administrative section of the soviet or the executive committee; where there are no such sections, the commission is formed by members of the appropriate soviets and executive committees. In urban communes and settlements where there are no police administrations, the commission is formed by the members of the presidium and the judicial - administrative section of the soviet. In municipalities and settlements where there are neither police administrations nor judicial-administrative sections of soviets, the work of the commission is performed by the presidium of the appropriate soviet. The functions of the commission are regulated by decrees of executive committees of the region and autonomous regions. The violation of obligatory ordinances of higher soviets in villages which call for more stringent penalties than village authorities are permitted to impose comes under the jurisdiction of the raion or city commission. Persons in military service who have violated ordinances are not fined but are reported to appropriate military authorities. All cases of violations have to be decided upon within a month, or the charges are cancelled. Prosecution of violations by judicial process has to be completed within two months. The entire process, including the imposition of a fine or penalty, the execution of the order, and the appeal from the decision, is not to cover a period exceeding five months; any deviation from this regulation voids the entire matter.

The order of appeal of fine or penalty has a definite procedure. The action of the village commission is appealed to the raion commission, and thence to the raion executive committee. The action of city and raion commission is appealed to city and raion soviets (presidium), respectively. The decision of the presidium can be appealed to the presidium of the appropriate executive committee. Actions of chiefs of police are appealed to appropriate commissions on administrative fines. The appeals have to be directed through the organ which imposed the penalty, within five days.

In general, decisions of the executive committees of the next higher soviets are final. Officials can be held to disciplinary responsibility for any irregularities in the imposition of fines.[12]

Obligatory Labor—General Provisions

In discussing labor in Soviet Russia one in confronted with the difficult task of making a distinction between forced labor, which is a penalty for a committed crime, obligatory labor, which may be required of citizens in every country under exceptional circumstances. and free labor, which in most countries need not be considered in a discussion of state coercion but which must be included, for reasons which will be given presently, in a treatise on Soviet Russia. Article XI of the Labor Code, upon which all coercive regulations as to labor are based, appears to be a reasonable provision, but it is at times interpreted in such a way as to exercise an evil influence on the conduct of free labor. The Article provides that in exceptional contingencies (struggle against calamities caused by the elements, lack of man power for the performance of work important to the state), all citizens of the R. S. F. S. R., with the exceptions stipulated in Articles XIII and XIV,[13] are liable to be called upon to perform obligatory labor service in conformity with special resolutions to be issued by the Council of People's Commissars or by other organs authorized to do so by the said Council. This authority for coercive action given to governmental organs calls for a discussion of the various practical applications of Article XI of the Labor Code.

Obligatory Labor in the Time of Elemental Disasters

The prevention of elemental disasters and the coping with problems after they have occurred are important duties of local executive committees under the supervision of administrative organs of the commissariat of interior. The local executive committees may issue obligatory ordinances of a general nature in this regard. In localities where the normal life has been disturbed by extraordinary elemental disasters, "exceptional order" (mild form of martial law) may be declared. In event of elemental calamities which cannot be prevented by ordinary measures of public safety, such as floods, snow storms, fires, etc., citizens may be drafted for duties of labor and transport by local executive committees. Only under extraordinary circumstances may lower executive committees exercise the same authority, and they must then at once inform the superior executive committees of this action. Village soviets possess that authority only in case of forest fires within a distance of ten miles from any of the local executive committees. The details of the law are carried out by the appropriate administrative divisions, regional committees, and village soviets. All persons who have been drafted for compulsory emergency labor must appear with the necessary equipment and tools. The failure to appear is punished in accordance with provisions of the Criminal Code.[14] Citizens may be compelled to render labor and transport duty only for the purpose of localizing and putting an end to a developing disaster. The drafting of the population for the purpose of prevention of elemental calamities is permitted only in exceptional cases when it is impossible to obtain voluntary labor, and the neglect of taking immediate measures would result in a catastrophe. The work must be paid for by those organs under whose supervision it has been performed. The wage scale is established every quarter by regional and local departments of labor in agreement with local councils of professional unions, and is confirmed by the appropriate executive committees, and must not be lower than the average wage of an unqualified worker (unskilled labor). Since 1927 the law permits the drafting of labor without compensation by central executive committees of republics, regions, and provinces, when it is in the interest of those citizens who are called to perform the labor. This rule also applies to disasters and the tasks ensuing therefrom. The differences which may arise in regard to damages suffered by those who are performing compulsory labor are decided upon by judicial process. The dependents of persons who have been injured incident to this work or who die as a result of it receive due compensation.[15]

ROAD BUILDING

When funds are lacking for the building and repairing of roads, the raion executive committees may draft all able-bodied persons residing in given rural communities within the limits of a raion to perform work in connection with building, upkeep, repair, and improvement of raion and village roads. The law stipulates, however, that before calling the village population to perform the task, the authorities must ascertain that the necessary financial means, materials, and technical personnel for the execution of the project are available. Employees and students are exempt from this duty, and it is within the discretion of the raion committee to increase the exemptions. The raion executive committees, however, are authorized to draft certain categories of employees who are partly occupied with agriculture. The superior executive committee must be informed of the draft. By special regulation of the R. S. F. S. R. and U. S. S. R., collective farms (kolchozy), agricultural artels and coöperatives, private trade and business associations, and other undertakings are also subject to this duty.

The raion executive committees may call all or certain persons in designated categories together with draft animals, wagons, and other equipment, or they may accept a financial settlement in lieu of work. This authority may be delegated to village soviets. The number of days of work with and without animals and financial substitution is decided on annually by the raion executive committee. The law permits discrimination against kulaks and private traders in favor of middle peasants (seredniaks) and poor peasants, etc., but in no case must the time demanded for road work exceed six days per year or financial substitution exceed 20 per cent of the agricultural tax and the income tax paid by a given individual. Upon refusal to perform the work or to pay the money, the sum is collected in administrative manner in accordance with the rules for tax collecting. Categories of those entirely exempt are (1) persons under eighteen years of age, men over forty-five years of age, and women over forty years of age; (2) sick persons during the period of illness; (3) pregnant women, eight weeks before confinement and eight weeks after; (4) nursing mothers; (5) women who have to take care of children up to eight years of age and have no one to take their place; (6) persons disabled by work or war; and (7) persons in the military and naval service, G. P. U., frontier guards, prison guards, and reserves of the Red Army performing their periodical service.

The raion executive committee under certain circumstances may use its own judgment in the matter of drafting persons for road work; thus it may decide to call only one able-bodied person from those peasant households which are exempt from the agricultural tax.[16] As in other instances this action must be communicated at once to the superior executive committee. Persons

called for road work may not be sent farther than fifteen kilometers from the place of their residence. Persons must not be
called for compulsory work at seasons when they are occupied
with agricultural work. The decisions of the village soviets may
be appealed to higher authorities.[17]

MISCELLANEOUS OBLIGATORY LABOR

Between 1921 and 1929, when the supply of labor exceeded the
demand of the Soviet industry, the obligatory labor provisions of
the Labor Code were rarely applied outside of emergencies, and
then only when it was impossible to obtain sufficient voluntary
labor to execute tasks considered of vital importance to the state.
In the last few years, however, the Communist Party has made
frantic attempts to develop industry, and consequently there has
appeared an acute shortage of labor. In their anxiety to carry
out the Five Year Plan, the aforementioned Article XI was interpreted by organs of government to cover the execution of any
phase of industry for which free labor could not be obtained. To
be sure every effort has been made to induce voluntary mobilization of labor, but frequently the natural disinclination of the
Russian peasant to coöperate with the government in carrying
out plans and the hostility of the so-called kulaks, who have not
lost all their influence by any means, have led to aggressive action
on the part of the governmental and party organs. This is regrettable since it has resulted in coercion of free labor.

The extent of this method of compulsion is hard to ascertain.
Reports conflict, and deductions from Soviet newspapers by
foreigners are frequently colored and influenced by their general
attitude toward the Bolshevik régime. One of the methods commonly used for the mobilization of citizens for obligatory service,
other than specifically provided by law, is the "self imposition"
of tasks by villages. Under this procedure each village is
assigned by the authorities of the next higher political subdivision
(such as the raion) certain tasks to be performed. A village
meeting is called, which is managed by the Party group of the
village soviet, farm hands, and poor peasants, whose loyalty
to the Soviet power is more or less taken for granted. The meeting is also attended by government officials under whose responsibility the projected task is to be carried out. This conference

prepares a preliminary plan of execution. If the nature of the work is such as to permit subdivision, quotas are assigned to various peasant families, the more difficult and larger tasks, of course, being given to the kulaks. The preliminary meeting is followed by a general meeting of all villagers, at which the plan is presented and, as a rule, adopted. Opposition is rare, since dissenters run the risk of being branded kulaks and counter-revolutionaries. After the meeting has accepted the plan, it is not safe for any individual to refuse to perform the task assigned to him, for this may expose him to prosecution under Article 61 of the Criminal Code, which provides severe penalties for "refusal to do obligatory service, national tasks, or work of national importance"; or the individual may also be prosecuted for counter-revolutionary activities in accordance with provisions of the Criminal Code.[18]

The scarcity of highly skilled workers or specialists, such as engineers and technically trained persons, has compelled the government to deal sternly with this class who refused to report to assigned places. Specialists were transfered from location to location as necessity arose. Many of them, however, belonged to the former middle class and were not at all anxious to see the Bolshevik government succeed, so that when occasion arose, they deserted their posts or failed to report to the positions to which they were assigned. To stem this desertion, which endangered the carrying out of the Five Year Plan, various decrees were passed which were at first mild in their provision of punishment; the methods of coercion were mostly indirect, such as expulsion from the trade union and assignment to places where conditions were disagreeable. Eventually, however, indirect methods of coercion were displaced by direct, and Article 61 of the Criminal Code was applied in recalcitrant cases. On September 24, 1930, the Union commissariat of labor resolved "to institute legal proceedings against specialists who resist mobilization, as well as against engineers and technicians who have been already removed from their former work, but have not yet proceeded to their new posts."[19] This resolution also applied to executives of undertakings who assisted specialists in evading orders to report for duty in enterprises to which they were transferred.

Compulsory Labor (Penal Labor)

In contrast to obligatory labor as described above, Bolshevik Russia employs the labor of persons awaiting trial or under sentence. The practice in itself is a step forward, but involves the question of the extent this kind of labor should be employed in industries which produce goods for the open market and are sold in competition with goods produced by free labor. In this field as in others, no reliable data are available; claims and counter-claims are made by friends and foes of the Soviets. Some prominent Communist authorities approve the use of such labor for reasons that during the period of reconstruction all available man power of the country, including that of prisoners, should be used; penal institutions availing themselves of compulsory labor are becoming self-supporting and in some instances showing a profit; persons under sentence are given a chance to acquire working class habits and even technical skill, which will be of lasting benefit to them after they have completed their sentence. Krylenko, the attorney-general of the Union, stated in the spring of 1931 that "In the sphere of penal labor policy, we are similarly facing production . . . . We have reconstructed everything, both penal labor camps, which are within jurisdiction of the O. G. P. U. and not within ours, and our penal labor institutions, both agricultural or factory and plant colonies, as houses for persons under age, and even the system of exile at compulsory labor on principles of production, and have made them assist the cause of socialist upbuilding. . . . We may well be proud of the fact that our places of confinement. . . . do not cost a single kopek to our proletarian state. . . . our timbering camps, our peat production enterprises, and our homes for criminals under age have been transformed into factory and plant educational institutions in order to produce after two and one-half years of study splendid cadre of qualified laborers."[20]

In this connection the Russian commissariat of justice issued two circulars on July 30 and August 30, 1928, respectively, which ordered judges to assign all prisoners, serving terms of less than one year, to compulsory labor without incarceration. These circulars also instructed that in the future, persons convicted of crimes which involved imprisonment for less than a year are to be sentenced to compulsory labor in preference to incarceration.

On January 19, 1929, the commissariat of justice directed that persons awaiting trial for none too serious crimes were to be compelled to work during the period of waiting. The commissariat of agriculture in June 1929, recommended the use of sentenced persons in timber work in forests and instructed lower state organs to see that the output of such labor be increased.[21]

In the years following the above mentioned instructions the Criminal and Corrective Code of the R. S. F. S. R. was amended, and the provisions for the assignment of persons awaiting trail to compulsory labor systematized. Furthermore, the categories of such persons were increased, and judges were ordered to impose compulsory labor sentences in preference to fines, confiscations of property, etc. Administrative rules were adopted, which tended to increase the number of such sentences.

The Criminal and Corrective Code of the R. S. F. S. R., as in force now, and administrative instructions based thereon divide all persons awaiting trial or sentence into two classes with respect to performance of compulsory labor: (1) those awaiting trial or under sentence who are to perform compulsory labor without the supervision of guards and (2) those awaiting trial or under sentence who are to perform compulsory labor under guard.

Prisoners sentenced to terms less than one year are not kept under guard. They serve out their sentence by performing labor either by the piece system or under the supervision of overseers. The law provides that such persons shall perform labor in the vicinity of their residence. Persons serving sentences not to exceed three months may not be detailed for work farther than ten kilometers from the place of their residence. Persons serving sentences of over three months and up to six months may, under exceptional circumstances, be sent to work beyond the ten kilometer distance from their residence. Convicts serving for a period longer than six months but under one year may be dispatched to other districts than their own, provided no work can be found for them in the vicinity of their places of residence. Convicts who are ordered beyond the ten kilometer radius to perform compulsory labor are entitled to transportation expenses and, in some instances, to living quarters and work clothes. Persons under compulsory labor sentences of less than a year, who are craftsmen, are permitted to work at their trade at home. In case of persons who work for hire, the work may be done at the places of previous employment. Short term compulsory labor may be used on state or collective farms in gathering fire wood or peat, and in the building or repairing of roads, railroads, bridges, etc. Compulsory labor may also be used in cleaning or improving of village streets, sewers, etc., under the supervision of village soviets. Generally, persons under short term sentences performing compulsory labor in their own homes do not receive compensation for their work; however, Article 33 of the Code provides that persons sentenced to compulsory labor, without detention under guard, at the place where they habitually work may receive up to 50 per cent of their wage while serving the term of sentence. All other persons sentenced to compulsory labor, without detention under guard, work as a rule without compensation.

Compensation is paid to prisoners only when expressly provided for in the court sentence, but the court must be "satisfied that the person has no other means of subsistence."[22] Those who are sentenced to terms of from one to ten years are generally compelled to perform labor under guard. Prisoners who are considered dangerous to the state are placed in solitary confinement. Practically all persons sentenced to long terms are placed in corrective camps or colonies. The tendency is to eliminate penal institutions where prisoners must be inactive. This policy is well described in a recent Soviet publication which states among other things: "Our principal form — corrective labor colonies—has been substituted for the complicated and uniform system of places of confinement. The places of confinement, in which existed sufficiently large industrial enterprises requiring much labor, have been transformed into colonies of a closed type (i. e. bounded by the walls of their respective places of confinement). Prisoners not engaged in work at such enterprises are taken out to places of mass work 'where they form open colonies engaged in agricultural, irrigational, mining, and road building work, etc.' Some of these colonies (for example those engaged at road construction and irrigation work) are considered as movable."[23]

The corrective labor institutions are usually either under control of the commissariat of labor or under that of the O. G. P. U.[24] In recent years a policy has been inaugurated to transfer all prisoners serving terms of more than three years to O. G. P. U. institutions, even if the crimes are not of a political character. As has been mentioned before, prisoners who are considered to be exceptionally dangerous to the state are either placed in solitary confinement or sent to labor colonies in remote parts of the country in order to prevent their corrupting others. Naturally the former bourgeois classes are frequently considered dangerous, and attempts are made to segregate them.

In recent years prison colonies have sprung up, and some of them are becoming profit-making industrial enterprises. Indeed, some of them are incorporated and registered, and have been extended the right of entering into contracts and of carrying out buying and selling transactions not unlike that permitted to free state enterprises. As an example of this policy may be cited the registration with the commissar of trade in 1930 of the "Combine of Factory Labor Colonies of the State Administration of Places of Confinement and Enterprises of the Committee of Assistance" under the abreviated name of "Combine F. T. K. Gumz." This organization is given the rights of a judicial person and, according to its statutes as approved by the central authorities, is "an independent economic entity operating on principles of economic accounting" and permitted to "conclude any kind of contract, obligation, and agreement pertaining to its economic and industrial activity." It is composed of thirteen labor colonies engaged in producing various kinds of merchandise. As a means of encouraging the increase in production, sentenced persons employed in labor colonies are allowed a small remuneration based on the amount of work performed by them. The food allowances of such persons are also "augmented according to the amount of energy expended." The profits of the labor colonies are used for various purposes: 40 per cent for the expansion of production in the labor colony; 12½ per cent for the improvement of the food supply; 15 per cent for assistance of ex-offenders; 20 per cent for the general correction fund of the R. S. F. S. R.; and 12½ per cent for payment of inspectors and for rewards to persons occupied with the organization of production.[25]

In addition to occupations already mentioned, prisoners who are members of the "Combine Gumz" are engaged in some such occupations as weaving, knitting, metal stamping, chemical and silicate manufacturing, mining, timbering, farming, etc. The Moscow Directory for 1930 published under the head "State Trade Collective Enterprises of the Moscow Place of Confinement" a list of corrective colonies, which included the following industries and enterprises: one peat gathering colony, one gravel producing colony, two brick plants, one camp for carpenters, locksmiths, radio equipment manufacturers, one stocking and knitted ware factory, and one photograph laboratory....

Most labor colonies according to a recent publication are engaged in timbering, farming, and manufacturing. The following table is illustrative of the development of the corrective labor colony movement:[26]

Type of Colony	Number of Colonies as of September 1, 1929	Newly organized and reorganized after September 1, 1929
Timber operations	6	19
Farming.	17	12
Factory and plant........	4	26

No accurate figures are available as to the number of persons performing compulsory labor in Soviet Russia. A pamphlet entitled "Convict Labor" and published in Moscow by the State Juridical Publishing Office of the R. S. F. S. R. in 1930 states that in the year 1928, 142,634 persons were sentenced by courts and 117,997 by administrative authorities to perform such labor, and that during the first half of 1929, 114,759 were sentenced by administrative authorities.

Before the conclusion of the discussion of obligatory labor, it must be mentioned that the category of labor, commonly called free labor, is in Soviet Russia controlled differently from that in most countries in the Western world. This important subject will be discussed later in connection with the Labor Code.

REQUISITION AND CONFISCATION OF PROPERTY

When the Bolsheviks came into power in the fall of 1917, they immediately proceeded to nationalize and municipalize that part of private property which they wished to withdraw from private control. Over one hundred decrees were passed regulating the requisition and confiscation of property ranging from railways, ships, and land to scientific instruments.[27] In this case as in other instances the onrush of the destructive forces of revolutionary enthusiasm did considerable harm. Irresponsible but zealous officials undertook not only to carry out the provisions of the nationalization decrees but forcibly expropriated property of persons of small means. Lenin, whose wisdom and surprising moderation frequently served as brakes on the actions of "hot heads", objected to the misuse of this power and employed influence and authority at the eighth Congress of the Bolshevik Party in forcing through a resolution, which prohibited irresponsible requisition and confiscation of property of the lower middle class. He insisted that all requisition must be carried out in accordance with the exact provisions of the law upon penalty of prosecution. Requisition in accordance with Bolshevik law means a forcible alienation or temporary withdrawal by the state of property in the possession of private persons, coöperatives, and societies. The amount of compensation for the requisitioned goods is to be decided on by the appropriate organs of authority. Confiscation is forcible alienation by the state, without compensation, of property which is in possession of private persons, corporations, and societies. The right to requisition of food products and manufactured products for the satisfaction of state needs was delegated to the presidium of the Supreme Council of Economy and commissar of foods, respectively. Although these two agencies could act directly, in practice, they exercised their authority through a special expropriation commission and through local organs. The presidium of the All-Russian Extraordinary Commission (Cheka), revolutionary tribunals, and people's courts were given the authority to use confiscation and requisition as punishment. Persons whose property was to be taken over were notified of the impending action in writing. Revolutionary tribunals and people's courts incorporated the decrees of confiscation in their judicial decisions.

Requisition of domestic objects, such as furniture, wearing apparel, shoes, dishes, etc., was prohibited. Special commissions, composed of provincial representatives, executive committees, provincial councils of people's economy, and provincial food committees were authorized in cases of extreme need to requisition domestic goods, but the appropriate superior central authorities had to be informed of the action. Persons hiding objects which were prohibited or permitted to be retained only in limited quantities were subject to arrest by administrative authorities. All confiscated and requisitioned goods were to become the property of the R. S. F. S. R. and had to be delivered by the agents within three days after collection. The officials who carried out requisitionary and confiscatory orders had to keep an accurate account of all objects collected. The payment for the requisitioned property was made by the governmental authority within a month after requisition. When confiscation was imposed as punishment, the offender was allowed to retain objects of domestic needs and instruments and tools of his profession and trade. Appeals could be made within three days to the presidia of local executive committees. To be sure the law provided that, in case of misuse of power in connection with the enforcement of this decree, officials could be called to account by the people's court, but at that time such provisions could hardly be enforced. Needless to say that in the early stages of the Bolshevik régime a great many people in moderate circumstances suffered from over-enthusiastic and frequently vicious agents of the government.

Between 1917 and 1921 the Soviet government passed a series of decrees regarding confiscation and requisition of property. The first decree, issued October 26, 1917, at two o'clock in the morning, abolished private ownership of land and theoretically nationalized all land, but in practice the holdings of peasants were not touched.[28] The same decree prohibited the damage of large estates, but the peasants, as might be expected, paid no attention to this, and in the midst of turmoil the properties of the land-owners were pillaged, and in some cases the buildings and movables which could not be carried away were burned. This decree was followed by another on November 28, 1917, abolishing the Land Bank of the Nobility and Peasantry. On November 30 of the same year, the government made a declaration of monopolistic control of all domestically manufactured as well as imported agricultural machinery. Industry, trade, and banking were nationalized on December 14, but the interests of the small depositors were to be safeguarded. Between October 1917 and

November 1918, 513 large undertakings in all branches of industry were officially accounted for as nationalized. Because of the unsettled condition and disarranged communication no complete figures were available as to happenings in the more remote parts of the country. On December 17, 1917, the government by a decree ordered all holders of safety deposit boxes to transfer moneys contained therein to a current account in the State Bank. All gold in coins and bullion was to be confiscated and transferred to the general state gold fund. The owners of boxes were instructed to appear within three days bringing their keys, on the penalty of being charged with maliciously refusing to submit to examination, and in that case their boxes were to be opened by the investigating commission and the contents confiscated by the State Bank. On the same day the "Society of Electrical Lighting of 1886" was declared the property of the Russian Republic. The government stated that for years this organization had received state subsidies and, in spite of this aid, had mismanaged its affairs. On December 29 the payment of coupons and dividends on private securities was suspended. All transactions in securities were prohibited on the penalty of prosecution followed by confiscation of all property. On January 23, 1918, all state loans of the previous governments were repudiated, this to be retroactive beginning with December 1917. The short term obligations of the state treasury were to remain intact, but no interest was to be paid on them. This order provided, furthermore, that these securities were to be used as currency. Persons of small means holding no more than 10,000 rubles worth (nominal value) of cancelled securities were to receive in lieu of them certificates of the internal loan of the Republic to the equal value. Deposits in savings banks were to remain untouched. Coöperatives, local governments, and other useful democratic organizations were to be compensated for any loss by the Superior Council of Economy, provided that they held the securities before the publication of this decree. The Superior Council of Economy was to decide which organizations were to be considered useful and democratic.

The Council of Workers', Soldiers', and Peasants' Deputies was to form commissions in agreement with local councils of economy to decide which of the citizens were to be considered belonging to the class of people of small means. These commissions were empowered to confiscate the savings of people, even if the sums did not exceed 5,000 rubles, if they deemed that the money was not obtained by toil.

On January 16, 1917, all capital stock of former private banks was confiscated, and the owners were ordered to deliver all securities to the State Bank on penalty of confiscation of all their property. In the same month the Merchant Fleet was ordered nationalized. In the following month, namely February 19, the large grain elevators were nationalized. A few days before, the "Liberty Loan Bonds" had been issued in denominations of one hundred rubles to be accepted as currency upon penalty of prosecution. On that same day a decree had been issued establishing the procedure that confiscations, requisitions, and nationalization were to be conducted under the authority of the Supreme Economic Council and the Council of People's Commissars only. On February 19, 1918, the All-Russian Central Executive Committee issued a decree in regard to socialization of land and at the same time repealed an earlier decree. This new decree gave instructions as to the exact procedure in carrying out the orders. A special gold committee was appointed by the Supreme Economic Council on March 3, 1918, which was to be in charge of the purchase of gold from gold mines. Four days later the annulment of state loans was proclaimed, and instructions were issued to grant annuities to persons who had 10,000 rubles worth of gold in safety deposit boxes which had been confiscated, provided however, that they had no other savings. On April 18 orders were issued for the registration at the State Bank of all stocks and bonds and securities held by private individuals and institutions. Five days later foreign trade was declared a monopoly of the state. By May 1, 1918, legislation reached into the most detailed phases of life, and the government declared the inheritance in real estate and movable property abolished, with the exception of property the value of which did not exceed 10,000 rubles and consisted of homesteads, furniture, and tools. This property could be inherited only by relatives incapable of working; all other property was to be appropriated by the state.

On May 3 and June 22, respectively, the sugar and oil industries were nationalized. By the decree of August 24, 1918, all private ownership of real property in cities was abolished. In cities of over 10,000 inhabitants all real property worth more than the amount established by local organs was declared forfeited. The former owners of the property were placed on the same status as renters. If, however, the former owner of real estate had no other income and was unable to work, he could be granted a subsidy in a lump sum not to exceed 10,000 rubles. On December 6, 1918, all unclaimed baggage, luggage, merchandise, and freight, the private sale of which was forbidden, was requisitioned. A short time before, namely on September 10, 1918, all private railways were taken over. On November 5, 1918, the Extraordinary Commission was ordered to transfer from warehouses to the government all goods and moneys taken from the bourgeoisie but was prohibited from distributing the goods, since it was not its purpose to serve as an agent of distribution but rather as an instrument in the elimination of the capitalistic class. In the meantime the Soviet government, in response to protests from foreign states, issued orders through the commissar of foreign affairs instructing the various expropriating agencies not to confiscate or requisition goods belonging to foreign governments, or under their management and disposal. Four days later, however, an order was issued for the liquidation of foreign banks. On November 5, 1920, the Council of People's Commissars ordered all movable property of persons who fled the country or who were in hiding forfeited to the state, for distribution to universities, museums, and other educational and public institutions and to the Goods Fund of the Republic. On January 3, 1921, a decree was issued enumerating the various valuables to be confiscated that were in possession of private persons and organizations who had no permission to retain them. These objects were (1) all coins (platinum, gold, and silver); (2) gold, silver, platinum, and other precious metals in bullion and otherwise; (3) bonds, with the exception of those which were used as currency; (4) diamonds, other precious stones above three carats, and pearls of certain size; (5) all products of precious metals that exceeded in aggregate the specified weight permitted each person, as (a) gold objects containing eighteen zolotniks (a zolotnik is a little over four grains) of gold, (b) silver three pounds. Exceptions were made in cases in which the gold was incidental to the purpose the object served, such as gold watches, glasses in golden frames, etc. Scientific instruments made of precious metals were not subject to confiscation.

Large sums of money found on private persons at once aroused suspicion that the sums might have been acquired by speculation. The money was sequestered and entered on the account of the owner in the State Bank until the case was decided by the people's court. A detailed record had to be kept of all confiscated goods and delivered in a short time after confiscation to the nearest agency of the commissariat of finance, but in the capital the goods had to be delivered to the State Depository of Valuables, at which institution they were checked in accordance with the records of the confiscation documents. The commissariat of finance or its local agencies had to decide within a week what parts of the sequestered valuables were to be confiscated or what portion was to be entered on the current account of the owner or what valuables were to be returned to the owner. The valuation of requisitioned goods and the payment for them was made in accordance with instructions issued on April 16, 1920, governing these cases.

Because of the scarcity of sanitary and hospital supplies the commissariat of health ordered the requisition and confiscation of all goods and properties necessary for the safeguarding of public health such as sanitary - technical; sanitary - hygienic and bacteriological equipment; disinfection apparatus and equipment for clinics and diagnostic laboratories; drugs, pharmaceutical and first aid equipment; medical instruments (surgical, dental instruments, x-ray and electro-medical instruments, etc.); and equipment for the care of the sick. It was provided, however, that property and objects as enumerated above which were necessary to the medical personnel in accordance with the established standards of the commissariat of health were not to be requisitioned or confiscated. The property of private medical institutions and laboratories, etc., approved by the commissariat of health could be exempted from requisition and confiscation at the discretion of the commissariat of health, which decided every case on its individual merits. The activities in this connection were carried out either directly by the commissariat of health or by its local agencies in accordance with rules laid down April 16, 1920.

The commissariat of public education had authority to requisition and confiscate objects of historical and artistic value, if attempts were made to take them abroad without permission. This rule also applied to objects left by owners. All kinds of scientific collections in museums, laboratories, libraries, and scientific educational equipment came under this regulation. Theatrical equipment, such as costumes, scenery, etc., musical instruments, and ritualistic objects of religious cults which had a historical and artistic value were subject to the same rules. These objects, however, were not to be requisitioned if they were necessary to the teaching personnel of middle and higher educational institutions; religious objects, if they were a part of churches and houses of worship and necessary for the ritualistic performance, were exempt from this rule.

Since the government had made foreign trade a monopoly, orders were issued to confiscate all goods which were destined to be exported by private individuals. That the government of Soviet Russia was very thorough in its policy can be seen from the enumeration of a great number of objects which were subject to confiscation; for example, arms, military equipment, and spy glasses found on travellers coming and going.[29] The confiscation decrees also included documents and deeds to property, documents which might damage the economical and political relations of the country, foreign currency if held without permission, and objects of art and antiquity.

The desperate situation of the country may be gauged by rules adopted at that time. Travellers were not permitted to have more than ten pounds of food supply per person, inclusive of half a pound of sugar, five pounds of baked bread, a quarter of a pound of tobacco, two hundred cigarettes, one cake of toilet soap, and a half a pound of laundry soap. Packages coming from abroad or going abroad, containing forbidden objects, were to be confiscated. On October 27, 1921, all undertakings and enterprises which had been taken over by governmental organs (central and local) were officially declared nationalized.[30] By the end of 1921 the period of wholesale confiscation was over; from then on there were only sporadic outbursts. In fact on June 15, 1925, the All-

Russian Central Executive Committee issued a decree of a retro-active character, declaring that the homes of those who had voluntarily joined the White Armies were to be left to their owners, provided the properties had not been subject to munici-palization and confiscation on March 28, 1921. This regulation was not, however, applicable to properties occupied by state organs or under management of communal departments.[31]

ADMINISTRATIVE EXILE

In criticising the Soviet government, the foreigner must bear in mind that many evils found in Russia today are not necessarily Bolshevik in origin and nature but are purely Russian; thus some repressive measures practiced by the Communists at the present time have their foundation in the past. In discussing the subject of administrative exile one must remember that a number of Western European countries still carry out this cruel practice. Before the Revolution, administrative exile was practiced in Russia in multifarious ways and for a variety of offenses. Thus persons who were under suspicions politically, or who did not possess passports, or persons who were deprived for some reason or other of the right to reside in a given area were exiled to distant and undesirable places.

Administrative exile in accordance with Soviet law is to be applied to persons who by their past unlawful acts have shown themselves dangerous to the safety of the "revolutionary order." Under this category are included members of counter-revolution-ary organizations. Moreover, the classification may be applied to a variety of people from monarchists to former social revolutionaries; likewise, to persons engaged in economic activities which the government considers counter-revolutionary and criminal, or to socially dangerous individuals who have not broken away from their groups. In the case of ordinary criminals, however, the law specifies that they may not be exiled until they have served at least two sentences.

Offenders may be sentenced to (1) exile from a given place with a prohibition to reside there, or (2) with a prohibition to reside in designated localities and provinces; (3) exile to a designated locality under official supervision, or (4) in a concen-tration camp for forced labor, or (5) exile abroad.

In general the period of exile does not exceed three years; the sentence carries with it the deprivation of all civil rights during that time. Exile is ordered by the local G.P.U. and special procurators of the organization. All orders must be confirmed by the central headquarters at Moscow. The mode of travel of the exile has not changed much from the days of the tsar; it is still the cruel Russian *etape*. It is not the purpose of this treatise to go into descriptive narrative; suffice it to say that the entire procedure is unworthy of a civilized government.[32]

Although families may not accompany the offenders, they are given permission to follow and live with them in the places appointed. Upon arrival in the designated place, the exiles must live at their own expense (a very small allowance is made by the government) and find work if they can. Severe punishment is imposed for unauthorized absences of more than three days or for returning to places in which residence has been forbidden.[33]

Extraordinary Condition and Martial Law

During the period of the civil war the part of Russia under jurisdiction of the Soviet government was ruled by martial law. The revolutionary tribunals and the Cheka had become the normal weapons in the revolutionary struggle. All the excesses and cruelty of revolution characterized those stirring times. Bloodshed became the order of the day, and the wrath of the unchained forces fell frequently upon the heads of the just and unjust alike. Regrettable as this was, yet it is hardly fair to condemn the Bolsheviks unreservedly, since they were in a desperate situation, and therefore, applied desperate means to overcome armed opposition; but when the civil war was over and the Soviet power was more firmly established, relatively normal conditions returned, and generally speaking, the application of martial law diminished and extraordinary measures were introduced to take its place. A decree issued on April 3, 1925, laid down the principles under which *extraordinary measures* could be applied: (1) in case of counter-revolutionary attempts to overthrow the Soviet power or its representatives, or under the circumstances of serious danger to the state; (2) in case of disasters which disturbed the normal flow of life; and (3) as a measure in a transitional period when a given area was recovering from a state of war.

The introduction of extraordinary measures is regulated in accordance with the provisions of the presidium of the executive committee of an appropriate republic. When, however, it becomes necessary to introduce extraordinary measures in two or more adjoining provinces which are a part of two different constituent republics, the step is taken by mutual agreement between the two respective republics. The civil authorities under extraordinary measures retain jurisdiction and operate through the local executive committee. At such times the committee is granted special powers in the matter of issuing compulsory ordinances, in imposing administrative fines, etc., within the limits decided upon by the legislative enactments of a given constituent republic.

In the R. S. F. S. R. the law provides that extraordinary measures are to be introduced by the order of the presidium of the All-Russian Central Executive Committee and the Council of the People's Commissars on the recommendation of the appropriate commissariat. In case of impossibility to communicate with the central authorities when delay may prove dangerous, extraordinary measures may be introduced by the central executive committees of autonomous republics and by the regional and raional executive committees and their presidia. The Council of Commissars of the All-Russian Central Executive Committee must be immediately informed that such action has been taken. No other local organs outside of those designated may undertake the introduction of extraordinary measures. In the declaration that an "exceptional condition" is existing, the locality affected must be clearly defined. The central authorities may appoint a special representative to serve under the appropriate executive committee. When extraordinary measures are introduced in regions and raions, representatives are appointed by the presidia of the appropriate superior executive committees to coöperate with local authorities. Generally, the duration of extraordinary measures does not exceed three months. The presidium of the regional or raional committee is granted, for that period, the right to issue obligatory ordinances pertaining to matters which are outside its competence. When local authorities act under special grants, they may impose administrative punishment in the form of imprisonment not to exceed two months and fines not to exceed 1,000 rubles in urban centers and 200 rubles in rural localities. The central government, however, usually issues permission for such authority when it is necessary for the safety of state and public security.

Furthermore, the presidia of the above mentioned executive committees have the authority during the critical period to banish from the limits of the region or raion or lesser areas, all persons who are considered dangerous to the public order. Moreover, the authorities may order undesirable individuals to definite places or regions, which they may not leave without permission. Public unions, organizations, and the press located in affected areas are also subject to the same restrictive regulation. In localities which have suffered from natural disasters, authorities may requisition property without previous permission of the central agencies and draft the entire population for duty. Lower executive committees and city soviets have the same rights as the superior executive committees with the exception that they cannot order exile. During the period of exceptional measures a representative of the procuracy is always present at all meetings of the executive committees and their presidia.

Martial law may be declared when the milder extraordinary measures are not sufficient to safeguard order or when a territory becomes the theater of military action assuming an important position from the standpoint of military strategy. Martial law may be declared in a territory, not actually in a state of war, only in accordance with general rules passed by the Central Executive Committee of the Union. The superior authority then is transferred by the Central Executive Committee to the Military Revolutionary Committee.[34] As soon as conditions have returned to normal, all obligatory ordinances issued at a time of emergency become automatically inoperative without further legislative action.[35]

CHAPTER XI

STATE LIABILITY AND LAW ENFORCEMENT

Liability for Unlawful Acts of Officials

The Bolsheviks, upon assuming power, abolished the Senate and other judicial institutions of the old régime.[1] Local justices were given authority to decide suits in the name of the Russian republic and issue their decisions and verdicts in accordance with the old laws, in so far as they were not changed by new enactments and were not contradictory to revolutionary "conscience and sense of justice." This last phrase is worth remembering since Bolshevik writers on law refer to it repeatedly. Soon after its inception the new government severed[2] all ties between Soviet justice and pre-revolutionary legislation, and decisions based upon tsarist laws were absolutely prohibited. A decree regulating the people's courts stated among other things that, in examining suits, the people's court must apply the rules of the workers' and peasants' government, and in those cases in which appropriate legislation was lacking or incomplete, the decisions were to be regulated by their socialist sense of justice.

Lenin, commenting on the changed order, stated that decrees are instructions calling the masses to practical accomplishments. "To be sure", he said, "there might be a good deal in the decrees which is useless and will not serve in practical life, but they have in them material for practical matters, and the task of the decree is to instruct those hundreds, thousands, and millions of people who listen to the voice of the Soviet power. This is an experiment in practical action in the field of socialist building in the village. Considered from that standpoint, much will come out of the collection of our laws and decrees. We will not look upon it as an absolute ordinance which must be carried out at once under all circumstances."[3]

In the early days of the new order, the Bolsheviks disavowed any intention to create a theoretical system of law. They rather wanted some elementary rules which would answer the practical necessities of life for the masses and assist in the carrying out of plans for the building of the Soviet state. As long as the revolutionary order was safe-guarded, any decree was to be considered good enough to serve as an administrative standard for the conduct of public affairs. The interpretation was left entirely to the socialist consciousness of the "toiling masses."

This easy going conception of law was not followed, however, when there was the slightest suspicion that the interests of the new government were in danger. Thus in the struggle between the Soviets and the counter - revolutionary movement, Lenin admonished earnestly that, "In order to bring an end to Kolchak and Denikin, it is necessary to observe religiously the laws and ordinances of the Soviet Power and watch over their execution. The smallest illegality, the smallest violation of Soviet order is a breach which will be felt instantly by the enemies of the toiling masses."[4]   From then on the government insisted that revolutionary legality must be first of all revolutionary discipline.

One of the first important acts in regard to the establishment of revolutionary legality in the period of military communism was an ordinance passed by the sixth All-Russian Extraordinary Congress, meeting on November 8, 1918, entitled "Under strict keeping of the laws." This legislation had in view the creation of revolutionary legal norms, which were to serve as the foundation of the laws of the R. S. F. S. R. and appealed to all citizens to obey implicity the law.

But the Bolsheviks were to find out that it was not a simple matter to establish revolutionary discipline. During the civil war, the various local units were in a habit of passing legislation which was contrary to the provisions of the central government. Bureaucracy came back with a vengeance that threatened to drown the state in a deluge of paper and red tape. Lenin, foremost among others, struggled to bring about some kind of order. Decree after decree was published, but very little attention was paid to them. Some decrees were issued in order to permit aggrieved citizens to appeal the action of local authorities who were carried away by revolutionary zeal and enthusiasm and not infrequently, by a desire for revenge of past injustices. In order to stem the wave of illegality, the sixth Congress of Soviets passed a resolution at the end of 1919, which authorized the Council of People's Commissars to call attention of the people by proclamation that it was their right to demand prompt action on their legal requests, and when officials insisted on excessive red tape, the petitioner was free to demand that a written record be made of the entire transaction . The resolutions moreover called to the attention of all officials the right of citizens to expect swift satisfaction of their legal demands. The written record was to be forwarded to the central authorities when the behavior of the local agents was appealed.

LAW ENFORCEMENT AFTER THE ADOPTION
OF THE NEW ECONOMIC POLICY

The adoption of the new economic policy, popularly called *Nep,* created additional difficulties in bringing about a unified system of law enforcement. In the days of military communism, law enforcement was closely connected with revolutionary discipline. Under the conditions of the *Nep,* the problem arose as to the relationship between the heavy state production and the small production of individual proprietors. It was not a question any longer of discipline in the Soviet governmental apparatus, but it became a problem of how to safeguard producers on the one hand and the right of citizens on the other. If these rights and the laws which defined them were different in various areas, no united support could be given the new policy in its attempt to develop a communistic economy in coöperation with private capital.

The changing role of revolutionary legality in the days of the *Nep* was remarked upon by Lenin in his letter to Stalin in which he said, "Legality must be one. The fundamental evil in all our uncultured condition is our tolerance of the real Russian point of view and habits of semi-savages which is attempting to save the legality of Kaluga in differentiation of the legality of Kazan.[5] Legality must be one, all Russian, and unified for the entire Federation of the Soviet Republics." Addressing the All-Russian Congress of Soviets on December 3, 1921, the great Bolshevik leader remarked, "As we enter conditions of sound and lasting power, the further goes the development of civil changes, the more it becomes insistently necessary to bring forth the hard slogan of 'bringing into existence the great revolutionary'."[6] Thus the Communists were confronted with the necessity of harmonizing the capitalistic tendencies of the *Nep* and the revolutionary conception of legality. Bolshevik leaders in general were loath to admit a change toward capitalism and attempted to rationalize. Thus Krylenko declared, "The difference between revolutionary and bourgeois legality is that our laws safeguard revolutionary order and a revolutionary state of advance, while the old law safeguarded the old order. The revolutionary legality in its final terms is that revolutionary legality and laws are themselves revolutionizing factors as expressed in the right of a new class marching forward and establishing new forms of living." But no matter how reluctant the leaders were in admitting a departure from communism, militant communism was in retreat.[7] The All-Russian Congress of Soviets attempted to sugar the bitter pill and issued a number of codes couched in the old revolutionary terms, but in reality created a new legality which was in conformity with prevalent capitalistic tendencies. These codes strengthened the judicial apparatus and reorganized legal defense and delegated to the procurator the supervision of law enforcement. It became the duty of the prosecuting magistry to supervise in the name of the state the legal actions of all organs of power, economic institutions, public and private associations, and private persons. All violations were subject to criminal prosecution. Thus the death knell of the revolutionary particularism was rung, and the grip of the central government was tightened on local units, who by their revolutionary enthusiasm were interfering with the general policies of the Soviet leadership. The procurators of the republics and the provincial or regional procurators and their assistants in local areas were assigned specific duties in connection with the enfocement of the new laws. To all outward appearance it was the duty of the chief procurator to call attention of the people's commissariats and central agencies to rules issued by them which were contrary to general legislation. The procurator could appeal the issuance of such rules to the people's commissariat of the Union and to the presidium of the All-Russian Central Executive Committee. This objection, however, on the part of the procurator was negative, since it did not stop the execution of rules contrary to the law. Local procurators, on their part, could suggest to executive committees repeal of regulations issued by them and their subordinate organizations which were contrary to law. Upon refusal of these agencies to comply with the request, they could forward complaints within two weeks to the chief procurator of the Union Council of Commissars and the presidium of the All-Russian Central Executive Committee.[8] The procurators had the right to be present at the meetings of the local executive committees and have a consulting vote.

When the chief procurator was designated as the state supervisor of revolutionary legality, some localities abolished the bureaus of complaints as superfluous. The R. K. I. (The Workman-Peasant Inspection) stopped this practice however, and the competence of the two organs was regulated in such a way as to reserve to the bureau of complaints the authority to examine and decide upon complaints and information of irregular, purposeless, and illegal actions and orders of officials; criminal acts subject to prosecution in accordance with provisions of the Criminal Code were exempted from its jurisdiction. Beginning with 1923, however, the operation of the bureau of complaints was modified by the activities of the R. K. I. The latter from then on accepted complaints of a limited scope pertaining to the needs of the "toiling masses", instances of bureaucratic red tape, etc. On August 11, 1927, the central bureau of complaints was given authority to accept and examine objections of the "toiling masses" in regard to activities of central and local organs and of individuals of the R. S. F. S. R.

The Unified Bureau of Complaints

After the fifteenth Congress of the Party in 1928, the R. K. I. of the U. S. S. R. decided to strengthen the central bureau of complaints by consolidating the Union bureau with that of the R. S. F. S. R. The work of this unified organization was to be carried out in the main with the help of workers', professional, peasant, and public organization. Therefore, from its very inception, the bureau attempted to attract to its main and branch offices workers in production. The goal of this activity thus was the elimination of bureaucracy and defects in the state apparatus. In 1929 the bureau mobilized 1,500 workers for the purpose of "raiding organizations without warning" in the city of Moscow. As a result overbearing officials and bureaucratic practices were discovered and removed. Raids were performed without special credentials. At a later date, 2,500 workers investigated the condition of employment agencies and food stores; the purpose of this inspection was to determine whether the long queus outside of the stores were necessary, and if so, find means for their abolition. At the end of 1929, the raiders invaded various undertakings and organizations. This practice spread to the urban centers of the provinces, and attempts were made to introduce similar activities in rural districts, but the response of the population was disappointing.

In 1930 the bureau of complaints organized conferences of worker-jurors in the large undertakings for the discussion of various phases of bureaucratic practices and discourtesy to customers in certain stores. The authorities made sure that the activities of the "raiders" were given wide publicity. This procedure had surprising results; officials, clerks, and employees of all kinds, who had lapsed into bureaucratic ways of the tsarist days and frequently had treated the public cavalierly, changed their way for the better. Although the groups of raiders were encouraged to act independently, they were nevertheless under the control of the R. K. I. When at the end of 1928 the central bureau sent out a call for "volunteers" for work of investigation, 4,000 persons answered the summons and promised to work without pay in their spare time. These volunteers were sifted and 1,100 retained, but since only ten per cent of this number were industrial workers, the bureau decided to discontinue its practice and introduce new methods of investigation. The bureau stationed at all plants and undertakings inspectors who were former workers; the inspectors in turn selected volunteers from among the workers who were divided into designated sections such as (1) agricultural; (2) industrial transport, production, and invention; (3) trade, coöperation, and publication; (4) administrative-legal and educational; (5) social insurance and health. These groups were given instructions in the methods of conducting investigations of complaints. They assisted the central bureau in the matter of confirming or reversing decisions of the lower bureaus. At the end of 1929 volunteer groups of ten members, headed by a foreman, were organized in the larger enterprises. The leaders formed an organization of their own. Volunteers were instructed to organize and carry out inspection raids. For a while these activities were salutary in their effects, but abuses developed so that the work had to be curtailed and a great many volunteers dismissed. The tried workers were frequently retained as inspectors. In general the bureau of complaints rendered a valuable service in supervising the execution of governmental and party orders.[9]

One of the important tasks performed by the unified bureau of complaints was to receive appeals from individuals and organizations who were dissatisfied with decisions of local bureaus. It was in some ways a court of last resort for thousands who suffered at the hands of cruel officials, as will be shown presently. In 1929 and 1930 the bureau received 22,661 and 20,923 petitions, respectively. These came from a variety of groups, workers, peasants, employees, students, disabled individuals, and members of the former middle and upper classes; also from state, public, and coöperative organizations. Most of the complaints coming from peasants were in connection with compulsory collectivization of their lands. Employees, on the other hand, complained largely of irregular dismissal from service.

The appeals coming from disabled individuals were termed "hopeless petitions", and illustrated the bureaucratic practices of some insurance organs in their dealings with questions of pensions. The petitions of organizations indicated the practices of red tape on the part of some authorities.[10]

It is interesting to note that, out of 2,195 complaints investigated which were directly under the supervision of the unified bureau, 1,011 were justified. It was, of course, humanly impossible for the unified bureau to investigate all complaints and claims; therefore, a great many cases were transferred for investigation to local bureaus, soviet organizations, and judicial organs. Frequently after the unified bureau transferred cases to some other agency for decision, no more was heard of them; there were 6,000 of such cases in 1929. The manner of procedure of the unified bureau was to examine the petition and, if the complaint was found justifiable, to attempt to correct the injustice. In 1929, as a result of investigating nineteen complaints, several guilty officials were removed from office, and forty-seven persons were subjected to administrative punishment. In 1930 ninety-nine persons were removed from office and eight-one were punished in the administrative manner. The work of the bureau is often retarded by the neglect of local bureaus in answering inquiries so that several requests must be sent before a response is received.

To illustrate the type of complaints received by the unified bureau, the following case may be quoted: a school teacher forwarded a petition in which she stated that she had taught for twenty-three years and was unable to obtain the pension due her. Among other things she wrote "....I am wearing myself out, and at present I am dependent upon charity, I stand in the market place with outstretched hand....they are driving me out of my room and they are waiting to see me end my life in the gutter." The local bureau, after a lengthy investigation, informed the headquarters that the facts as stated in the petition were correct and that the school teacher's sufferings were due to red tape and procrastination. The official guilty in causing the suffering of the teacher was sentenced to a term in a penal institution.[11]

PROCEDURE OF ENTERING COMPLAINTS

As far back as December 30, 1919, a decree issued by the Council of People's Commissars[12] worked out a procedure by means of which a citizen could appeal against any decision of governmental bureaus and institutions. Complains upon action of the cantonal administration were directed to the district executive committee and from there to the provincial executive committee and thence to the Council of People's Commissars and to the Council of Workers' and Peasants' Defense. A final appeal could be made to the All-Russian Central Executive Committee. The supervision of the organizations of all the governmental agencies which had authority to receive complaints and forward them to the appropriate authorities was delegated[13] at first to the State Control. Later this function was transferred to the Workman-Peasant Inspection (R. K. I.).[14] As has already been mentioned a central bureau with branches in the several republics was organized in connection with the R. K. I. The local bureaus of complaints were headed by persons recommended by the local party and by professional organizations. Representatives of local workers' and peasants' organizations were invited to take part in the work of the bureaus. In all instances the examination of complaints was to be in charge of representatives of the "toiling masses."

Complaints and information could be forwarded by aggrieved citizens personally, in written or oral form, or through the mails. The authority of the bureaus extended to all the complaints and information concerning illegality and unsatisfactory action. The departure of officials from local rules, excessive red tape, discourtesy, etc, were also subject to the jurisdiction of the bureaus. Furthermore, these complaints could be initiated not only by those who suffered directly from the acts of officials but also by persons and organizations who did not suffer themselves. The bureaus, however, had no authority to receive complaints in regard to regulations of the Council of People's Commissars or of the All-Russian Executive Committee. Claims which grew out of the actions of individual people's commissariats or irregular and illegal action on the part of higher authorities were outside the jurisdiction of local bureaus and subject to provisions of general legislation.[15]

The regulations in regard to complaints attempted to shield the petitioner from all kinds of unpleasantness or hindrances. It was stipulated that all complaints entered without any intention of malice or slander would be kept in confidence, and complainants were guaranteed absolute safety. A circular issued by the presidium of the All-Russian Central Executive Committee on June 30, 1921, commented on the fact that in district and provincial cities not only the individual complainants but also delegates from cantonal and village soviets had met with difficulties in their attempt to reach headquarters. Moreover there have been cases in which those who had complained to the central government were subject to arrest and other repressive measures in their own localities. This circular stated emphatically that such procedure was absolutely contrary to the customs of the Soviet power and under no circumstances must complainants be pun-

ished; those appealing with malicious intent were to be prosecuted by judicial process only.[16]

While it was within the jurisdiction of the local bureaus to
receive complaints, they had no authority to set aside any of the
regulations complained about but could only petition for a post-
ponement of execution of decisions by appropriate agencies and
persons whose actions had been appealed. By 1921 the bureaus
were given the right to stop the execution of administrative regulations[17] and, provided this action was approved by the manager
of the local R. K. I., it became binding on authorities. This provision was later amended,[18] and the R. K. I. was permitted to
stop the execution of regulations only when the latter were
obviously illegal and were liable to cause material and financial
loss to the state.[19]

In 1924 the procedure of entering complaints was further
regulated by the people's commissariat of the interior,[20] so that
citizens, groups of citizens, and institutions, even if they were not
the aggrieved parties themselves, could enter complaints in regard
to action of the administrative organs which they considered
illegal, irregular, or complicated by red tape. The petitions could
be directed to designated judicial organs, prosecuting attorneys,
appropriate executive committees, and appropriate superior
organs. Appeals of actions of presidents of village soviets and
village militsia, cantonal executive committees, and cantonal
militsia (police) were to be directed to cantonal executive committees and the district administrative division, respectively. Complaints on the action of persons connected with the district
administrative division and their assistants, and on the official
action of persons heading the provincial administrative .division
and their deputies and assistants were to be directed to provincial
administrative divisions and to the commissariat of interior,
respectively. The decisions of all other official personnel of the
district, or provincial or administrative departments could be
appealed to the official in charge of a given division and forwarded by him to superior organs. The head of a division could
not refuse to accept and examine a complaint.

Appeals could be made either in written or verbal form. If
they were made verbally, they had to be registered by an
employee of the agencies appointed for that purpose by the

authorities receiving complaints. A receipt was issued to the petitioner stating the date of action, the number of applications, and the date set for the petitioner to appear in order to receive a reply. There was no definite limit of time for entering complaints. When a petition was received by an agency whose action was being appealed, it had to forward within three days the complaint, including all data and documents and a statement of its own side of the case, to the appropriate superior authority. The receipt held by the petitioner had to indicate the time when the petition was to be forwarded and in case of any delay, the reasons for it had to be given. The petition had to be examined by the appropriate organs within a period not to exceed seven days after its reception. On examining the complaint, the superior organ had a right to demand immediate explanation from the institution whose action was being protested, or order an investigation by competent persons who were not subordinate to the official or institution whose action was being investigated. In case the complaint proved genuine, the action complained about was not only to be changed but, depending upon the character of the irregularity, the guilty person could be prosecuted by judicial process.

Punishment of Officials

The Bolsheviks after coming into power attempted to obliterate all outward signs of the autocracy, but they found that they could not eradicate *volokita* (red tape) so beloved of the old Russian official. The central authorities made superhuman efforts to eliminate unfair treatment of citizens by officials. Tons of circulars were sent out and numerous regulations passed, which threatened dire punishment of officials who were delaying the examination of complaints and were careless about forwarding explanations in regard to the complaint to higher authorities. Local authorities were informed that not only were they subject to disciplinary action but could be prosecuted in accordance with provisions of the Criminal Code. The Russian's delight in procrastination was not, however, to be spoiled by mere official regulations. As a last resort the dreaded Cheka was called in to enforce obedience. This agency was granted extensive authority in the matter of irregularities of civil service employees and was instructed to impose severe punishment. This the Cheka proceeded to do. In the early years of the Soviet régime over 50 per cent of accused officials were executed by that organization.[21] By 1927, however, this punitive procedure was softened, and since that time capital punishment is very seldom applied in cases of neglect in office.

With the gradual elimination of the unfit in the civil service and the return of normal conditions, prosecution of officials was transferred to criminal, civil, or disciplinary tribunals. Some service violations were placed either under the jurisdiction of regional courts or under the people's courts composed of a judge and two co-judges (jurors). Other infractions by government agents were punished in the administrative manner. Complaints against irregularities in connection with requisition of property and suits against district executive committees or city soviets of district towns are to be entered against them as such and not against any of their departments. Likewise, claims against central institutions and provincial committees are to be made directly against them in superior courts and not against their bureaus and divisions. Regional courts have jurisdiction of litigation in connection with agencies of people's commissariats.[22] Soviet legislation recognizes two kinds of official violations: (1) violations which are to be punished in accordance with the provisions of the Criminal Code by judicial process; (2) violations of rules of an internal character which had been issued in accordance with general enactments in regard to labor and specified as punishable in a disciplinary manner. Whether an unlawful act of an official comes under the first provision or the second depends upon whether or not the act is detrimental to public weal at that particular time. Thus, for instance, even serious offenses, such as misuse of power and negligent attitude toward the service, may be punished in the milder disciplinary manner, provided that the offense was not practiced by the official habitually or his behaviour motivated by selfish interests, and the actions did not result in serious consequences. The provisions of the Criminal Code are reserved for cases in which social defense is involved, *i.e.* counter-revolutionary activity.

For the guidance of authorities in case of doubt as to whether a given violation was merely a disciplinary matter or a crime[23] punishable by judicial process, special rules were passed which specified the kind of punishment to be imposed.[24]

A decree issued on July 4, 1927, states that disciplinary penalties are imposed by superiors in accordance with the established rules of internal management of a given institution. This applies to all employees and responsible workers.[25] The superiors are permitted to impose a variety of disciplinary penalties varying in degrees of severity; namely, "remarks on the action", "reprimand", and "strict reprimand", transfer to other positions in the same institution, and finally, dismissal from the service. Transfer and dismissal from service is within the jurisdiction of the managing authority of a given bureau of officials and organs on whom the appointment or selection for the position depends, without further confirmation by superior authorities or of the superior who had the authority to confirm the appointment to a given position, or of all superior organs in accordance with their degree of subordination. Disciplinary penalties can only be imposed after the accused has been given opportunity to make an explanation of his behavior. This explanation can be given in written form within a period of one week from the time the accused has been informed of his alleged misconduct; he can, however, appeal within a week to superior authorities through the appropriate immediate superiors. In case of appeal of dismissal, action is to be held in abeyance until final decision by the superior authorities. Disciplinary action may be taken against an employee not later than one year after the offense has been committed; however, if during that period of time the employee has not given cause for new disciplinary procedure, the record of his accusation is expunged.[26]

In March 1932 a supplementary decree was passed which systematizes the entire process of responsibility of officials in regard to service neglect, misdemeanors, and those violations of labor discipline which are not subject to prosecution in accordance with provisions of the Criminal Code. Those who are not subject to disciplinary punishment are (1) officials who have authority to hire and discharge employees; (2) classes of responsible workers, designated by the commissariat of labor of the R. S. F. S. R. in agreement with the All-Russian Central Union of Professional Unions; and (3) elective officials (members of administrative staffs of coöperative organizations, people's judges, etc.). All other official persons working for wages are to be responsible for their violation in accordance with rules of internal management and the attached schedule of penalties.

The agencies which have the authority to impose penalties are (1) organs or persons who have authority of appointment; (2) organs which have elected the official persons involved; and (3) superior organs or persons in the order of jurisdiction.

Disciplinary punishment is imposed upon initial recommendation of organs or persons who, in accordance with legislation, have the right to make authoritative suggestions in regard to imposition of disciplinary penalties. Penalties imposed are ranked to suit the violation namely, (a) remark, (b) reproof or reprimand, (c) demotion to a lower rank for a period not to exceed one year, and (d) dismissal from office (in case of an elective official, recall by the organ which elected him).

An elective official may be removed from office by appropriate authority while his case is pending. Disciplinary penalties are not to be imposed without first giving the accused an opportunity to explain his action. The explanation may be made in writing within five days after the accused has been informed that he is to be called to answer for a stated offense. The law provides that the disciplinary penalty must be imposed within a month following the time the offense has been uncovered, and in case of a criminal process, within five days after the trial has been concluded. In cases of criminal prosecution, however, the time between the discovery of the offense and the conclusion of the process must not exceed six months, exclusive of the time taken for the preparation of the case for trial. The decision in disciplinary cases must be based on good reason and communicated to the offender and to the institution in which he is employed. A decision may be appealed to higher authorities within ten days.

The appeal, however, does not stop the execution of the original sentence except in cases of dismissal. At the expiration of the time for appeal, if the sentence is sustained by the high authorities, the decision is entered upon the record of the guilty person. Disciplinary punishment does not exclude criminal prosecution, but the imposition of disciplinary punishment may be postponed until the criminal trial has been completed. In the less serious offenses, if the punished official has not been subject to new penalties within a year, the record of his offense is expunged. In case of dismissal three years must have elapsed before this action is taken.

Members of local soviets are subject not only to disciplinary punishment for offenses in connection with their offices but also for offenses unconnected with the exercise of official duties, if the acts are of such a nature as to reflect unfavorably on their social position and are unbecoming to a Soviet official. In less serious cases not subject to criminal prosecution, members of local soviets and executive committees may be punished for their offenses by any one of the following authorities: the plenum of appropriate soviets, executive committees and their presidia, Council of People's Commissars, central executive committees of autonomous republics, Council of People's Commissars of the R. S. F. S. R., and the presidium of the All-Russian Executive Committee.

Members of presidia of local soviets and executive committees are disciplined by superior executive committees in the order of superiority up to the presidium of the All-Russian Executive Committee. Members of local soviets, executive committees, and their presidia who do not hold other official positions are subject only to remark and reprimand. Members of soviets who hold official positions are subject to the entire range of punishment as described above, in accordance with the provision of the law.[27]

Responsibility of State Institutions

Responsibility of state institutions for damage caused by irregular action of their employees is established by Soviet law only in cases in which such action is subject to judicial or administrative punishment. The institutions are free from responsibility when the party whose interests have been damaged has not entered complaint within a specified period of time. Institutions have a right to deduct from the pay of their employees the sum which has been paid to the persons who have suffered the loss.[28]

The responsibility of state institutions for the acts of their employees has created considerable confusion. Therefore, a new enactment was passed according to which state institutions are made responsible for acts of their employees, only in those cases

in which the acts were committeed strictly in the line of duty
upon direct orders, and for certain irregularities which are recognized by judicial and administrative organs as illegal and
criminal.[29]

The Criminal Code[30] enumerates specifically cases in which
state institutions are responsible, an outstanding example of
which is the illegal requisition or confiscation of property.
Finally, in accordance with the law of March 28, 1927, the state
is liable in cases in which persons have suffered from illegal
requisition or confiscation of property. The aggrieved person
has the right to demand the return of the property and to ask
for compensation by means of legal action against the institutions and civil servants who were responsible for requisition or
confiscation.[31]

The Workman-Peasant Inspection in Relation to Law Enforcement (R. K. I.)

As indicated above, the R. K. I. has had considerable influence
in the eradication of certain evils in the Soviet state ; it is therefore,
necessary to describe somewhat in detail the organization of this
commissariat. The Soviet state apparatus is based largely upon
theories which the Bolsheviks brought with them from exile, and
during the years of their rule they have undertaken a variety of
reforms and considerable reorganization. Lenin himself declared
that the Soviet machinery was an inheritance from the old order
and is consequently full of the flaws and shortcomings of an
antiquated culture. In the struggle with bureaucratism, the Communists rather distrust and have a contempt for Western
European principles of public administration. Yet certain of their
writers who have had the advantage of training are frequently
looking back to some of the bourgeois countries and publicists.
Lenin, probably the most rational of Soviet leaders, repeated time
and again that one may drive out the landlords and the
capitalists, but bureaucratism in a peasant country will be eradicated only by a slow and never-ceasing effort to uproot this evil.
It is well for the Western observer to remember how easy it
is for officials of any country to become bureaucratic. The
Bolsheviks were faced with the old *chinovnik* system, phases of
which remained in the new Soviet state even after attempts to

rebuild the entire state apparatus had been made. Unfortunately, at the time when the old structure was razed, there was nothing new to take its place. In their efforts to reorganize the government, the new rulers under the leadership of the Gosplan (State Planning Commission) applied a system of planning in public administration fashioned after their economic planning.

The immediate instrument by means of which the Soviet state apparatus is being reorganized upon principles of Socialist state building is the remarkable people's commissariat of Workman-Peasant Inspection, popularly known as the R. K. I. Historically the predecessor of the R. K. I. is the State Control, which was nothing more than a recording department for the registration of fiscal data. When at the height of counter-revolution and general chaos the government found itself swamped by inefficiency, the All-Russian Central Executive Committee issued April 12, 1919, a decree attempting to broaden the activity of the State Control and draw into its circle the masses of workers and peasants to serve as a kind of state auditing agency. This organ was slated to become an instrument of popular socialistic control, a clearing house of experimentation in socialist building, and the headquarters for reorganization activities of the Soviet mechanism. The decree of April 12 transferred to the State Control (Goskon), among other things, the task of submitting for examination to the central authorities projects for the simplification and reorganization of the state administration, based upon observation and investigation. The crying need was the abolition of overlapping, thriftlessness, and official red tape, but this machinery was to go through additional transformation before any actual improvement in the state structure was to be materialized. By 1920 the new government was sufficiently experienced to proceed drastically against its greatest enemy, inefficiency. On February 7, 1920, the All-Russian Central Executive Committee created the Workman-Peasant Inspection, which was instructed to proceed to the immediate reorganization of all organs of the State Control. New elements were drawn into its work, and it was given authority to exercise control over all organs of state administration, economy, and public organs. To be sure the adoption of the new economic policy complicated the work of the R. K. I., and enormous tasks of financial, controlling, revisionary, and rationalizing character were assigned to it. Nevertheless the organization vigorously began the work of investigating incomes and expenditures of all the people's commissariats in the light of the new economic developments, and attempted to harmonize legislative practice with the economic realities of the time. It collected materials and data which might be useful in framing new enactments for regulation of the economic life of the Union. The R. K. I., attempting to reorganize the administration in accordance with Communistic principles, was faced, however, with the task of applying socialist principles to a capitalistic economy created by the *Nep*. The result was chaos; in fact the great masses of men and women who were brought into the organization were dismissed, and it looked as if another failure was to be recorded. Some leaders advocated that the R. K. I. base its work on the old idea of the State Control or suggested that it be transformed into a plan inspection bureau for the more important branches of industry. The central government made gigantic efforts to hold the organization together through the year 1922.

On December 6, 1923, a new decree was issued whereby the R. K. I. was to make a study of theoretical and practical problems of administration, which would point out the shortcomings and advantages of all organs of administration. It was to recommend the abolition of some bureaus and the strengthening of others, and introduce experiments leading to the creation of undertakings for the rationalization of the technique in all phases of administration. It was to work out the more efficient forms of accounting, calculations, etc., and indicate principles for the changing of the structure of the state apparatus with a view to bettering its work. Finally, it was to create agencies for state supervision of public and governmental activities.

The decree stipulated that the work of the R. K. I. was to be conducted upon the principle of scientific organization of industry, production, and administration, uniting the principles of scientific theory with practical experiment for the purpose of bringing about practical results.[32] To insure the carrying out of its task, the R. K. I. was authorized to conduct inspections, demand materials and data, and call in managers and co-workers of institutions for personal explanations or for consulting purposes. It had authority to propose to various state institutions, undertakings, and organizations certain changes for the purpose of rationalizing their apparatus and to dismiss employees for thriftlessness and inefficiency. These seemingly broad grants of authority were weakened by the fact that instructions of the R. K. I. were mostly advisory. The directors of institutions and undertakings had the right to express their disagreement with the suggestions of the R. K. I., but they were obliged in that case to inform it at once of their disagreements and leave to the legislative organs the final decision in any controversy. The intervening years proved that if the R. K. I. was to remain an advisory body only, it could not possibly fulfill the purpose for which it was created. Therefore a law was passed May 4, 1927, which broadened the authority of this body. State institutions henceforth were obligated to accept its decisions as final and execute them, provided they were in such fields of activity as (1) the simplification of registration and accountancy; (2) the abolition of superflous organs and representatives; (3) the abolition of superfluous members of staffs; (4) lowering of expenditures; (5) changing of the building plans of individual departments of institutions and undertakings; and (6) disciplinary punishment and dismissal of employees for confirmed thriftlessness, bureaucratism, and red tape. The R. K. I. was to be in close contact with the party control organs, and operate in the several republics through the people's commissariats of the R. K. I. of the appropriate republics, and function in the larger political subdivisions of the republics through local branches. For the purpose of carrying out its work of administration and rationalization in individual bureaus and institutions, the R. K. I. created special subordinate organs whose task it was to make a study of the technique, organization, and the work of the administration and to submit projects which were to simplify these organs and bring them in nearer contact with the masses. The sixteenth Congress of Soviets authorized the Central Executive Committee and the Council of Commissars of the U. S. S. R. to appoint a commission consisting of the president of the Council of Commissars, the secretary of the Central Committee of the Bolshevik party, the president of the R. K. I., the chairman of the Union of Agricultural Collectives (Kolchozcentr), and representatives of other important organs for consultation purposes. Similar commissions were created in connection with commissariats of the various autonomous republics and the regional executive committees, which were to be in close contact with the R. K. I.

In 1931 the Central Committee of the Bolshevik Party and the Council of Soviet Commissars of the Union joined in the effort to better the state apparatus [33] and to encourage the R. K. I. in initiating thorough check-ups and investigations of all governmental institutions. These investigations are frequently followed by "purgings" which take the form of dismissal of employees. In the more serious inefficiency cases, members of the staffs may be exiled, and under circumstances of certain grades the extreme penalty of death may be applied. The R. K. I. has become a well established department of government, and the impartial observer cannot help but admit that in consequence of its efforts, the Soviet Union is evolving fairly efficient administrative machinery in accordance with Soviet principles.

CHAPTER XII

CIVIL LIBERTY

INTRODUCTION

In attempting to describe the concepts of civil liberty under the Soviets, one is confronted with difficulties and paradoxes. The temptation to compare the state of affairs in Russia with that in Western Europe, especially conditions as they exist in the Anglo-American world, drives one nigh to despair. It is only when one constantly keeps in mind the historic background of Russia, and conditions under which the Russian people have lived for centuries that he can understand the philosophy of the Bolshevik state. There never was any liberty in Russia; the people from the very beginning of their political existence were ruled by some autocracy or other; the great movements, such as the religious revolts in the fifteenth, sixteenth, and seventeenth centuries, and political revolutions in the eighteenth and nineteenth centuries which rocked the foundations of the Western world, never penetrated Russia. Sporadic attempts by small idealistic groups were crushed ruthlessly with much blood and cruelty. Thus the traditional conceptions of liberty, such as are an integral part of the West, were known to only a very few in Russia, and those were far removed from the masses socially and economically. The revolutionary movement of the nineteenth and the first decade of the twentieth century was confined to a narrow intellectual group who, after great sacrifices, succeeded in persuading a minority of the skilled workmen in the larger centers of the empire to join. Since the majority of the population consisted of nearly 85 per cent of peasants, illiterate and superstituous, engaged in a terrific struggle to keep body and soul together, there could be no question of mass movements for liberties as are known to Western Europe. To be sure there were peasant uprisings in Russia, but the desire of the peasant was for more land,

and had the autocracy possessed a minimum of social intelligence and granted the peasants some concessions in this connection, it is doubtful if the present government would be entrenched in the Kremlin. Yet even if the autocracy had wanted to use reason, it would have been stopped by the granite wall of a powerful, corrupt, and selfish landowning aristocracy, who had not progressed very far from the days when the majority of the peasants were serfs. To be sure the granting of the Duma, and later the constitution of 1905, was a degree of political concession, but anyone even slightly acquainted with Russian conditions knows that the autocracy soon repented of its concession, and the October Manifesto was practically annulled. At the opening of the World War, Russia was an autocracy. The tragic interlude between March and October 1917 was an attempt to graft Western European institutions into the gnarled stump of the Russian body politic, and the result was a dismal failure.

The Bolsheviks, notwithstanding their high sounding rhetoric, are realists and, coming to power with the full knowledge of Russian history and conditions, proceeded to establish a state which, distasteful as it is to the Western mind, fits the majority of Russians. Only in a rigid absolutism now called "The Rule of the Proletariat", could Russia with its cultural backwardness progress. Yet the Bolsheviks do not intend to create a particular ruling class but to abolish all classes and create a classless state of proletarians, as is shown in the following quotation from Lenin's *State and Revolution:* "The dictatorship of the proletariat—that is the organization of the advance guard of the oppressed as a ruling class for the purpose of crushing the oppressors, cannot produce merely an expansion of democracy. Together with an immense expansion of democracy—for the first time becoming democracy for the poor, democracy for the people, and not democracy for the rich—the dictatorship of the proletariat will produce a series of restrictions of liberty in the case of the oppressors, exploiters, and capitalists. We must crush them in order to free humanity from wage slavery; their resistance must be broken by force. It is clear that where there is suppression there must also be violence, and there cannot be liberty or democracy.... Only in Communist Society, when the resistance of the capitalists has finally been broken, when the capitalists have disappeared, when there are no longer any classes (that is, when there is no difference between the members of society in respect to their social means of production) only then does the state disappear, and can one speak of freedom. Only then will be possible, and will be realized, a really full democracy, a democracy without any exception. And only then will democracy itself begin to wither away by virtue of the simple fact that, freed from capitalist slavery.... people will gradually become accustomed to the observance of the elementary rules of social life, known for centuries, repeated for thousands of years in all sermons. They will become accustomed to their observance without force, without constraint, without subjection, with the special apparatus of compulsion which is called the State."[1]

With this description of Bolshevik ideology in mind, the application of the Bolshevik conception of civil liberty may be stated.

PERSONAL GUARANTEES

INVIOLABILITY OF HOME AND PERSON

The first months of the Bolshevik revolution witnessed some irresponsible actions on the part of zealous workers; indiscriminate arrests, prosecutions, and executions were the order of the day. But in December 1917 there was an attempt made by the commissar of justice to regulate arrests, searches, and other coercive measures. The arrested persons, in accordance with the new regulations, had to be taken to designated prisons, and the charges and legality of arrest investigated within forty-eight hours.

The All-Russian Congress of Soviets meeting on November 6, 1918, ordered the release of all persons arrested, who were not to be prosecuted within two weeks for taking part in a conspiracy to overthrow the Soviet power, or preparing for such act, or being part of the organization of White Guards, or assisting those groups and parties which had for their purpose an armed uprising against the Soviet power. It was also decided to free all hostages, with the exception of those retained as a precaution for the safety of Bolsheviks who had been captured by the "Whites", and these were delivered into the exclusive jurisdiction of the "Cheka." The period between December 1918 and the end of the civil war was characterized, however, by unusual severity on the part of the authorities, frequently expressed in illegal action, which may be blamed on the critical condition of the government and demoralization of the entire life of the community.

At the end of the civil war and the coming of relatively normal times, which permitted the building up of machinery for the safeguarding of the state, there manifested itself at least a theoretical tendency for personal liberty. Thus the Criminal Code of R. S. F. S. R. stipulated that persons could be deprived of liberty and placed under arrest only in accordance with legal provisions. Judges and prosecutors were admonished to free all persons under guard who were arrested without legal sanction of appropriate administrative organs or kept under guard longer than provided by law. Severe penalties were provided for illegal action on the part of officials. Persons suspected of wrong doing were to be arrested by investigating officials in cases designated by law,[2] and a report of the proceeding had to be sent to the investigating magistrate or people's judge of the precinct within twenty-four hours. Within forty-eight hours after receiving the report, the investigating magistrate or people's judge was obliged either to hold the suspect for trial or release him. Unfortunately some of these humane provisions were on paper only; in practice the suspected person was, and is still, frequently held for a longer period of time than specified by law. This is especially true in rural districts where the distances are enormous and militsia (police) personnel is inadequate.

As the law stands now a person may be admitted to bail if vouched for by a professional, or workman-peasant public organization. No property or cash bond is accepted as bail. Persons suspected of counter-revolutionary activity, those engaged in traffic of women, and illegal manufacturers and sellers of alcoholic beverages may be arrested without a warrant. All other law breakers may be arrested only under orders issued by appropriate authorities. Persons may, however, be arrested without special orders, if they appear intoxicated in public places.

In taking up the provisions as to the inviolability of the home, we find on paper liberal provisions, which are regulated in detail and which stipulate that the militsia (police) may enter into a private dwelling place (1) when in the act of apprehending a criminal who has been in a private dwelling; (2) when a crime has been, or is being committed in a private dwelling; (3) when the public peace is being disturbed; (4) when an official summons is served; and (5) when it is necessary to make a search (in accordance with rules laid down by law). Searches are made by police officers in accordance with the provisions of the Criminal Code, which authorizes chiefs of police and other persons to issue such orders. The law, however, provides that searches may be made, if the police officers have good reasons to believe there is danger that evidences of law violations may be hidden or destroyed.[3]

In rural districts, where there are no representatives of the militsia (police), the chairman and members of the local soviet may demand from a householder the delivery of material evidence which will assist them in the detection of a crime. Upon refusal a search may be made, provided the crime comes under the classification of theft, robbery, cattle rustling, arson, murder, assault, and home brewing for commercial purposes. The search must be made at the time when the culprit is caught in the act or soon afterwards, and when there is reason to believe that the material evidence may be hidden and the traces of crime destroyed.[4] A report of the entire transaction must be made to the police administration within twenty-four hours, and a similar account must be sent to the investigating magistrate.[5]

Freedom of Movement

THE SYSTEM OF PASSPORTS AND IDENTIFICATION

The passport is an old Russian institution. It goes back to the days when the per capita tax and compulsory military service were introduced into Russia, and a passport then served as a means of keeping track of every inhabitant. An order issued by Peter the Great stipulated that all persons who did not have with them passports or letters of identification were to be considered "evil persons or out and out thieves." The passport also served as a means of keeping the great mass of Jews cooped up in the notorious *Pale*. A husband could refuse his assent to the issuance of a separate passport to his wife and thus keep her with him against her will, as no human being was allowed a legitimate existence without this sacred document.

The Bolsheviks introduced the work book to take the place of the passport for all persons who lived on unearned increment, that is, income from property or interest on money; for those who employed help for the purpose of profit; for private traders, middle-men and jobbers; for professional people who did not exercise a socially useful function; and for all persons who did not have definite occupations, such as former army officers, lawyers, etc. The holders of these so-called work books had to report at least once a month to the local soviets, in order that entries could be made as to fulfillment of public tasks which were imposed upon them. The work book was indispensible for the above classes if they desired to move from one community to another, and without it no food cards were issued to them.[6]

The discrimination against a particular group lasted only a short time, and soon a general work book was introduced for the entire population. A decree issued by the All-Russian Central Executive Committee stated that all persons who were sixteen years of age and were citizens of the R. S. F. S. R. were obliged to have work books. The possession of this document proved that the possessor of it was usefully occupied and it served as an identification within the limits of Russia, enabled the holder to obtain food cards, and made him eligible for compensation in case of disability and unemployment. With the coming of the new economic policy the work book lost its significance, and the limitation on movement was practically abolished.[7] In fact, on January 24, 1922, the presidium of the All-Russian Executive Committee issued an order to permit all citizens free movement throughout the republic. Until 1923, however, persons were required to possess a special identification certificate, issued by the commissar of the interior, but this rule was given a liberal interpretation so that between July 1927 and January 1933 a citizen of Russia could, for the purpose of identification, present one of the following documents: (1) the special identification card, (2) birth or marriage certificate, (3) house registration card, (4) service or work book, (5) union membership card, (6) student or graduation certificate, or (7) any other official document.

The above applied to adults only; minors up to sixteen years of age were included in the identification of the parents or guardians, or included in the rolls of the institutions in which they lived. In exceptional cases, a child between twelve and sixteen could receive an identification certificate on the petition of his parents or guardian, or on the petition of the minor himself. This provision harmonized with the Bolshevik ideology of permitting adolescents to start life independent of their parents or guardians.

In January 1933 a decree was issued which, when carried out, will reinstate conditions existing under the tsarist régime. By this decree all persons residing in the larger towns of the Union will have to make application for the issuance of passports. It is understood that only persons of "proper" social origin, who are at the time of application employed in useful occupation, will be granted passports. Persons to whom passports are denied will have to leave the city and move to rural communities not nearer than sixty miles from the urban center in which they formerly resided. The authorities hope that this regulation will result in the elimination of overcrowded conditions of industrial centers, and provide housing for the workers employed in necessary industries. Moreover, it is hoped by the authorities that the persons who were forced to leave the cities will turn to agricultural pursuits and help to increase the production of food stuffs.

Even before 1933 every person having taken residence in a dwelling within the city limits had to report within three days to the house committee and present a document of identification. The house committee then entered the tenant in the house register and reported to the appropriate department of the militsia (police).[8]

The mode of control as described above was, in practice, rather lax before January 1933, as far as Russian citizens were concerned, unless they stopped at hotels.[9] When, however, Soviet citizens desired to leave and foreigners to enter the country, they faced stricter regulation than in any other country in Europe. In recent years the Soviet government has been encouraging tourist trade, and hence has relaxed some of the stringent conditions as far as foreigners entering the country in groups are concerned. The average individual foreigner desiring to enter the country must receive the approval of the authorities in Moscow, which, of course, consumes considerable time. Foreigners must have entrance and exit visas, without which they cannot enter or leave the country. Russians desiring to leave the country, unless sent on official business, face an impossible task at the present time. It is only rarely that visas are granted to them, and then at exorbitant rates. Foreigners desiring to prolong their visits in Russia (the usual visa is for four weeks) must receive extension from the authorities. There is a fine of 500 rubles or forced labor for one year attached to any attempt to leave or enter the Soviet Union without authorization. Yet, strange as it may seem, the constitution of the Soviet Union provides for the right of an asylum for those persecuted for political activity or religious persuasions;[10] to such persons the provisions as to passports and visas do not apply.

The Right of Assembly and Organization

Before 1905 the people had no right of assembly and organization without the expressed permission of the government, and from a legal standpoint Russia before 1905 was a *Police State*. The constitution of 1905 did provide, however, for freedom of assembly and organization. Unfortunately for the Russian people this freedom did not last for long. Soon after the grant of the constitution, temporary rules were passed which considerably curtailed the rights granted. Thus between 1905 and 1917 there was very little freedom of assembly and organization as understood in the Western world. The short-lived Provisional Government attempted in this, as in other matters, to introduce Western European practices, but the coming of the Bolsheviks and the fierce struggle that followed the inception of the Soviet régime introduced new conceptions which are at variance with Western views in these matters. Thus the constitution of the R. S. F. S. R. makes provision for freedom of assembly and organization by stating that "For the purpose of enabling the workers to hold free meetings, the Russian Socialist Federated Soviet Republic offers to the working class and to the poorest peasantry furnished halls, and takes care of their heating and lighting appliances. The Russian Socialist Federated Soviet

Republic, having crushed the economic and political power of the proprietied classes and having thus abolished all obstacles which interfered with the freedom of organization and action of the workers and peasants, offers assistance, material, and other assistance to the workers and the poorest peasantry in their effort to unite and organize."[11]

This, of course, is in perfect agreement with the Bolshevik class ideology, and is valiantly defended and justified on the grounds that such restriction as the provision implies is a safeguard against usurpation of these rights by a small bourgeois ruling class, at the expense of the toiling masses which constitute the majority.

The Bolshevik authorities encourage the organization of voluntary societies, but they must be within the scope of Soviet control. To be sure in the early years of the Bolshevik régime there was a fair opportunity for dissenters, such as the Social Democrats and Social Revolutionists, to meet and organize. Indeed up to 1920 these groups retained their organizations openly and published their own newspapers. As may be expected they had to register with the Cheka and frequently met with difficulties in the matter of obtaining places for meetings; but when the civil war broke out, many of the moderate socialists joined the armed forces of the opposition. As a result, after the Soviet army defeated the opposing forces in 1920, this semi-tolerance to opposition organizations was withdrawn, and none but associations loyal to the Soviet power were allowed to remain in legal existence. In a decree issued by the All-Russian Central Executive Committee on August 3, 1922, the entire matter of right of assembly and organization was regulated. To meet new conditions these rules have been amended from time to time, but not with the intention of lessening the control of the government in these matters. Finally a decree entitled "A Decree in Regard to Associations and Unions which do not have for their Purpose the Obtaining of Profits"[12] issued on February 6, 1928, made a careful enumeration of the class of organizations allowed legal existence. It authorized the founding of voluntary associations of citizens which have a definite coöperative purpose, and are in no way connected with material gain of the members or the satisfaction of their economic needs. Under this category belong

educational, artistic, literary, sport, fire-fighting associations, etc.
These organizations are differentiated from private economic
associations and from coöperative societies which are regulated
by special legislation.[13]

The voluntary associations which are not organized for the
purposes of profit may undertake all kinds of economic projects,
provided these projects are a part of the purpose of the organization. Moreover they are permitted to conduct commercial and
trading transactions within the limits of their original purpose.
They may operate some such enterprises as publishing houses,
laboratories, experimental stations, etc. The decree of 1928 also
permits the organization of unions of associations. A union is
defined as a consolidation of two or more associations which do
not have for their purpose the obtaining of profit. The consolidation may take place under the general rules passed for the
organization of individual associations.

In accordance with the limits of their activity, voluntary organizations and unions may be of a merely local character, operating
within the limits of a single city or village and having no
branches in other political areas such as federal, regional, raional,
etc.[14]

The members and the elective executive organs must be composed of citizens who have reached their eighteenth year and
have not lost their right to be electors of soviets. Persons who
have lost their civil rights by judicial process and the privilege
to hold offices in public organizations cannot be members of the
associations during the period in which they are deprived of their
rights. Provided it is not contrary to their statute of incorporation, corporate bodies may become members of unions of associations. Voluntary associations and unions must have an
approved constitution and comply with the regulations in regard
to registration. No organization may legally operate until it has
registered with the appropriate authorities and its constitution
has been approved.

The constitutions of associations which operate throughout the
territory of the Soviet Union must be confirmed by the Council
of People's Commissars of the Union, and those that operate
in Russia proper, by the commissariat of interior of the R. S.
F. S. R. The articles of provincial and local organizations must

be confirmed by their appropriate executive committees or the presidia of the city soviets.

The administrative divisions and the presidia of the city soviets may not confirm the constitutions of those associations and unions which conduct activities beyond the limits of the territory of the given executive committee or city soviet, since those organizations are under the jurisdiction of superior organs. An association in order to obtain legal approval must have no less than ten members. A union must contain at least two registered associations. To the application for the approval of the constitution must be attached a list of the organizers, minutes of the meeting, and the project of the constitution which must contain the following information:

1. The name of the organization, its purpose, the place of location, and the form of its activity.
2. The rules for joining and resignation of members.
3. The financial sources of organization and the order of their disbursement.
4. The membership fees and the manner of their payment.
5. The staff and the organization of the executive organs, their location, and the manner of their organization.
6. The time and order of calling executive sessions of congresses.
7. The manner in which the association expects to report to the registering authorities in regard to the activity of the organization or union, and the names of all their members furnished in the established form.

The appropriate organs which are to confirm the constitution may not refuse the acceptance of the constitution for examination, and within a period of two months they must either issue to the organizers a copy of the constitution with an indorsement of confirmation or refuse to confirm, indicating reasons for refusal. The refusal to approve the constitution may be upon grounds that the purposes or the methods of the constitution are contrary to the laws of the Soviet Union or the R. S. F. S. R. Constitutions of organizations which threaten public peace and safety, or arouse racial antagonism and enmity, or have for their purpose the study of mysticism such as occultism, spiritualism, etc., or have no clear or definite purpose are refused permission for legal existence. The refusal of confirmation may also be based upon the reason that the association or union asking approval is duplicating organizations already in existence in the same district or locality.

The deciding authorities consult, in each separate case, in regard to the confirmation of a constitution either the appropriate people's commissariat or the divisions of executive committees within the district in which the association or union is to operate. If the superior organs fail to make a decision within one month, the confirming authorities may suggest changes in the activity of the union or association, or the substitution of some of the organizers by others as conditions for approval.

Within two months from the day of confirmation of the constitution, the associations and unions, inclusive of country wide organizations, must register with the organs which approved their constitution. Prior to registration, the activity of the organization must be limited to organization, recruiting of members, and the calling of a general meeting for the purpose of electing executive organs. Active operation does not begin until after registration of the association or union.

For the purpose of registration, associations and unions are required to forward to the registering authority a petition, the records of the election of executive organs, the location, a list of all members of the executive organs, and a list of all members of the organization. Within two weeks from the date of application for registration, the appropriate authority must issue to the executive body of the association or union the necessary papers. The responsible authority may suggest the elimination of some members as well as of some organizers. The local divisions of associations and unions must register in the administrative division where they are located, the executive officers appearing in person for that purpose.

Voluntary organizations and unions, desiring to enlarge their activity outside the limits of a given constituent republic, must apply for registration to the Union Council of Commissars. If they desire to operate in the R. S. F. S. R., approval by the commissariat of the interior of the republic is necessary. Unions and associations in their activities within the territories of the several republics must regulate themselves by the rules and laws of the respective republics. In case of disagreements with subordinate authorities, appeals may be made in a definitely established manner.

Thus refusals to permit the operation of unions and associations (1) by presidia of city soviets may be appealed to the appropriate higher executive committee; (2) by administrative divisions, to that executive committee whose division made the decision; (3) by the people's commissariats of autonomous republics, to the central executive committees of the respective republics; and (4) by the people's commissars of the Russian Republic, to the Council of the People's Commissars of the R. S. F. S. R.

The questions of corporate rights of voluntary associations and unions is delegated to the registering organs, and also to the people's commissariats, and the departments of executive committees under whose jurisdiction the activity of a given association or union is to be found. Branches of nation-wide organizations which operate within the limits of R. S. F. S. R. are also supervised by the above mentioned governmental agencies. The registering organs have a right to familiarize themselves with the affairs of the associations and unions, their financial condition, etc., and also to receive periodical reports of their activity.

Should the authorities find associations and unions to be deviating from the provisions of their constitutions without, however, violating existing laws, the registering authorities have the right to suggest to the organization that they eliminate, within a certain period of time, the various violations of their constitution. If the offense is in violation of existing laws, or the associations and unions have ceased to be active, appropriate authorities may liquidate the organizations. Local authorities are not permitted to stop the activities of All-Russian or Union associations. In case of necessity, the administrative organs may recommend to the appropriate people's commissariat of the R. S. F. S. R. that certain organizations be disbanded but must not act until an answer from the higher authorities has been received. Branches of associations and unions located in the R. S. F. S. R. whose constitutions have been confirmed by the Union Council of People's Commissars may be interfered with only by the Council of People's Commissars of the R. S. F. S. R. The Council of Commissars of the U. S. S. R. must be informed of this action immediately. The disbandment of unions and associations is resorted to only in cases designated by law or by the order of the Council of Commissars of U. S. S. R.[15]

The convening of congresses and meetings of associations are regulated by a decree of the All-Russian Central Executive Committee, dated June 12, 1922. National congresses must receive preliminary permission from the commissariat of the interior. Local congresses and meetings may be called by the permission of the provincial executive committee.

Organizations which intend to call congresses or meetings must send to the commissariat information as to the confirmation of their constitution and registration of their association, the time, the place, and the purpose of the congress, and also an exhaustive report as to the ratio of representation and the number of delegates expected. This information must be in the hands of the appropriate authorities not later than one month before the meeting of local congresses, and two months in case of a national congress. The appropriate authorities may use their own discretion as to permission or prohibition of the meetings of congresses. The replies, favorable or unfavorable, are usually sent within two weeks after application if it is a local congress, and within a month if it is a national congress.

The organization of public meetings, processions, and manifestations or parades is regulated by the laws of the various local units, based upon the general enactments of the Federation in accordance with Article VI of the constitution of the R. S. F. S. R., and must be in harmony with the provision of obligatory ordinances of local executive committees.

CHAPTER XIII

THE CHURCH AND THE STATE

"Orthodoxy and Autocracy are the Siamese Twins; one without the other could not survive." Thus spoke a professor of ecclesiastical law back in 1906, and this statement aptly characterizes the history of the Russian Orthodox church. Any discussion of the pre-Revolutionary church must make clear that her teachings and polity remained medieval. Persecution, torture, and exile were the lot of the non-conformists and heretics of Russia. While in Western Europe, the eighteenth and nineteenth centuries brought religious tolerance, the Russian church experienced no change until 1905, and even then the Orthodox church was the state church having the first and dominant place in the body politic. The tsar was the head of the church and the highest defender and guardian of the doctrines of the dominant faith. Russian subjects who did not belong to the Orthodox church had very little chance to advance themselves; in fact, they were excluded from many professions and occupations. In order to appreciate the church situation in Soviet Russia, one should bear in mind that there are excellent reasons for the hatred which the Bolsheviks and revolutionists in general nurture for the Orthodox church, a hatred, which in their ignorance of any other church, is carried over to all religious sects. To them, God as interpreted by the Orthodox church is merely an expression of oppression. Without doubt the "darkness" of the Russian peasant can be directly traced to a superstituous clergy, domineering and intellectually blind, to whose advantage it was to keep the people in ignorance. The higher clergy had very close contact with the autocracy, since its opulent existence was dependent upon the continued welfare of absolutism, and it worked hand in glove with the worst autocracy in the history of the modern world. When the Bolsheviks came into power, one of the important

decrees issued was the one of January 28, 1918, which provided
for an absolute separation of the church from the state. The new
régime made clear its refusal to serve as protector of church
institutions and as patron of ecclesiastical establishments.

The Soviet government rejected any tie with the church, which
it considered a weapon for the oppression of the masses. The
leaders believed that the people of the Soviet Union had "no need
of authoritative fantastic religious powers; the state wants no
interference from God or gods in any way or manner."[1] This
decree of 1918 covered all ecclesiastical communities and confes-
sions and all private religious organizations already existing or
newly organized. It applied to all associations which stipulated
that their member must belong to one faith, and also to organizations which were founded under the guise of mutual help,
philanthropy, and educational aims which had for their purpose
the help and support of any kind of a religious cult, or maintenance of servants of any religious organization, etc. The decree
of 1918, together with the prohibition to discriminate between
citizens in accordance with religious persuasions, provided that
no privileges be attached to any religious persuasions, or any
official cognizance be taken of them in making out of official
papers, and that citizens did not have to profess any religion if
they did not desire to do so. All the disabilities connected with
religious persuasion or absence of religious persuasion were
abolished. The decree furthermore encouraged anti-religious
propaganda. In fairness to the Bolsheviks it may be said that the
various excesses perpetrated by private organizations were frequently disapproved by the government, which favored educational campaigns against religion in preference to physical
force.[2]

The decree of 1918 prohibited the constituent republics from
passing legislation for the purpose of handicapping or limiting
freedom of conscience. The free execution of religious rituals
was guaranteed insofar as they did not interfere with public
order and were not encroaching upon the rights of citizens. In
accordance with the provision of the constitution of the R. S. F.
S. R. there is religious freedom in the country, and the citizens
are granted the right of anti-religious as well as religious
propaganda.[3]

Religious organizations could use their rituals and also preach sermons insofar as these were a part of their worship, and could do so without previous permission, provided that the contents of the sermons were of a purely religious nature. Prayer meetings could be conducted without previous permission in buildings dedicated for that particular purpose without limitation as to the numbers of worshipers. Meetings could also be held for the purpose of discussing the support of the church and the management of the ecclesiastical property.[4]

Permits for religious parades and any kind of public religious performance upon the streets and squares were to be issued by local authorities only on special request. All religious symbolism such as ikons, pictures, or statues of a religious character were removed from state and public buildings. The religious vows and oaths were abolished. The keeping of vital statistics, which before the Revolution was in the jurisdiction of ecclesiastical authority, was transferred to civil authorities.

In consequence of the separation of the church from the state, no citizen could excuse himself from performing civil duties on account of religious beliefs; however, citizens who belonged by birth and training to sects whose teachings forbade them before 1917 to serve in the army could be exempted from military service by order of the provincial courts.[5]

With the separation of the church from the state, the schools were also severed from the church. Any kind of religious instruction in state, public, or private schools was prohibited, with the exception of those schools which were especially dedicated to theological study. All clergymen, no matter to what religious cult they belonged, were prohibited from holding office in any school. Citizens could be instructed in religious subjects only privately; persons under eighteen years of age were not to be permitted to attend organized instructions in religious subjects.[6] For persons over eighteen years of age there could be organized theological courses with a view to preparing them for the church provided, however, the course be limited entirely to a theological curriculum. Special lectures, reading courses, and discussions could be organized for persons over eighteen years of age on questions of religious matters, provided they did not have the character of systematical school instruction. Citizens could form "groups of believers" or organize religious associations for the satisfaction of their religious needs. If believers desired to use houses of worship and did not care to enter into a more cohesive group, they could organize a group of no less than twenty persons and obtain the use of a building for that purpose. These so-called "groups of believers" were not to constitute collectives and were not to be considered from a juridical point of view. They were to be merely an aggregation of individuals, united only by a mutual agreement, having an executive committee to make arrangements for the use of the meeting place or other cult property, the contractual relationship being individual with collective responsibility.

The law, however, provided for the organization of religious associations.[7] Religious organizations could obtain the confirmation of their constitutions from provincial, circuit, and regional administrative departments. Religious organizations had to register with the appropriate civil authorities in their particular locality. The application for registration had to indicate (in case their membership was less than fifty) whether any of the local citizens had been deprived of their rights by judicial process, and whether the rules of the associations and method of their activity were contrary to the constitution and the laws of R. S. F. S. R. In contrast to other associations and unions, which did not have for their purpose the exaction of profit, religious organizations were not to enjoy the rights of juridical persons and were to hold no title to property. This provision was for the purpose of preventing ecclesiastical and religious organizations from concentrating in their hands economic and financial powers and creating in that manner a reactionary "state" within the Soviet state. The decree of 1918, in regard to the separation of the church from the state, has remained the guiding principle of all subsequent Soviet regulation of religious bodies.

Transactions connected with the use of the congregation's property, such as construction of buildings, hiring of singers, purchasing and supplying of fuel and books, and the renovation of buildings, could not be consummated collectively but by individual transactions.

Religious organizations were permitted to name delegates to carry out the orders and directions of general meetings of their organizations, and transact the necessary business within the limits of the law. These representatives were not juridically the organs of the association but the attorneys of the citizens who composed the association within specified limits of their commission. Since religious organizations did not possess the rights of juridical persons, they could not carry out judicial, punitive, or taxing functions, or order compulsory levying of taxes and impositions for ecclesiastical and religious needs; nor could they make use of punitive measures in disciplining of their members. Religious organizations and their representatives could collect voluntary offerings for the purpose of defraying expenses in connection with the use of the congregation's property, but the imposition of compulsory membership dues was proscribed. Ecclesiastical and religious organizations were not entitled to assistance or subsidies from the state or from local governmental organs. All state organizations were strictly forbidden to support any religious associations, or give preference to one class of ecclesiastical authorities over against another or some religious groups over against others by means of administrative intervention. The religious organizations of all faiths were equal before the law. No religious organization could interfere in the activity of another against its will. The local authorities had to see that there was an orderly and a free exercise of the religious needs of the citizens and hold all disturbers to strict legal accountability.

The religious organizations of a cult could organize provincial and national congresses, but congresses of religious organizations below that of provincial congress were prohibited. The congresses were permitted to elect executive organs. The faithful could voluntarily submit to the central hierarchical authority within the limits of internal church discipline, assent to the rules concerning economic management of the cult's property, and carry out the duties in connection with ecclesiastical employment. The congresses could not impose obligatory taxes. The above bodies were not permitted to accept church property of the organization or negotiate any kind of contracts relative to property.

The commissariat of the interior and its local organizations supervised the activities of the religious bodies and their congresses. The liquidation of religious organizations was carried out in the same manner as in the case of other organizations.

All property of church and religious establishments was declared by the decree of the separation of the church and the state as belonging to the state's domain, and that included properties of all descriptions, movable and immovable.

Buildings and such paraphernalia which were necessary for the ritual were transferred, not to the clergy but to the groups of believers organized and registered in accordance with the provisions of the law.

Local executive committees which had received all church property after the nationalization could transfer the property, such as buildings, to the groups of believers and religious organizations free of charge, provided the property was used for religious needs only, the congregation being responsible for all damage during the time of use.[8]

If it was found that a church group had taken part in counterrevolutionary activity or had been damaging church property wilfully, the contract between the authorities and that group was to be cancelled.   This action could, however, be appealed, the All-Russian Central Executive Committee being the final authority in determining a controversy of this kind.   The central authorities or their representatives had a right to order the cessation of public worship, if the gathering of worshipers threatened public peace or if the overcrowding of the building might cause its collapse.

Church property could be taken in a given locality for dwelling, sanitary-medical, and cultural-educational purposes, and also requisitioned by popular request for other public uses provided, however, there were no other buildings available in the locality.

In order to manage church affairs more efficiently the All-Russian Central Executive Committee established on May 30, 1931, permanent and local commissions for the investigation of religious questions and disputes.   A permanent central commission was attached to the presidium of the All-Russian Central Executive Committee.   This body is to have charge of general directions and the supervision and execution of the policies of the Party and government.   The commission is to apply the laws in regard to ecclesiastical bodies over the entire territory of the R. S. F. S. R.   The central commission is composed of a chairman who is a member of the presidium; a responsible secretary, members appointed by the presidium, and a staff of workers and advisers. The duties consist of drafting of legal projects in regard to the supervision of cults, conducting preliminary discussions of the same, and reaching conclusions and decisions. These projects together with conclusions are to be forwarded to the presidium for investigation and examination. The central commission is obligated to see that commissariats, central executive committees, autonomous republics, and regional executive committees are applying the law in regard to ecclesiastical establishments. Moreover, the commission is to assist the various governmental bodies with explanations and directions in the application of the law.

To the central commission is delegated the task of systematizing all legal acts and decisions of the Central Executive Committee and Council of the People's Commissars of the R. S. F. S. R. in regard to matters connected with church organizations. Furthermore, this body is to render advice to the Central Executive Committee, and investigate complaints on actions of executive committees in regard to treatment of religious bodies, such as closing of ecclesiastical buildings and breaking of agreements on the part of governmental agencies with religious organizations and groups of believers.[9] The commission is instructed to keep a unified record of all religious unions and gather statistics based on data supplied by local organs. It may demand from local organs information in regard to religious bodies, and print and publish materials in connection with legislation relative to ecclesiastical organizations. The commission is authorized to establish sub-commissions for the discussion of special questions. All organs of the R. S. F. S. R. must consult the commission before making any decisions in regard to ecclesiastical organizations, and the decision of the central commission must be obeyed by all local organs.

Republican and regional commissions are formed in connection with the presidia of executive committees. A member of the presidium is chairman; the rest of the membership is composed of one representative of the procurature, the commissariats of education of the autonomous republics, the regional departments of education, party and professional organizations, and other interested agencies, respectively.

The local commissions supervise the application of laws by lower organs and conduct preliminary investigations, upon requests of raion executive committees and city soviets, in regard to opening and closing of ecclesiastical buildings. They investigate requests for permission to hold ecclesiastical congresses within the limits of the autonomous republics, regions, and raions. They pass on requests for the use of printing presses and seals by ecclesiastical bodies. The commissions also investigate complaints on the action of raion executive committees and city soviets in regard to broken agreements, taxes, and similar subjects.[10] They keep a record of the religious bodies within their respective territories. They may call in representatives of commissariats attached to departments of executive committees to assist their regular staff. All agencies within their respective territories must consult the commission before taking action. Cities constituting independent raion units are permitted to form commissions under the chairmanship of the presidents of the city soviets. The duties of the lower commissions are identical with those of the higher bodies within the limits of their respective territories. Raion executive committees may be given authority to establish such commissions.[11]

The anti-religious attitude of the Bolsheviks as described above is the same to date, although the mode of procedure in agitating against religion has changed. The Communist is learning the age-old lesson that excessive zeal in persecution makes martyrs. They have checked the terrific speed with which they were creating an atheistic society. The enthusiastic denunciation of priests and the fanatical and frenzied abuse of the church and all her servants have changed into more scientific, cool, but steady educational campaigns carried on by means of exhibits, statistical material, and charts. All these activities are for the purpose of proving that the church was a tool in the hands of autocracy and capitalism, diverting untold treasure into the pockets of the hierarchy. Objects reputed to have miraculous qualities, which were used by the clergy to hold the superstituous masses in subjection, are exhibited and explained.

Miraculous mummifications of saints have been publicly exposed, and frequently proved to be nothing more than a collection of animal bones cleverly assembled to resemble a human skeleton. The most important work is done among the new generation in schools. Only the future can tell the result of this educational process. The old Russian church is dead ;[12] even the Bolshevik in his fury against the old church realizes it, and consequently the wiser heads among the leaders have concluded that the small communions of believers, unless they constitute an economic or political impediment, may be left to themselves and time.

CHAPTER XIV

THE SUPERVISION OF THE PRESS
AND POPULAR AMUSEMENTS

THE LEGAL STATUS OF THE PRESS

A free press in the democratic sense never existed in Russia. From the introduction of printing in Russia in the middle of the sixteenth century, the printing and publishing trade was controlled and harassed. In fact, the deacon Ivan Feodorac, who introduced the printing press into Russia, had to flee from Moscow on the peril of his life. Some authority always supervised and censored the printed word; the clergy at first, and later on, the police. To be sure, at some periods of Russian history before the October Revolution there were temporary respites of censorship. Indeed, a short while after the Revolution of 1905, the administrative chains were taken off the Russian press for a little while, but in a short time a reaction followed, and the press was muzzled as effectively as ever. Underground presses, however, flourished in Russia, and the revolutionaries knew ways and means to continue their existence in spite of raids and arrests. The short-lived Kerensky government established freedom of the press, but with the coming of the Bolsheviks conditions changed.

An understanding of the ideology of Russia is necessary for an intelligent discussion of the press. Any repression or control which the Soviet government exercises is, in accordance with the Bolshevik doctrine, a guarantee of liberties for the "toiling masses" over against the "exploiting elements", which are not necessarily the bourgeois but may be certain workers themselves. In short, it is not merely the protection of the existing form of government or the safeguarding of the state, but an assurance of the dominance of the Communist Party over all elements. It is unblushingly a dictatorship that knows no bounds in its intolerance of opposing ideas. In fairness to the Soviets it must be said, however, that the repressions are no more drastic than those of other dictatorships or of some periods of the tsarist régime. The traditions of Russia are not those of a free country in the Western sense of the word.

LEGAL PROVISIONS IN REGARD TO THE PRESS AND PUBLICATIONS

The origin of the present control of the press dates back to October 28, 1917, when the Council of People's Commissars issued its first decree regulating all non-Bolshevik publications. There was violent opposition to this decree from all non-Bolshevik sources. In answer to the protests the new government stated that behind the liberal screen was hidden the liberty for propertied classes only, which appropriated the lion's share of the entire press for the purpose of poisoning the minds of the people and of bringing confusion to the masses. Among other things, the new government stated that at the critical moment when the power of the masses was just being consolidated, it would be madness to leave this powerful weapon, more dangerous than machine guns and bullets, in the hands of the enemy. It added, however, that as soon as the new order was firmly established, the administrative repression against the press was to be abolished, and complete freedom established subject only to judicial responsibility in accordance with broad and progressive legislation. Lenin, in a speech before the All-Russian Executive Committee on November 4, 1917, suggested that a commission be appointed to investigate the dependence of the bourgeois press on banking institutions. He believed that there ought not to be liberty of the press which depended upon capital. On December 18, 1917, there was established, in connection with the revolutionary tribunal, a press tribunal with jurisdiction over crimes committed against "the people" by the use of the press. The local divisions of the Cheka organized subdivisions, which began to collect newspapers and other publications and to mark the more radical outbursts against the Soviet government. The Cheka had authority to arrest responsible editors and transfer their case to the press tribunal.

This struggle with the press continued until the summer of 1918 when, after several cases had been tried by the press tribunal, the Soviet authorities concluded that the various non-Bolshevik papers were opposed to the Soviet régime and ordered all remaining opposition papers to cease publication. Since that time, *i.e.* 1918, there has been only one press and that is the Party press. The constitution of the R. S. F. S. R. stipulates that "in order to secure for the laboring masses real freedom in expressing their own opinion, the R. S. F. S. R. destroys the dependency of the press upon capital and transfers it into the hands of the working classes and poor peasantry, together with all technical and material resources for the publication of newspapers, pamphlets, books, and all other printed matter, and guarantees their free circulation throughout the country."[1] Lenin, in commenting on the above provision of the constitution, remarks caustically, "Liberty of the press also serves as one of the main battle cries of pure democracy. Nevertheless, the workers know, and the socialists of all countries have admitted millions of times, that this freedom remains a deception as long as the best printing presses and the largest reserves of paper remain in the hands of the capitalists, and as long as that is true the power of capital will continue to rule over the press"....He continues, "In general, real freedom and equality can only be brought by a régime which will not permit the press to be subordinated, directly or indirectly, to the power of money...."[2]

This, in short, is the attitude of the Bolsheviks towards freedom of the press. The Soviet government was not slow in realizing the advantages of an absolute monopoly of all news agencies. Thus beginning with 1918 the Soviet printing output, in spite of mechanical difficulties and scarcity of paper, assumed gigantic proportions. In 1919 the various governmental and coöperative publishing agencies united into one great publishing corporation, the Gosizdat, which became a part of the Narkompros (commissariat of education). The president of the editorial collegium at the head of the Gosizdat had direct access both to the Council of People's Commissars and the presidium of the Central Executive Committee.

Thus practically the entire machinery of publication, private or official, scientific, technical, or literary, was controlled by this mammoth publishing organization. Since the publishing of any work was dependent on the Gosizdat, it is clear that "non-conformist" literature had slight chance. Furthermore the Gosizdat controlled not only the publication but also the machinery and paper supply. Hence all work connected with the publishing business, directly or indirectly from planning of paper reserves to the circulation of printed matter throughout the country, was concentrated in one gigantic state organization. Beginning with January 1, 1921, books, newspapers, journals, pamphlets, and other printed matter were supplied to all organizations and institutions free of charge. The New Economic Policy, however, put an end to this scheme. On account of the economic changes following the adoption of the *Nep* policy, the Council of People's Commissars issued a decree on December 12, 1921, permitting the opening of private publishing firms that were given the right to own and operate printing presses, offices and editorial staffs, warehouses and shops, etc. The issuance of permission was subject to the authority of the Gosizdat. The organization of coöperatives was favored and encouraged. The new policy brought about changes in the organization of the Gosizdat, which lost its planning and regulative functions and became merely a state publishing agency. A new super censorship board (Glavlit),[3] the functions of which will be described later, was created under the jurisdiction of the commissariat of education with branches all over the country. The control over foreign news and foreign correspondents is under the jurisdiction of the commissariat of foreign affairs. All news coming into the Soviet Union from abroad and all the news from anywhere in the Union goes through a telegraph news agency which is absolutely controlled by the Soviet government.

The G. P. U., which is represented in the Glavlit, has authority to arrest violators of regulations and may confiscate printed matter even after it has been censored, if it is found to be contrary to public weal. Various committees, established for the control of dramatic, musical, and film productions in the several republics, have also been granted censorship authority. In addition, the post office department, under the direction of Glavlit and G. P. U., has a right to withhold or return prohibited printed matter. A kind of an "index expurgatorium", kept in the receiving bureau of the post office, is augmented as occasion arises.

The Glavlit, the chief censoring board, is headed by a superintendent, who is assisted by two deputies, appointed by the commissariat of Education with the approval of the representatives of the Revolutionary Military Council (Revvoensovet) of the Union, G. P. U., and the Council of People's Commissars of R. S. F. S. R. In the larger centers, branches of the Glavlit are to be found, which must act in conformity with the regulations of the main office. The Glavlit directs the preliminary examination of all manuscripts and printed matter, which includes periodicals, books, films, drawings, music, maps, etc.—in short, everything that is to be published in Russia or imported from abroad. The Glavlit and its local branches carry on all kinds of censorship—military, political, ideological, etc.

This amazing censorship board and its branches also have the authority to issue permits for the opening of publishing houses, and for the issuance of periodical and non-periodical literature, and special literature for public use. Moreover, it passes rules in regard to circulation of printed material and conditions upon which manuscripts may be published. It compiles lists of all publications; those which may be sold to the public and those forbidden. The repertoire of theaters, printing presses, libraries, bookstores, and warehouses also come under its jurisdiction. The grounds upon which the Glavlit may forbid publication and circulation of printed matter are regulated in detail by law. Some of the reasons for prohibition are counter-revolutionary agitation, divulging of military secrets of the Union, the arousing of public opinion by means of falsehoods, the inciting of racial and religious fanaticism, and pornographic character of the publication involved.

The Glavlit may furthermore stop individual editions, cut down circulation, close publishing houses if their activities are found to be in violation of law, and initiate judicial prosecution, or it may transfer the matter to the G. P. U. which, as was mentioned, may on its own initiative stop the circulation of publications. The "underground" publications, the importation of publications from abroad, and the sale of Russian and foreign literature which have been proscribed by the Glavlit receive the strictest attention from the G. P. U.[4]

Every publication issued in the Soviet Union must bear the stamp of the Glavlit or its branches and the name of the publishing house, its address, the year of publication, the name and address of the printing press, and the number of copies published. Periodical literature must, in addition, name the responsible editor and the year in which the publication was issued.

A "book chamber" (palata),[5] located in Moscow and organized in the early years of the Bolshevik régime, collects and registers copies of all printed matter published in the Union. This chamber issues and distributes copies of publications to all state libraries and retains the original copy. A certain number of copies of all publications must be sent to this chamber by all printing presses engaged in producing any kind of reading matter.

All advertising was declared a state monopoly in November 1917, and only Soviet publications were allowed to carry advertisement. Private periodicals were forbidden to accept advertisements. Any publication violating this law was stopped, and the responsible parties were punished and fined. At the present time paid advertising may appear not only in governmental, but in professional, party, and coöperative publications; strictly private publications, however, are still prohibited to accept paid advertising.

The manufacture of school equipment is governed by special rules. All school supplies such as textbooks, readings, tablets, maps, and pictures can be manufactured only by permission of the state educational council (G. U. S.) of the commissariat of education, and all requests in connection with this matter must be directed to that organization. School supplies issued without permission of the educational council are subject to confiscation by judicial process. Those confiscated materials which are deemed suitable for the use of institutions are distributed free of charge by the commissariat of education to labor and other organizations; the remainder are converted by authority of the state publishing board into pulp for the manufacture of paper.[6] It is safe to say that nearly the entire publishing, printing, and printing supply trades are under the control of the state.[7]

A rigid supervision is exercised over all undertakings connected directly or indirectly with the printing and publishing business. The book trade by private persons is strictly regulated and is entirely prohibited in all localities outside of the larger cities. By a decree issued on July 13, 1927, all establishments, public and private, in any way connected with the manufacture or distribution of printed matter, must register with the trade department of the executive committee of the locality in which they happen to transact business. The manufacture and distribution of statutes, badges, photographs, etc. of the leaders of the Revolution are permitted only to state organizations. Other organizations and private persons must have special permission of the Glavlit or its branches and the commissariat of the interior.

The federal regulation of the entire printing trade and its collateral branches is under the authority of the coördinating committee on publication of the Union commissar of trade. This committee is composed of four members appointed by the Union commissariat of trade; one of the members is appointed by agreement with the commissars of trade of the several constituent republics.[8]

SUPERVISION OF POPULAR AMUSEMENTS

Closely connected with the regulation of the press is the supervision of amusements. The decree which created the Glavlit stipulated that the supervision of amusements and theatrical performances was to be delegated to the directors of regional educational departments. For the purpose of controlling the repertory, a special committee was formed under the supervision of the Glavlit. The committee (repertkom) at present consists of a chairman and two members appointed by the commissariat of education. The duties of this body consist of issuing permits for stage, dramatic, musical, and motion picture performances, and compiling periodic indexes of all permitted and prohibited plays. The committee has the authority to control the repertory of all amusement establishments and to close, by judicial and administrative means, all of the performances, should they violate the established rules. No play can be performed without the permission of the appropriate committee or the authorized local organs.[9] The issuance of permits for the exhibition of motion pictures is under the exclusive jurisdiction of the committee.[10] While permits are issued for an indefinite period, yet as a rule plays and motion pictures are not permitted to run, without a renewal, longer than eight months. Films which have not met with the approval of the committee are confiscated by the organs of the commissariat of the interior and are transferred by them to the commissariat of education. Imported films may be returned to the exhibitors for the purpose of restoring them to the owners abroad. All works permitted by the committee may be staged anywhere without special permission by the local organs; any change in the text of plays, however, is strictly forbidden. The permission to give a public performance does not free the manager from the responsibilitty of registering the performance with the local organs of control. Organizations, institutions, and private persons who intend to sponsor a public performance must report to the local organs their repertory not later than three days before the performance is to be given, and describe in detail the program of the intended exhibition. In case of a repertory planned for a longer period of time, a permit may be obtained for the entire season, but no changes may be made after permission has been granted.[11] The commissariat of the interior is responsible for the carrying out of the regulations of the committee (repertkom) and must govern itself by the index of prohibited and permitted plays as made out by the above committee. The violations of this rule carry with it a heavy penalty.

Performances by collectives in villages are governed by special rules. For the purpose of exercising artistic-ideological control and censorship of all traveling companies of artists playing in villages, special revisory commissions have been established in connection with raional and regional political-educational organs. The membership of these commissions is composed of various educational and cultural committees of the appropriate administrative divisions. The commissions censor all of the works intended for public performances in the village by theatrical organizations — professional and amateur groups, and clubs coming from headquarters or elsewhere, or local provincial talent. Only those are exempt from this censorship who have a special endorsement from headquarters (*Glavpolitprosvet*). Similar revisionary commissions are created in connection with the lower cultural-political committees, whose duty it is to go over all performances which are to be staged in a given district. These revisionary commissions censor the performances not only from an ideological standpoint, but they also decide whether the content is suitable for village audiences, and pass judgment upon their artistic-literary value and clearness. The approval of the revisionary committees, does not, however, dispense with the necessity of obtaining permission from the organs of central authorities (Glavlit). The local authorities are enjoined to examine carefully all artistic organizations coming into the village, and not to permit any performance without the sanction of the appropriate authorities.

Circus performances, concerts, motion pictures, cabarets, expositions, menageries, sport tournaments, public picnics, shooting galleries, skating, racing, merry-go-rounds, dances, and games, provided they are not of a hazardous kind, may be managed by state, professional, coöperative and private associations and by private persons. Permission for this purpose must be obtained in the more important cities from the appropriate administrative divisions of soviets; in other urban communes, from the presidia of the city soviets; and in rural communes, from the village soviets. Organs of authority, upon receiving applications for permission to conduct the above described recreations, must give a favorable answer within a month or inform the applicants that approval has been refused. Needless to say the entire amusement field is strictly under the control of the governing authorities, excepting those sponsored and vouched for by state organizations.[12]

CHAPTER XV

THE POLICE
(Militsia)

POLICE FUNCTIONS

Bolshevik writers, in discussing the police in the Soviet state, designate it as a class institution officially known as the Workman-Peasant Militsia and Criminal Investigation. The main function of this class organ, it seems, is to guard the revolutionary order and the safety of the toiling masses. Previous to the abolition of the commissariats of interior in the constituent republics, the police administration was attached to these commissariats. In 1930 the old police establishment was reorganized into "The Chief Administration of Workman-Peasant Militsia[1] Administration and Criminal Investigation" and placed in close connection with the councils of people's commissars of the R. S. F. S. R., constituent republics, autonomous republics, regional and raion executive committees, and city soviets. This reorganization, according to Bolshevik interpretation, creates a structure which is built from below and will culminate in an efficient centralized organization, that will strengthen discipline in the ranks. At the same time it will improve conditions of the ranks all around. The police in its new organization is to become as strong a rampart of the proletarian dictatorship as the Red Army.[2]

THE CENTRAL ORGANS

The central organs of the police administration are attached to the council of people's commissars of the respective republics, and are under the direct supervision of a newly created chief administration of police and criminal investigation. The local organs of administration are located in regions, autonomous republics, raions, and cities.[3] The chiefs of local police administrations are under immediate jurisdiction of the superior police organs and are responsible to them for the condition and activity of their respective departments. Yet in actual operation the local departments govern themselves by the regulations of those organs of government to which they are attached: to wit, councils of commissars of autonomous republics, local executive committees, and city soviets.

The chiefs of republican police administrations are appointed by the council of people's commissars of the respective republics. The heads of the lower political units, such as regions and autonomous republics, are appointed by the executive of the central republican police administration. In cities and raions of the R. S. F. S. R. the heads of police administration are appointed by the chiefs of regional or autonomous republican police administrations; in other constituent republics, by the chiefs of the central republican police administrations. Councils of people's commissars of autonomous republics, local executive committees, and city soviets may take exceptions to these appointments. A decree passed May 25, 1931, authorizes councils of people's commissars of constituent republics to issue regulations for the guidance of central police administrations of constituent republics and also of the local police departments. The chiefs of the central republican police administrations are authorized by a recent decree[4] and other current legislation to decide upon regulations pertaining to (1) general service regulations, (2) disciplinary regulations, (3) conduct of police educational institutions, and (4) supplementary instructions for the departmental police.

The General Division of Police

The Police is divided into two general branches, the General Service and the Departmental Police.

I. THE GENERAL SERVICE

The General Service is composed of (1) the rank and file, who execute post duty and carry out the operative work in safeguarding order and public safety; (2) those who are employed in the political training of the line personnel; (3) the administrative staff; (4) persons employed in the administrative-economic staffs, who operate in connection with economic and medicosanitary sections of the police; and (5) the educational personnel employed in police training schools. The divisions of commanding rank and file are again classified into three categories, namely—(1) senior, (2) intermediate, and (3) junior.

The rank and file of police are not covered by general labor legislation. The conditions under which they work, the order of appointment, time on duty, and dismissal from service are regulated by special police legislation.[5] Generally, the rank and file who are on line duty work eight hours a day, and those who are engaged in office work spend six and one-half hours in continuous service.[6] In fact they are expected to perform continuous watch duty for the same length of time, whether they are on duty day or night. In case of necessity, police employees working on regulated time schedules are expected to work over-time without extra pay. Under certain circumstances, such as holidays, members of the police must work on the day of their weekly rest, but in that case they are permitted to substitute another day of rest. Annual leaves are granted in accordance with the kind of work a given individual is performing, but they do not generally exceed twelve working days.

Women employed in police departments engaged in intellectual or office work are granted a leave of forty-two days before and forty-two days after confinement. Women engaged in physical labor may have fifty-six days before and fifty-six days after confinement. Women who are in the fifth month of pregnancy may not be detailed for night duty or to other than their usual places of occupation. Nursing mothers are allowed sufficient time to nurse their infants.

Police employees upon entering the service must give a written promise to serve two years and this is repeated at two-year intervals thereafter. Employees of the police who have received the benefit of special training in a police educational institution must serve two months for each month of training, and in general no less than a total of two years. Unauthorized separation from the service may result in trial by court martial. The members of police establishments are under military discipline and must carry out all instructions of superiors in the line of duty with military precision, unless such commands are obviously illegal. If the subordinate carries out an illegal order, both he and the superior may be held responsible. The members of the police force assigned to active service must wear the prescribed uniform, insignia of rank, and regulation arms.

For outstanding service in the line of duty the members of the police establishments are rewarded in accordance with the degree of meritorious service. The classes of reward are as follows:

(1) Citation in orders.
(2) Increased leave.
(3) Monetary reward.
(4) Reward by a special gift.
(5) The issuance of a letter of honor.
(6) The award of decoration.

Service Infractions

Service infractions which are not serious enough to be prosecuted in accordance with the Criminal Code are punished as follows:

(1) Remark.
(2) Reprimand.
(3) Strong Reprimand.
(4) Confinement to official quarters.
(5) Extra duty.
(6) Arrest for twenty days.
(7) Reduction in rank.
(8) Dismissal from service.

Additional disciplinary measures are provided in the general police disciplinary regulations. For more serious offenses the members of police departments may be tried by military courts, as well as by civil courts.

The members of the police are supplied with arms, ammunition, and material equipment. The standard of supplies which is administered by a central agency is the same as that furnished for militarized guard. The uniforms of the members of the police force are identical throughout the Union.

The expenses in connection with police service (with exception of departmental police) are carried on the budgets of the constituent republics, regions, autonomous republics, raions, and cities. The funds, which are appropriated for the support of the police by budgets of autonomous republics and local units, are administered by central authorities and are at the disposal of the central police administrations of the constituent republics.

II. THE DEPARTMENTAL POLICE

This branch is organized by agreement between the central police administrations of constituent republics, regions, autonomous republics, and state and public organs. The duties of departmental police consist, in general, in rendering special protection of separate undertakings, structure, and properties of the organs involved. The departmental police acts upon authority of general police legislation and provisions; additional instructions are issued as circumstances and conditions demand them. The departmental police is supported by those institutions which use its services. The funds used in this connection are entered into the current account of those police administrations as a special tax of the organs to which the given departmental units are attached.

COMPENSATION OF MEMBERS OF THE POLICE FORCE

The salaries of the members of the police force are very low. In rural districts the pay of the ordinary policeman is about forty rubles per month; in urban centers the compensation is somewhat higher.[7] The salaries of the commanding personnel range from fifty-nine to ninety-three rubles. There is also provision for the issuance of an annual allowance of eighty-four rubles and ninety kopeks for equipment, but in most localities only fifty rubles is granted. Some of the privileges attached to the service, however, give the individual members of the police the standard of living of the average manual worker. The law provides for regular increase in salaries; thus after three years of continuous service a policeman receives a two per cent increase; after six years, 20 per cent; nine years, 30 per cent; and twelve years, 50 per cent. Time spent in training school counts for double. The members of the police force are forbidden to occupy any other remunerative positions, with exception of certain activities of a public nature which do not interfere with their official duties. Members of senior, intermediate, and junior commanding personnel may accept employment as specialists in state and public organs, but permission for such activity must be obtained in each individual case from the chief of the appropriate police administration. Employees of the police department who are not in the regular line of service or on the administrative-economic staffs are subject to the general provisions of the Labor Code. All members of the police force have a right to be members of professional unions. The usual local committees are not to be found in the police organizations, but in their place are the social - cultural commissions, which are organized upon the authority of special regulations issued by the All-Union Central Council of Professional Unions, in agreement with the chiefs of the main police administrations in the constituent republics.

BENEFITS AND PRIVILEGES
OF MEMBERS OF THE POLICE FORCE

The senior, intermediate, and junior militsiamen of the commanding staffs and their families are entitled to all the privileges awarded to the members of the Red Army of equal rank and their families. The administration of these privileges is under the jurisdiction of the chiefs of the main police administrations. The other members of the police force are entitled to all the privileges of the regular social insurance provisions on equality with manual laborers. In addition, however, the rank and file of the police force are insured at public expense in state insurance organizations, a provision which entitles them to death benefits and payments in case of accidents in the line of duty.[8]

The members of the police and their families are entitled to all advantages in the line of education, use of land, agricultural taxes, and housing, on equality with the members of the Red Army and their families. In fact city soviets and local executive committees are instructed to set aside five per cent of the housing fund for the erection of new dwelling places for members of the police force. Their food rations are equal to those of industrial workers, and the Union commissariat of supplies is in the process of constructing a chain of "closed" dining rooms for members of the police force.[9]

POLICE SCHOOLS

On January 23, 1931, the chief police administration of the R. S. F. S. R. issued an order for the establishment of schools for highly qualified police employees. The order recommends the increase of schools in regions, with a minimum of at least one

school in each region, for the training of intermediate commanders. It urges the improvement of existing schools, the training of personnel for regions inhabited by national minorities,
and the establishment of extension courses for senior, intermediate, and junior commanding staffs. The order further
recommends the attachment to the police of all persons who have
graduated from police schools, and encourages improvement in
the efficiency of all members of the police force. It urges the
organization of at least one school in each consolidated region for
the training of junior commanders, and lastly, recommends the
increase of short term courses for the training of persons who
wish to join the police force.

The Field Activities of the Police Force

The activities of the police may be divided into three general
groups of duties: (1) prevention of crime, discovery and investigation of crimes and violations within the limits of the law; (2)
coöperation, in accordance with existing law, with state institutions and officials in connection with the carrying out of duties
assigned to them; (3) the extending of protection and assistance
to those in need within the scope of police power, as provided by
law. In executing their functions the members of the police
force must strictly obey the directions of the existing regulations
of the central and local authorities.

The members of the force must report immediately counter-
revolutionary practices of citizens; namely, the posting of
counter-revolutionary proclamations, the delivery of counter-
revolutionary speeches on the streets, the distribution, sale, or
appearance of posters, and the distribution of counter-revolutionary literature in general. The police must also prevent the
removal by force of the Soviet shield and flag, and the display
of flags and emblems of any kind which are inimical to the Soviet
power. Upon the discovery of counter-revolutionary activity
the members of the police must report at once to the appropriate
authorities and to the nearest branch of the G. P. U. and hold all
guilty parties, together with material evidence such as literature,
flags, emblems, etc. All counter - revolutionary manifestations
within the precincts of a given police station, such as meetings of
armed counter-revolutionary detachments or separate armed men

who have counter-revolutionary intentions, must be stopped by the police. All interference with and damage of telegraph and telephone wires, coming to the attention of the individual policeman on the beat, must be reported to the police station and to the G. P. U. and to the nearest military detachment as soon as possible. Before the arrival of an armed force, the police must take all means to find out the extent, the character, and purpose of the activity. The members of the police force must arrest and hold all ring leaders and the more active participators in riots.

For the purpose of detection and prevention of crime and violations of public order, safety, and welfare, the members of the police are instructed to collect information in regard to all suspicious places and persons on their beat. They must also watch them and take notice of all occurrences and report to the authorities; in certain cases reports must also be sent to the nearest agent of the criminal investigation bureau. Furthermore, the individual policeman must be on the lookout that property stolen or obtained illegally is not sold or exchanged in public fairs or market places, taverns, boarding houses, etc., and if possible, apprehend the persons who are engaged in such trade and activity. In rural districts the duties of the police include the safeguarding of the people against bands of thieves, robbers, and bandits by sending immediate information to the chief of the rural units of police, and in the meantime they must make every effort to protect the population by arresting the perpetrators of crime.

In urban communes, the district police inspectors (nadziratel) are instructed to make frequent inspections of dwellings, check the tenants by means of the registration book,[10] and be on the alert for persons who are not registered or are deprived by judicial process of the right to live in a given locality. The inspectors are duty bound to be present at all mass meetings of citizens in the streets and public places. If any violation of the law is detected, the inspector must at once inform the citizens and ask them to comply with the law, explaining to them that in case of non-compliance, he will act in accordance with the provisions of the law.[11] In order to facilitate the discovery and investigation of misdemeanors and crimes and bring the guilty to justice, the members of the police force are duty bound (a) to take oral or written depositions of persons and public institutions in regard to crimes and violations committed, and to obtain testimony from persons who have suffered damage from the attempts of violators; (b) to examine the persons who are under suspicion of having committed a crime; (c) to conduct investigations in regard to crimes committed.

The police must be ready to receive information of violations and intended violations of law at any time, day or night, without exception, inclusive of holidays. Every written record (protokol), which has been made by a member of the police in regard to a crime or violations of public order and safety, must contain the following information: the date when the record was made, the official status and the name of the person who has made the record, the reasons for making the record, the time and the place the violation was committeed, the nature of the violation, the name of the person who suffered from the act, the name of the alleged violators, the name and place of residence of every witness of the act, and the extent to which every witness can testify as to a personal knowledge of the violation.

The record is made, whenever possible, in the place where the crime was committed, as soon as it has been discovered or reported. Every deposition must be signed by the informant, and if for any reason the informant refuses to sign it, this fact must be recorded. The record then must be signed by the officer in charge and his official status indicated. The members of the police must demand the identification of persons who are suspected of violations of the law, and require from them identification papers. Any document may serve for identification, provided it was issued by a state institution or professional union and contains the name and place of work or employment or place of residence. If the suspected person or violator has no such documents or if he has presented a document which is irregular or of dubious character, and if the identification of the person cannot be substantiated by third parties who happened to have been at the place at the time when the crime was committed, the members of the police must require the accused person to accompany them to the police headquarters for identification. In case of refusal the policeman has the right to take him into custody.

This procedure does not imply, however, that such conduct on the part of the suspected persons is to be punished with the deprivation of liberty. Moreover the Criminal Code limits this procedure only to cases in which the alleged crime is of a nature coming under the classification of "social defense."[12] Persons, however, who are suspected of having committed violations and crimes which do not come under this classification cannot be compelled to accompany the officer to the police headquarters against their will.

The identification of persons who have been taken into custody may be made by means of investigation at the place of their employment and residence, and also by calling of witnesses who may be able to identify the suspected persons; but suspects must not be kept in custody without charges longer than twenty-four hours. When information cannot be obtained because his residence and working place are in different cities, the citizen must be freed at once. If there is no cause to hold a suspect for investigation or for trial, the Criminal Code provides that a record of the case be made in accordance with the testimony of the suspected person, and he is warned that giving false information may be punished as stipulated in Article 187 of the Criminal Code.

The police conducts investigations on all matters which are provided for in the Criminal Code, such as the violation of rules of public health, public safety and order, violations of rules of administration, offenses against personal dignity, and in general, all the violations of order, safety, and welfare which are provided for in obligatory decrees or other legislation of the Soviet power, and which are punishable in judicial or administrative order.

The police is obligated to coöperate with every state institution in connection with carrying out of decisions of the Soviet power, and also with every official person in the exercise of his duties and in the operation of obligatory ordinances of local authorities. Official persons who do not belong to the police force have a right to demand from the members of the police coöperation in all those cases in which they are carrying out official duties and meet with opposition or difficulties from citizens. The orders of the commissariat of the interor are carried out directly by the police; other departments, however, may call for assistance of the police in certain designated instances only.

The police coöperates with the military authorities in the apprehension of deserters, assists in the drafting of persons who are subject to military service, and coöperates in carrying out orders for mobilization. Fiscal agencies and finance inspectors may call for assistance of the police in connection with assessments and examination of business and trade records. They may also call upon the force in case of refusal of those engaged in trade to comply with legal tax requirements. The collection of taxes and arrears in taxes, public sale of defaulting taxable property, closing and padlocking of stores and other places of business, delivery of tax notices and tax lists, etc., are outside the scope of police duties.

The police coöperate with custom house officials in their searches for contraband goods beyond fifty kilometers of the custom house, and take part under limitations in the searches by the agents of the custom departments for contraband goods in cities and villages. Execution of orders of custom agencies in connection with imposition of fines is not within the competence of the police.

The people's commissariat of transportation may request the police to arrest persons and to impose fines for riding without tickets on railroads and water ways and for entering on the platform without tickets. Other departments of government may, under certain circumstances, call upon the police for the performance of certain duties only with the express permission of the central authorities.

Citizens may appeal directly to members of the police force for aid in cases of personal or property damage and other violations of legal interests. Members of the police, when they are appealed to by citizens, must protect them from assault or attempt at assault. If the assault is of a criminal nature, the reconciliation of the two parties does not stop prosecution, and the police officers must make a record of the offense and permit the matter to take its legal course. Under certain circumstances the policeman may use his discretion, depending upon whether the assault has taken place in a private or public place. If it has taken place in public, the violator is accused of rowdyism; if however, it has occurred in a private dwelling, the officer simply stops the assault and informs the aggrieved person that he can prosecute the violator in accordance with the law, but no record is made of the occurrence.

Persons who have suffered from violence, accidental or natural misfortune, or persons who have found themselves in a public place on account of a stroke or sickness can expect the members of the police to render them first aid, call an ambulance, or take them to the nearest hospital or drug store, or call medical help. The members of the police are obligated to save drowning individuals, attempt resuscitation, and take care of all other accidents which may occur in public places. Mentally deranged persons who may be dangerous to themselves or to their fellow men must be sent to a hospital. Abandoned children are sent by the police to the nearest foundling institution, and lost children are conducted to their homes or to the nearest branch of the police headquarters.

For the purpose of safeguarding the legal rights of citizens, the police must receive complaints in regard to lost objects, animals, etc., and attempt to return the lost object to its rightful owner. In the exercise of their duties the members of the police must strictly observe all the provisions of the law, and not take action which is embarrassing to citizens unless it is absolutely necessary for the carrying out of their duties. Police officers are permitted to call citizens to headquarters for the purpose of informing them of minor violations of law, but this is permitted only under exceptional circumstances, and even then the summons must be considered as an invitation. The appearance of citizens in compliance with such a request is not obligatory, and the refusal to comply with it is not punishable by law.[13]

In the exercise of their duties, the members of the police force may ask for assistance of house porters (dvorniki) and night watchmen in urban and rural communes. The coöperation of the house porters with the police is carried out as follows: (1) They assist in the detection of all kinds of violation of public order and safety within the limits of the house where they serve, and transfer all the violators to the jurisdiction of the police. (2) They send information to the police in regard to any violation of public order and safety, if they themselves cannot prevent the act. (3) They apply to various medical institutions for first aid for persons who have met with accidents and see that the victims are transferred to hospitals designated by the police or some other institution, but the police must be informed of the action at once. (4) They conduct suspected persons to police headquarters unless an armed convoy is necessary. (5) They take the place of a policeman on his beat should the latter become ill or find it necessary to absent himself in the line of duty. The same duties are imposed upon night watchmen; in addition, they must protect their premises from robbers.

Under certain circumstances the police officers may request coöperation from citizens. Obligatory coöperation on the part of the citizens can be expected (1) when the police is attempting to hold intoxicated persons and rowdies who are resisting; (2) when the services of citizens are needed as witnesses in searches, inquests, and other actions which the police performs in the line of investigation; and (3) when vehicles are commandeered by the police in the exercise of its duties. In all other instances the coöperation of citizens can be expected only as a voluntary action. Persons refusing to coöperate with the police without due cause may be punished.[14]

A member of the police force may use fire arms in the exercise of his duties under the following circumstances: (1) when he is set upon by armed persons or answered with armed opposition in carrying out legal orders; (2) when his life and liberty are threatened by an unarmed person; (3) when assaulted for the purpose of liberating persons in his custody; (4) when attempts are made to take from him property, money, papers, or arms entrusted to him, provided all other means of defense have been exhausted; (5) when it is necessary to defend citizens from violence endangering their lives and general safety, if any other means of protection could not be used; (6) when attempting to prevent illegal appropriation of property, if this act cannot be checked otherwise; (7) when pursuing a criminal who has broken away from his guards, provided he cannot be stopped by other means.[15]

In case of necessity the police may call out the military for coöperation but this recourse may be taken by the civil authorities only under circumstances of disaster approaching a calamity, a counter-revolutionary conspiracy or up-rising, an attempted violent robbery of property and the threatening of public safety (pogroms), and an extreme development of banditism which is threatening to assume calamitous proportions.

The authority to call out the military in ordinary and extraordinary circumstances belongs to the presidents of local executive committees. Under conditions of martial law, when the location is not in the sphere of military activity, the chairman of the military committee (Revkomov) performs this task. The request is directed to the chief of the local garrison, and the military must respond immediately. Upon the arrival of the military the civil authorities explain the situation to them, and after that, in the exercise of their duties, the military act of their own authority. The civil authorities and the police must direct all their demands to the chief of the military unit and not to any detachment or to separate persons.[16]

POLITICAL POLICE

THE STATE POLITICAL ADMINISTRATION (G. P. U.)

Thus far the discussion of the police in the Soviet Union has been confined to the uniformed branch found in every civilized country. The G. P. U.[17] is an institution which is based in part on the old tsarist *Ochrana* and the later Soviet Cheka. These names inspire fear in the average Russian and a feeling of uneasiness in the foreign visitor. Yet when one remembers the Marxian conception of the state as a committee of the ruling class, and considers that the Bolshevik régime came into existence by force and had to wage a terrific struggle against external and internal enemies, the existence of both the Cheka and G. P. U. can be understood without in any way approving of its activities. The Soviet government is a child of revolution, and revolutions have always been cruel and merciless to their old enemies over whom they have triumphed. The Bolshevik apologists for the activities of the Cheka and G. P. U. claim that the very existence of the Soviet state is due to the watchfulness of the Cheka in the past and the G. P. U. at present.

The Creation of the G. P. U.

The ninth All - Russian Congress of Soviets meeting in December 1921, passed among other matters a resolution abolishing the extraordinary commission, commonly known as the "Cheka." This commission was an extraordinary tribunal created in the days of civil war for the purpose of crushing opposition at any price. It spread terror among all classes of people, especially among the members of the former bourgeois and nobility. The Cheka was not subject to any constitutional control. With the coming of more normal times, it was decided to re-organize this fearful institution into the G. P. U. (State Political Administration).[18]

Nominally, this new secret police differs from the old Cheka in that the G. P. U. is under constitutional control. A decree issued on February 8, 1922, abolished the Cheka and instituted a state political administration (G. P. U.) attached to the commissariat of the interior. Departments of the G. P. U. were instituted in the various political subdivisions of the Russian Federation and were under the jurisdiction of the central organ in Moscow. When the Union was formed in 1923, a general provision was made for the legal status of the G. P. U., which stipulated that, for the purpose of combining the revolutionary efforts of the constituent republics in the struggle with political and economic counter-revolution, etc., the O. G. P. U. was to be established in connection with the Council of People's Commissars of the U. S. S. R. The president of the organization was to be a member of the Council with a consulting voice. The central organization was to direct the work of the local organizations through its representatives attached to the councils of people's commissars of the several republics. The procurator of the Union Supreme Court was to supervise the legality of the actions of the O. G. P. U. in accordance with special regulation of the Central Executive Committee of the U. S. S. R.[19]

In practice, the authority which controls the work of this amazing political police is the Polit-bureau[20] and the Central Executive Committee of the Party.[21]

ACTIVITIES OF THE G. P. U.

Arrests by the G. P. U. are regulated by a decree issued on February 6, 1922. The number of the G. P. U. is estimated at 100,000 uniformed men and many thousands in the secret service. Its jurisdiction is extended to all offenses which are considered subversive to the Soviet régime and include in detail counter-revolutionary activity, brigandage, espionage, contraband, crossing of borders without permission, and looting on railroads and waterways. It also assists, as already mentioned, as a censoring board in the matter of publications appearing in the Soviet Union. The official organization finds numerous helpers in the ranks of the Communist Party and other elements of the population who serve as informers.

The G. P. U. may not only arrest but may exile and imprison accused persons without a judicial trial. It may also include in its action the extreme penalty of death, the latter, however, only with the approval of the Central Executive Committee. While no one is immune from the authority of the G. P. U., certain classes of people are endowed with special guarantees in regard to arrest. Members of the Union and All-Russian Central Executive Committees may not be arrested and confined and their premises searched by administrative or judicial orders without special sanction of the respective presidia of the committees. In extraordinary circumstances, the chairmen of the committees may give permission for such action, and report it to the appropriate presidia.[22]

The Soviet régime, having been established on a revolutionary foundation by force, is for that reason extremely sensitive to any opposition. The activity of the G. P. U. is concentrated on the anti-Soviet elements composed of the old aristocracy, the former intelligentsia, private traders, irreconcilable priests of the old church, some socialistic factions which refused to join the Bolsheviks, anarchists, and certain elements of the Communist Party formerly led by the exiled Trotsky.

In the nature of things the work of the G. P. U. is secret, and arrests are usually made late at night. The agents in plain clothes are generally accompanied by uniformed, armed soldiers. The arrests are made with authorized warrants. The agents of the G. P. U. are not beneath setting traps for suspected persons, which usually take the form of stationing operatives on the premises of suspected persons for some days. The G. P. U., whose leaders are tried Bolsheviks, have learned a lesson or two from the tsarist *Ochrana* and have improved on it.

In accordance with the decree on February 1922, the agents of G. P. U. are authorized to undertake arrests, searches, or seizures without special permission of higher authorities in cases of persons caught in the act or within forty-eight hours of having committed a crime. All other arrests, searches, and seizures are only permissable by special authorization of higher organs. The prisoner must be indicted not later than two weeks after arrest. At the expiration of two months after the day of arrest, the G. P. U. must either free the prisoner or ask special permission from the Central Executive Committee for a longer period of detention. This may be granted at the discretion of the Central Committee if circumstances in the case warrant such action; otherwise, the case must be transferred to the courts. The majority of violations in connection with speculation and dereliction of official duties and similar offenses, which were under the jurisdiction of the Cheka, are now transferred to the jurisdiction of revolutionary tribunals or regular courts.

The above decree further provides that, at the discretion of the commissar of justice, all general offenses in connection with illegal acts directed against the Soviet régime, or other violation of the law of the land may be dealt with exclusively by the courts.[23]

Unfortunately the provisions as stated above are not adhered to in practice, and most political cases originating with arrests by the G. P. U. are dealt with administratively and not by regular judicial procedure. Economic cases, on the other hand, are turned over to the courts. The G. P. U. may also exile a person involved in offenses against the state. A sub-committee of the central organ in Moscow, in coöperation with a prosecutor appointed by the Union Central Executive Committee, takes charge of administrative exile. The prosecutor, who is a federal officer, supervises the legality of the action of the G. P. U. and guards the prisoner against illegal action. Any disagreement between the sub-committee and prosecutor is settled by the Union Central Executive Committee.

The organization in the various republics is similar to that of the central organ and is directed by the Union agency. A prosecutor appointed by the central executive committee of the respective republic is in charge of the activity in that state. The local G. P. U. may appeal any disagreement with the local prosecutor to the Union Central Executive Committee. All activity of the local units of the G. P. U. must be reported to the central headquarters in Moscow. The Central Executive Committee is the last resort in any change of sentence. In conclusion, it may be said that the severity of the political police is due, to a great extent, to fear on the part of the present régime of plots hatched in and outside of Russia.[24]

In recent years there have been in Soviet publications complaints of the low educational qualifications of militsiamen. There is also considerable criticism of the character of the police force. In some cities members of the police force had to be disciplined for drunkenness, failure to execute orders, desertion of their posts, discourteous treatment of the public, etc. There is considerable agitation for the increase of salaries and betterment of living conditions in order to attract superior types of men into the service, and in recent legislation passed in 1931 some of these demands have been met. However, with the exceptions of the activities of the G. P. U. as described above, all fair observers and students of Soviet Russia agree that the Soviet police is not more unreasonable than the police the world over. The Bolshevik policeman is certainly no less courteous than the policeman in the United States, and generally speaking, the life of the citizen is as well protected from criminal acts in the Soviet cities as it is in other countries. There is one phase of Russia life, however, which cannot be duplicated in any other country unless it is in Italy or Germany, and that is the insistence on political orthodoxy, which is justified by Bolsheviks as an absolute necessity in a proletarian state, constantly plotted against by internal and external foes. The state in its fight for existence, they argue, must use all means to protect itself. The G. P. U. is a guarantee of safety and when enemies inside and outside of the Soviet Union cease to hatch plots for the destruction of the régime, the G. P. U. will then no longer be necessary.

CHAPTER XVI

SUPERVISION OF ECONOMIC AND SOCIAL LIFE

INDUSTRY, BUSINESS, TRADE, AND AGRICULTURE

As soon as the Bolsheviks established their authority in Russia, they were confronted not only with the task of establishing a government but with the gigantic problem of economic reconstruction. On the one hand the workingmen, under the mistaken idea of liberty, proceeded to interfere with the entire machinery of production by attempting to apply anarchistic, syndicalistic, and other destructive measures in the administration of industry; on the other hand, former owners and technical staffs were obstructing by sabotage the operation of industrial plants. Between 1917 and 1920 the government made superhuman efforts to establish a Communistic dictatorial organization, which eventually eliminated the destructive interference of labor and technical staffs. It furthermore created a highly centralized organization which unified, regulated, and controlled the entire economic life of the country. But the ruling powers seemed to have conceived the idea that the most important task was to create organization; hence organs continued to multiply so that at one time there were fifty-nine administrative organizations in existence, in addition to the National Economic Council. All these bodies set to work producing plans for the economic regeneration of the country, but a great number of the overlapping organizations had to be abolished before progress could be made. By February 1920, 4,273 industrial undertakings, which employed over a million workers, had been nationalized. Over 400 small scale enterprises, employing over a quarter of a million workers, were still to be nationalized. Nearly 3,000 nationalized plants, which were under the immediate control of the National Economic Council and were organized into 179 state trusts, were operating under a centralized financial administration and unified supply of raw

250

materials and fuel. Local organs and provincial economic councils controlled the rest of the nationalized industries, which, however, were subordinate to the uniform policies of the National Economic Council, and had to deliver the products to central distributing depots controlled by the central organization.

On the face of it, the plan was theoretically perfect, but because of the inexperience of workers and technical staffs in mass production and the continued obstructionist practices of the old technicians, the plans put into operation failed to produce results. Moreover, the country was faced with civil war and intervention, which further disrupted the economic life weakened by four years of war and revolution. The consequences were disasterous; consumers' goods disappeared from the markets, and the peasants, unable to obtain manufactured goods from the town, refused to deliver food products, and thus the urban centers were facing starvation. The peasants in their primitive manner retired into their "deaf" villages and lapsed into even a more elementary existence than had been theirs during the tsarist régime. In the nature of things the whole economic experiment of the Bolsheviks was dependent upon the urban industrial centers, but starvation sapped the energy of the workingmen, and it looked as if the new state was to be sunk by the unsocial attitude of the half-savage peasants. Requisitioning and punitive expeditions into the rural districts for the purpose of obtaining hoarded products resulted in sporadic uprisings of the peasants, which were suppressed with a heavy hand. It appeared as if New Russia would perish in a flood of blood as a result of war between city and country.

The Bolshevik leaders, even before the Revolution, were not at all certain of the coöperation of the peasants. When they came to power they fully intended to abolish private property in land, but realizing the impossibility of performing this task at once, they went about the process slowly. Theoretically the land was nationalized; practically, the right of confiscation was delegated to communities of rural soviets, who were responsible to the provincial committee and eventually to the national agricultural committee. These committees, however, were not inclined to act; the land of the great landowners were expropriated by the peasants at the beginning of the Revolution and they meant to keep it. The government, finding itself up against a stone wall of resistance, founded small administrative collegia, composed of from three to five reliable persons, whose task it was to see that governmental decrees in regard to state monopoly of agricultural machinery, the prohibition of private trade in agricultural produce, and the socialization of the land were to be carried out. But the Russian peasant was not willing to give up private holding of land and the right to dispose of the fruits of his labor; hence a long struggle, which will be described later, ensued between the Communistic government and individualistic peasants, and this conflict is still being carrried on. To be sure the government attempted to organize state farms, but they did not at first thrive; later, however, they were more successful, especially after the government succeeded in inducing millions of peasants by fair or foul means to join farm collectives. In the meantime the urban population had to be fed. A period followed which is perhaps one of the most tragic and yet heroic in the annals of the modern world.

A government undertook to feed millions of people, and those who were expected to supply the food refused to give up the life-giving substance. Strict rationing was introduced, under which the former propertied classes suffered unspeakable tortures. By a decree issued on December 15, 1918, the population was to be divided into the following classes: (1) workers, (2) state employees, (3) families of workers and state employees, (4) the armed force, (5) the general civil population, (6) the rural population. The workers and employees, with their families, who were engaged in various industries, transport, and supply were to be considered first, and the principle, "If a man will not work, neither shall he eat", was to be emphasized. On April 30, 1920, a decree was issued which established a new system of rationing based not upon social origin but upon the kind of work one performed. The people's commissariat for food distribution and its organs took charge of the rationing. Food was distributed by these agencies free of charge to the classes entitled to subsistence, which included manual workers, state employees, disabled soldiers and workers, mothers, pregnant women, families of men serving in the Red Army, etc.

This gigantic task necessitated a stringent policy of requisitioning by the government, but the more force the government used, the more obstinate the peasants became; they buried or destroyed their crops. In addition the peasants introduced a policy of passive resistance by abstaining from sowing so that, in some of the most fertile parts of Russia, the areas sown fell to one-fourth of the pre-revolutionary acreage. The continuation of this state of affairs could result only in colossal disaster. In fact, it appeared that nature itself had conspired in the destruction of the suffering people. For in addition to the nearsightedness and stupidity of the peasantry, a terrific drought visited the most fertile parts of the land, and by 1922 a population estimated at nearly forty millions was starving. The passive resistence of the peasants, together with the policy of requisitioning, consecutive crop failure, and abnormal drought, exhausted the grain reserve and brought the country to the brink of despair. The assistance of the American Relief Administration and European labor organizations saved millions from death by starvation, but even at that countless thousands perished. In the wake of famine came epidemics of pestilence and scurvy which took a terrific toll of human lives.

In the face of disaster, civil war, and intervention, the Bolsheviks decided to execute a "retreat" which is commonly known as the *Nep* (New Economic Policy). Lenin, in his characteristic manner, announced at the tenth Congress of the Communist Party meeting in April 1921, that they had made a mistake. He declared that it was apparent socialism could not be introduced into Russia without a transitional period and proceeded at once to suggest measures for the rectification of mistakes which had brought the country to the brink of chaos. In the face of dire necessity theory was forgotten, and for the time being, Russia returned to partial capitalism. In fairness to the working class it must be said that, after years of suffering for the creation of socialism, it showed itself well disciplined when it had to give up everything it had gained by the Revolution, but this change of policy saved Russia.

The *Nep*, in general, authorized the leasing of small enterprises to private persons. The small domestic industries were freed of state control, and only the large industries remained under the control of the government. With the introduction of wages, money was restored as the medium of exchange. A state bank was organized and a budget introduced. Taxes in kind took the place of requisitioning. The decree authorizing the *Nep* provided for free exchange of goods, sale and trade of surplus agricultural products, and a relaxing of the restriction on private trade and manufacture in general. A decree passed by the Council of People's Commissars on May 24, 1921, regulated in detail the exchange, sale, and purchase by individuals and coöperatives of consumers' goods and agricultural products. The new rules provided for the conduct of trade in markets or fairs and other public places, and at counters, stands, and shops. After April 26, 1922, the rules were further relaxed and persons who desired to open private business establishments needed only to register, obtain a business permit from police headquarters indicating where the business was to be conducted, and attach to the application an order from the communal division of the city soviet. The police had no authority to refuse permission and was ordered to issue licenses without unnecessary delay. By an order of the Council of People's Commissars issued October 31, 1924, the conduct of private trade was further regulated, whereby private business could be conducted by citizens in all kinds of goods excepting the trade in certain commodities, such as the articles which were taken out of private circulation, and those that were not subject to an excise tax; food products which were detrimental to health, and did not bear the stamp of inspection, or which were obtained through illegal means,[1] or were prohibited to be sold in designated localities for protection of the native population from business exploitation by private traders.[2]

The regulations further stipulated that the trade in spiritous liquors, in medicines, in hunting arms, in printing presses and printed matter, and the distribution of revolutionary emblems were subject to special restrictions. The supervision of rules governing artisans, private commercial undertakings, and individual traders was placed under the jurisdiction of departments of the various commissariats. Thus the inspection of business was delegated to the commissariat of trade; financial inspection, to the commissariat of finance; sanitary inspection, to the commissariat of health; the technical inspection, to the National Economic Council, the various administrative departments, and the militsia. The administrative organs of the commissariat of the interior had the jurisdiction of the general supervision and execution of rules in regard to the opening and closing hours of business and trade undertakings, weights and measures, prices, and the order of trading in market places and in places of public use. The same department had the authority to issue licenses for any business enterprises which required special permission, and had direct supervision of such commercial establishments.

The local executive committees and presidia of city soviets were authorized to pass special rules in regard to hours and sanitary conditions of trade. The legal provisions in regard to weights and measures were made by the bureau of standards, and were inspected by local branches of that bureau. The militsia was to see that detailed execution of these provisions was faithfully carried out. The prices of goods were regulated by the commissariat of trade, and the militsia was to see that the prices as established by the commissariat were not raised by the traders. A committee elected by all the traders in a particular market was to have supervisory authority over the orderly conduct of business. Since 1927 the issuance of permission to form such committees in urban communes has been transferred from the commissariat of the interior to the presidia of city soviets. The committees were responsible for the sanitary conditions of markets and the carrying out of rules pertaining to them. They coöperated with state authorities in the enforcement of all the rules and regulations passed for the conduct of trade. The general supervision and control of the activities of these market committees were transferred by the new law from the administrative department of the militsia to the agencies of the commissariat of trade. By a decree issued July 14, 1922, the trade in drugs was turned over to coöperative public organizations and private persons. The wholesale trade in drugs by the state, coöperative and public organizations, and private persons was regulated by the commissariat of health in agreement with the commissariat of trade of the R. S. F. S. R. Licenses for this purpose were issued to establishments and individuals who had previously obtained permission for wholesale trade in drugs. The wholesalers, however, were permitted to sell drugs only to health departments, drug stores, hospitals, sanitary organizations, and establishments which had the right to conduct wholesale or retail trade in drugs.

The retail trade in drugs was limited to state and coöperative undertakings which had the right to operate wholesale business, and to certain coöperative organizations situated in localities where there were no drug stores or state stores dispensing sanitary or hygienic products. Coöperative organizations, which were not permitted to trade in drugs by the wholesale but were allowed to operate retail stores in drugs, had to register with the local organs of public health within two weeks after the opening of their business. Other stores were permitted to sell certain drugs which are commonly obtainable without a physician's prescription.

The conduct of business in fire arms and hunting supplies was rigidly limited and allowed only by special permission of the administrative divisions in agreement with the organs of the G. P. U.[3]

Departures From Socialism and Their Consequences

It should not be deduced from the above description that Soviet Russia was permanently re-establishing the individualistic capitalistic system. The concessions made to private trade and industrial enterprises were merely temporary and considered at best a nuisance to be tolerated for a short period to tide over a crisis. It is necessary to remember that, even at the height of private trading, large industrial and commercial undertakings and foreign commerce remained a state monopoly. Between 1929 and 1930, after the government attained considerable success in collectivization of agriculture, certain elements in the Party began to advocate a complete socialization of the economic and social life of the country. From 1930 onward, the private traders have been disappearing. In the following year the Soviet government was able to organize under more favorable conditions its economic life.[4] Any intelligent observer has learned that the Bolsheviks are opportunists, and that while they are committed to ultimate socialization of all resources and production, yet in case of necessity, they do not hesitate to leave the main road of socialism and seek refuge in bypaths. Thus from the very beginning of its existence, the Soviet régime has compromised with petty copitalism whenever circumstances forced it to do so, as at the time of the *Nep* and in later concessions. The most recent deviation took place in the spring and summer 1932, when decrees were issued, legalizing the sale of agricultural products by collectives, the details of which will be discussed later in connection with the agrarian policy of the government. A short time later a decree was passed permitting individual tradesmen and artisans to manufacture whatever they pleased and sell their goods on the open market at their own price. This new departure from the main road is expected to increase the supply of most necessary commodities, such as clothing, cloth, boots, tinware, and hardware. The new great plants were originally intended to supply all the necessary household articles and wearing apparel, but the demand is far exceeding the supply, and hence the government again must call on the individual tailor, cobbler, and tinsmith to supply the goods, which they had for the most part produced before the Revolution and during the *Nep* period.

It is natural that the artisan, who was a few years ago urged and sometimes forced to join coöperatives and large plants, and set to work to produce machine parts for the heavy industries, will hesitate to accept the new proposal, although naturally a great many of them will be tempted by the larger earnings in private trade. In some quarters this new policy is regarded as the resurrection of the *Nep*, but again hasty conclusion must be withheld when one remembers the previous actions of the Soviet government. Moreover, while during the *Nep* period there developed a large class of middlemen, in the present instance, the government itself serves as the middleman. In addition, the new regulations do not authorize the employment of hired labor, and the government has absolute control over the supply of raw materials which the artisans will need in their work. In conclusion it may be said that, in the present departure from socialism as in the past, the Soviet government is simply making use of the tools of capitalism to meet an emergency, and that as soon as the emergency is passed, the government will not hesitate to crush all individualistic production and return to the main road of communistic endeavor.

Agrarian Policy

BEFORE THE REVOLUTION

The history of the Russian peasant is a chronicle of want and privation extending over many centuries. From the earliest times onward, the peasant had to fight not only the vicissitudes of natural conditions but also the steadily encircling force of the powerful landlord, who sought to enslave him and eventually succeeded in doing so. In order to escape from the clutches of serfdom, many of the more courageous and adventurous peasants took refuge beyond the settled pale of the established communes into the wilderness and there mixed with Tartar nomads. These groups of rebels eventually formed communes of their own on the Don, the Dneper, and the Volga, which later became known as Cossack settlements. These warriors did not hesitate to attack the estates of their erstwhile lords and masters. Later on, ironically enough, after coming to terms with the tsarist government they were the main props of the autocracy, and are remembered as the most bloody suppressors of peasant uprisings. From the sixteenth century onward, revolts of serfs destroyed life and property in a horror inspiring manner, but these uprisings were in turn suppressed with utmost cruelty. By the beginning of the eighteenth century, the Russian upper classes had acquired some superficial Western European polish and succeeded in uniting themselves into a cohesive group loyal to the sovereign, but became more dangerous to the welfare of the mass of peasants, by this time completely enserfed. The very existence of the serf was at the mercy of the noble landlord; cruelty and torture were within the jurisdiction of the lord, who was the supreme master and was not held responsible for any acts of oppression, even death. The serf had no recourse to higher authorities, and complaints of ill treatment were punished by flogging and exile to Siberia. These conditions continued with some mitigation until the middle of the nineteenth century. In 1861 the private serfs were given their personal freedom and "the right of bondage over the peasants settled upon landlords' estates and over the courtyard people, is forever abolished." Theoretically the statute of emancipation of February 19, 1861, provided not only for personal freedom of the millions of serfs, but also for the grant of land. In reality the law in this connection was so muddled that no one could interpret it. While the government was reluctant to create a large landless peasant class, yet it was unwilling to touch the estates of the landlords. In consequence, one group of liberated serfs, the so-called household serfs, were forced to seek employment in towns or engage in the uncertain occupations of farm hands. All other serfs were given the opportunity to buy from the masters, at a set price, the huts which they occupied and a very small allotment of land, frequently of the lowest grade. The law did not make it obligatory for the landlords to sell the land, but whenever the masters were willing to sell, the government furnished four-fifths of the purchase price, on condition that the serfs provided the remainder. The peasants were to return the loan in installments during a period of forty-nine years. It is not to be understood, however, that the individual ex-serfs became landowners. The government was careful in this transaction not to turn the land over to the individual peasants but to a village *mir* (Commune) upon whom was imposed collective responsibility for the payment of redemption installments and taxes. The *mir* redistributed the land as occasion arose, but in doing so reverted to the primitive custom of assigning land not in single plots but in strips of varied quality, and this practice, of course, stood in the way of agricultural progress. In fact the Russian peasant, because of such a policy, remained as primitive in his methods as his ancestors in the dim past. A peasant could "buy" himself out of the commune upon payment of his share of indebtedness and other duties. These archaic methods were continued until the peasant disturbances of 1905. The government, after a half century of muddling and temporizing, decided to pass a law permitting individual peasants to separate themselves from the community, and take possession of the amount of land received at the last redistribution without special payment to the *mir*.

Generally the entire distribution of land to the freed serfs was unfair, and was bound to create continuous dissatisfaction and ferment and to end in disaster. The so-called agrarian reforms of 1906-1910 were typical of all tsarist reforms, in that no sooner was a measure undertaken to ameliorate conditions, economic or political, than it was sidetracked for fear that the people might actually be benefited at even a very slight expense of the small privileged groups. In the years following the emancipation, small numbers of peasants, by shrewd trading and terrific exploitation of their families whom they worked like slaves, succeeded in acquiring some capital for the purchase of additional land. This class came to be known as kulaks (fists). A less prosperous group worked itself up to the middle status, but the majority of the peasant class was "poor," probably the least favored of any agricultural class in the civilized world. The standard of living of the average Russian peasant was a little above that of his savage ancestors.

To add to his troubles, the peasant was prolific, and therefore the land holding between 1861 and 1917 of the average *moujik* was further reduced. Thus on the eve of the Revolution the peasant, outside of the small kulak group, was confronted by lack of land and was on the verge of starvation, not infrequently being obliged to mix tree bark with flour for his sustenance. It must not be forgotten, however, that this situation was not due to a natural "land hunger," since Russia possessed a tremendous agricultural area, but developed because most of the best land was in possession of the nobility, the imperial family, and the church. The reader should not, therefore, pass too harsh judgment on the following events, remembering that not only were the majority of the Russian people kept in serfdom for many centuries, but when they were freed, they were not supplied with sufficient land to support themselves, and the pitifully small allotments bought by them from their former masters were obtained at prices far exceeding their real worth.[5]

UNDER THE BOLSHEVIKS

The March Revolution did not settle the land question; the Provisional Government, weak and fearful, announced that the land was to belong to those who actually tilled it, but left the decision to the Constituent Assembly. When after several postponements this body was finally convened, the Bolsheviks had already overthrown the Provisional Government, and the Assembly was duly dispersed by the new authority. The Bolsheviks coming into power nationalized the land in the first days of their rule, but this action, as will be shown, remained largely on paper. The peasant, with the first news of the March Revolution, proceeded to expropriate the great estates of the nobility and the holdings of the richer peasants. The newly acquired land was divided among the peasants and their children, and by the time the Bolsheviks took charge of affairs in November 1917, little remained of landlord estates outside of a few million acres of land, which the Soviet government converted into state farms. These above happenings, however, were far from satisfactory to the new government, which did not mean to create an economic system based on a large conservative group of small backward landowners. It hoped to transform a primitive agricultural community into a modern industrial country, and this could not be accomplished if the peasants were to be permitted to settle down to a backward agricultural life, which would not enable them to purchase machinery or engage in mass production. It was furthermore the opinion of Lenin and his followers that only by a planned economy could Russia be rescued from the stagnation of the middle ages. This planned economy, however, involved the absolute control by the government of all resources and means of production of the country. When in 1920, Lenin began to think seriously of the electrification of the country, the State Planning Commission (Gosplan) was delegated to collect, examine, and correlate data for this purpose. As a result of its work, this body brought out a preliminary draft for a Five Year Plan to cover the period of 1927-1932. After the draft underwent numerous corrections and amendments, it was adopted as a basis for the Five Year Plan to begin October 1, 1928, and to be completed September 30, 1933. A detailed explanation of this most difficult undertaking need not be given here, but it should be stated that the plan made provision for the development of every phase of national economy which, of course, included agriculture. If the Bolsheviks were to carry out the plan, they had to be reasonably certain of agricultural production, and this could not be when the industry was in charge of millions of individual proprietors, whose main purpose was personal gain. This then very briefly constitutes the Bolshevik agrarian problem, and it is no exaggeration to state that the success of the Communist experiment depends on the satisfactory solution of this question. This should be kept in mind as the description of the Bolshevik agrarian policy is given.

The Communist Party was committed to coöperative agriculture, but this in itself was not new to Russia. As far back as 1910 there were 27,000 agricultural coöperatives in Russia of all forms and degrees.[6] Since 1921, however, there have developed in Russia various types of coöperatives, the most important of which are (1) Agricultural Associations, (Tovarishtestvo), (2) the *Artel,* and (3) the Commune. An agricultural association is merely an organization for the purpose of increasing the yield of the land, by means of pooling the work in the cultivation of the land and by the joint use of all machinery and draft animals of the members of the association. The association secures credit, manages the marketing of the products of the members of the association, and furnishes the individual member with agricultural information. The land, machinery, and draft animals are not absorbed by the association but remain the property of individual members. The members of the *artel* on the other hand pool all their resources such as land, agricultural machinery, and draft animals, but retain individual possession of their homes, small domestic animals, and fowls. In the commune, which the Bolsheviks favored, the members are required to pool all their resources, inclusive of homes, the members sharing everything in common through a system of communal kitchens, dining rooms, nurseries, laundries, etc. The peasant, being an individualist, was not inclined to join a commune, and if he joined a collective at all, he preferred the association or artel type.

There is one more form of socialized farming necessary to mention, and that is the state farm (Sovchoz). These farms were established in 1917 by the government on the land seized from the landowners. They are owned and operated by the state. They were intended to serve as experimental stations and models of large scale farming organizations, and to supply information of a cultural and agricultural nature. Unfortunately for the Bolsheviks, these state farms were far from being model after 1921; this was, however, on account of general disorganization of the country. The rest of the collective farms were lost in the mass of individual holdings, as collectivization in the early years of the Bolshevik régime could not be carried out on account of intervention, civil war, and other disrupting factors. The peasants were left their individual holdings, and the grain necessary for the sustenance of life in cities and towns had to be collected by requisition. The coming of the *Nep,* which was after all a compromise with the capitalistic tendencies of the trader instinct in the peasant, retarded whatever collectivistic development there might have been found among the rural population. In the years between 1921-1927 the class of peasants commonly called kulaks became prosperous by controlling agricultural production; collectivization on the other hand was at a standstill. By 1927 the supply of agricultural products reached such a low level as to actually threaten the very existence of the state. The industrial workers were living on starvation rations, and there was no way open to bring about an increase of production, if the old Russian system of primitive individualism was to be continued. The government was in a desperate position. In the Party councils various plans were advanced, the most notable one by Trotzky, who advised an energetic collectivization campaign and the ruthless suppression of the kulaks. Stalin, however, whether for reasons of personal jealousy or honest conviction, opposed the plan and suggested a substitute for it, a program which called for encouragement of coöperative farming and a control of the activities of the kulaks. It will be seen presently that eventually Stalin had to give up his program and turn to the policy of his enemy, Trotzky. The adoption of the Five Year Plan, which among other things provided for expansion of collective farming and to some extent the improvement of individual farming methods, brought with it also a terrific repression of kulaks by every means available to the ruling powers. This brought criticism of the *right* opposition, who claimed that it was feudal in its nature and detrimental to the increase of agricultural products. Stalin, however, had the Party behind him and succeeded in retaining his position and leadership.

The fifteenth Congress of the Communist Party, meeting in 1928, gave Stalin full support and adopted his program, which consisted of an endeavor to increase the agricultural production and encourage socialized agriculture, both state and collective, at the expense of individual farming. For the purpose of carrying out this program, two policies were adopted, namely, (1) the development of the socialized sector of agriculture by 1933 so that its production would equal and, if possible, exceed the production of the "upper section" of individual farmers in 1928; (2) and a provision for the betterment of individual farms by the introduction of modern agricultural machinery, improvement of methods of farming, and the supplying of better seeds and fertilizers. The increase in production of agricultural products was not only to supply the domestic needs but was to create a surplus for export, and at the same time the government was to be freed from dependence on the upper strata of individual farmers, and thus the way would open for a decisive struggle against the kulaks.

Even before the fifteenth Congress collectivization was advancing, but by 1929 there was a notable increase of collective farms. While in 1927 there were 15,670 collective farms with a population of 1,000,000, in 1929 there were 61,000 collective farms with a population of 4,680,000. Soon after the fifteenth Congress there began a concerted attack on the kulaks, who, realizing that collectivization would mean their extinction, proceeded by every means, fair and foul, to stave off the disaster, and attempted to dissuade the poor and middle peasant from joining collectives. Failing in this, they engaged in murder and arson, and thus the "class" war was in full swing in the villages. The government responded with severe repressions, and in 1928 deprived the kulaks of their franchise. This was followed by other legislation which discriminated against them as far as division and utilization of land were concerned.

On February 20, 1929, a law was passed establishing the single agricultural tax which, when applied to the kulaks, was very burdensome. Stalin, after scoring a smashing victory over the *right* opposition who opposed the treatment of the kulaks, proceeded to issue orders (through the proper agencies) for the complete liquidation of the kulak class. The village authorities were ordered to consider the liquidation of the kulaks as part of their work in the process of collectivization. "Shock brigades" of workers commandeered from industrial centers proceeded, together with the local authorities, to collectivize farms within given sections. The result was that "class" war in the village became intense. The land and machinery of the kulaks, however, were confiscated and they were deprived of the right to rent land; in addition they were not permitted to enter into the newly formed collectives which had taken over their property. The kulaks, enraged, began to slaughter their cattle in preference to delivering them to collectives, to murder Soviet officials, and set fire to Soviet properties. Since the kulaks could not join collectives, it was suggested that they be sent to the lumber camps of Siberia and Northern Russia. As on previous occasions, the rank and file of the Party who went out to execute the commands of the central authorities permitted enthusiasm to run away with their better sense, and unfortunately there was no Lenin to call them back to rational action. Although individual party men deplored the hardship of the individual kulak, and the intimidated opposition attempted to criticize the actions of the Party, yet as a whole the Communists approved of this policy. By March 1, 1930, nearly 55 per cent of the peasant holdings had been collectivized, but at a terrific price. The countryside was demoralized to the extent that dissatisfaction was created not only among the chief sufferers of this policy but also among the middle and poor peasants. If the government intended by collectivization of the farmer to create a "link" between the peasant and the urban proletariat, it was surely using a wrong method. If anything, the peasants' antagonism was aroused against the Soviets and all their agents, and this was true not only of the kulak element but also of some of the more prosperous classes of peasants. In addition, local authorities, vying with one another in the work of collectivization, actually attempted to promote this policy in remote and wholly unprepared sections of the country. Failing to accomplish this, they frequently created "paper collectives", which had not actual existence. Stalin, by that time, became alarmed at the danger which such a policy might bring to the Soviet state, and in an article published in the *Moscow Izvestia* March 1930, he issued a warning to his co-workers, and proclaimed among other things the now famous phrase "Dizziness from Success." He stated that in their behaviour some of the Party members were playing into the hands of the enemies of the Communist régime. He called a halt to further extreme collectivization, and condemned "paper collectives" and the carrying out of the collectivization policy by intimidation and military force. At the request of the Central Committee of the Communist Party, Stalin issued ten propositions to *Comrade-Collecti-vists* on April 3, 1930, in which he gave an analysis of the mistakes of over-enthusiastic Communist village workers. He decried the repressive measures used against the middle peasants, who had often been mistaken for kulaks. Stalin did not deny that "repression is necessary and useful in the struggle against our class enemies; it is dangerous and forbidden with respect to the middle peasant who is our ally." He reminded the local Communist authorities of Lenin's injunction, that the collectives can only become permanent when they are voluntary; hence, forced collectivization can be at best only temporary, without practical lasting results. Some of the peasants, after Stalin published his "Dizziness from Success", began to with draw from the collectives. These, he warned, were acting against their best interests, for only in collective farming would the peasant find deliverance from poverty and ignorance. It is not to be understood that the Soviet government abandoned the fight on the kulaks; this was, as Stalin stated, merely an interval or breathing spell in order that the forces might be consolidated for a renewed struggle in the village. As was stated before, Stalin was facing opposition from factions in the Party, yet on March 15, 1930, the Central Committee of the Communist Party issued a decree which was in line with Stalin's analysis of the agrarian situation. The decree forbade the departure from the party policy in the collectivization movement. Among other things it instructed local party organizations to refrain from applying force in the establishment of collectives, and it forbade the transformation of an artel into a commune, without approval of higher authorities, and the compulsory socialization of homes, livestock, and poultry. The decree instructed that a revision be made of the lists of persons who had been deprived of their lands and franchises, prohibited the practice of closing local markets, and granted permission to individual peasants and members of collectives to sell their produce in the open market. The decree ordered the discontinuance of the practice, incidental to collectivization, of closing churches without a special request of the majority of the village population, and ordered the replacement of all officials and party workers who were not willing or able to carry out the exact party provisions.[7]

The New Collectives

The action of the government, however, was not merely negative, for even before the work of collectivization was slowed down, the Central Committee of the Communist Party issued a decree on January 6, 1930, ordering the commissariat of agriculture to prepare a model charter for the organization of collective farms of the artel type. Accordingly on March 2, 1930, the government published a charter[8] which provided for the organization of collective farms of peasants voluntarily united who, "by combining means of production and labor, would establish a large collective farm, and thus guarantee a real and final victory over the kulaks, over all exploiters and enemies of the workers, over need and ignorance, and over the backwardness of the small individual farmer, and thus create a high productivity of labor and establish a marketable surplus." Under the model charter, land, agricultural machinery, draft animals, farm buildings, and seed reserves are socialized. The houses of the members, sheep, swine, and implements necessary for work in gardens and orchards are exempt from socialization and remain individual property.

QUALIFICATION FOR MEMBERSHIP

Working persons who have reached the age of sixteen are eligible to enter an artel. Kulaks, priests, former members of the bourgeoisie, gentry, and other members of the disfranchised classes are barred from membership of the artel; exceptions, however, may be made in cases of families who have members serving in the Soviet armed forces, or as village teachers. The initial fee for entering an artel is a cash payment of from two to ten per cent of the value of property, both socialized and individual. This fee may be returned when a member leaves the artel, although the land remains the property of the artel. Former members of the artel, however, may apply for an allotment of land from unoccupied state land reserves, depending on the availability of land. One-quarter to one-half of the value of the socialized property is set aside as a reserve fund, which may not be divided, to be used for various purposes of improvement and extension of the artel.

The Administration of the Artel

The administration of the artel is vested in the general meeting of the members, and in an executive council elected annually. The executive council apportions work among the members of the artel, of both a managerial and productive nature. The members of the organization are entitled to receive, in the course of the year, an advance of their earnings, in kind or cash not to exceed 50 per cent of the amount earned by them. The final settlement is to be made at the end of each fiscal year. In accordance with the provisions of the model charter, each artel is to become a member of the Union of Agricultural Collectives (Kolchozcenter), and must deliver its marketable produce to designated state organizations and coöperatives. The state and coöperatives in return supply to the artel such necessary implements and goods as tractors and other farm machinery and manufactured goods. They also extend credits to the artel and supply them with technical advice and assistance. The government, anxious for the development of collectives, extended to them privileges not accorded to individual peasants. Thus the individual tax law of February 23, 1930, repealed the provision in the regard to progressive taxation as far as collectives were concerned. It furthermore differentiated between various types of collectives, in such a way as to tax the commune collective at the lowest rate. In April 1930 the government issued a decree exempting for two years from the single agricultural tax all collectives in which draft animals and other inventory were socialized, and freeing from taxation all socialized draft animals and all livestock and fowls, both socialized and those remaining in individual possession of members of collectives. The individual farmer, whose eventual collectivization the government was planning, also benefited by the new legislation, since he was still necessary at this stage of agrarian economy. The tax law of February 25, 1930, provided for the exemption of all land sown in excess of the acreage of the foregoing year. In case, however, a peasant should decrease the sown area without good reason, a tax would be levied on a sown acreage equal to the previous year, and the land which was left unsown was to be turned over to the original owner. Many peasants, who mistook the retreat of the government for weakness, failed to take advantage of the privilege offered him and reduced the sown area considerably. This was true of the peasants who had not joined the collectives and those who had left the collectives, but the government was in dead earnest and hence declared on April 12, 1930, that the tax laws of February 25, 1930, would be enforced, but at the same time directed members of collectives to assist individual peasants after completing their own work.

The Soviet government realized that its very existence depended on a solution of its agricultural problem, and therefore it distributed during the years 1929-1930 nearly a billion and one-half of rubles in investments and credits among various farm organizations and individual peasants. In return the government expected a supply of agricultural products to feed its urban population and an exportable surplus. To that end it has in recent years inaugurated a policy of contracting with collective farms and individual peasants for the delivery of produce. The grain contracted for is to be turned over after the harvest to grain coöperatives, which in turn are to deliver it to the Central Agency (Soyuzchleb) for storing and milling. The population receives its flour and bread from the consumers' coöperatives. The government encourages individual farmers to form coöperatives for the delivery of the grain to the state agencies, and hopes in this way to create a desire in independent peasants to join a collective for production.

The New Departure

The procurement of grain was conducted by the Soviet government in the aforementioned manner until May 1932, when the Communist again beat a tactical retreat and legalized the sale of agricultural products by collectives. Under the new law the peasants, both members of collectives and individual farmers, are allowed to retain a large part of their harvest and sell it at the open market for what it may bring. For this purpose the government has requested local communities to supply market facilities, lodgings, dining rooms, and other necessary accommodations for the peasants who come to town to dispose of their produce. This seeming return to *Nep* policies was necessitated by a scarcity of food in many parts of the Union, which could not be attributed so much to a bad harvest as to the faults in the machinery of government procurement. Furthermore under the old system the peasants, who were required to give up all their grain supplies to the state soon after the harvest at a fixed price, usually a low one, found themselves frequently without bread later in the year, and had to buy at a high price wherever they could. Frequently zealous young Communists in their enthusiasm would collect all the reserves of grain, so that the peasant was left no seed for the next sowing season. When they were supplied seed by the government, a large part of it had to be used for food. In addition, young zealots and the individual farmers, who were anxious to fulfill the plan of procurement, required the collective to sell to the state every available ton of produce, with no regard for the peasant's need of food for himself and his livestock. The policy brought disastrous results. Under the May law the peasant is able to sell all surplus on the open market, although the amount of produce sold to the government will be made at the usual fixed price. This policy, however, is merely temporary, and no doubt as soon as the Bolshevik leaders deem the time ripe, they will return to the road of communism.[9]

CHAPTER XVII

LABOR LEGISLATION

It is not the purpose of this treatise to discuss the conditions of labor in the Soviet Union in detail, yet for the sake of coherence it is perhaps necessary to indicate in general terms the conditions of free labor, since of late many contradictory reports have been current on this important subject. In the chaotic days following the Bolshevik Revolution, in the stress and strain of counter-revolution and civil war, labor was called upon to make many sacrifices. The commissar of labor of the R. S. F. S. R. speaking before the fifth Congress of Labor Unions in September 1922, admitted that in those dangerous and tragic days the assignment of work was conducted in arbitrary fashion; the workers' preferences were not consulted. With the coming of more normal times and the inauguration of the *Nep*, the conditions of labor improved. In the R. S. F. S. R. a Labor Code was adopted in November 1922. The Union, despite the power conferred upon it, has not up to the time of this writing availed itself of this right. Each constituent republic has its own labor code which is, however, modeled after the Code of the R. S. F. S. R. For all practical purposes then the Code of the Russian Republic is also the Code of the Union. In fact, it was made so by a resolution of the Union Central Executive Committee on July 13, 1933. To be sure, by decisions of the Central Committee of the Communist Party and the Central Union of Professional Unions, new projects of labor legislation are being considered.

A discussion of the provisions of the Bolshevik Labor Code is better understood if one keeps in mind that the standard of living of the Russian worker was the lowest in Europe. The average worker had no decent place to live; in the small urban centers the workers lived in mud hovels, and in the large cities, even in the two capitals, many workers could not afford to rent living space, but slept on benches and tables in the workshops. Others, more affluent, rented "sleeping corners" in crowded rooms occupied in common by men, women, and children. Some rooms were shared by as many as twelve people of both sexes and various ages. The census of 1912 lists 300,000 such corners in Moscow, and in other large cities the conditions were not any better. In the years 1911-1913, 27.3 per cent of all babies born of the lower classes died in infancy. Other conditions, both economic, and social, were equally bad. Such was the state of affairs that the new government inherited, and although the present régime has many glaring faults, yet at least it attempts to eradicate harmful conditions and create better ones. A study of the Labor Code leaves the impression that it is a carefully planned document. It contains provisions relative to wages, standards of output, rest periods, treatment of working women and minors, the prevention of industrial accidents, etc. It also forbids the transfer of workers from one enterprise to another or from one locality to another without their consent. Chapter 15 of this Code, devoted to labor unions, recognizes them as representatives of the workers, and specifies the general duties of the unions to consist of (1) the making of collective agreements as representatives of the workers; (2) the election of labor inspectors; and (3) representation of the workers through the medium of the factory committee, or by an authorized delegate of the union instead of the committee.

It further describes the duties of the trade unions in connection with the enforcement of labor legislation as follows:

1. They decide, in agreement with the commissariat of labor, the order in which unemployed workers are to be referred to employment.

2. They determine the period of validity of collective agreements.

3. They may terminate any labor agreement between employer and employee.

4. They coöperate in drawing up rules of employment.

5. They fix standards of output in agreement with the management.

6. They determine the remuneration for work, if wages have not been fixed by agreement.

7. They must approve any refusal of leave to workers.

8. They take part in specifying the groups of workers who may be exempted from the eight-hour day.

9. They approve overtime work and the number of hours of overtime in excess of the hours fixed by law.

10. They assist in fixing a weekly rest day and annual holidays and in specifying the undertakings in which work must be carried on uninterruptedly, even on rest days and holidays.

11. They coöperate in drawing up a list of specially strenuous and unhealthful occupations and of the maximum weights which may be carried.

12. They coöperate in fixing the period of apprenticeship and the number of apprentices allowed in each undertaking.

13. They regulate night work for women.

14. They coöperate in fixing the minimum number of minors to be employed in the various branches of industry.

15. They assist in issuing regulations in regard to night work.

16. They visit all workshops, departments, and laboratories through the members of factory committees or their authorized delegates.

It is the particular duty of the trade unions, through the medium of the factory committee (a) to watch over the strict observance by the management of the legal standards for the protection of the workers, social insurance, the payment of wages, hygiene, safety, the prevention of accidents, etc., and to collaborate with the public authorities in the protection of labor; (b) to take steps to improve the cultural and material position of the workers.[1]

The Code recognizes two types of collective contracts: (1) the general contract, which embraces an entire branch of industry within the territory of a constituent republic, and (2) a local contract, which can be entered into only in the absence of a general contract, or under provisions contained in a general contract. In addition to the two major types of contracts, the Code also refers to "contracts of work" or individual written agreements entered into between the employer and employee, under which the latter agrees to place his labor at the disposal of the former for a certain remuneration. The terms of the individual contract, however, must not be less favorable than the collective agreement of a similar trade. The Code provides for settlement of disputes by "wage appraisal and dispute committees," "arbitration courts," and "ordinary people's courts" sitting in special labor sessions. Labor unions are always represented in these tribunals. The Code makes provision for labor exchanges which are agencies of the commissariat of labor. Originally all employees were to be hired exclusively through these agencies, but in 1925 this provision was modified and now hiring "at the gate" is permitted. Until recently freedom of action of the workers in the Soviet Union depended upon the policies of the labor exchanges. These exchanges, through which the workers obtained employment, were the organs of the Union commissariat of labor. This control has been, of course, eliminated since the enterprises have been permitted to hire labor "at the gate." The labor unions stand between the workers and employees and are a very important factor in the economic system of the country. The law empowers the commissariat of labor (1) to regulate labor markets and agencies for employment of labor, the manner in which labor is to be recruited and transferred, and the means by which agricultural laborers in masses or in groups are to be directed to seasonal work outside of the village; (2) to determine jointly with the Union Central Council of Labor Unions the manner in which specialists are to be registered; (3) to regulate wages and administer the enforcement of its own schedule of minimum wage scale; (4) to determine the wages and personal allowances of the workers of state institutions and enterprises of the country; (5) to issue certain regulations in regard to registration of collective contracts and the manner in which various organs for the settlement of labor disputes are to be created; (6) to assist in the elimination of unemployment and lend its coöperation in the erection of workers' dwellings, the "rationalization of labor utilizations," the regulation of social insurance, etc.; (7) to direct and supervise the activity of the commissariats of labor of the constituent republics.[2]

Refusal of Employment and Its Consequences

Workers were frequently found to refuse employment for various reasons, preferring to depend on the unemployment dole. In order to eliminate this condition the law provides a penalty for a worker (1) who refuses employment in a trade in which he is skilled as a specialist, because the wage is lower than that he received previously in a similar position; (2) who refuses to accept temporary employment in a trade in which he is unskilled and rejects employment of a nature in which he is not skilled, even though for an extended period of time there has been no demand for workers in his own trade; (3) who if unskilled, refuses work which his physical condition renders him fit to perform; (4) who, without a family or with a family of not more than two persons, rejects permanent employment of a nature in which he is skilled in a locality other than his permanent residence; (5) or who refuses to participate in public works organized by labor exchanges, or to undergo a training period for a particular trade. The law provides that the names of persons guilty of these offenses are to be removed from the register of the labor exchanges and such workers are not to be permitted to register at a labor exchange for a period to be determined by the labor exchange committee. These persons are furthermore deprived of their unemployment payments and this action is to be entered upon their union cards.

Obligatory Free Labor

The statement is frequently made that there is no free labor in the Soviet Union. It is further stated that certain provisions of the Labor Code, though appearing reasonable, have been at times interpreted in a way that practically enslaves free labor. The provision in question reads as follows: "In exceptional contingencies (struggle against calamities caused by the elements, lack of men for the performance of work important to the state) all citizens of the R. S. F. S. R., with the exceptions stipulated in Articles XIII and XIV, shall be liable to be called upon to perform obligatory labor service in conformity with special resolutions to be issued by the Council of People's Commissars, or by other organs authorized to do so by the said Council." No fault can be found with the wording of this provision, as some such stipulations are to be found on the statute books of all civilized countries. It is true that the interpretation of this Article frequently results in coercion of free labor not to be found in other countries, but it is to be remembered that certain conditions exist in Soviet Russia which are not to be found anywhere else. Between 1929-1931 the productive machinery of the Soviet Union was laboring under the terrific strain of the Five Year Plan. The shortage of labor, poor living conditions, and the natural slothfulness of the Russian workingman have been interfering with the carrying out of the Five Year Plan, the success of which was to determine the very existence of the present order. The Bolshevik leaders, in their desperate effort to carry out succssfully their plans, have at times ignored the human quality of labor, and have adopted tactics which to the outsider were nothing short of the abolition of free labor. Means were employed, at variance with the conceptions of free labor, which will be discussed presently. The commissar of labor, speaking before the Central Executive Committee of the U. S. S. R. on January 1931, stated that the "labor exchanges with their former functions must be considered antiquated in the face of the needs of the present moment; the labor exchanges are now confronted with absolutely new tasks....the labor exchanges having been reorganized into management boards for the preparing and training of labor forces, into headquarters, as it were, for opening up sources of labor and distributing it in a plan-governed way....are to attend to new tasks, to questions of organizing labor at the producing concerns, to questions of plan-governed distribution of labor, and to the opening up of new sources of labor man power in the towns as well as in the villages."[3]

About the same time the commissar of labor of the R. S. F. S. R. declared that it was necessary to bring about "a radical remodeling of the entire system of work in the sphere of procuring labor man power and utilizing it," and "the task is, that from a mere passive regulation of the labor market, we must go over to the system of its active organization, the object being to draw the entire labor man power employed, into the orbit of plan devising and regulation work, on the basis of its most suitable utilization and distribution. I think that the difficulties which are experienced at present in regard to labor man power should prove only an impetus and a stimulus. . . . in the matter of bringing out those latent reserves of labor man power, which we actually have in sufficient numbers."

In accordance with the above utterances the government proceeded to carry out a campaign for labor recruiting. For the purpose of examination of methods employed by the government in planned distribution of labor, the workers may be conveniently divided into three main groups: (1) workers engaged in free labor, that is, workers performing tasks not assigned to them in accordance with obligatory labor provisions (Article XI), or by sentence imposed by courts or administrative organs; (2) workers performing tasks in accordance with obligatory labor provisions of the Labor Code; and (3) workers performing tasks of a compulsory nature, in accordance with sentence imposed upon them by courts or administrative organs. (In this connection only free labor will be discussed as it is affected by Article XI of the Labor Code. The other two groups are dealt with in another place.)

Since the entire economic life in the Soviet Union is monopolized by the state or coöperative organizations,[4] the available places of employment in the Soviet Union may be classified as follows:

1. The apparatus of the Communist Party, the government, the labor unions, the coöperative, and other public organizations, which altogether employ approximately 4,000,000 persons.

2. Industrial (non - seasonal) transport and communication enterprises, which are in most instances state owned and are operated by state trusts subordinate to various commissariats; persons therefore, employed by them, about 8,000,000 in number, may be in a sense considered state employees, although not a part of the actual machinery of government.

3. Seasonal industries, such as timbering, fishing, peat gathering, the building and construction trades, sowing and harvesting; these industries employed in 1930, 6,000,000 persons, and the plan for 1931 called for 10,000,000 workmen.

4. Agriculture: (a) employees in state farms (sovchozy), who number about 1,400,000; (b) members of collective farms, who

were estimated at 40,000,000 in 1930;—in the last two years, as already mentioned, the government has made extreme efforts to increase the number of collective farms under the centralized authority of the Collective Farm Center (Kolchozcenter); (c) farm hands and laborers employed by individual peasants numbering about 1,000,000 persons;—this class is for the most part extinct, since the "liquidation" of the kulak class and their absorption in the collective farm system; (d) the extremely poor peasants, (bedniaki);—this class has been absorbed by the collectives but in the year 1930 this group constituted 35 per cent of the peasant population; (f) middle peasants (seriadniki) who constituted the bulk of the Russian peasant class;—a great percentage of them has also been absorbed by the collectives; and (e) the wealthier peasants;—this class has been destroyed by liquidation and their number is unknown.[5]

In recent years there has been an increasing demand for skilled and semi-skilled labor in establishments using machinery. The peasant has always in the past served as the reserve labor supply in Russia. Hundreds of thousands flocked to the cities and industrial centers, where they swelled the population of the poor quarters and tended to hold down wages and living standards. Various factors have contributed to the development of an acute labor shortage in recent times. Poor food and living conditions in industrial centers have slowed down the flow of the peasantry into the cities; the great enlargement of the timber industry and the development of construction in remote places have diverted many of this element to those enterprises; collective farms have retained groups of peasants which formerly supplied the needed labor in industries; and the tendency to wander from place to place in search of better living and working conditions has added to the scarcity of man power. In order to overcome this handicap that interfered with the carrying out of the Five Year Plan, the government has undertaken the gigantic task of a systematic distribution of labor. In carrying out this undertaking it has employed such methods as declaring a suspension of the unemployment dole; abolishing of employment agencies and establishing in their places labor offices under the jurisdiction of the commissariat of labor, which were charged with registration, training, and distribution of workers, and the strengthening of discipline in the various industries. In general then the distribution of labor in the Soviet Union is regulated by the stipulation that follows: workers must be selected from the list of those registered in the labor offices, with the exception of administrative workers and specialists whose assignments are arranged by special agencies of the government. This also covers farm hands and apprentices.

The following groups may be registered upon the lists in the labor offices:

I. Labor union members.

II. The following non-members:

1. Children of laborers and minors from children's homes, even though they have never worked for hire.

2. Government employees and soldiers, wives, divorced wives, and widows of laborers.

3. Students, though they have never before worked for hire, and others members of the same category.

4. Laborers and government employees who have not worked for some time.

5. Demobilized soldiers, provided they appear within one year after mobilization.

6. Labor and war invalids fit for certain types of work.

7. Workers in production, and coöperatives who have been employed in workshops and enterprises of the coöperatives for at least three years, provided they apply six months after leaving the coöperative.

8. Children of workers in production, coöperative organizations, and individual handicraft workers.

9. Farm labor hands and poor peasants.

10. Collective farmers.

11. Inventors.

12. Ex-convicts belonging to the labor class prior to the sentence, who apply for work within six months after the expiration of their term of imprisonment.

13. Employed persons who are not working at their specialty and who wish to be transferred to their particular line.[6]

Persons in the categories above mentioned were to register at labor offices located nearest their permanent residences. Collective farmers were to register at the headquarters of the collective farms. The dispatch of workers registered at labor offices to places of employment had to take place within three days. The demobilized Red Army soldiers had to be dispatched to work on the day of registration. Persons guilty of desertion or breach of discipline were to be punished by prohibition of working in industries and transport for six months. There were also penalties prescribed for refusing work assigned.

On account of the difficulty in obtaining farmers for industrial work, collective farms were induced by Soviet authorities to enter into contract for furnishing to industrial enterprises a fixed number of workers at specified dates. Economic enterprises could obtain workers on collective farms only with the consent of the commissariat of labor, and when members of collective farms refused to deliver their quota of workers, they were made to feel the pressure of the higher authorities. They were branded as kulaks, and were ousted from the collective farm or prosecuted for counter-revolutionary tendencies. The official attitude toward recalcitrant collective farms may be gleaned from the following: "Collective farms which conceal their labor power, or refuse to take part in lumber operations under various pretexts are not to be tolerated on any account. They are in substance pseudo-collective farms, inasmuch as one cannot imagine collective farms or their leaders who do not go hand in hand with the general line of Party policy, and who do not take into consideration the basic fact that lumber operations are the most important economic and political tasks in the northern regions."[7]

Various methods were used in order to prevent workers employed at free labor from leaving their places of work: (1) the deprivation of the right to work in industry and transport for a period of six months;[8] (2) the exclusion from labor unions of workers who desert and discrimination against such workers in the distribution of living quarters, food, etc.

TERMS OF EMPLOYMENT

No bargaining was permitted between worker and state-owned enterprises; it was customary for the worker to sign an individual agreement in prescribed form embodying the terms of a collective contract, the contract to last for one year, but later legislation permitted the extension of time to three years.

Definite methods of maintaining discipline were adopted, and the official definition was given: "Labor discipline means a careful and conscientious fulfillment by a laborer of all obligations assumed by him as a participant in the socialistic upbuilding of the U. S. S. R. as defined in the collective and personal labor contracts and in the rules regulating the internal life of enterprises."[9]

The following acts constituted the breach of labor discipline: tardiness, loafing, wasting time by personal matters during the time of work, distracting other laborers, leaving work too early, sleeping during working hours, and reading or talking during working hours; violations of rules in regard to visitors such as preferential treatment of certain visitors and rude treatment of others; drunkenness while at work and quarreling; replacement of one workman by another; non-fulfillment of orders of the management to perform work provided for by collective contract or the law (including overtime and night work); rejection of temporary legal transfer to other work; insulting and threatening of managing personnel by laborers and *vice versa;* violation of safety rules and sanitary regulations; "the non-execution without justifiable reasons of the work ordered and of the quota's output"; production without justifiable reasons of defective goods, "exceeding the normal percentage of defective goods"; loss and carrying away of tools, equipment, documents, etc.; damaging of machinery and equipment; utilization of obviously defective materials; utilization of working clothes while not at work; rowdyism; making of false statements concerning illness, and the deliberate causing of unfitness for work by self-inflicted injuries and feigned illness.

The following penalties were provided for breach of discipline: (1) reprimand to be published and note made in the personal document of the person concerned; (2) withholding of wages (for tardiness, absence from work, or loafing provided the record of the person concerned is not bad); (3) the collection by the management from the worker of the amount of losses caused by violation of labor discipline; (4) discharge by management without notice and without payment of discharge allowance, together with a forfeiture of the right to be employed before expiration of six months in industrial and transport establishments; (This latter penalty was to be imposed in "cases of systematic and willful violation of labor discipline") ; (5) deprivation of the right to receive goods of which there is a scarcity in the canteen ;[10] (6) trial before "comradely tribunals", who may impose fines, order expulsion from labor unions, transfer to less agreeable work at lower wages, dismissal from work, public reprimand in the wall posters or the press; and (7) prosecution in criminal courts.[11]

A number of the restrictions as above described, especially those concerning the hiring of labor only through the medium of labor offices, have been abolished in a recent decree. It goes without saying that the system worked out by the Soviet government to control the distribution of labor does not operate perfectly. It is easy enough to pass laws for the control of millions, but it is another story to enforce them. The Bolsheviks have used every resource at their command to bring about the utilization of all the forces of the country, human and otherwise, since the carrying out of the Five Year Plan is the very foundation of their existence, but the one hundred millions of human beings of working age, in spite of all pressure, have not become complete automata. To supervise millions of workers by one centralized agency is a task of such gigantic proportions that it cannot but fail. Managers of enterprises, despite severe penalties prescribed for failure to observe the correct procedure in obtaining workers, found themselves compelled by contingency to hire "at the gate". Workers, regardless of dire punishment expressed in the loss of preferred status, were nevertheless deserting from the places of their employment, and were attempting and succeeding in the task of obtaining work under more advantageous conditions.[12]

THE PROFESSIONAL CLASS

The "white collar" class in Russia has gone through a long period of hardship since the Revolution of 1917. Reduced to an inferior position and constantly under suspicion, the engineer, the physician, the teacher, the scientist, and the intellectual class in general felt themselves outcasts to be prosecuted and punished for offenses which were frequently outside of their control. The best they could hope for was a mere toleration because of their indispensibility in the carrying out of the communistic plans. To be sure, in some ways the intellectual and professional classes brought a good many of the evils upon themselves, since they, as a whole, never really recognized the Soviet government, and at the least opportunity were willing to assist in its overthrow. In the critical years of 1917 to 1921 they were active in joining the "white" ranks or, if they remained passive, took a mentally hostile attitude toward the Soviet government in the struggle for its very existence. Consequently, when in 1921 the Bolsheviks succeeded in vanquishing their foreign and domestic foes, the lot of the intellectual was not an enviable one. As the years went by, the young generation of the intellectual class became aware of the task that the Communist was attempting to perform, and hence there was a split, not in the intellectual class alone, but in families, where children rose against their fathers and their philosophy. The Bolshevik government for many years made no attempt to reconcile this valuable element of the population; in fact the behaviour of the government was such as to further estrange the intellectual. Experienced technicians of the professional class were frequently replaced at important tasks by youngsters whose superiority consisted in their acceptance of Bolshevik ideology. Experienced engineers and professional men, if they succeeded in retaining their positions, were frequently subordinated to the authority of young Communists of limited accomplishments. Here and there engineers and other responsible technicians were apprehended in plots. This brought with it fearful repressions, and thousands of the intellectual class were exiled and imprisoned. In addition, the Soviet government was in perpetual fear of capitalistic foreign invasion and constantly suspected plots on the part of this class, not without reason. The climax was reached in 1930, and from then on the wave of persecution receded, so that by 1931 there was a noticeable change for the better. On June 23, 1931, Stalin delivered a speech which brought great comfort to the intellectual class. He said among other things that the dominant class cannot get along without the intellectuals, and he decried specialist-baiting and all inimical attitudes toward the intellectual workers. Soon after, to be exact on August 31, a decree was issued, by which engineers and the technical personnel in general were given equal status with the industrial workers. They became eligible to all the privileges as to food, clothing, housing, and medical care received by workers.

Their children, furthermore, were admitted to schools on equality with the children of the laboring class. The G. P. U. was given to understand that there must not be indiscriminate arrests of engineers. In general then since August 1931, the lot of the intellectual workers has improved considerably. The intellectuals have won the respect of the proletarian, but on the other hand the professional class is beginning to realize the tremendous accomplishment of a class which it hitherto had despised.

Labor Unions

Labor unions before the Revolution were more or less underground organizations, tolerated by the government at times for its own purposes, and destroyed as soon as their usefulness to the government was at an end. For the most part labor organizations existed illegally. The Bolsheviks, coming into power, found strong organizations which had developed in the brief interlude between the fall of absolutism and the establishment of the Kerensky régime. These they proceeded to reorganize to suit their own purposes, with the result that the Party and the Soviet government dominated their councils. Contrary to usages accepted in other countries, labor unions under the Soviets are not organized according to individual trades but for entire industries. Thus the only union existing in a steel mill is the metal workers' union. Anyone employed in such a plant, regardless of what work he might be performing, belongs to that union and is not permitted to join any other union. The membership in the union depends, then, on the industry in which a worker is employed. Thus if a machinist is transferred from a steel mill to a textile factory, his membership is automatically transferred to the textile workers' union. The primary unit of labor unions is the factory committee, which is to be found in every enterprise in the Soviet Union. This committee consists of members of the union who are elected annually to these positions by a collegium of delegates which is in turn elected at a general meeting of all employees of the enterprise; the non-union members are not barred from voting. The collegium of delegates holds at given intervals meetings, at which it discusses and approves, or disapproves, reports of the committee. The committee also appoints a number of sub-committees designated as cultural-educational, production, labor protection committees, etc. In small undertakings, the members of the factory committees devote only a part of their time to union activities, for which a proportional compensation is paid them, but in larger enterprises the members of the committee give all their time to labor union business. The higher steps in the labor union structure are the urban, raion, regional, and republican committees, culminating in the All-Union Central Committee. Each of the aforementioned divisions of the labor unions holds congresses at certain intervals and selects a labor union council which represents the labor unions in various governmental organs requiring such representation. The All-Union Congress of Labor Unions meets at least once every two years, and is composed of delegates elected from labor union congresses of the lower administrative divisions of the U. S. S. R. Between sessions of the Congress, the All-Union Central Council of Labor Unions, which is elected by the Congress, represents the authority of the Congress. However, most of the administrative and executive work is carried out by a presidium, elected by the Central Council from among its members. This presidium by agreement with the All-Union Central Committee of Labor Unions, appoints representatives of the Central Committee to various regions where they are charged with directing the work of local union organs. The Central Committee has authority to conclude collective contracts in the name of the unions and authorize the organization of strikes. All local, urban, and district organs of labor unions are in direct touch with factory committees operating in the geographical area under their control, and work under the direction of the Central Committee. The All-Union Central Council of Labor Unions is the highest labor union organ of the U. S. S. R. and coördinates the work of the various labor unions. The decision of the Council is mandatory upon all the unions which constitute the labor union structure of the country. This Council has the authority to expel persons and organizations connected with the labor union movement who do not carry out its orders; its power is almost autocratic.[13] In accordance with recent statistics there are forty-six unions in the U. S. S. R. with a total membership of 18,000,000.

The Communist Party, Soviet Government, and the Labor Unions

The Party and the government maintain control over the labor unions in various ways: (1) They select Party members for labor union officials (the higher labor union officials according to the statutes of the Party must be trusted Communists). Theoretically these officials are elected by the appropriate labor union organs, but in actual practice only those are elected who are nominated by the Party factions and the organs. These Party factions receive their orders from the Party leaders. If the labor leaders show lack of proper responsiveness to the will of the Party, they are usually removed from office by the so-called "purging" process. The party factions are composed of members of the Communist Party and the various labor union organs. Their duties, according to the statutes, are "to strengthen the influence of the Party in a non-party environment and to assure party control of the work of the organ." (2) The labor unions jointly with the apparatus of the state are a part of the governing machinery. In certain cases the apparatus of the labor union enters into and becomes a part of the state apparatus, as for instance (a) when the labor unions assist the commissar of labor in working out regulations regarding the hiring of workers; (b) when they take part in the activities of the people's courts, and in the formation of arbitration courts, conciliation boards, etc.; (c) when their representatives participate in central legislative and executive organs of the U. S. S. R. and constituent republics; (d) when their representatives take part in the work of the state, economic, and labor organs, as well as in the administration of state owned trusts, syndicates, trading organizations, etc.; and (e) when the central organs of the labor unions issue orders jointly with the highest economic and labor organs of the state, which are binding upon both state and labor union organization. The union structure, not unlike the government itself, is highly centralized.

While unions are voluntary organizations, yet there are so many privileges attached to the membership in the union that practically everyone who can qualify becomes a member. A union card serves as a proof of citizenship and certifies the possession of civil rights. The loss of civil rights deprives the victim of his union card and frequently of employment. Certain elements of the population, such as former police officials, clergymen, private traders, and others who have been deprived of civil rights, may not become members of unions. The union card entitles the holder to a ration book, membership in a coöperative organization, and the opportunity to earn a living; hence, one's very existence depends upon this precious document. The members of the unions pay two per cent of their wages as dues which are used for administration expenses in connection with the Union administrative machinery, for financial aid, and for cultural-educational purposes of the members. While frequently the provisions of the Labor Code are disregarded under stress and strain incident to the carrying out of the Five Year Plan, and while the labor element is treated as a commodity and the human element is disregarded, it must be admitted, nevertheless, that labor conditions in Soviet Russia are in general superior to those of tsarist Russia. The worker is constantly reminded that he is working for himself and not for any individual capitalist, and is promised that as soon as circumstances permit, the various provisions of the Code will be carried out. How long the transitory period will last no one is foolhardy enough to foretell. One can only hope that the lot of the workingman in Soviet Russia will be improved to such an extent as to permit him to live a decent human life.

SOCIAL INSURANCE

The Bolsheviks came into power with a certain well defined conception of social insurance and welfare. As far back as November 1917, they pledged themselves to social insurance for all workers and for the poor in cities and rural districts. The various projects for social legislation included insurance to all toilers in city and country in case of incapacitation for work on account of sickness, accident, disability, and old age, or incident to maternity, widowhood, orphanhood, and unemployment. The employer was to carry the entire cost of insurance, and the compensation was not to be less than the wage earned by the worker if not incapacitated or unemployed. The insured were to administer the insurance institutions. In the last two months of 1917, decrees were passed which established organizations and set aside funds to take care of contingencies. Theoretically it was an admirable scheme. Unfortunately civil war, invasion, and other misfortunes prevented the carrying out of this tremendous project. In addition, since all industry was nationalized, the class that was to contribute the funds was deprived of its property. Yet in spite of difficulties which would have discouraged most governments, the Bolsheviks set to work in the latter part of 1918 to supplement the original legislation. A decree issued in 1918 provided for the creation of a form of social insurance consisting of certain aids for workers who were disabled but had retained their social-economic status. The task of carrying out the provisions of the decree was assigned to various Soviet organizations, the Soviet state making itself responsible for all expenditures in connection with rendering these aids. Special agencies were to be created for the purpose of administering medical care, which was to be subsidized by a central state organization. Since these free services were to be confined to the class of "actual workers" who were unemployed or incapacitated, soldiers in the Red Army, Soviet employees, and members of their families unable to work, all other classes of society such as members of professions, independent craftsmen, and peasants had to make personal contributions in order to be entitled to the various benefits.[14] Private traders, middlemen, and employers were entirely excluded from these benefits.

In 1919, the third All-Russian Congress of Soviets ordered the various provisions for social welfare to be incorporated into a Code. Under the provisions of the Code, it became obligatory for all citizens between the ages of 19 and 50 to engage in some useful labor, exceptions being made in cases of disabled persons, pregnant women, and the feeble minded. The Code set forth in detail the right of every capable citizen to work at his own trade and the compensation he was to receive for performing his task. The Code enumerated the conditions under which employees could be transferred or dismissed, and provided for a notice of dismissal. Labor exchanges and unions were assigned the duty of coming to the assistance of the employed and acting as mediators in controversies and frictions which might arise. All employment was divided into definite cadres and paid in accordance with a scale determined for the category of labor. Wages were paid in money or in kind, which was in the form of food, living space, and other necessities. The working hours were limited to eight for day workers and seven for night workers for mature persons; younger persons were limited to six hours. Every employed person was entitled to forty-two hours of leisure and two weeks' vacation every six months. A minimum output of work was, however, stipulated by the Code. The commissariat of labor was assigned the task of instituting an inspection service by a trained personnel, whose duty it was to see that the health of all employed in economic tasks was protected, and factory committees were elected in all industrial establishments, whose task it was to carry out permanent supervisions.

As might be expected, the provisions of the Code were not always carried out in practice, yet the government spent millions of rubles in executing the plans of insurance and social aids in the year of 1920 alone. Most of the millions in the insurance fund and all benefits under the public welfare provisions have gone to workers. Hospitals, rest-houses, schools, and various institutions served them first of all; the whole economic and political apparatus of the state seemed to exist only for the purpose of serving the former under-dog, the proletariat. The leaders appeared over-anxious to serve the proletariat and failed to remember the natural slothfulness of the Russian masses. In spite of the millions spent and untold toil given to these projects, the masses at first did not realize that only by increased production would they be able to maintain what they acquired by revolution and confiscation. Instead they slackened in their work, refused to coöperate, and were quite willing to live on the "payok" or ration to which they were entitled as workers. It was after an extremely painful experience that the Russian workman was to learn the truth that one cannot keep consuming without producing. Before the Bolshevik leaders were able to start on the main road to Socialism, they had to put the people through a discipline of labor. Famine, civil war, and the *Nep* which emerged scrapped the systems inaugurated in the days of revolutionary enthusiasm. Increased production was now the watchword, since only through it could the state be saved from utter destruction. The peasant had to be given something in return for the necessities of life. The *Nep* brought with it difficult problems, since under the new order, private, semi-private, and coöperative enterprises were started, and the state had to see that the workers received protection under the new order by insurance and, if possible, shift the cost of this protection to the machinery of the *Nep*.

In November 1921 a law was passed and later on supplemented by the Labor Code of 1922 and other legislation, which provided for compulsory insurance for all wage-earners. In accordance with the scheme as worked out by the Bolsheviks, the entire administration was unified and the same standards prevailed in all the territories of the Union. Chapter 17 of the Code provided that all wage-earners were entitled to insurance. This classification in theory covered all employees in all state, public, coöperative, mixed, or private undertakings from the very first day and the entire period of employment. Such an ambitious plan of insurance would naturally fall short of the ideal in practice; however, since 1923, the number of insured has almost tripled, and it is estimated to be near twelve million persons. The insurance provided the following classes of benefits:

MEDICAL BENEFITS

The dispensing of medical aids is organized under the so-called Unified Soviet Medical Service and is administered by the commissariat of public health. Any insured person is entitled to medical attention, which is given free to the insured and his family by the local agency of the commissariat of health. In case of necessity the insured and his family may be admitted for treatment into hospitals, clinics, sanatoria, health resorts, and other similar institutions. On account of a scarcity of physicians and hospital equipment the service is not as yet functioning perfectly, and frequently patients have to be turned away.

FINANCIAL AID

The law provides for the payment of benefits during temporary disability resulting from accidents, ill health, pregnancy, child birth, quarantine, and for the care of sick relatives. Under this provision the temporarily incapacitated worker is paid the equivalent of his daily wage for the entire period of incapacity[15] and until such time as he comes to a disability pension. In case of women the law provides an allowance equivalent to their wage for eight weeks before and eight weeks after confinement, if engaged in heavy physical labor; women who are performing light work receive the allowance for six weeks before and six weeks after confinement. Other allowances consist of subsidies for the providing of baby clothes, and nine monthly allowances for nursing mothers, and funeral benefits.

The law furthermore provides for the following six classes of persons who are disabled by an industrial accident or by occupational diseases: (1) disabled persons who are not only unable to work, but are dependent on outside assistance and care in their daily needs; (2) disabled persons who are unable to work, but require no special assistance and care in their daily needs; (3) disabled persons who are not only unable to work at their trade, but are incapable of performing any regular labor, and can only engage in temporary, occasional, and light occupation; (4) disabled persons who are compelled, because of their disability, to change from higher paid trade to that of a lower; (5) disabled persons who are compelled to give up their previous trade and change to another, which, however, pays the same compensation, but who need assistance in the transitional period; and (6) disabled persons who can continue in their original trade with a lowered earning capacity.

The first three classes receive full, three-fourths, and one-half of wages respectively. The last three classes receive one-third, one-sixth, and one-tenth of wages respectively. If the disability is not the result of occupational disease, classes one, two, and three receive two-thirds, four-ninths, and one-third of wages, respectively.

Provision is also made for minor children under sixteen years of age, brothers and sisters, widows, and parents who are incapable of working or have to support children under eight years.[16]

UNEMPLOYMENT INSURANCE

Unemployed persons who have been previously employed for a period varying from six to thirty-six months immediately preceding,[17] must have registered at the labor exchange or at the local office of the trade union, if there is no labor exchange in the locality in which they lived. The recipients of benefits must be destitute, and in case their casual earnings for any one month amount to more than 150 per cent of the basic compensation or if they have regular incomes, they are not entitled to unemployment benefits for that month.[18] If the aggregate earnings and benefits of the unemployed total 75 per cent of the average monthly earnings of the beneficiary when working, he is deprived of the compensation. Should any member of the unemployed have access to an unearned income, or the total earnings of the rest of the members of the family exceed the sum of 180 rubles in the first district and varied lower sums in the other five districts, he is not entitled to benefits.[19] The amount of compensation is determined by a decree which divided the unemployed into three classes. The first class receives from 12 to 27 rubles; the second from 9 to 20 rubles, and the third from 7 to 15½ rubles. The compensation is increased 15 per cent for one dependent, 25 per cent for two, and 35 per cent for three or more. Skilled workers receive a maximum of nine months' unemployment compensation, and unskilled, no more than six months' for any one year. The total continuous period of unemployment compensation may not exceed eighteen months for skilled workers and twelve months for unskilled laborers. Persons who are supported by a husband or wife, or who receive an unearned income, or who have other sources of income, or who earn wages above 72 to 120 rubles a month, depending on the zone, are not included in the provision. Since 1930 the unemployed have been reduced to negligible number, but this situation is fraught with danger to the individual, since in accordance with a decree issued by the commissariat of labor, no person can refuse work on the pretext that it is not in the line of his training, exception being made only of those who have a certificate from a physician testifying to the disability of the unemployed. Thus persons unused to heavy physical labor must accept any job offered them, even if it is of the commonest unskilled labor variety.[20]

OLD AGE INSURANCE

Old age insurance is still largely a theoretical scheme. Only a few classes of workmen are entitled to its benefits, and they are (a) workmen in mining, metallurgical, electrical, chemical, textile, printing, glass, china, and tobacco industries; and (b) workmen in rail and water transport.

Men to be entitled to old age pensions must be sixty years of age when they have stopped working and must have been employed in industry for not less than twenty-five years. Women may retire at the age of fifty-five, but they must have worked for wages no less than twenty years. Workers engaged in underground occupations in the mining industries may retire at the age of fifty, provided they have worked no less than twenty years, ten years of which they must have spent in underground work. The Allied Council of Social Insurance, may, however, reduce the work period and the age limit of persons in other dangerous occupations. Old age pensions are awarded irrespective of the capacity to work. The pension must be no less than half of the wage previously earned by the workers.

It is the intention of the Soviet government to broaden the scope of old age insurance. To be sure the largest part of the population is still excluded from the benefits of old age pensions, yet great strides have been made in procuring economic security of workers. It remains to be seen whether in the course of years the pension policy of th Soviet government may not be broadened, so that there will be no longer any discrimination between the manual workers and other classes of wage earners.[21]

CHAPTER XVIII

WOMEN AND CHILDREN

The New Woman

If one were to point out the most amazing transformation achieved by the Bolshevik Revolution, one would have to point to the Russian Woman. From the days of ancient Muscovy, woman was considered inferior to man in every respect. The Orthodox church had taught the evil of woman's influence upon man. The invasion of the Tartars brought to Russia even lower conceptions of woman's place in society. Thus for centuries the Russian woman of the upper classes lived an isolated life. She was debarred from all education and political and social life. Locked up in a *terem*, an isolated portion of the house, she became merely an object for man's physical satisfaction. The women of the lower classes were beasts of burden and brood mares at the same time. To be sure, Peter the Great, eager to transform backward, Asiatic Russia into an European state, compelled the men to allow their women to come out of their seclusion and appear at public functions. This, of course, met with terrific opposition, but Peter was not a man who could be disobeyed with impunity, and a new era for the women of the upper class was ushered in.

Eventually Western European customs of chivalry were introduced in Russia, and superficially the Russian upper class woman became the equal of her European sisters. In the course of the nineteenth century, however, the Russian woman of the intellectual and upper classes showed an amazing development. In the revolutionary history of Russia, woman's part stands out as a great monument to the courage of young Russian womanhood. Women underwent all the danger and asked for no privileges. They walked to the gallows unflinchingly and died by the hundreds in uprisings and prisons. Men and women were equals in the revolutionary circles of Russia. But the story of the masses of working and peasant women is one of tragedy and suffering. Abused and exploited by husband and father, without recourse to law, since the traditions and customs were fully supported by the law and authorities in this connection, beaten, harassed, and exploited in every way, they became old hags before they reached the early thirties and sometimes earlier. The Bolsheviks, nurtured in the revolutionary traditions of equality of sexes, when they came into power, swept away by legal enactment all limitation upon the rights of women, and declared their complete political equality with men. All offices and appointments are open to them, and if there is any discrimination, it is not against them as women but as members of an economic-social class which the Bolsheviks consider inimical to their order. In offices of the national, state, and local governments, on the judicial bench, in diplomacy, and in the army women can be found holding positions of importance. All authority which a man could exercise over his wife and all limitations imposed upon her have been eliminated by law. In fact, the law recognizes no difference between man and woman in meting out punishment for political or other crimes. The social limitation imposed upon women by even the most civilized nations is unknown in Bolshevik Russia. In clubs, in schools, in trade unions, and other institutions and professions, woman is the man's equal. Yet in spite of this concept of equality, the Bolshevik government from the first day of its existence has recognized the necessity of protecting women, and hence has passed laws to safeguard their rights.

Between 1921 and 1926 new laws were enacted for the special protection of women. Under present legal enactments, no woman can be discriminated against on account of her sex, and no woman is permitted to work longer than eight hours a day. Night work for women is prohibited with exception of cases involving light office work. The employment of women in especially heavy labor is discouraged. Women employed in certain positions[1] are permitted sixteen weeks' vacation, eight weeks before confinement and eight after; all other employed women are allowed twelve weeks' vacation with pay. In cases of abortion, women are allowed three weeks' vacation with pay. Arrangements are made during the year after birth of a child for a working woman to leave her place of employment without deduction of pay at intervals of three hours in order to nurse her baby. Working women, unemployed at the time of pregnancy, who are looking for positions receive small allotments from the Social Insurance Fund. Other classes of women are also entitled to aid at the time of confinement. Wives of workers, soldiers, or of injured workers are entitled to assistance during confinement. Women who have no claim to social insurance may receive aid upon payment of fees and, if by reason of poverty they are unable to pay, may receive free medical care.

BIRTH CONTROL AND ABORTION

A law passed in 1920 legalized abortion under certain well defined limitations, such as that the operation must be performed by a qualified physician and that drugs may be used only under exceptional circumstances. The law provides for a three-day confinement after the operation and abstention from work for two weeks. The performance of an abortion for the first pregnancy is prohibited, unless the giving birth to a child would endanger the mother's life. No abortion is to be performed after two and one-half months of pregnancy. Qualified physicians may advise against the operation, but must not refuse to perform it, for any other cause than first pregnancy and time limitation. Small fees are to be charged to those persons who have no claim to social insurance.

The law further recommends that the operation be performed in a hospital having a special section for that purpose. Midwives and other persons are strictly prohibited from performing the operation. Private physicians and other individuals who performed an abortion which resulted in death may be prosecuted for manslaughter. Finally there is a provision in regard to discouragement of abortion, if a woman with less than three children has sufficient means to support another child, and her health would not suffer from giving birth to another child, and if in general the economic, social, and physical conditions do not demand an abortion. In recent years the government and health authorities have engaged in a campaign against abortion in favor of birth control. Local points of consultation have been established where women can obtain the necessary information.

CARE OF MATERNITY

Institutions have been provided for the care of pregnant women where they may receive necessary information and medical attention. Pregnant women are entitled to privileges in regard to supplies, and are issued certificates for the necessities of life. Pregnant women are released from work two months before and two months after confinement, and under certain circumstances may be released for the entire duration of pregnancy.

MARRIAGE UNDER BOLSHEVIK LAW

The Soviet law regulates that cohabitation constitutes marriage and carries with it all the responsibilities of marriage. A casual relationship, however, is not to be understood as synonymous to marriage. Certain facts must be proved, such as the establishment of a household, the fact that two persons have lived together, a joint rearing of children, and the acknowledgment of the fact of marriage upon other grounds; but it is recommended, for the sake of the children which may result from the union, that the marriage be "inscribed" in the registry office, not to avoid illegitimacy, for all children are legitimate in Russia, but to establish the responsibility of the father for the support of minor children.

THE RIGHTS OF WOMEN IN MARRIAGE AND DIVORCE

In entering upon marriage the woman may retain her own name or take the name of her husband. Hyphenated names are forbidden by law, as they create difficulties in census taking. In case of divorce, the husband and wife indicate what name they want to retain, and if a dispute arises, each of them retains the pre-marital name. Contrary to the law of old Russia, the wife need not follow her husband to any destination she dislikes, and may adopt any profession or occupation she desires. In the general conduct of their lives and in the rearing and education of children, the wife's opinions have the same weight as the husband's.[2]

In case of divorce, the parents must decide to whom the custody of the children is to be given; if they can come to no agreement, the courts decide the question from the standpoint of the children's welfare. The woman retains her Russian nationality when marrying a foreigner.

In Urban Communes

The law differentiates between (1) property acquired by each party before marriage, and (2) property accumulated jointly. Both parties retain the ownership of the property belonging to them before marriage. The property of the wife is not subject to any services in consequence of judicial decisions against the husband, either for personal debts or delinquent taxes. It may not be confiscated if her husband is convicted of a criminal offense. It is exempt from any services in connection with debts or crime of husband.[3] The property belonging to the wife before her marriage remains with her in case of divorce. Property accumulated jointly during the period of marriage is disposed of by the court in case of divorce, in accordance with the special circumstances of a given case.

THE SUPPORT OF THE WIFE DURING MARRIAGE
AND AFTER DIVORCE

A needy and incapacitated wife must be supported by her husband; on the other hand if the wife possesses means or is earning wages, she is not entitled to the support of her husband. If unemployed, however, the wife has a right to demand support, even if she is not physically incapacitated. The two parties decide upon the amount to be received by the wife. In case of disagreement, the matter is decided by court. Upon divorce, the wife, if she is in need and is incapacitated, may demand support for a period of one year after the divorce, within the husband's financial capacity. If the wife is not incapacitated but happens to be unemployed, she may demand alimony for a period of six months, but the sum demanded must not exceed the amount she could obtain from the unemployment fund. The wife retains the right to alimony independent of support of children by their father. While the non-payment of alimony for the children is a criminal offense, the failure to pay alimony to a divorced woman cannot be prosecuted by law.

PROPERTY RIGHTS OF WOMEN IN RURAL DISTRICTS

Even more significant is the change in the situation of the rural woman. Before the Revolution the wife of a peasant had no rights to her husband's property. Under the new law the woman receives a full share of her husband's estate, provided the woman contributes her labor in the management of the household. All the property which she has brought with her remains her own. In case of separation, she is entitled to a part of the estate in proportion to the labor she has contributed. Frequently a peasant, who did not desire to expose his property to division, entered into a non-registered union with a woman, and later on ran her off his land without even a payment of wages. Soviet courts, however, do not differentiate between registered and non-registered marriage, and hence a woman entering a non-registered union is entitled to all the rights of a legal marriage.

If a woman has stayed only a short time, she is adjudged proper compensation for her labor. A peasant woman is not entitled to special support from her husband, since husband and wife share equally in the property. Exceptions are made when the husband leaves the household and the wife is unable to manage the property without his help. In case of divorce, the wife is not entitled to alimony, if she has received her share of the property. If, however, her share was not sufficient, she may ask for alimony for one year if she is unable to work, or for six months if she cannot obtain employment. In urban districts at the death of her husband, the wife shares equally with the children in the estate of the deceased, but retains her own original share intact.[4] This, however, does not deprive a husband of the right to will his entire property to his wife. In rural districts, on the other hand, the wife has no right to her late husband's share, but it is divided among all the members of the household.[5]

EFFORTS TO INTEREST WOMEN IN PUBLIC AFFAIRS

In spite of all efforts on the part of the central authorities to induce women to join in public activities, women have not, generally speaking, fully realized their opportunities. Complaint is heard in some quarters that women have not as yet undertaken heavy responsible burdens in the conduct of public affairs as they should. It is said that women who attend meetings are not politically active to the extent they should be. Bolshevik leaders urge that the women members at present active in various public institutions should attempt to attract millions of their sex into active coöperation, and thus increase the competition in plants, factories, collective farms, and state farms. The attention of women members in city and village soviets must be directed to mobilization of internal resources for the purpose of bettering the living conditions of women. Bolshevik leaders claim that a good deal could be accomplished by women workers and women peasants who would bring their initiative and their organizational ability to the service of the state and public institutions. It is urged that women members of soviets, leading women workers in factories and collective farms should be promoted to responsible positions in public life. There is yet considerable of the old Adam in Russia and the old superiority of male over female is frequently expressed by even highly placed officials in the Soviet structure. To be sure women in European Russia have made gigantic advances, but the contrary can be said of the women in the East where old traditions and inhabitions are still adhered to. It is pointed out as a hopeful sign that the political activity of women during election campaigns increased from 49 per cent in 1929 to 60 per cent in 1930. However, the number of women elected to office is not commensurate with the degree of their activity, although the membership of women in soviets has risen from 19 per cent in 1929 to 20.4 per cent in 1930. In conclusion it may be said that a New Woman is rising in Soviet Land, a woman the like of whom has never been known in the history of mankind.[6]

Children

Anyone acquainted with conditions of rural and lower class Russia of the pre-revolutionary period is bound to admit, in spite of whatever prejudice he may have, that the care of children in Russia has improved to an incalculable extent. Since detailed discussions of the care of children have been admirably set forth by others,[7] it is sufficient to state at the outset that the chances of the infant to live, even in the remote districts of Russia, have increased tremendously. Such an innovation as the day nursery (créches), where food is scientifically dispensed and provisions are made for the physical and mental development of the child, is sufficient proof. In addition, the mortality of infants has been considerably reduced by giving the Russian mother of the peasant and working class lessons in the care of children and the preventative measures necessary in safeguarding health. The children in the larger urban centers receive daily medical examinations, which have contributed to the checking of epidemics, that were so prevalent in years gone by and that frequently annihilated thousands of children, or left them disfigured and handicapped for life.

The Bolshevik régime has established various classes of nurseries. Some of them are open between 7:30 A. M. and 10:00 P. M. These nurseries receive children up to three years of age, after which they are sent on to the kindergarten. The larger factories and establishments have organized nurseries for the care of children while their mothers are at work. Higher schools frequently have nurseries to take care of children while their mothers are at study. In rural districts, at harvest time and other busy seasons, nurseries are established in connection with collective farms, so that the adults may give their time to the pressing work. It is fair to note that, before the Revolution, infants were left to themselves or taken to the fields to be exposed to dust and wind and weather. A movement has been started in some territories in Soviet Russia to organize nurseries to take charge of children in the evenings, so that their parents may take advantage of various cultural-educational opportunities after working hours. It is not to be understood from the above description that Russia has transformed itself into a paradise for children, but whatever judgment is passed upon Russia must be made in the light of past conditions, for it is only from this point of view that justice can be done for improvement or blame assessed for deterioration.

Homeless Children (Bezprizornost)

As far back as the period of Peter the Great, Russia has had the difficult problem of child vagrancy. In his attempt to modernize Russia Peter established, in Moscow and other cities, institutions in connection with churches for the purpose of taking care of infants "of women and wenches" who had given birth illegally to children, and who had out of fear of social condemnation abandoned them to perish.[8] It was the purpose of this order to encourage mothers, not able or unwilling to take care of their infants, to bring them without being observed to those institutions. The order provided a grant for nurses of three rubles a year and a certain amount of flour a month for the support of these children, but in practice this provision was never carried out.

Later, Catherine the Great established foundling asylums which were to train the foundlings to become mechanics, artists, scientists, rich merchants, and even efficient administrators. The provisions for these foundling asylums were very liberal; no questions were to be asked except whether the child had been named and baptized. The infants did not have to be delivered directly to the asylums, but could be left with parish priests or at monasteries and convents any time of the day or night. Anyone bringing an infant into an asylum received a compensation of two rubles in silver.

The children were to be brought up and educated in these institutions, and after reaching a certain age, they were to intermarry in accordance with mutual agreement. After marriage the couple was to live in the institution for three or four years, and after that period, in order to pay for the expense of upbringing, they had to consent to work in a state controlled industry. Upon leaving the institution each charge received new clothes, consisting of several shirts, ties and handkerchiefs, cap, hat, socks, shoes, boots, a suitcase in which to carry away these gifts, one ruble in cash, and a passport which entitled him to live anywhere in the empire as a free man. From the moment of leaving, the wards of the state were under the special protection of the state and their descendents became free people. They had a right to buy houses and vacant lots in cities for the purpose of conducting business, building factories and foundries, or exercising their trade. They were free of the per capita tax and military service. This was theoretically the plan as outlined by one of the favorites of Catherine the Great, but in reality the picture was different. There was an overcrowding in foundling institutions, and in the first year the death rate reached 98 per cent. The government then gave up the idea of raising exemplary settlers, rich merchants, and efficient administrators and proceeded to distribute the children to various peasant homes in villages.[9]

Following the World and the civil wars came famine and the destruction of economic life. Social and family relations and ties were loosened in Soviet Russia; hence there was a tremendous increase of child vagrancy. On the eve of the October Revolution there were already a great number of children who were not taken care of, such as orphans and semi-orphans, and victims of the war and the difficult economic conditions of the country. From the very first days of its existence, the Soviet government attempted to ameliorate the tragedy of these children by opening institutions in which were kept hundreds of thousands of children. But the plan for this work was interrupted by the famine of 1921 and 1922. Incomplete data show that nearly seven and one-half million children perished in that time (not counting those in Ukraina), and there were six million children in need of immediate help. Under such conditions there was no possibility of a plan for normal physical and mental development of children. The cry of the time was that the children had to be saved from starvation, death, and physical degeneracy. Relief was undertaken by various children's organizations, which were crowded by a continuous stream of newcomers. In 1922 there were 6,063 children's homes with a population of 540,000 children, but even in these institutions there were no adequate means to take care of them. The children were half dead, physically degenerated, sick, and constantly in a semi-starving condition. There was a lack of an efficient nursing staff and of buildings in which to house the homeless waifs. Only at the end of 1924 had the wave of child vagrancy receded, and then the children's homes were placed upon a solid foundation, and a compaign against child vagrancy was started. On March 8, 1926, a decree was issued regulating measures for safety, help, and upbringing of young homeless charges who had not reached the sixteenth year, and who were living under conditions dangerous to their physical and social development. The child vagrants were divided into two categories: (1) those that were in need of complete care and upbringing, and (2) those that were in need of protection only. To the first category belonged the complete orphans, children who had lost all contact with their parents and relatives, and children who because of mistreatment had been taken away from their parents by judicial process of children's bureaus. This group was divided into children up to three years of age and those above three years of age.

The work of taking care of abandoned children up to three years of age was carried out in connection with safeguarding of motherhood and infancy, and was conducted by the organs of the people's commissariat of health, which provided care and refuge for the woman before confinement and later a home to take care of the child and mother. The same authorities were also taking care of orphaned and abandoned nursing infants. Up to 1927 the number of abandoned children was still very large; in fact, up to 1929 fifteen thousand infants were abandoned every year. A three-year plan was formulated and confirmed by the All-Russian Central Executive Committee and the Council of People's Commissars for the purpose of suppressing child vagrancy. Arrangements were made to appropriate funds from local budgets to take care of vagrant children in cities and villages, and a campaign was mapped out to fight the practices of abandoning infants. For this purpose an organization was to be established to take care in a coöperative way of the unmarried mothers in homes, and give deserted mothers material and judicial help. Dormitories were established for friendless mothers, and arrangements were made for the return of mothers and children, deserted by their husbands and fathers, to places of their original residence. The campaign to befriend uncared for children, three to sixteen years of age, was taken charge of by the organs of the people's commissariat of education which were to make provisions for children's homes. The systematic upbringing of the child in a children's home was considered absolutely indispensable in the struggle against child vagrancy. But since the demands upon the local budgets were heavy, there was a tendency on the part of local communities to eliminate these institutions. Between 1926 and 1927 there were in the U. S. S. R., 2,510 children's homes with a population of 201,955. The All-Russian Central Executive Committee and the Council of People's Commissars suggested that local executive committees avoid reducing the number of their children's homes and also the appropriations in the budget of 1926 and 1927 for the purpose of supporting these institutions.

The important task of the organs of education was to turn the waifs toward productive labor, transform the homes for children into normal working institutions, and qualify the children as efficient workers. For this purpose the pupils in homes, up to fourteen years of age, were sent to schools for apprentices, and those who had reached the sixteenth year, into productive labor. Furthermore, the organs of education were given the right to place pupils from children's homes as apprentices in coöperative unions and with individual mechanics in cities and in rural districts. The organs for popular education assumed the financial responsibility for support for one year. After that time the employer paid all expenses. A law passed April 5, 1926, authorized the distribution of pupils from children's homes among individual households of peasants. This new method replaced a previous regulation in use during the famine, whereby the children were distributed to the cantonal executive committees and led an unsupervised existence, wandering from family to family. Now, however, there is a definite agreement between the authorities and the individual peasant household; the general provisions of the agreement are to the effect that the child must be treated on equality with other members of the family, and taught how to become an efficient farmer, and given an opportunity to acquire knowledge and political development.

A peasant household receiving a child secured certain privileges, namely the right to obtain a portion of the pupil's allotment of land from the reserve land fund for use, and an exemption of that allotment from taxes for the first three years. In addition the peasant household was entitled to other assistance. Moreover the peasant household, which conscientiously carried out its duty in regard to the child given to its care, was eligible to additional reduction in taxes.[10] Minor law breakers who did not respond to medical-pedagogical treatment were to be placed in industrial homes, colonies, and other institutions of the commissariat of the interior.

In addition the law provided for the organization of a children's social inspection bureau. The inspectors were obliged, under certain circumstances, to place minors in children's institutions. All of the administrative organs were to coöperate with the inspectors in their work of elimination of child vagrancy. A commission for the betterment of lives of children was organized by the central authorities to coöperate with state organs in this work. The provisions were made for funds to be set aside by state and local budgets to be used in the campaign for the improvement of the living conditions of children. In addition federal and local funds, collected in the name of V. I. Lenin for the purpose of assisting vagrant children, were also available. Means were provided by various public organizations interested in the struggle against child vagrancy, and by other associations already in existence or newly organized in connection with children's institutions.

In spite of all efforts the government has made, Soviet Russia is still struggling with this sad problem. Since 1930 the Union government has appropriated sums derived from the Union budget for the purpose of eliminating child vagrancy. By a decree issued by the Council of People's Commissars on July 11, 1931, commissions for minors were established in all regions, cities, and raions. In the autonomous republics these commissions work under the management of the commissar of education. The membership of these commissions in urban centers is made up of an educator, who acts as chairman, a physician, a people's judge, an inspector, and a representative of the Young Communists, the Association of Children's Friends, and the council of professional unions, respectively. The regional commissions are composed of the manager of the regional department of education who acts as chairman, and representatives of the court, department of health, Young Communists' Organization, professional unions, and Society of Children's Friends of that political division. Representatives of other organizations are invited to take part in the meetings of the commission and are granted a consulting voice.[11]

As late as October 1931, however, the problem of child vagrancy was far from being solved; in fact, Moscow was facing an influx of homeless children from other centers. Conditions became so serious that the All-Russian Executive Committee issued an order on October 10, 1931, to instruct local authorities to remove homeless children from Moscow and its environs. The executive committee of the Moscow region was ordered to take energetic measures to relieve the situation, by organizing unified receiving and distributing points to take care of wandering children between the ages of four and eighteen. The local authorities, however, found it impossible to carry out the instructions and appealed to the Russian commissariat of education for assistance in the matter of finding homes for youthful vagrants in other regions. Children arriving in Moscow unaccompanied by adults were taken in charge by agents of the regional committee. The children's commissions of the Central Executive Committee were called upon to supply the necessary funds for this emergency. Executive committees of all autonomous republics and regions were requested to forbid public and state organizations sending children to the capital for the purpose of having them placed in institutions. All children's agencies were informed that they would be held to strict accountability for disobeying orders.

In the motley crowds of ragged and hungry children coming into Moscow were many who, by years of wandering without supervision, had developed into accomplished criminals. Some of them were diseased. There was great danger that, if they were placed in institutions, the children already there would be exposed to physical and moral hazards. To avoid this, the chief of the militsia of the Moscow region was directed to take charge of the newcomers, and, if possible, isolate those who were criminally inclined and place them in special institutions. All children found diseased were placed in isolation wards for treatment. Institutions were ordered disinfected in the briefest possible time. Before the new "invasion," plans were made to gradually reduce the number of children's homes, but in the face of the emergency orders were issued for the establishment of additional institutions. Inspectors were appointed to serve as protectors of children in Moscow and other areas having large numbers of children's institutions. The wards in institutions who had completed the apprenticeship and were employed in industries, or who attended training schools were ordered removed from the homes, and were placed in dormitories or newly built homes established by various economic organs. Whenever possible, wards were

removed from the Moscow region. The National Economic
Council was directed to supply by October 15, 1931, sufficient
materials for necessary remodeling of institutions.[12]

The Soviet government is not unmindful of the existing problem of child vagrancy. The central authorities have for a long
time decried the indifference of institutions and the public toward
the problem of homeless children. There are a number of organizations in the Soviet Union and in Moscow, such as the Association of Children's Friends, Young Communists, and other associations, which are taking an active part in this most necessary
work of housing and training of youthful vagrants, but the public
in general is indifferent. This attitude may be traced to many
years of suffering before and after the Bolshevik Revolution.
The years covering the civil war period were full of stark horror.
The average Russian has been conditioned to look on gruesome
scenes with a detachment that leads the American observer to
hasty conclusions as to his character. There are perhaps no people
in Europe who have seen so much tragedy and experienced so
much sorrow as the Russian. They have seen members of their
families faint because of hunger and had nothing they could give
to save them from death by starvation. Parents were separated
from their children in the days immediately following the establishment of the Bolshevik régime and the outbreak of the civil
war. At that time areas changed rulers once a week; no sooner
was a counter-revolutionary commander received with "bread and
salt" as the saviour of Russia than he was driven out by a Red
Army, which in turn was put to flight by some "White" leader.
The civil population stayed or fled with the faction with which
they sympathized politically. Frequently people were bewildered
and did not know what to do. If they had helped to welcome a
"White" force, the "Red" army on entering would mete out
punishment, and *vice versa*. In this bedlam, human misery knew
no bounds. People who have always lived under the blessed,
orderly conditions of America cannot quite understand the so-
called "hardness" of the Russian in the face of human wretchedness. Fortunately, as conditions improve, and time in its mercy
heals the wounds of the past, and new generations grow up who

do not remember the horrors visited upon their parents, the natural kindliness of the people will assert itself.

No one can accuse the Bolsheviks of not having attempted to ameliorate the evils in connection with child vagrancy, but because of lack of financial means, administrative inefficiency, and the terrific pressure of economic and social problems upon the authorities, they were not always able to carry out their plans. The question of child vagrancy still presents a tremendous task to Soviet Russia, but the government has the situation well in hand.

CHAPTER XIX

SOCIAL EVILS

In attempting to control and eradicate such social evils as prostitution, alcoholism, pauperism, and rowdyism, the Bolshevik government has introduced some interesting and courageous experiments, which deserve more than passing notice.

PROSTITUTION

BEFORE THE REVOLUTION

Russia before the War had one of the worst records for prostitution of all countries in Continental Europe. Unspeakable poverty, and the monotony and drudgery of small town and country life were fertile soil for the procurer. Jewish girls, compelled to live under the wretched economic and social conditions of the "pale of settlement," were frequently victims of the traffic. The pitifully low wage scale of the women workers and domestic servants in Russia, which prevented them from creating any reserve whatsoever in the case of seasonal or temporary unemployment, together with the total defenselessness of that class, was conducive to the successful activity of traffickers in vice and swelled the ranks of prostitution. The notoriously corrupt Russian police administration fell easily for bait in the form of bribes which the panders offered in exchange for protection.

A brief sketch of the attitude of tsarist Russia in this matter is necessary for an understanding of measures undertaken by the Bolsheviks to suppress and eradicate prostitution, since the new régime has inherited this problem of the ancient profession from the old order. Peter the Great, in his characteristic way, issued an order in 1716 commanding that the various military reservations were to be purged of all women who were there for immoral purposes. The women in question were to be delivered to the

310

public executioner, denuded of their apparel, and publicly driven out. The entire business was performed in a barbaric manner, without consideration for the causes which brought the victims to their unfortunate profession. Two years later the chief of police of St. Petersburg was ordered to "round up" all unprotected women and investigate their records. Sometime later, to be precise in 1771, an order was issued to "round up" all "useless wenches" and draft them for compulsory labor in factories. This policy continued far into the nineteenth century. In the forties of the last century, the attitude of the government became less savage, but the entire system was delivered into the hands of none too honest or scrupulous police officials.[1]

Under this rule, women who were suspected of practicing prostitution were deprived of their documents and were issued in exchange a special identification card, the notorious "yellow ticket." The holder of this "yellow ticket" was automatically excluded from engaging in honest labor. The fact that a woman might have engaged in the practice on account of temporary or seasonal unemployment in order to save herself from starvation had no bearing on the case.[2] "The yellow ticket" chained her to the "profession" for the rest of her life and followed her no matter where she was or what she did. She ceased to be a woman; she was a "prostitute," at the mercy of police agents. If she left one place and went into another locality, the "yellow ticket" followed her. If she managed to obtain honest occupation and was later found to be the holder of a "yellow ticket," she had to go back to her original disgraceful trade. In some of the cities prostitutes were forbidden to live in certain streets, and the renting of dwelling places to them was permitted only by special order of the police. In many instances this measure compelled unfortunate women to deliver themselves in despair into brothels, and thus the last tie between them and the outside world was broken. To be sure the woman who plied her trade individually was not prevented from doing honest work, but the conditions under which she lived in "houses" killed in her every habit of honest labor.

The new regulations mentioned above provided for periodic medical examination of defenseless women suspected of being prostitutes. The poverty stricken classes were, however, singled out for this regulation, as the law provided that the supervision should be confined to the lower classes. The police rules of Riga and Warsaw may serve as cases in point. In the former city only the women of the lower classes were subject to examination, while in Warsaw all women were subject to examination who did not have sufficient means for subsistence and were under fifty years of age, even those who were pregnant. Servant girls finding themselves out of work were subject to this compulsory examination. An investigation of prostitution in St. Petersburg in 1896 brought out the facts that women taken in police raids were composed of peasant girls and women who had come to the capital to look for work, and after exhausting all their means and not having obtained employment, were forced to take the choice between prostitution and starvation. Frequently these victims were very young girls who came to the city with their mothers, or apprentices who, because of cruel treatment, had run away from their masters and mistresses. The police, in arresting girls of that class, did not listen to argument, but took for granted that they were professional prostitutes and acted accordingly. Another cruel way of practically forcing women into prostitution was the regulation in some Russian cities that proprietors of beer halls, cafes, restaurants, and factories were to be responsible for the female employees. A chief of police of Warsaw at one time actually demanded from proprietors a guarantee that their female help and workers were not prostitutes. If no such guarantee was given, the women employees were compelled to report to police headquarters twice a month for medical examination. By these means it was sometimes possible for proprietors to threaten any woman worker with this terrific punishment if she refused his will. On the face of the matter it would appear that such stringent control would result in the eradication of disease, but in practice there developed a terrific moral and financial exploitation by police officers of defenseless and often innocent working girls. Whereas the proprietors of brothels, procurers, and panders received protection for a price, all unprotected, suspected women were treated alike and herded together in abominable police stations. Innocent girls easily became the victims of police agents and were treated worse than animals, subject to blackmail and persecution of petty police officials. Very few girls, once having fallen into the clutches of the police, could escape the "yellow ticket."[3]

UNDER THE BOLSHEVIK REGIME

The Revolution of October 1917 swept away the old order. The period of militant communism with its compulsory labor laws made prostitution impossible, since anyone who refused to perform honest labor was severely punished, and prostitutes refusing to work were interned in concentration camps. The dreadful famine which visited Russia, together with the social-economic upheaval incident to the Bolshevik Revolution, threw a great number of girls and women upon their own resources. Starvation was stalking the land, and people were willing to sell their bodies for a handful of rice. As if the famine was not sufficient to plague the people, a great wave of unemployment, caused by the disorganization of industry and the inauguration of the New Economic Policy, affected women workers sooner than men and revived the old evil of prostitution. The breaking of old ties and a general demoralization due to difficult living conditions, which were accentuated by the loosening of family discipline and other forms of control, served as contributory factors in this matter. The Bolshevik government made desperate attempts to stop the spread of prostitution.

A joint circular of the commissariats of health and interior dated December 25, 1922,[4] warned the managements of publicly controlled industries not to discharge women employees before making a thorough investigation of their economic circumstances, and to regard carefully the economically unprotected women. The situation was further aggravated by the fact that thousands of children were left orphaned and abandoned by the casualities of the World War, revolution, and civil war, and thus girls in their early teens drifted into the ranks of prostitution. In its attempt to suppress and eradicate prostitution, the Bolshevik government emphasized the terrible disgrace of tolerating professional prostitution in a workers' republic, since, in accordance with communist ideology, prostitution is merely an outgrowth of the capitalistic economic order.

It is to the credit of the Bolsheviks that in adopting policies for the suppression of prostitution they have not reverted to the barbaric customs of the autocracy. The measures taken by the decree of 1922 and later enactments for the eradication of social evils are humane and are carried out in an enlightened manner. The various instructions emphasize the great physical dangers of the occupation and the shamefulness of exploiting the human body for such purposes. The local authorities are ordered to exercise a strict administrative supervision of all places where women might possible be tempted into prostitution. This supervision is to be carried out by civil authorities in coöperation with women's organizations and professional unions. Under no circumstances are the authorities permitted to revert to tsarist methods, such as raids, prosecution, compulsory examination, etc. These methods, the Bolsheviks claim with truth, were not in Russia used for the protection of women and public welfare, but were merely the expression of police arrogance. Under no circumstances, they said, must the fight against prostitution be considered a persecution of the individual prostitute. The suppression of procurers, panders, and middlemen in commercialized vice is carried out relentlessly. A strict supervision is kept over places which might serve as camouflaged brothels or houses of assignation, and administrative rules provide for their immediate closing and the arrest and punishment of keepers. In all these activities local governmental, as well as social and professional agencies, are invited to participate. A central council, composed of representatives of administrative organs, provincial professional unions, and women's organizations, the representatives of the commissariat of health, the superintendent of the venereal section of the commissariats of health and interior, the All-Russian Central Council of Professional Unions, and the women's section of the Central Committee of the Communist Party, has been created. The police has been ordered to coöperate in ferreting out agents of prostitution, to close all kinds of haunts of corruption, and to arrest persons connected with such activity. The police furthermore has been authorized to undertake periodical inspections of establishments of public amusement, cafes, beer halls, restaurants, etc., and to examine without opposition all rooms, chambers, and enclosures. The police is in charge of the supervision of public baths, promenades, and parks, and may enter private dwellings when there is sufficient evidence that they are serving as haunts of corruption. All persons apprehended in connection with exploitation of women are subject to judicial prosecution in accordance with the provisions of the Criminal Code, and their establishments are immediately closed. The police authorities are, however, warned that in the carrying out of duties delegated to them, they must not use repressive measures against the prostitutes and their patrons outside of compelling them to appear as witnesses in their particular cases when called into court.[5]

The government does not confine itself in the control and suppression of prostitution merely to legal police measures. A campaign of education is carried on among the masses of Russian youth. As in other social evils the shame and unworthiness of exploitation of weaker, fellow human beings is inculcated into the minds of the young. In addition, from the very beginning of the attempt to eradicate prostitution, the Bolsheviks have emphasized that the patrons of prostitutes deserve the most decided social condemnation; however, the authorities have not as yet found it feasible to make the offense punishable by law.[6] The Bolsheviks claim that this ugly means of satisfying sex desires was left as a heritage from the old régime and is not due to criminal intention, but is the result of ignorance and lack of understanding. Moreover the disrespect for women, which permits her to be used as an object of purchase and sale, is a consequence of centuries of male sex irresponsibility, and cannot be eradicated by legislative repression but only by a planned educational agitation which will clear the way to a new consciousness in this matter.[7] The patron who is willing to pay, directly or indirectly, the keepers of brothels, panders, and middlemen who recruit women for this occupation is after all the mainspring which puts the entire system into operation. The commercial agents, against whom all the forces of law are concentrated, are only the auxiliary of the patron for whose satisfaction they recruit and keep women in prostitutional subjection. The Communists claim that it is the demand which makes possible the existence, not only of the procurers and middlemen but also of the very institution of prostitution. As long as it is advantageous for a man to satisfy his sex desires by means of buying a woman's body, prostitution will continue its existence, but should it be possible to create a social order in which the demand ceases, prostitution will cease. This ideal will be realized when the economic and social conditions are such that no offer to pay for a woman's body would be possible or necessary. The Bolsheviks hope to create such a frame of mind in the people that the very idea of the purchase of women will result in such unspeakable revulsion and odium that even those inclined to exploit women for their own purposes will find it socially advantageous to abstain from such acts.

That the campaign is not confined to mere talk may be gauged by the fact that the government has undertaken a definite program for the rehabilitation of prostitutes. Institutions are provided in the large urban centers where these women receive medical treatment. They are given an opportunity to learn a trade, and at the completion of their training they are provided with employment. During the period of training, efforts are made toward their mental rehabilitation through lectures, which point out the evils and dangers of their former trade and emphasize the dignity of honest labor. Even after the inmates leave the institutions, the authorities do not lose sight of them until they have habituated themselves to a life of self-respecting labor. Although some of the women return to their former profession, Bolshevik authorities claim that the majority continue in their new occupations. This claim, to the foreign observer who has come to Russia by way of Paris, Berlin, and Warsaw, is not at all incredible, since in comparison with these and other European cities, the streets of the Russian cities are quite free from the solicitations usually made by the hordes of women promenading main thoroughfares. Whether the assertion of the Bolsheviks that prostitution is merely a result of economic need is to be fully accepted or not, it is nevertheless true that to outward appearance Russian cities are free from the usual "street walkers."

In addition to the education of youth to shun exploitation of women, the inculcation of the idea in the mind of male youth that women are in no way inferior to them, together with a sane and tolerant sex attitude on the part of the authorities, is no doubt a contributory factor in the remarkable decrease of professional prostitution. It is too early to predict permanent results in this connection. The institutions of the land of the Soviets are still in a period of flux, yet it is somehow impossible for the student of Russia to imagine the return of pre-revolutionary conditions in regard to prostitution, if the programs for its suppression as carried out at the present time are consistently continued.

Alcoholism

Russia of the tsars was cursed by drunkenness. The government and manufacturers of alcoholic beverages were in league, and since the excise taxes brought considerable income to the public treasury, the authorities constantly urged the increase of sale of alcoholic beverages. Thus the vodka shops and government combined in the impoverishment and demoralization of the people, and temperance movements were frowned upon by the authorities. In the fifties of the nineteenth century, there began in Russia a temperance movement, which met with the opposition not only of the secular authorities but also of the chief procurator of the Holy Synod, and since the government had farmed out its excise taxes to private individuals, the minister of finance issued an order prohibiting meetings for the purpose of advocating temperance. By the end of the nineteenth century, the liquor trade became a government monopoly, and from one-fourth to one-third of all the government income came from that traffic. In 1912 the State Duma worked out a project for the purpose of fighting drunkenness, and provided for the right of village and city assemblies to forbid the sale of strong liquors. This project, however, was never to see daylight, as it was buried in the files of the State Council. In 1914, the tsarist government, then in the throes of war, remembered the statement of the Japanese military leaders that the Russian drink shop had helped them to defeat Russia, and issued an edict prohibiting the sale of liquor for the duration of war. The upper classes approved of this measure because more than half of the distilleries were in the war area. In addition, the increased demand for denatured alcohol for military purposes gave the liquor interests a chance to become enriched by supplying the army. With the cooling of patriotic fervor and the gradual deterioration of living conditions, the masses took refuge in drink, and since vodka was difficult to obtain, denatured alcohol, varnish, polish, cologne, and other substitutes were used, and on the frontiers and important towns a brisk illicit trade developed. The rural population soon found a solution for prohibition and proceeded to manufacture home-brew, which proved to be far more powerful than the old liquor produced by regular distilleries, and the consumption of it assumed gigantic proportions. Every household became a distillery. In general, the prohibition experiment, which Russia forced suddenly on a hard-drinking people, was a complete failure.

When the Bolsheviks came into power, they opposed the use of alcohol, for they realized that only a sober people could help them carry out their plans, but they could not stop under-ground trade in liquors and home-brewing, which by this time had developed into an institution. Not unlike other govern-ments, they attempted at first to stop this evil by legislation; hence after two years of struggling, the Council of Commissars issued a decree prohibiting the manufacture, without permit, of any kind of alcoholic beverage and the sale of drinks which had alcoholic contents, and stipulated that wines must not contain more than 12 per cent of alcohol. Furthermore the same decree prohibited the consumption in public places of drinks illegally manufactured. Appearance in an intoxicated condition in a public place could be punished by imprisonment for one year and by compulsory labor for not less than one year. The coming of the New Economic Policy invalidated some of the provisions. New regulations permitted the sale of vinous beverages containing 14 per cent of alcohol; later the percentage was raised to twenty, and by 1924 it was permissable to sell spirituous liquors containing 30 per cent of alcohol. The state distilleries and their ware-houses were permitted to sell cognac and other liquors having alcoholic content up to 30 per cent. The manufacture of vodka was renewed as a government monopoly by a decree issued August 28, 1925, by the Central Executive Committee and the Council of People's Commissars of the Union. From then on the alcoholic content of beverages was steadily increased until beverages containing from 40 to 60 per cent of alcohol were permitted to be manufactured. Until 1927 permits for the sale of alcoholic beverages were issued by the administrative divisions of the provincial and circuit soviets (the sale of beer was under the jurisdiction of the district and cantonal police).

Since 1927, the permission to sell liquor in rural districts must be obtained from district (raion) and cantonal executive committees. The government also started an active campaign against home-brewing and provided heavy penalties for infractions of the law. In accordance with a law passed on December 27, 1927, a fine of 500 rubles was imposed for the preparation of home-brew and the manufacture and sale of machinery for its production.[8] Using the Union decree as a basis, the All-Russian Central Executive Committee and the Council of People's Commissars of the R. S. F. S. R. issued regulations on January 27, 1928, prohibiting (1) the preparation and storing of home-brew even if there was no intention of sale; (2) the disposal of home-brew, commercially or otherwise; and (3) the preparation, storing, repair, and sale of machinery for the preparation of home-brew, commercial or otherwise. Individual cases could be punished in administrative manner by a fine of one hundred rubles and compulsory labor for one month.[9] The executive committees of the lower political units were authorized to impose penalties in accordance with general enactments in the form of fines of twenty-five rubles and compulsory labor of two weeks. In recent years the Soviet government has undertaken a hard fight against alcoholism. The backwardness of the masses of the people, lack of decent living conditions, and ignorance were important factors in the increase of drunkenness in Russia.

In the struggle against this ancient foe of Russia, the government agencies are authorized to compel persons who have become a social danger, on account of the misuse of alcohol, to undergo treatment.[10] The law further stipulates that persons who have become mentally unbalanced because of the abuse of alcohol or who have become a danger to the community, their families, and neighbors, and persons who have become chronic drinkers and in this state of intoxication squander and destroy property are subject to compulsory medical treatment, after a preliminary investigation and examination by a special commission under the jurisdiction of the department of health. Relatives, guardians, or police officers are delegated to bring the patient to a designated medical point if he refuses to appear voluntarily. Appeals against the decision can be made to higher authorities. Local executive committees are authorized to form public commissions for the purpose of studying problems in connection with alcoholism in their respective localities, and to approve measures of local organizations interested in the temperance movement. They must endeavor to bring the masses of workers and peasants together in the discussion of problems in connection with alcoholism, and find means to organize prophylactic-medical and cultural institutions for the purpose of fighting alcoholism.

The central government in its attempt to limit the sale of spirituous liquors passed a decree on March 4, 1927, permitting local executive committees (not lower than provincial and circuit) to prohibit the sale of spirituous liquors in cities and rural districts and entire areas of a given administrative-economic unit, on holidays, evenings, and the eve of a holiday. The same authorities had the right to prohibit entirely the sale of alcoholic beverages, if such action was decided upon at a general meeting of the citizens of a given rural settlement, or at general meetings of workers in individual plants and settlements. The sale of spirituous liquors to minors or those in an intoxicated condition was absolutely prohibited. The sale of all spirituous liquors at refreshment stands, theaters, motion pictures, clubs, and cultural-educational institutions and organizations was strictly forbidden. The violation of the rules was to be punished at the first offense by administrative order in accordance with obligatory ordinances passed by local executive committees, and at the second offense by judicial process in accordance with Article 109 of the Criminal Code.

The question is frequently asked how the government monopoly of spirituous liquors is to be reconciled with its campaign against alcohol. The apologists for the Bolshevik régime state that the monopoly was established merely for the purpose of controlling the sales of liquor. If the retail sale had been taken over by individual traders, the government not only would have lost control of this lucrative business yielding an income of probably five hundred million rubles a year, which it can make use of in carrying out the economic program, but it also would have no assurance at all that private retail would in any way help in reducing the consumption of liquor. Furthermore, it is declared that the monopoly is merely a temporary measure and will be given up as soon as the government finds additional sources of income for the development of the national economy. It is hoped that in the near future the manufacture of alcohol will be reduced to a minimum for technical and industrial purposes only, and eventually the sale of alcoholic beverages will be "liquidated" entirely.[11] The Bolshevik leaders, however, know from past experience that in a country such as Russia, with a peasantry and people addicted to drink, national abstinence is not an easy task to accomplish. A rigorous campaign is carried on by the government and by societies against drink; in fact the government as one measure of control, is making liquors more and more unpalatable. The hope lies in the new generation who are trained in the new ideology. It is vain to expect that the millions of middle-aged and old men and women, habituated to the conditions of old Russia, will change in this respect. Tremendous efforts are made, to be sure, but prohibition forced by law has failed in countries far more advanced than Russia; hence the Bolshevik policy of education is probably the only feasible way of sobering a people of heavy drinkers.

Pauperism

The beggar was always a part of the Russian scene. He could be found at church doors, public buildings, parks, and places of public amusement. The cry "alms for Christ's sake" is familiar to all who have visited Russia. The development of professional mendicancy in Russia in the eighteenth century brought with it repressive measures. Peter the Great issued a decree in 1718, regulating that beggars apprehended for the first time were to be whipped mercilessly and sent back to their native villages; if apprehended for the second time, they were to be punished corporally in a public place and sentenced to hard labor. Women were to be sent to textile factories, children were to be whipped and apprenticed to weavers and other craftsmen. Landowners, proprietors, and various authorities were to be fined five rubles for each man apprehended who was under their supervision. In the same year, Peter issued an ordinance forbidding the giving of alms, and fining donors five rubles for the first offense and ten rubles for the second. Later on there were sporadic police drives on beggars, but in general they were tolerated and frequently respected by the religious masses. In general Europe considered professional begging a criminal offense and yet tolerated it. The Bolshevik government at first was too busy to pay attention to the beggar, although in the period of military communism, mendicancy was considered as equivalent to industrial desertion, and there were attempts to enforce the constitutional provision which stipulated that "he who does not work shall not eat."[12] Accordingly, provincial and district commissions, established for the purpose of fighting industrial desertion, were given the power to impose upon beggars administrative fines, and to transfer cases which deserved more severe punishment to the disciplinary courts, people's courts, or revolutionary tribunals. The abolition of the commission for the suppression of industrial desertion on December 14, 1921, and the coming of the New Economic Policy put an end for a while to prosecution of beggars.

Since that time there has been no definite policy is regard to begging. Regulations were never more than sporadic, and thus even the casual observer could see multitudes of paupers assailing the public and begging for alms on the streets of Soviet cities. The police, to be sure, were supposed to prevent able-bodied persons who refused to work from seeking refuge in begging as a profession, and to take measures to prevent vagrants and beggars from using any kind of deception in order to arouse the sympathy of the public. The Soviets, furthermore, had actually reverted to the policy of the old government and sent back to their native villages paupers of peasant origin who were stranded in cities. In some instances destitute persons were concentrated in colonies.

On April 6, 1926, the All-Russian Central Executive Committee issued instructions that the struggle against pauperism and vagrancy was to be conducted on the lines of concentration into colonies, and that appropriations be made for that purpose from state and local budgets. Again in 1929, the Central Executive Committee and Council of People's Commissars ordered an increased activity in the liquidation of pauperism and vagrancy, and recommended the rehabilitation of professional paupers by placing all beggars incapacitated for work in institutions. Here they were to be given an examination, upon the result of which they were to be divided into categories and placed temporarily in dormitories until their cases could be finally disposed of. It was urged by the central government that assistance be rendered to persons who had fallen into temporary distress. In some instances, these persons were to be returned to their original communities where the local authorities were to take charge of them. In other instances, temporarily destitute persons were to be assisted in obtaining work. It was recommended that able-bodied professional beggars be sent to working colonies, industrial or agricultural, where they could be trained in the habits of useful occupations. Detained beggars, who were found to be malicious or connected with criminal elements, were to be placed in institutions of compulsory labor under specal supervision.

This work of eradication of beggary was to be conducted under the supervision of the commissariat of social security of the R. S. F. S. R. For the purposes of coördination, periodic conferences of poor-relief agencies and organs of social security were to be called. It was further recommended that the various agencies coöperate with committees of soviets, urban and rural organizations for mutual help, and similar groups. These organizations were to attempt to get in touch with relatives of indigent persons who were legally responsible for them. The various executive committees of political divisions were urged to coöperate with the agencies of social security in their struggle to eliminate beggary and vagrancy of adults.

All reasonable assistance in the matter of supply of raw materials, equipment, etc., was to be rendered to the various relief institutions which conducted work shops. These institutions were also to be freed from taxes and other obligations. The rents paid for buildings in which such work shops were located should not exceed the rate charged to institutions caring for the incapacitated. In order to facilitate this work of rehabilitation, inmates of institutions before leaving were to be registered at employment agencies and supplied with work. The appropriate commissariats were instructed to set aside necessary sums in their annual budgets for the purpose of inaugurating a "five year plan" of organizing institutions for the rehabilitation of beggars. Local executive committees were requested to set aside certain sums in their budgets for such purposes as enumerated above. The local authorities were ordered to make provisions for medical and sanitary services for these institutions.[13]

Before 1931, when there was considerable unemployment in Soviet Russia, begging was tolerated, and police officers winked at the evil, permitting the general public and the occasional tourist to take care of the multitude of paupers to be found on the streets of Russian cities. Although begging is still prevalent in Russia, in the last few years, there has been a considerable decrease due to a more liberal policy in the matter of supplying work to the classes who are not of proletarian origin. Indeed, there are attempts made at present to provide work for every one, irrespective of social origin.

Rowdyism (Chuliganstvo)

The word *chuligan,* which is probably derived from the English "hooligan", as used in Russia includes any one engaged in anti-social activity, from those participating in pogroms to the neighborhood and village bully. The Russian hoodlum, before the Revolution, was frequently made use of by the government in general, and police in particular, whenever officials wanted to intimidate the more liberal elements of the population. The hoodlum was the tool in the hands of police, and the outrageous acts committed by the "Black Hundred" of the pre-revolutionary memory were carried out by hirelings recruited from this stratum of the Russian population.

The short-lived Kerensky Republic suffered from this element, and the Bolseviks in their first years of existence were powerless to stop the outrages committed on railroads, in suburbs, in villages, and on city streets. When the Criminal Code was adopted, it specifically provided penalties for the acts of the *chuligani*. The Code declares rowdyism (chuliganstvo) an unsocial activity and inimical to public welfare. Anyone apprehended in the act of rowdyism for the first time could be prosecuted in an administrative manner or by judicial process. When rowdyism expressed itself in disorder and riot in spite of warnings issued by authorities, and the rowdies not only refused to desist from their activity but responded with abuse, the perpetrators were to be prosecuted by judicial process. For the purpose of taking effective measures against rowdyism, the Council of People's Commissars of the R. S. F. S. R. issued in October 1926 a decree, which instructed various authorities and lower executive committees in regard to cultural and educational campaigns for its eradication, and indicated the administrative and judicial method which they were to follow. In the line of education it was proposed to organize club houses, tournaments, and excursions, and to give the unruly youth of the working and peasant class access to lectures, shows, concerts, motion pictures, etc., and to impart to these activities an amusing and educational character. It was also recommended that idle young men be given a chance to obtain work, and boys in their teens encouraged to attend school. In the field of administrative and judicial activity, it was urged that local executive committees issue obligatory ordinances which would simplify procedure in dealing with rowdyism. In order to centralize the activity in the struggle against rowdyism, it was recommended that the higher executive committees grant the district and cantonal executive committees the authority to impose administrative fines within the limit of the law for all violations of order. Unless otherwise delegated to higher authorities, current legislation authorized lower executive committees to impose administrative fines for disorderly conduct. The punishment in administrative manner was to be confined to those forms of rowdyism which expressed itself in profane language and insulting remarks to citizens in public places, rather than in physical violence against persons and destruction of state and private property. All other expressions of rowdyism which were dangerous to the community were to be prosecuted by judicial process. The obligatory ordinances, issued by lower executive committees for the purpose of suppressing rowdyism, gave the police the right to impose a fine of three rubles for minor offenses which had been committed in factories, clubs, theaters, cinemas, on the streets, and in other public places. The fine was to be collected at once at the time and place where the violation had been committed, and a receipt was to be issued, although no written record was to be made of it. If the violator refused to pay at once, his fine could be increased five-fold. When serious acts of rowdyism had been committed, the police was instructed to make a record and forward it at once to the special chamber organized for that purpose in all larger administrative centers. If the case was serious enough, the perpetrator had to be brought before the people's court. Acts of rowdyism which were to be punished in an administrative manner were decided upon in accordance with the record of the deed made by a police officer and signed by the violators. Individuals who had been prosecuted for rowdyism were deprived of the right of carrying fire arms and other weapons, and any arms found in their possession were to be confiscated and the permit for carrying them, annulled.

CHAPTER XX

THE ADMINISTRATION OF EDUCATIONAL, CULTURAL, AND HEALTH INSTITUTIONS

Many able studies on the educational, cultural, and health institutions are available to the interested reader. This chapter will, therefore, confine itself largely to a consideration of the legal enactments.[1]

In recent years the Soviet government in its task of building cultural and educational institutions has departed somewhat from its general policy of centralization. Until 1927 the administration of all public institutions was highly centralized. Now localities are encouraged to establish cultural, educational, and social welfare institutions. The establishments found throughout the country are classified as all-union, republican, and local, depending upon the sources of support and administration. If a given institution serves mainly the inhabitants of a particular area, it must be supported by local funds and administered by local organs. This regulation applies to small rural communes as well as larger territorial divisions, and includes schools, hospitals, and other public establishments. The purpose of this ruling is to develop close ties between the local population and the institutions which serve it, and arouse local civil pride and desire to support and improve local schools, hospitals, and other public institutions. It was found that in small areas, when institutions are supported by the funds granted by higher units, the local population makes no effort to supplement the grants, and frequently neglects establishments entirely.

This tendency toward devolution was further strengthened by a decree issued in 1927, which directed that the entire network of those institutions of public education, health, and social welfare having no state significance was to be transferred to the supervision of those executive committees upon whose territories they were located. In addition, it was proposed that the cultural institutions of local significance which had been supported by state budgets were to be transferred to the local budgets, granting them, however, a subsidy equal to the amount formerly expended by the state for their support. It was provided that local units were to support only those institutions which directly served them, and the administration and direction was to be concentrated in the hands of local authorities.

The general supervision of public health was to remain under the jurisdiction of higher authorities. Thus village and other rural medico-sanitary institutions were to be directed by superior departments of health. In raions, the medical departments were to take under their direction the entire field of medico-sanitary work. Before 1927 the administration of cultural institutions was incumbered with a good deal of red tape, and the transfer of documents from one organ to another was extremely complicated.

Schools in villages and rural areas, supported by local funds, were to be supervised and directed by the authorities of the raion. The direction of higher educational institutions, however, was to be retained by the superior authorities. It is argued that the transfer of the higher educational institutions to the lower units of government is at present inadvisable on account of the absence of qualified personnel who are capable of taking charge of them. The direct supervision and conduct of technical institutions which are located in provincial and district administrative units were to be retained by the commissariat of education and other commissariats, irrespective of the sources of their financial support.

The laws of July 27 and August 30, 1927 respectively, simplified the process for the establishment of cultural, educational, medical, sanitary, and social institutions within the limits of the general plan. Executive committees of localities that appropriated funds for the operation of these establishments were granted considerable jurisdiction. Thus the dismissal and transfer of the immediate pedagogical personnel in public, educational, and medico-sanitary institutions, and of responsible administrative staffs in medical institutions was delegated to their authority.[2]

The appropriate departments of the superior executive committees retained, however, the right to dismiss managers of cultural, educational, and medico-sanitary institutions which had been appointed by the lower executive committees. Village soviets and local executive committees had the right to suggest and reject candidates for the office of directors and for the pedagogical personnel of public institutions supported by them. By the law of 1927, confirmation of plans for the management of these institutions by higher authorities was no longer required. All records were to remain in local archives which might be inspected and corrected at regular intervals. Considerable superfluous paper work was eliminated, and the influx of streams of circulars sent out by higher authorities, which frequently resulted in confusion, was stopped. Thus as present local authorities are managing their own institutions. While these institutions are not permitted individual accounts and budgets, yet the tendency is toward decentralization, from which may develop a more normal local institutional life.

Public Education

As in other attempts to rebuild the country, the Soviets have encountered passive opposition and negligence on the part of the rural population. The older peasants, never having had the opportunity of learning even to read and write, could not be transformed overnight into zealous advocates of popular compulsory education, especially if there were any financial outlays connected with it. Local soviets frequently neglected to expend even the meagre appropriations for educational purposes. In 1929-30 only 68.4 per cent of the appropriations for primary education was expended, 67.8 per cent for reading-huts and 36.7 per cent for capital repairs. The erection of proposed school buildings was not completed in time, and there has been an unusually high percentage of truancy of pupils because of the lack of equipment and adequate teaching staffs. The same negative results may be found in the movement for the abolition of illiteracy. Everywhere there are to be found procrastination and neglect on the part of persons responsible for the execution of projects. In 1930 there were still millions of peasants who were illiterate and millions of children who had no school to attend. Yet when one considers this lack of interest on the part of the masses and the fact that before the War two out of every three Russians were illiterate, the achievement of the Soviet government becomes nothing short of gigantic.

In the fiscal years of 1930-1932 compulsory primary education has been introduced in the Soviet Union, and the attendance of children in primary grades has increased 50 per cent. It is estimated than twenty million children attended the primary grades in the fall of 1932, which is three times the number of children in school in 1913-1914. This, of course, required almost superhuman effort in the matter of arousing backward localities to action. In 1930 there was a change in the educational system, and the so called "unified system" of polytechnical education which applied to all grades was introduced. Under this system, schools were directly connected with factories and farms, which were to serve as laboratories and give the older pupils a chance to participate in the actual work of farms and plants. In some instances, it was found that the collective method employed in Soviet schools, which was the organization of groups to perform definite tasks, not unlike "brigades" of workers in industry, reacted disastrously on certain types of children who required individual attention. To remedy this situation the Central Committee of the Communist Party issued a decree on August 25, 1932, in which it instructs the commissar of education to eliminate certain defects in methods and propose new ways. It also recommends the strengthening of school discipline as outlined in a decree issued in September 1931. The teacher, who under the previous methods practically lost his authority, is reinstated in his position. The decree shows further a more prudent attitude toward the teacher. Hitherto the teacher had been looked upon with suspicion and considered more or less a remnant of the old bourgeois intelligentsia; but under the new regulation the teacher becomes eligible to receive food products and manufactured articles on equality with industrial workers.

The living conditions of teachers and their families are to be improved and their wages paid regularly. The teaching profession is to receive consideration in regard to rest and other necessities. The State Publishing House has been instructed to publish special sets of books in various branches required by teachers, and to sell them at reduced rates.

It is proposed by the decree, eventually to lengthen compulsory education from seven years to ten. Plans were made to spend in the Soviet Union over three billion rubles on education in 1932. Soviet authorities report that in 1931, 100 per cent of the city children between eight and twelve years were attending school, and 86 per cent of the children in rural districts. On September 20, 1930, the Central Executive Committee of the U. S. S. R. issued a decree in regard to reorganization of higher schools and technical institutions. Since 1928 the number of students in the higher educational institutions has tripled. The number of universities and institutions for higher learning has been increased. The entrance requirements for universities and higher technical schools have been raised. All candidates for admission to higher institutions are required to take an examination in mathematics, physics, chemistry, language, and social science. The curricula have been revised and methods of teaching improved. The requirements for candidates to pedagogical positions in scientific institutions have been raised. A special engineering academy is being planned for the training of specialists for the various new construction projects. A new departure from Bolshevik practice is the prohibition of student organizations to interfere in the administrative and educational direction issued by the teaching staffs. In general a stricter régime has been adopted in regard to disciplinary matters, such as attendance of classes, etc. In order to improve the teaching staffs, heads of departments henceforth are to be appointed by various commissariats as a result of competitive examinations. The schedule of salaries of the teaching staffs is to be raised, the new scale to be based on training, type of teaching, and length of service. The decree of September 20 finally provides for the organization of a committee of higher technical education in connection with the central education committee of the U. S. S. R. This committee is to exercise general supervision and control over the technical schools.[3]

PUBLIC HEALTH AND WELFARE

In a discussion of the details of public health in Soviet Russia, it is well to remember that Russia before the Revolution, not unlike other countries in Eastern Europe, did very little for public health of the masses. Whatever institutions existed were of a private-philanthropic character. To be sure here and there were found agencies in charge of public health, but like all governmental institutions of that time, they were thoroughly bureaucratic in their nature and inefficient in the carrying out of their tasks. Whereas the Russian people as a whole were not personally more careless in the habits of physical cleanliness than those of other nations, yet because of extreme poverty and ignorance of the masses, and indifference of the government, sanitary conditions in the poorer sections of the cities and in rural communities inspired revulsion in the Western visitor who happened to stray from the more exclusive parts of the urban centers. It is not to be understood that the Bolsheviks have succeeded in eliminating the evils accumulated in the centuries of poverty and indifference; on the contrary, because of the extremely crowded conditions of city dwellings, one is frequently unpleasantly impressed by unspeakable filth. The difference lies in the fact that from the very beginning of the Soviet régime, colossal attempts have been made by posters, lectures, and practical application to drive out filth and unsanitary conditions. Furthermore, agencies have been created which are making almost superhuman efforts in the face of a difficult situation to inculcate in the minds of the masses habits of cleanliness. Especially is this true as far as the oncoming generation is concerned. Sanitary supervision agencies have been established for the safeguarding of the life and health of the masses, and serious attempts are being made to eliminate unsanitary conditions. Organizations have been created for the struggle against contagious, social, and occupational diseases in the Soviet Union. Staffs of sanitary experts, stationed in districts in rural localities, cities, precincts, and suburbs, and on railroads and water fronts, are waging a courageous fight to overcome the century-long inertia of the masses. Sanitary corps have been placed in charge of special departments for the purpose of inspection of dwellings, and are given authority to enter buildings and courtyards of all state, public and private buildings, institutions, and undertakings, for the purpose of inspection. Dwelling places may be entered from eight o'clock in the morning to eight o'clock in the evening, and places of public use, such as night asylums and penal institutions, state, public, and private institutions, etc., at any time of the day or night. If conditions justify such action, the agents may order the elimination of unsanitary conditions and forbid the violation of the sanitary rules within a certain period of time. The sanitary inspectors may initiate administrative and judicial prosecution of all persons refusing to carry out their instructions. The sanitary service may order the withdrawal from sale of all objects, products, and drinks which are considered dangerous to health, and may even destroy them, if they constitute a special danger to public health. The sanitary service may temporarily close all buildings, rooms, and undertakings, if such are obviously dangerous to the health, until such time as the entire matter is decided by appropriate judicial or administrative organs. Patients having contagious diseases or symptoms of a contagion may be isolated, if they are a menace to those near them or if there is danger of the infection spreading. In carrying out the supervision of the sanitary organs, its agents take part in all the attempts of the state in executing the measures to safeguard the life and health of the population. Regional and provincial departments of health have the authority to compel those suspected of being victims of venereal disease to undergo an examination, and to place all infected persons under compulsory treatment, should they refuse to do so voluntarily.

This right of compulsion is vested in the organs of public health only, and not in the police organs. The following categories of persons may be compelled to undergo medical treatment: (1) persons who have been found diseased by the medicosanitary establishments; (2) diseased persons who live in circumstances that constitute a danger to those around them; (3) persons who work under conditions which expose to infection all those who serve them or work with them; (4) pupils in schools, on the authority of the school health supervision; (5) persons who serve as wet nurses or domestic servants, upon recommendation of health authorities; (6) pregnant women who have acquired syphilis in any period of the disease, after a diagnosis by competent medical authority; (7) all other persons who refuse to undergo treatment in spite of the advice of medical authorities.[4]

A quarantine service has been established to guard against the infiltration of infectious diseases from abroad. In cases of the appearance of infectious diseases in the territory of the Soviet Union warnings are sent out to neighboring countries. The quarantine guard at the borders is under the authority of the commissariat of health of the republic within whose territory the sanitary bureau is located. In their activity in the guarding of boundary lines against the influx of disease and the consequent spread of contagion, the commissariats of health of the constituent republics are regulated by Soviet rules and laws as well as by international sanitary agreements entered into by the Soviet Union and other countries. Medical authorities are under obligation to send by way of the local sanitary organs information to the commissariat of health of the appropriate republics concerning all infectious diseases that come to their knowledge. Health authorities are responsible for the isolation of the sick in hospitals or at home, disinfection of property and persons who have come in contact with sick rooms and hospitals, and the extermination of rodents. They may prohibit the transfer from localities where epidemics are raging of any objects which have not been disinfected. Special sanitary points in various localities, water fronts, and railroad centers and ports are established for the purpose of guarding against and eliminating disease. Ships arriving from foreign ports must undergo sanitary inspection; if unwilling to submit, they must leave at once. Vessels, however, may be permitted to unload their cargo if they are willing to isolate the ship, the crew, and the passengers. Passengers who land must undergo sanitary inspection in accordance with legal enactments of sanitary and health organs.

Since 1930, the Soviet government has increased its effort in the field of public health. In March 1930, there was convened an All-Russian Congress of Health Departments for the purpose of finding ways and means for the betterment of health service, especially in the rural districts where health activities have been operating under extreme difficulties. The authorities claim, and correctly, that only by enlisting public opinion can the task of bettering sanitary conditions be accomplished. Improvement is noticeable, since the death rate, which was a century before the War never less than 25.27 per thousand, has decreased in 1928 to 18.23 per thousand; (the lowest death rate in 1928 was to be found, however, in the cities of Russia proper, which was 16.2 per thousand). This, of course, is still high when compared with the deaths in England, France, and the United States which average about 12 per thousand. Infant mortality on the other hand, has been reduced to an astonishing extent. Before the War there were 270 to 280 deaths per 1000 births; in 1928 this high mortality was reduced to 167 per thousand.

The shortage of trained medico-sanitary personnel, equipment, and institutions has been the greatest obstacle in the struggle for better health conditions. Every attempt has been made to increase the number of trained health workers. The budget of the commissariat of health for the fiscal years of 1930-1931 as over against that of 1929 has increased 67.2 per cent.[5]

NOTES AND REFERENCES

NOTES AND REFERENCES

PART I

CHAPTER I

INTRODUCTION

1. Article 98.
2. Article 99.
3. Article 2.
4. Harper, *The New Electoral Law for the Russian Duma*, pp. 9-13.
5. The table of ranks was abolished on December 10, 1917.
6. Later the Senate was reformed and a department of cassation was established and served as the highest court in civil and criminal matters.
7. *Fundamental Laws,* Volume XVI; Zelitch, *Soviet Administration of Criminal Law,* pp. 381-405.
8. See page 5.
9. Gagen, *Uchebnik Administrativnovo Prava,* pp. 116-228.
10. The term Zemstvo comes from the Russian word *zemlya,* land, and is generally associated with organizations connected with land, landed nobility, and peasants.
11. Kisevetter,*Mestnoe Samoupravleniye;* for a detailed description of the activities of the Zemstvos during the World War, see Polner, Obolensky, and Turin, *Russian Local Government during the War and Union of Zemstvos.* Kolesnikov, *Administrativnoye deleniye gosudarstva.*
12. For a description of Russian municipal government and activities during the World War, see Astrov, *Municipal Government and the All-Russian Union of Towns* in *The War and the Russian Government.*

CHAPTER II

1. The word *Soviet* in Russian means council. The revolutionary origin of this institution is traced to the upheaval of 1905, when a council of delegates from factories and trade unions was elected to meet in St. Petersburg. The leadership was supplied by some of the radical intelligentsia (Trotsky was a prominent member). This council was in the vanguard of the labor movement in Russia and actually organized a general strike. Not much was heard of this organization until March 1917, when a body of some two thousand delegates elected in various ways by factory workers, peasants, and revolutionary military units met at the State Duma in Petrograd and elected a provisional executive committee. Soon soviets were organized in other parts of Russia, at the front, in factories, etc. Presently the word soviet came to mean a revolutionary assembly for discussion and action. At first it was composed of the "left" groups, made up of Constitutional Democrats (Kadets), Social Revolutionaries, Mensheviks (minority socialists), and Bolsheviks (majority socialists). The Constitutional Democrats, who were mainly bourgeois liberals, lost their influence with the increase of revolutionary fervor. The Bolsheviks at first constituted a minority of the membership, the Mensheviks and Social Revolutionaries, in most cases, dominating the council. Eventually the Bolsheviks became predominant, and the Petrograd soviet, being near the center of activity, served as the leader. Eventually out of these local bodies developed larger bodies, such as district, provincial, regional, etc., to which representatives were elected from the lower soviets. The chain of soviets culminated in the All-Russian Congress of Soviets. With the coming of the Bolsheviks into power, these came to be denoted as governmental organs. Chamberlin, *Soviet Russia*, pp. 28-30; Graham, *New Governments of Eastern Europe*, p. 42; Batsell, *Soviet Rule in Russia*, pp. 20-22.

2. In the early years of the Soviet government Stalin headed the Department of Nationalities, but he gave up that position to become Secretary General of the Party.

3. *The Declaration of the Rights of Laboring and Exploited Masses* was incorporated as a preamble to the Constitution.
4. Batsell, *Soviet Rule in Russia,* pp. 304-309.

CHAPTER III

1. *Union Constitution,* Article 7.
2. *Decree of the Central Executive Committee and Council of People's Commissars; Polozheniye o grazhdanstv Soyuza S. S. S. R.* (issued April 22, 1931). *Sobraniye Zakonov* (May 5, 1931), No. 24. Previous legislation of May, June, and November 1930 was repealed. The above instructions were issued to the commissariat of foreign affairs in agreement with the Unified State Political Administration.
3. Tepper, *Election in Soviet Russia,* in the *American Political Science Review,* Volume XXVI, p. 330, (October 1932); *Instruktsia o Vyborach v Sovety i na s'ezdy Sovetov R. S. F. S. R.*
4. In some cases autonomous republics have been annexed by regions; in instances where they have not, the autonomous republican congresses elect delegates to the All-Russian Congress.
5. *Instruktsia o Vyborach v Sovety i na s'ezdy Sovetov R. S. F. S. R.*
6. Cypin, *Voprosy Vnutriapartiinoi Demokratii;* Volosevich, *Organiztsionnye Printsipy Bolshevisma;* Kaganovich, *Kak Postroena V. K. P.* (b).
7. *Kalendar-Ezhegodnik Kommunista Na 1931 god,* p. 351.
8. Named in honor of the October Revolution (old style).
9. For an excellent study on the subject, see Harper, *Civic Training in Soviet Russia,* and *Making Bolsheviks* by the same author.
10. As quoted in Batsell, *Soviet Rule in Russia,* pp. 705, 706.
11. Batsell, *Soviet Rule in Russia,* p. 706.
12. *Constitution of the Communist Party.*
13. *Constitution of the Communist Party,* Article 66.
14. *Constitution of the Communist Party,* Article 67.

15. Exceptions may be made by the Central Committee and presidium of the Central Control Commission.
16. See Batsell, *Soviet Rule in Russia,* Chapter XIII.

CHAPTER IV

1. *Soviet Union Review* (November 1932), p. 200.
2. Chugunov, *Gorodskiye Sovety,* pp. 7-9.
3. Although in some cities, such as Kronstadt and Krasnoyarsk, the Soviets of Workers' and Soldiers' Deputies became the actual ruling power.
4. Chugunov, *Gorodskiye Sovety,* pp. 16-17.
5. This provision applied only to cities of at least 50,000 inhabitants. Smaller cities did not have to comply with this regulation.
6. In Moscow and Petrograd the executive committee could contain as many as forty members.
7. *Constitution of the R. S. F. S. R.,* Chapter 11, Articles 57-60.
8. Chugunov, *Gorodskiye Sovety,* p. 19.
9. Between 1922-28 the Union and the All-Russian Central Executive Committees were very much concerned with affairs of local government. During that time ordinances were issued which modified the provisions of 1922 in regard to details of city rule. For a collection of resolutions and ordinances passed by various congresses of soviets and Union and All-Russian Central Executive Committees, see Michailov, *Mestnoe Sovetskoye Upravleniye,* Appendix, Parts I-III.
10. While this study concerns itself primarily with the cities of Russia proper, practically the same may be said of city government throughout the Soviet Union.
11. Moscow and Leningrad are permitted only one deputy for every 400 voters.
12. This also applies to permanently residing foreigners of the same class.
13. Some members of these groups may under certain conditions obtain the right to vote by petitioning the appropriate central executive committee.

Kulakov, *Konstitutsiya S. S. S. R. v. Schemach,* pp. 73-80. Bolshevik writers are indignant at the accusations abroad that only a small part of the adult population is permitted to vote. The figures of the 1926 municipal elections show that in 360 urban communes in R. S. F. S. R. only 4.8 per cent of the population was denied the vote. Whereas in 1923 about 92 per cent of the people of over eighteen years of age was allowed to exercise the franchise, in 1926 practically 95 per cent of the adult population took part in the elections.
Chugunov, *Gorodskiye Sovety,* pp. 34-35.

14. By a law passed in 1928 and elaborated in 1929, cities of over 100,000 inhabitants are permitted to organize ward (raion) soviets. Deputies may be members of both ward and city soviets. *Sobraniye Uzakonenii,* No. 85, Article 354.

15. The commission may appoint a sub-commission to compile lists of the non-organized elements of the community in various parts of the city.

16. In recent years regular electoral campaigns have been conducted and candidates recommended by means of advertisements in the press and the distribution of campaign literature. It is interesting to note that the non-party elements are largely represented in city soviets and frequently form a majority, although the leadership is still with the Communists.

17. An unusual phase of soviet elections is that alternates are also elected.

18. *Polozheniye o Gorodskich Sovetach* (1925), Chapter 6.

19. City soviets frequently meet at factories and shops for the convenience of members and private citizens.

20. *Polozheniye o Gorodskich Sovetach* (1925), Chapter 4.

21. The actual carrying out of measures is left to the militsia (police) and G. P. U. (State Political Administration).

22. This provision applies only to cities which are seats of governmental divisions.

23. *Sobraniye Uzakonenii* (May 30, 1932), No. 44, Section 196.

24. The city soviet must also take care of the cultural needs of national minorities within its territory.

25. *Polozheniye o Gorodskich Sovetach* (1925), Chapter 3.

26. See the writer's article on *Municipal Government in Soviet Russia,* in the *National Municipal Review* for December 1929.

27. This provision was applicable only to municipalities which constituted seats of governmental divisions, but this number practically included most cities and towns of any importance; *Polozheniye o Sovetach* (1922), Sections 8-9.

28. In practice a group of three members of the presidium, variously known as the bureau of the presidium, the working trio, etc., represents the city in all its official business; this smaller collegial executive is generally composed of the president, his deputy, and secretary.

29. The vice-president of the city soviet is frequently the director of this department.

30. *Polozheniye o Gorodskich Sovetach* (1925), Section 19. *Sobraniye Uzakonenii,* No. 11, Section 119. Some Bolshevik writers on municipal government are dissatisfied with this linking of city management with county and provincial machinery. They urge more freedom in city affairs and lessening of cumbersome supervision by higher soviets. See Chugunov,*Gorodskiye Sovety,* p. 89; Elistratov, *Administrativnoye Pravo,* p. 92. Conversely, others justify it on the grounds that the creation of an independent city executive committee would create misunderstandings between it and the higher executive committee located in the same territory. The obvious reason for this arrangement, however, may be found in the reluctance of the Soviet central authorities to permit too much local independence, especially since the suffrage has been widened to an extent as to permit non-party majorities in city soviets.

31. *Sobraniye Uzakonenii* (1929), No. 11, Article 119.

32. *Polozheniye o Gorodskich Sovetach* (1925), Chapter 5, Sections 45-61.

CHAPTER V

1. From the above statement, it may be deduced that the city soviets have only nominal authority in budget making, the real power being lodged with central authorities.

2. City soviets may, however, appeal rulings of higher soviets to central authorities, but while action is pending, appealed decisions are not suspended. The Financial Decree designates in detail the classes of taxpayers and those exempted or granted reduction of taxes.

3. *Sobraniye Zakonov* (January 24, 1932), Part I, No. 2.

4. City soviets may negotiate with state coöperative institutions, and private persons in the Soviet Union and abroad; the latter, however, is out of the question at present. They may also issue bonds and certificates of indebtedness.

5. Some Bolshevik municipal authorities suggest that the following sources of revenue should be transferred to cities:

    Profits from mineral resources within the jurisdiction of the cities.

    Parts of profits from state enterprises which have been delegated to city management.

    Taxes on incoming and outgoing freight, transported by rail or water.

    Fees paid on business transactions at various exchanges located in city territory. See Chugunov, *Gorodskiye Sovety*, pp. 145-147.

6. Special schools for the study of history, civics, and social ethics from a Marxian standpoint.

7. Th state supplies part of the funds for this purpose.

8. The Financial Decree instructs executive committees to authorize city soviets to widen their fields of activity only in proportion to the increase of their financial resources.

9. This does not apply to the expenses in connection with the election to the city soviet itself, but to congresses of soviets only.

10. These accounts are kept separate and are not included in the budget.

11. The practical administration of the funds is in the hands of the directors of the municipal branches of executive committees.

12. Urban land utilization, like any other activity, is controlled by the central government. See *O Zemlinich Poryadkach v Gorodach.*

13. It is interesting to note the meaning of the legal provision in regard to land under the jurisdiction of city soviets. The special decrees of the commissariats of agriculture and interior, issued July 18, 1923, in connection with the promulgation of the Land Code, explicitly stated "that all those lands are to be considered under the jurisdiction of city soviets and included in the urban domain which are given over by order of city soviets to the use of the city population through the agency of various coöperatives or organizations. In this class are also to be included lands which were used for parks, playgrounds, etc., and lands which were subject to municipal taxes and assessments prior to August 1, 1922." On the the other hand, "city plots which are in use by city dwellers for agricultural purposes, meadows, pastures, and truck gardens by permission of city soviets are not included in city territory, if they were made use of for such purposes prior to August 1, 1922."
Some of the instructions are not quite clear and are contradictory, as they take for granted the existence of municipal organizations throughout the Soviet land. As a matter of fact very few cities had municipal governmental organization prior to 1925. See Chugunov, *Gorodskiye Sovety,* pp. 157, 158.

14. This provision complicates the situation, since certain agricultural lands adjacent to new urban centers, though outside of the city limits, were subject to city authorities. Yet under the new ruling these lands may still be used by municipal agencies and remain a part of cantonal (volost) territory. It also may be noted that prior to 1927 city boundaries in many urban communities had not been determined at all. To be sure, by the decree of December 7, 1925, the All-Russian Central Executive Committee and the Council of People's Commissars, all municipalities in Soviet Russia proper were ordered to establish boundary lines by January 1, 1929. Compliance with this decree was, however, retarded by litiga-

tions on the part of users of agricultural lands opposed to city annexation.

15. This provision, however, operates only in part, since it was passed on April 13, 1925, previous to the last municipal decree.

16. Any disagreement is settled between various interested parties and the provincial executive committee.

17. The authorities under whose jurisdiction the above properties are placed must come to an agreement with municipal authorities in regard to measures of public welfare, such as fire prevention, sanitary rules, etc. All misunderstandings are decided by the commissar of the interior.

In cases of certain lands set aside for local or state institutions, coöperatives, etc., the municipal bodies are limited in their authority by certain provisions. From the above it is clear, therefore, that certain sites of city lands may be held by general legal provisions, by special regulations of central authorities, by local ordinance, and by agreement between municipal authorities with the users of the land.

18. More than a hundred cities in Soviet Russian have already worked out definite plans which are followed in carrying out of new constructions.

19. The city may charge for lots in cemeteries.

20. The project of the State Planning Commission calls for removal of industrial plants to the outskirts of the city. Whereas this is frequently impossible in the case of old cities, it is followed in the planning of the so-called new cities.

21. *Sobraniye Uzakonenii* (1929), No. 10, Article 111. Sobraniye Uzakonenii (1929), No. 1, Section 1.

CHAPTER VI

1. *Sobraniye Uzakonenii,* No. 82, Section 827.

2. *Sobraniye Uzakonenii,* No. 51, Section 333.

3. *Land Code,* Article 52.

4. The secretary does not necessarily have to be a member of the village soviet.

5. *Sobraniye Uzakonenii* (1924), No. 28, Article 266; No. 2, Article 25; No. 8, Article 78. *Instruktsia N. K. U. D.* (June 27, 1927). Elistratov, *Administrativnoye Pravo,* pp. 84, 85. *Sprvochnik Selskovo Soveta* (1930).

6. *Land Code,* Article 28.

7. *Sobraniye Uzakonenii* (1929), No. 3, Article 32; No. 1, Article 3; No. 28, Article 292.

8. *Osnovnye Polozheniye ob organizatsii selskich Sovetach v S. S. S. R. ot 3 fevralya 1930 g., Isvestiya* (1930), No. 65. *Polozheniye o selskich Sovetach R. S. F. S. R. ot 1 yanvarya 1931; Vlast Sovetov* (March 1931), No. 8.

CHAPTER VII

1. Raions which have highly developed local industries and considerable communal property may, with the permission of the presidium of the All-Russian Executive Committee, form a technical department of road building.

2. Chelyapov, (ed.) *Osnovy Sovetskovo Stroitelstva,* p. 160. *Sobraniye Zakonov* (June 9, 1931), No. 36; *Sobraniye Uzakonenii* (March 26, 1931), No. 11.

3. *Vlast Sovetov* (1931), No. 12.

4. From the newspaper *Kolotushka* (May 1930), as quoted in *Administrativnye Organy v Novych Uslovyach,* p. 36.

5. Chelyapov, (ed.) *Osnovy Sovetskovo Stroitelstva,* Chapter VII.

6. See Elistratov, *Administrativnoye Pravo,* pp. 143, 144.

7. For an account of subjects upon which local organs may pass decrees see pp. 110, 111.

8. The judiciary is not separated from the political functions of the state, but as will be shown later, has been created for the purpose of administering not impartial but proletarian justice. The issuance of normative acts by various departments of governments is still characterized by an absence of uniformity. Elistratov, *Administrativnoye Pravo,* pp. 146, 147.

CHAPTER VIII

1. Michailov, *Mestnoye Sovetsckoye Upravleniye*, pp. 39-41.
2. *Constitution of the R. S. F. S. R.*, Section 58.
3. This is, of course, true of the identical organs in all other republics.
4. This differentiation between obligatory decrees and instructions and circulars seems to contradict the rule stated by Bolshevik jurisprudence in regard to the issuance of obligatory decrees; namely, that obligatory decrees are applied equally to private persons, to state institutions and undertakings, and to public organizations, and that officials are subject to the same punishment for violations as private persons. Soviet publicists attempt to reconcile this seeming contradiction by stating that this rule has no intention whatsoever to mix the obligatory ordinances for citizens and instructions for officials; that is, it is intended for those instances in which certain obligations that have been established by obligatory decrees happen to be the same for citizens and officials; as for instance, removing rubbish and snow from streets and yards is obligatory for private owners, house administrations, and the management of buildings occupied by state institutions and undertakings. These special instances do not in any way destroy the principal difference between obligatory decrees and instructions. Kolesnikov, *Vlast Sovetov* (1923), Nos. 8 and 9, p. 13. Elistratov, *Administrativnoye Pravo*, pp. 141, 142.
5. *Constitution R. S. F. S. R.*, Article 3.
6. *Constitution R. S. F. S. R.*, Article 44.
7. In practice this rule is not observed.
8. *Constitution R. S. F. S. R.*, Article 26.
9. *Constitution R. S. F. S. R.*, Article 33.
10. This also applies to the rest of the constituent republics of the Soviet Union.
11. Did not become a full fledged commissariat until 1932.
12. Decree in regard to the creation of the commissariat of communal economy (Narkochoz) was issued December 10, 1931, by the All-Russian Central Executive Committee and Council of People's Commissars, based on legislation of the Central

Executive Committee of the Union. *Sobraniye Uzakonenii* (January 18, 1932), No. 3.

13. Practically all these provisions apply to all other constituent republics and to a more limited extent to the autonomous republics.

14. *The Constitution of the U. S. S. R.*, Chapter V.

15. Ananov, *Ocherki Federalnovo Upravleniye S. S. S. R.*, Chapter V; *Polozheniye o narodnom komissariate po inostrannym delam S. S. S. R.* A translation of this document may be found in Batsell, *Soviet Rule in Russia*, pp. 622-627.

16. In time of war there is appointed a Commander-in-Chief of all Armed Forces, who is perhaps the most important member of the Council.

17. Ananov, *Ocherki Federalnovo Upravleniye S. S. S. R.*, pp. 81-88.

18. *Polozheniye o norodnom komissariate vneshnoi torgovli S. S. S. R.*; Ananov, *Ocherki Federalnovo Upravleniye S. S. S. R.*, pp. 98-105.

19. February 27, 1932; *Sobraniye Zakonov* (March 5, 1932), No. 16.

20. Ananov, *Ocherki Federalnovo Upravleniye* pp. 93-96, 164-168.

21. Ananov, *Ocherki Federalnovo Upravleniye,* pp. 118 and 122; *Polozheniye o narodnom kommissariate truda S. S. S. R.*

22. Ananov, *Ocherki Federalnovo Upravleniye,* pp. 124-134; *Polozheniye o norodnom kommissariate rabochekrestyanskoi inspectsii S. S. S. R.* An English translation of this decree may be found in Batsell, *Soviet Rule in Russia* pp. 611-618.

23. Decree of the Council of People's Commissars of the U. S. S. R. (August 21, 1923). For English translation see Batsell, *Soviet Rule in Russia,* pp. 620-622.

24. For a discussion of this body see pp. 245-249.

25. One of the outstanding members of the S. T. O. is Stalin, who entered its membership in 1930.

26. Batsell, *Soviet Rule in Russia,* pp. 618-620.

CHAPTER IX

1. The people's commissariat of Workman-Peasant Inspection, also known from its abbreviations as *Rabkrin,* or *R. K. I.*

2. Elistratov, *Administrativnoye Pravo,* p. 125n.

3. *Sobraniye Uzakonenii* (1917), No. 3; (1918), No. 15, Article 217; (1921), No. 62, Article 792; Elistratov, *Administrativnoye Pravo,* pp. 123-125.

4. *Sobraniye Uzakonenii* (1927), No. 59, Article 588; No. 97, Article 647.

5. *Sobraniye Uzakonenii* (1926), No. 66, Article 502; No. 77, Article 627.

6. The following services are exempt from the above rule: the postal-telegraph service (with exception of those employed in the central bureau); teachers, lectures, librarians in all scientific, educational, and social institutions; artists and musicians in state theatres and studios; physicians in various institutions of the people's commissariat of health; agricultural experts, surveyors, entomologists, and various technicians in experimental stations of the commissariat of agriculture; *Sobraniye Uzakonenii* (1924), No. 1, Article 2.

7. Exceptions are made in many cases of scientific, technical, and educational activities such as lecturing by experts, writing for and editing periodicals, medical practice, and accessory service in coöperatives of a given department. Membership in special and permanent commissions of inter-bureau or bureau character may be permitted if in accordance with rules laid down by the directorates of the respective departments. The participation of experts of other departments in the work of the Gosplan (State Planning Commission) is encouraged. Elistratov, *Administrativnoye Pravo,* p. 127n.

8. *Sobraniye Uzakonenii* (1926), No. 63, Article 494.

9. The learned professions, service in the militsia (police), G. P. U., and military forces are regulated by special decrees. The service in the learned professions is regulated by a decree on January 21, 1924, and positions of instructors in labor faculties by a decree of June 28, of the same year.

10. Since 1925, common-school teachers, librarians, and other educational workers have received pensions after twenty-five years of service. Those remaining on duty after the specified period receive half the amount of their pension. Upon the death of the pensioner, his dependents are entitled to specified parts of the pension. Generally, teachers' pensions amount to about two hundred and forty rubles a year.

11. For a statistical survey, see *Gosudarstvennyi Apparat S. S. S. R.* (1929); Vladimirova and Syrkin, *Chistka Gosapparata i Borba s Burokratismom.*

12. *Polozheniye o Sudoustroitstve,* in *Sobraniye Uzakonenii* (1922), No. 69, Section 902; (1926), No. 85, Section 624; *Sobraniye Zakonov* (1924), No. 21, Section 185; No. 25, Section 216; (1930), No. 2, Section 10, Part 1; Krylenko, *Sud i Pravo v S. S. S. R.* Parts I and II; Zelitch, *Soviet Administration of Criminal Law,* Chapter II.

13. The above is a free translation of some of the passages of Krylenko's interpretation of the preamble to the decree in regard to court structure; Krylenko, *Sud i Pravo, Part I,* pp. 27, 28.

14. In autonomous republics the superior court is known as the highest or principal court. Changes in the organization required by special, cultural, economic, and administrative conditions may only be made by permission of the presidium of the Central Executive Committee of the U. S. S. R.

15. Whatever is said of this court in Russia proper also applies to the supreme courts in all other constituent republics.

16. *Ugolovno-Protsesualny Kodex R. S. F. S. R.* (1927), Section 449, sub-sections 1 and 2.

17. The Cassational division of the Supreme Court, unlike the cassational division of the intermediate courts, is authorized, subject to approval of the presidium of the Central Executive Committee, to reduce the original sentence below the minimum provided for by the Criminal Code.

18. *Judiciary Act of 1926,* Section 59, sub-section a., as quoted in Zelitch, *Soviet Administration of Criminal Law,* p. 123.

19. Zelitch, *Soviet Administration of Criminal Law,* pp. 115-128.

20. Zelitch, *Soviet Administration of Criminal Law,* pp. 128-135. Since private practice by lawyers has been abolished, there has been organized a *College of Advocates* which is supervised by the courts. It is the purpose of this organization to render advice and aid to the population at a stipulated honorarium, or free of charge in cases where the clients are, in the opinion of the court, too poor to pay for the services. The College of Advocates is at present merely under sufferance, and many arguments are advanced for its abolition. Some Bolshevik leaders claim that in a proletarian state no lawyers are necessary and all legal advice should be rendered by labor and professional organizations.

21. For a discussion on this point see Zelitch, *Soviet Administration of Criminal Law* pp. 98-104.

22. The Supreme Court also has original jurisdiction in civil cases in the matter of disputes between constituent republics.

23. The decision of the regular criminal and civil departments and the special session cannot be appealed by way of cascation, but a complaint may be made to the plenum of the Supreme Court of the Union, under specified restrictions.

24. Military tribunals are organized at the various military divisions. The judges are appointed and dismissed by the military division of the Supreme Court of the Union. These tribunals have jurisdiction over a variety of military offenses.

25. *The Constitution of the U. S. S. R.,* Chapter VII; *Polozheniye o Verchovnom Sude S. S. S. R. i prokuraturi Verchovnovo Suda S. S. S. R., Sobraniye Zakonov* (1929) No. 5, Section 445. Zelitch, *Soviet Administration of Criminal Law,* pp. 95-111.

PART II

CHAPTER X

1. The authority to issue these ordinances was given to local organs (executive committees) in a circular of the presidium of the All-Russian Central Executive Committee dated May 11, 1921; *Sobraniye Uzakonenii,* No. 52, Article 310.

2. The decree of June 23 did not apply to the Cheka and other extraordinary commissions and tribunals and to localities under martial law. Elistratov, *Administrativnoye Pravo.*

3. *Sobraniye Uzakonenii* (1929), No. 13, Article 148.

4. Now abolished.

5. In the chief cities of the oblast the heads of the oblast administrative division exercise the authority of imposing administrative punishment.

6. Non bis in idem.

7. Elistratov, *Administrativnoye Pravo,* pp. 153-158.

8. *Ispravitelno-trudovoi Kodeks,* Articles 23 - 43. *Sobraniye Uzakonenii* (1926), No. 6, Article 462.

9. Officials may be punished for wrongfully imposing fines. Fines may also be imposed for law breaking as stipulated by the Criminal Code in connection with violation of special regulations of various governmental organs. Certain serious disregards of law are also punished by fines in administrative order, as for instance, smuggling (first offense), poaching, breaking of sanitary, fire, and labor regulations, and the failure to register births. The total number of persons who were subject to administrative penalties between July 1, 1924 and June 30, 1925 in Russia proper was 1,023,106; for the same period between 1925-1926, 1,532,795 (an increase of almost 50%); between 1926-27, 1,520,818; after that period there was a noticeable decrease. The average fine in the second half of 1924 amounted to eleven rubles, eighty-eight kopeks, which decreased the first half of 1927 to an average of five rubles, sixteen kopeks. Between January and June 1927, the

administrative fines imposed in Russia proper amounted to 3,191,000 rubles. 53% of this sum were fines in rural districts. Elistratov, *Administrativnoye Pravo*, p. 162 n2.

10. See Borodin, in *Administrativny Vestnik* (1927), Nos. 7 and 8, pp. 17ff.

11. The chiefs of the militsia (police) of Moscow and Leningrad may impose fines not to exceed ten rubles; chiefs of militsia in general may impose fines not to exceed five rubles in towns, and in other urban settlements not to exceed three rubles.

12. *Sobraniye Uzakonenii* (1931), No. 17.

13. Persons under eighteen years of age, men over forty-five years of age, women over forty, women with children under eight years of age, and persons incapacitated by illness or injuries may be exempted by special order of appropriate organs.

14. Article 61. The first refusal, administrative penalty imposed by appropriate authority within the limits of the law; second time, deprivation of liberty not to exceed six months or a fine as defined by law for that category of infraction. If a group of people by a previous understanding refuse to render the service, they may be punished by compulsory labor not to exceed one year or a fine the double of one imposed on individuals for the same category of offense.

15. *Decree of the All-Russian Central Executive Committee and Council of People's Commissars,* dated June 18, 1927.

16. Usually poor peasants.

17. *Decree of All-Russian Central Executive Committee,* dated April 1, 1929.

18. *Lumber Operations of the Third Year of the Five Year Period, Sobraniye Uzakonenii* (1930), No. 9, Section 107.

19. Reported in the Moscow Za *Industralizatsiiu* (September 25, 1930).

20. *Sovetskaya Yustitia* (April 10, 1931), No. 12.

21. *Moscow Bulletin of Financial and Economic Legislation* (1929), No. 8, p. 56; No. 26, p. 35.

22. *Corrective Code,* Article 34.

23. Shirvindt and Utevsky, *Soviet Corrective Labor Law.*

24. The O. G. P. U. is in charge of the various categories of political criminals.

25. *Corrective Labor Code,* Article 79.

26. Shirvindt and Utevsky, *Soviet Corrective Labor Law.*

27. An enumeration of the subject matter of the decrees will give the reader an idea of the magnitude and revolutionary character of the legislation. I communication: (1) railways, (2) ships and shipping, and (3) telephone; II financial: (1) banks and banking, (2) coupons and dividends, (3) currency and valuable papers, (4) interest bearing papers, (5) gold and platinum, (6) societies of mutual credit, and (7) state loans; III foreigners (non-residents); IV industry: (1) general, (2) chemical, (3) fur, (4) grain elevators, (5) mining, (6) rubber, (7) sugar, and (8) textile; V inheritance; VI insurance; VII land and real property; VIII personal property: (1) agricultural machinery, (2) automotive property, (3) baggage, merchandise, freight, (4) coupons and dividends, (5) interest bearing papers, (6) liquid capital, (7) metals, (8) personal property of bourgeoisie in warehouses, (9) property of expatriates or persons in hiding, (10) property and creditors of deceased persons, (11) safe deposit boxes, and (12) scientific, literary, musical, and artistic productions and creations; IX trade: (1) general and (2) foreign.

28. This decree was modified by later legislation.

29. All valuables enumerated before as subject to confiscation could be taken from travellers.

30. The above data were obtained from the *Collection of Laws and Decrees of the Workers'-Peasants' Government,* published in Moscow in 1921.

31. *Sobraniye Uzakonenii* (1925), No. 43, Section 322.

32. For a good journalistic description see Baldwin, *Liberty Under the Soviets,* Chapter 16.

33. The fines and punishment vary from one month to one year of imprisonment, and a fine up to one hundred rubles imposed in administrative order.

34. Martial law may be declared on railroads, factories, plants, and warehouses in accordance with special rules.

35. *Sobraniye Uzakonenii,* No. 29, Article 225; No. 21, Article 249; *Polozheniye o chrezvychainich merach ochrany revolutsionnavo poriadka,* dated April 3, 1925.

CHAPTER XI

1. *Decree of November* 24, 1917.

2. November 30, 1918.

3. Lenin, *Collected Works,* Volume XVI, p. 149.

4. Lenin, *Collected Works,* Volume XVI, p. 303.

5. Names of Russian provinces.

6. Lenin, *Collected Works,* Volume XVIII, Part 2, p. 415.

7. There has been considerable difference of opinion in regard to the conception of unity of revolutionary legality. Some Bolshevik authorities claim that the revolutionary legality demands the revision of the norms of law from the standpoint of revolutionary expediency and therefore the question of expediency ought to rule over the form of law. See Solc, *Isvestiya C. I. K. and Pravda* (November 24, 1925). Other Bolsheviks, on the other hand, agree with Lenin. See Krylenko, *Statyi o revolutsionoi Zakonnosti;* and Yachontov, in *Sovetskoye Pravo* (1926), No. 1.

8. Obligatory ordinances of the lower executive committees must be forwarded to the prosecuting attorney not later than two days after their issuance.

9. *O Borbe s Nedostatkami Gosapparata.*

10. A number of organizations in Moscow apply directly to the R. K. I. for the solution of some of their difficulties.

11. *O Borbe s Nedostatkami Gosapparata.*

12. *Sobraniye Uzakonenii,* Nos. 1 and 2, Article 7.

13. *Decree of the All-Russian Central Executive Committee* (April 9, 1919).

14. See p. 129.

15. *Sobraniye Uzakonenii,* No. 23, Articles 271 and 272.

16. *Sobraniye Uzakonenii,* No. 23, Article 271; No. 49, Article 254.

17. *Circular of the All-Russian Central Executive Committee,* dated June 30, 1921.

18. January 9, 1932.

19. *Sobraniye Uzakonenii,* No. 32, Article 384.

20. *Cirkular ot 9 oktyabraya 1924,* No. 459; *i 1925 goda* No. 1.

21. The Soviets inherited from the tsarist régime the old state apparatus composed for the most part of inimical elements and therefore, the Soviet government has ever been suspicions of its civil servants.

22. *Civil Code,* Articles 23, 24, and 21.

23. *Criminal Code,* Articles 112, 120, 128, 113, and 121.

24. The above mentioned disciplinary rules provide for penalties for violation of labor discipline which cannot be considered as misdemeanors, as for instance conversations during working hours, the appearance in an intoxicated condition, discourtesy to visitors, etc. Disciplinary penalties are imposed upon civil service employees. The term civil service does not necessarily mean only those persons who are employed by the Soviet governmental bureaus; in accordance with the Criminal Code, civil service employees are defined as persons who are permanently or temporarily employed in state institutions, organizations, and associations which are in accordance with the provisions of law, created for the carrying out of definite tasks of economic, administrative, and professional nature, and others of a general state character. In addition to that, employed persons and officials of professional unions may be held responsible under these rules for embezzlement, bribery, etc. Up to recent times, disciplinary penalties were imposed either by special disciplinary courts or by superiors, but at present the regular courts have jurisdiction in the more serious violations.

Disciplinary courts were organized in 1923 in order to deal with service negligence, misdemeanors, and any irregular activity of employees who were occupying responsible positions in governmental institutions, in all cases where their action would not justify prosecution in accordance with criminal law. At first there was organized a chief disciplinary court under the All-Russian Central Executive committee and disciplinary courts under the provincial and regional executive committees. In 1926 there was organized a group of disciplinary courts in circuits and in districts. In order to eliminate any kind of privileges for the workers in the apparatus, the disciplinary courts, in accordance with a resolution of the fifteenth Congress of the Communist Party, were abolished, and all the state employees became responsible equally with others to the general civil courts. There has been a tendency among some organizations to soften the punishment of party members, but Lenin's opinion that communists, if apprehended in any service misdemeanors ought to be punished more severely than those who are not communists, no matter how high a position a person may hold, is generally put into practice at the present time. *Izvestiya N. K. truda S. S. S. R.* (1926), Nos. 45 and 46. *Polozheniye o dissudach 14 iuna 1926.* Sobraniye Uzakonenii, No. 36, Section 291.

25. Earlier laws passed in 1921 stipulated at the first offense a subordinate was to be publicly reprimanded, which action was to be published in the press, and he might also be subject to arrest not to exceed two weeks; but a short time afterwards the arrest was abolished, and consequently the only disciplinary action a superior could take in regard to the irregularities of subordinates was a public reprimand.

26. The provisions of the disciplinary decrees do not cover all of the state employees. In accordance with the special enactments, persons who are in the ranks of the Red Army performing compulsory service, members of the militsia, employees of penal institutions, and members of the G. P. U. may be subject to arrest in the line of disciplinary punishment.

27. *Sobraniye Uzakonenii* (March 20, 1932), No. 32.

28. *Polozheniye o disciplinarnoi otvetsvennosti v poryadke poschinennosti; 4 Iyulya 1927; Civil Code,* Article 407.

29. That is, cases in which a person has transferred property to institutions or to a civil employee, in accordance with the demands of the law, judicial decisions, or cases in accordance with regulations established by appropriate officials which later were adjudged illegal by competent authority.

30. Article 406.

31. *Sobraniye Uzakonenni* (1927), No. 38, Article 248. See Elistratov, *Administrativnoye Pravo*, p. 280.

32. *Postanovleniye VTsIK i S. N. K. o reorganizatsii N. K. R. K. I.*

33. See Chelyapov, *Osnovy Sovetskovo Stroitelstva*, p. 202.

CHAPTER XII

1. As quoted in Baldwin, *Liberty Under the Soviets,* pp. 19, 20.

2. *Ugolovno-protsesualny Kodeks R. S. F. S. R.,* Articles 100 and 103.

3. This last clause, of course, opens a way to abuse, and tends to nullify a rather liberal legal provision as to the inviolability of private dwellings.

4. *Sobraniye Uzakonenii* (1928), No. 5, Section 43.

5. For a discussion of the police, see Chapter XV.

6. *Sobraniye Uzakonenii,* No. 73, p. 792.

7. The work book also served the purpose of a census on available labor resources of the country at a time when the Soviets were engaged in a life and death struggle.

8. The practice under the tsarist régime, to exile all persons who did not possess permission to live in certain districts to places of their birth, was abolished by law in 1923.

9. This statement will have to be considerably modified if a news dispatch dated January 21, 1933, is to be given credence. In accordance with the dispatch all persons living in the larger cities will have to obtain passports by January 25, 1933. This reversal to the method of tsarist days is excused on the ground that great numbers of "socially" useless

persons have crowded into the cities and have usurped space belonging by right to those engaged in necessary work. Hence only certain classes of population will be issued passports; the rest, to whom the issuance of passports will be denied, will have to leave the cities for smaller communities.

10. *Constitution of the R. S. F. S. R.,* Article 12.

11. *The Constitution of the R. S. F. S. R.,* Articles 15 and 16, in McBain and Rogers, *The New Constitutions of Europe,* p. 388.

12. This decree does not apply to professional unions, since these are provided for in the Labor Code. See *Labor Code,* Articles 151 and 152.

13. Some Bolshevik writers state that this characterization is misleading since not only cultural organizations are devoid of profit purposes, but also in certain cases, stock companies are not organized for the purpose of profit; for example the articles of incorporation of some stock companies provide that no profit shall be distributed among the members, but be devoted to cultural, educational, and other similar purposes. The same may be said of certain industrial artels, which are organized for the purpose of pooling physical and mental effort. They are conducted under a coöperative agreement, and the remuneration which is received is merely wages for actual labor performed, and hence there cannot be any talk of profit. See Danilov, *Osnovy Sovetskovo Prava,* pp. 214, 215.

14. National organizations are regulated by a special Union decree issued May 9, 1924.

15. On the first of July 1924 there were in R. S. F. S. R., not counting the autonomous republics, 545 associations; in 1925 there were 933; in 1926 there were 1137; the first of January 1927, 1,209. Within a period of two and one-half years the number of associations has been more than doubled. More than 33 per cent of all the organizations were of an educational and scientific-technical character; over 19 per cent, of mutual aid; and 18 per cent, of a cultural educational nature. These three groups represent three-fourths of all the existing associations. The associations which operate throughout

the territory of the Soviet Union comprise over 5 per cent of all associations, over 36 per cent operate within provincial and regional territory, over 28 per cent are urban associations, over 24 per cent are of circuit and district extent, and 5 per cent operate in canton and economic districts and in individual rural localities. The majority of these organizations, nearly 65 per cent, are independent, the others are branches of Central Unions. The members in the majority of all the associations, in fact over 74 per cent, are employees and persons who perform intellectual labor; the rest of the associations are composed of laborers and peasants. The communistic element composed over 33 per cent, and non-party over 66 per cent. Elistratov, *Administrativnoye Pravo,* pp. 232, 233.

CHAPTER XIII

1. Krassikov, *Na cherkovnom fronte,* p. 41.

2. See *Circular of the people's commissariat of justice of the R. S. F. S. R.,* dated January 3, 1919, and also Gidulianov, *Otdeleniye cherkvi ot gosudarstva v S. S. S. R.,* p. 657.

3. *Constitution of the R. S. F. S. R.,* Article 4. The original provision of the constitution was far more liberal in regard to religious freedom, but the extreme Bolsheviks have pointed out that this provision is of bourgeois nature; they further pointed out that Marx in his mature years was opposed to this middle class conception and insisted upon anti-religious propaganda. However, the permission for religious propaganda must not be taken too seriously, since it merely means that sermons may be preached in established houses of worship, provided these sermons are not making too many converts.

4. See *Instruction of the people's commissariat of justice and the people's commissariat of interior,* dated June 19, 1923.

5. *Zakon ob obyazetelnoi voyennoi sluzhby* (September 18, 1925), Article 216.

6. This, of course, does not include church attendance or religious instruction at home.

7. *Sobraniye Uzakonenii* (1929), No. 35, Article 353.

8. Churches and buildings of historical, artistic, or archeological significance were transferred by special instruction to the people's commissariat of education. This action was to safeguard national monuments, art, and history.

9. The decisions of this commission are subject to confirmation of the presidium.

10. The action of these commissions are subject to confirmation of the central executive committees of the autonomous republics and regional executive committees.

11. *Sobraniye Uzakonenii* (June 15, 1931), No. 37, Section 248.

12. This may also be applied to Jewish synogogues and institutions of other religious faiths.

CHAPTER XIV

1. *Constitution of the R. S. F. S. R.,* Article 14.

2. Lenin, *Collected Works,* Volume XVI, pp. 39, 40.

3. The full designation is *Glavnoye upravleniye po delam leteratury i izdatelstv; Sobraniye Uzakonenii* (July 5, 1931), No. 31, Section 273.

4. In cases of special publications not to be found in the index, the G. P. U. refers the question to the Glavlit.

5. *Sobraniye Uzakonenii* (November 30, 1931), No. 71.

6. *Sobraniye Uzakonenii,* No. 24, Article 167.

7. Elistratov, *Administrativnoye Pravo,* p. 211. *Sobraniye Uzakonenii,* No. 93, Article 614.

8. *Sobraniye Uzakonenii* (1928), No. 2, Sections 16 and 17.

9. Exceptions are made in cases of well known popular artists who are permitted to perform in plays without previous censorship.

10. Local organs have no authority in this matter.

11. In order to facilitate the censorship of performances, all places of public amusement must reserve seats, not farther back than the fourth row, for the representatives of the censorship committee and the G. P. U.

12. Occasional performances may be given in places generally used for such purposes without special permission; however, information to that effect must be given three days before the performance. The local executive committees may issue detailed regulations as to the conduct of performances. In case of systematic violation of the rules by the performers and owners, their performanc may be stopped by the order of the appropriate executive committees or urban soviets. *Instruktsia N. K. V. D.* (October 29, 1927), No. 401.

CHAPTER XV

1. The Russian term for police is *militsia,* but in this discussion we shall use in most instances the more familiar term, police.

2. *Prikaz Glavnovo Upravleniye Militsii i U. G. R. O. pri S. N. K. R. S. F. S. R. ot 23/1 1931,* No. 7.

3. If conditions warrant, inter-raion police administrations may be organized with permission of chiefs of central militsia administration.

4. June 25, 1931.

5. *Decree of May 25, 1931,* Section 16.

6. The working schedule of the commanding staff is not definitely regulated.

7. In the Moscow region the pay of policemen is considerably higher; thus in the city proper, the pay of the ordinary policeman in sixty-one rubles and in rural districts, fifty-five rubles.

8. These benefits do not affect the benefits and pensions from the regular social insurance organs.

9. *Polozheniye o Rabotche Krestyanskoi Militsii; Sobraniye Zakonov S. S. S. R.* (May 31, 1931), No. 33; (February 21, 1931), No. 8.

10. Tenants moving into an apartment are entered by the porter (dvornik) into a registration book, which is taken at intervals to the police station to be checked and recorded.

11. These violations may be punished by arrest not to exceed three months or a fine not to exceed three hundred rubles.

12. *Criminal-procedural Code,* Article 100-103 and special instructions issued to organs of police, especially in regard to the activities of district inspection.

13. See *Circular of the commissariat of the interior* (January 13, 1927), No. 16. Of course, under certain circumstances, citizens must appear—such as in case of persons who were called out as witnesses or experts, or those called to report for mobilization or to render the necessary labor required by the state.

14. Women and invalids and persons of insufficient physical strength can be called upon only for purposes of summoning the nearest policeman, house porter, night watchman, or other officials, although they may also be used as messengers.

15. Soviet authorities are careful to differentiate between criminal (prestupnik) and prisoner (arestant); in the first instance are meant persons who have already been convicted by a court and adjudged guilty to be punished; in the second instance are meant persons whose cases are being investigated by the organs of prosecution and are being kept in detention. Thus arms are not to be used against persons who have not as yet been subject to investigation, although suspected of a crime.

16. *Prikaz Ts A. U.* (1924), No. 145. Elistratov, *Administrativnoye Pravo,* pp. 302-314.

17. The full designation is *Gosudarstvennoye Polititseskoe Upravleniye,* which means the *State Political Administration.* Very little reliable information is available on this subject. Several exposès have been published by alleged former members of the organization, but since it was impossible to check on their authenticity, no use was made of them in this work.

18. In 1923, after the formation of U. S. S. R., it became known as O. G. P. U., the "O", first letter of the word, signifying unified.

19. *The Constitution of the U. S. S. R.,* Chapter IX, Articles 61-63, and the *Decree* dated November 15, 1923 of the Central Executive Committee of the U. S. S. R. A good English translation may be found in Batsell, *Soviet Rule in Russia,* pp. 609 and 610.

20. The directing group of the Bolshevik Party.

21. The uniformed branch of the O. G. P. U. has received praise even from the opponents of the Soviet régime for its efficiency in preserving public order; but quite the contrary is said of the plain clothed agents, whose general practice is frequently reminiscent of the *Ochrana* of the tsarist days.

22. The generally accepted provisions of International Law as to immunity of diplomatic representatives are incorporated in Soviet law. This also applies to foreign merchantmen in Soviet ports. *Sobraniye Uzakonenii* (1928), No. 5, Articles 47 and 48; No. 52, Article 348.

23. *Decree of February 8, 1922,* as translated by Batsell in *Soviet Rule in Russia,* p. 608.

24. For a view on this point by an American writer, see *Anti-Soviet Concentration in Paris* by Pierre Van Paassen in *The Nation* (December 2, 1931), pp. 602-603.

CHAPTER XVI

1. The meat products were subject to examination in cities and larger villages. Black bread was not permitted to be sold for consumption before four hours had expired after baking.

2. For instance, the buying and selling of raw furs in designated rural regions of the country.

3. The rules in regard to the obtaining of hunting arms are closely related to the rules of hunting itself. All citizens who have reached majority, who have received a license, and have

paid the hunting tax have the right to hunt. Persons engaged in professional hunting in certain regions are exempt from these rules. The commissariat of agriculture has authority to issue licenses for this purpose. The old order, whereby the people desiring to purchase hunting knives had to register with local militsia, was repealed in 1927, and at the present time the permission to obtain hunting knives is issued by local administrative divisions.

4. A description of Internal and Foreign Trade may be found in Hoover, *The Economic Life of Soviet Russia,* Chapters V and VI.

5. For an excellent study of the Russian peasant before the Revolution see Robinson, *Rural Russia Under the Old Régime.* A short sketch on the same subject may be found in *Russia's Agrarian Problem* by Vera Micheles Dean, in *Foreign Policy Association Information Service* (July 23, 1930), Vol. VI, No. 10.

6. For a description of coöperative agricultural societies in Russia before the Revolution see Kayden and Antsiferov, *The Coöperative Movement in Russia During the War,* Chapters V and VI.

7. *Izvestia,* March 15, 1930.

8. The text of this model charter may be found in *Economic Review of the Soviet Union* (April 1, 1930), p. 127.

9. In an Associated Press news dispatch dated January 20, 1933, it was stated that the Soviet government has once more changed its tactics in the matter of grain collection. In accordance with this dispatch a decree was issued on January 20, 1933, whereby the entire system of grain collection has been scrapped and a tax in kind substituted. Under the new method a special tax in kind would be levied from each hectare sown by collective and individual farmers, the latter paying a higher rate. The prices for the levied product are fixed by the government; all that remains after paying the tax can be sold on the open market. Heavy penalties are provided for non-compliance with the law.

CHAPTER XVII

1. *The Industrial Life in Soviet Russia,* (published by the International Labor Office).

2. Local agencies of the Union commissariat of labor are established in the subordinate political units. *Sobraniye Zakonov S. S. S. R.* (1929), No. 69, Section 645.

3. *Moscow Izvestia* (January 11 and 13, 1931).

4. There are, of course, left very limited groups of persons engaged in private trade, manufacture, domestic handicraft work, etc. Most of the professions, such as medical, dental, and legal etc., are employed by the state. The clergy is in a class by itself.

5. The Soviet Union population is approximated at 160,000,000 persons, about 30,000,000 of whom reside in urban communes, and about 130,000,000 in rural or sparsely settled districts.

6. *Resolution of the people's commissariat of labor of the U. S. S. R.* dated December 23, 1930; *Moscow Bulletin of Financial and Economical Legislation* (January 7, 1931), No. 1, p. 56.

7. *Lumber Operations of the Third Year of the Five Year Period,* Archangel (1931), p. 40.

8. *Izvesttia* (December 18, 1930).

9. *Izvestia* (December 30, 1930).

10. The extent to which this punishment is imposed is unknown.

11. *Order of people's commissariat of labor of the U. S. S. R.,* dated December 17, 1930; *Moscow Izvestia* (December 1930).

12. After reading much material pro and con on so-called slave labor by free unconvicted men, I find myself unable to come to any definite conclusion since most of the data which have come to my attention were based on prejudiced conceptions one way or the other. It is a subject which ought to be investigated by impartial, scientific men who understand the ideas of Sovietism and its ultimate aims.

13. In accordance with a recent decree the central organizations of the labor unions have been joined with the commissariat of labor.

14. Exceptions were made for special classes, such as victims of counter-revolution and those injured in natural disasters, such as fire, floods, famine, etc.

15. The maximum allowances vary from 120 to 180 rubles a month, depending on the region.

16. See *Sobraniye Uzakonenii* (1928), No. 17, Sections 143, 146, and later amendments; (1929), No. 63, Sections 597-9; No. 65, Section 596; No. 63, Section 581.

17. A widower may also be granted a pension if he was dependent on his deceased wife.

18. Trained workers, technical experts, persons under eighteen years of age, former Red Army Soldiers, and a few other classes are exempt from this provision.

19. For the purpose of administering the social insurance schemes the country is divided into six geographical zones or districts.

20. *Resolutions of people's commissariat of labor of U.S.S.R.,* dated February 1927 and September 1928. The unemployment dole is practically suspended at the present time.

21. *Labor Code,* Chapter 17, Part I, Section III; *Sobraniye Zakonov* (May 1929), No. 32, Article 289.

CHAPTER XVIII

1. Factory workers and manual laborers, telegraph and telephone employees, physicians and nurses employed in certain institutions and villages, dentists, trained workers in institutions for defective children, teachers in villages and certain designated institutions, masseuses, athletic directors, artists, actors, newspaper workers, women connected with business enterprises, travelling inspectors and instructors, and post office employees.

2. In the question of division of opinion in regard to selection of schools for children, etc. the matter may be referred to the authorities for decision.

3. The law prescribes in detail the procedure which the wife must pursue in case of any danger to her property because of indebtedness or criminal offense of her husband.

4. Furniture and other household goods are retained by those who lived in the same household with the deceased.

5. A husband may not will, outside of his personal effects, his entire property to his wife. His share must be divided equally among all the members of the household, unless he and his wife were the only members of the household. In case of divorce the latter loses all the rights to her husband's share.

6. *Vlast Sovetov* (April 20, 1931), No. 11.

7. Field, *Protection of Women and Children in Soviet Russia.*

8. It frequently happened that unfortunate, unmarried mothers killed their babies in fits of despair.

9. M. G. *O vospitatelnich domach v Rossii, Archiv sudebnoi mediciny 1868,* Nos 1 and 4; *and 1869,* Books 1 and 3, as quoted in Elistratov, *Administrativnoye Pravo,* p. 345.

10. By a new decree issued on February 6, 1928, the question of finding patrons for the vagrant children was elucidated; executive committees were given the right to make agreements with peasants for a period of time no less than three years. The executive committees were supposed to supervise, in the interest of the children, the relation between the children and the patrons, to conduct a systematic supervision and control, and to draw into this work various public organizations, cantonal executive committees, and village soviets.

11. *Sobraniye Uzakonenii,* R. S. F. S. R., (July 1931), No. 38.

12. *Sobraniye Zakonov* (October 28, 1931), No. 61, Section 446.

CHAPTER XIX

1. In Russia in the time of Nicholas I there was organized a morals police after the French manner.

2. An official investigation made in 1889 brought out the fact that most of the prostitutes were women whom the economic order had thrown out of work, helpless women who found themselves far away from friends and relatives, and young girls, minors, who had not as yet developed strength of character and became easy victims of procurers and panders.

3. An ordinance in one Russian city stated that the best way in which a woman who held a "yellow ticket", could free herself from the stigma was for her to die. Bronner and Elistratov, *Prostitutsiya v Rossii.*

4. *Bulletin NKVD* (1923), No. 2.

5. Elistratov, *Administrativnoye Pravo,* pp. 324-333.

6. This does not apply in the case of the use of minors for immoral purposes, which is punished severely.

7. *Materialy mezhduvedomstvennoi kommissii po borbe s prostitutsiei* (first edition, 1921), p. 11.

8. The law, however, differentiates between the purely commercial enterprises and the individual home brewer who manufactured for his own use or for occasional sale because of poverty and unemployment. In the latter case the penalty is less severe.

9. By a decree passed April 8, 1929, the punishment for repeated illegal trade in alcoholic beverages was to be by summary criminal process and carried with it exile from the given territory. *Sobraniye Uzakonenii* (1929), No. 30, Section 316.

10. Educational campaigns are conducted, and various psychiatric and medical institutions are being made use of in this struggle against alcohol.

11. See *Izvestiya C. I. K.,* No. 261. The struggle against narcotics is being waged in Soviet Russia. At a scientific conference meeting in Moscow in December 1923, this entire question was discussed. It was found by the Moscow commissions that a great number of minors have been using

cocain and that there were persons in Soviet Russia who were willing to enrich themselves by the sale of this dangerous drug to anyone. The Criminal Code makes provisions for severe punishment of this type of vender. The manufacture of narcotics is concentrated in the hands of a state trust that works in connection with the people's commissariat of health which decides the annual output of narcotics necessary for medical purposes in the Soviet Union. The importations from abroad and purchases from native sources are directed to the people's commissariat of health and are delivered only by special permission of that commissariat. *Sobraniye Uzakonenii,* No. 85, Article 867.

12. Article 18.

13. *Sobraniye Uzakonenii* (October 8, 1929), No. 67, Section 659.

CHAPTER XX

1. Goode, *Schools, Teachers, and Scholars in Soviet Russia.*
   Nearing, *Education in Soviet Russia.*
   Wilson, *New School in New Russia.*
   Haines, *Health Work in Soviet Russia.*
   Harper, *Civic Training in Soviet Russia.*

2. Exceptions are being made in cases of institutions which are supported by village and cantonal budgets. The appointment, dismissal, and the transfer of personnel are retained by the economic district and district organs of public education and public health, respectively.

3. *Soviet Union Review* (September-October 1932), pp. 117-180; *Soviet Union Review* (November 1932), pp. 209-211.

4. Persons who are aware of having a venereal disease, and in spite of this knowledge, have had sexual intercourse with other persons may be punished by law.

5. *Ezhegodnik Sovetskovo Stroitelstva i Prava na 1931 god,* pp. 265-284.

BIBLIOGRAPHY

Administrativno-Territorialnoye Deleniye S. S. S. R. ("Adminis-trative-Territorial Division of the U. S. S. R.")

Administrativnyi Kodeks U. S. S. R. ("Administrative Code of the Ukraine S. S. R.")

Ananov, I. N. *Ocherki Federalnavo Upravleniye S. S. S. R.* ("Outlines of Federal Administration of the U. S. S. R.")

Archipov, K. *Sovetskiye Avtonomnye Oblasti i Respubliki* ("Soviet Autonomous Regions and Republics").

Archipov, I. *Zakon v Sovetskom Gosudarstve* ("The Law in the Soviet State").

Baldwin, Roger N. *Liberty Under the Soviets.*

Batsell, W. R. *Soviet Rule in Russia.*

Berezin, N. *Economitseskaya Politika S. S. S. R.* ("Economic Policy of the U. S. S. R.")

Brandenburgskii, Ia. N. *Iuriditseskaya Pomosht Nasileniyu* ("Legal Aid to the People").

Bronner, V. W. *Prostitutsia i Puti yeyo Likvidatsii* ("Prostitu-tion and the Ways for Its Eradication").

Chamberlin, William H. *Soviet Russia;* a living record and a history.

Chelyapov, N. (ed.) *Osnovy Sovetskavo Stroitelstva* ("Prin-ciples of Soviet Construction").

Chernytov, A. *Zakony o Rabote Selsoveta i Evo Sectsii, 1930* ("Laws in Regard to the Activities of the Village Soviet and Its Sections").

Chugunov, S. *Voprosy Organizatsii Nizovovo Sovetskovo Apparata—Gorsovety* ("Problems of Organization of the Lower Soviet Apparatus—City Soviets").

Chugunov, S. *Voprosy Organizatsii Nizovovo Sovetskovo Apparata — Selsovety* ("Problems of Organization of the Lower Soviet Apparatus—Village Soviets").

Cifrinovich, B. Osnovy Zadatsi Sovetskich Yaceiek ("The Ele-ments of the Problem of Soviet Cells").

Cypin, G. *Voprosy Vnutripartiinoi Demokratii* ("Problems of Inner-Party Democracy").

Deistvuyushteye Zakonodatelstvo o trude Soyuza S. S. S. R. i Soyuznych Respublic, tom II, 1931 ("Operative Legislation in Regard to Labor in the U. S. S. R. and Union Republics, Volume II, 1931").

Drezen, *Rukovodstvo po organizatsii upravlentseskavo apparata sovetskich uchrezhdenii* ("Directions in regard to Organization of the Administrative Apparatus of Soviet Establishments").

Eckhardt, Hans von, *Russia* (Translated by Catherine Allison Phillips).

Elistratov, A. I. *Administrativnoye Pravo* ("Administrative Law").

Essen, A. *Puti Stroitelstva S. S. S. R.* ("The Roads of Construction of the U. S. S. R.")

Ezhegodnik Sovetskovo Stroitelstva i Prava na 1931 god (za 1931 god) 1931 ("Year-Book of Soviet Construction and Law for 1931").

Field, Alice W. *Protection of Women and Children in Soviet Russia.*

God Raboty Pravitelstva (Pervyi God Payatiletki) (1928-1929) 1930. ("A Year of Work of the Government—First Year of the Five Year Plan—[1928-1929] 1930").

Gosudarstvenny Apparat S. S. S. R. ("The State Apparatus of the U. S. S. R.")

Grishin, (ed.) *V Borbe s Nedostatkam Gosapparata, 1931.* ("In the Struggle with the Deficiencies of the State Apparatus, 1931").

Gurvich, G. S. *Osnovy Sovetskoi Konstitutsii* ("Principles of the Soviet Constitution").

Harper, Samuel N. *Civil Training in Soviet Russia.*

Harper, Samuel N. *Making Bolsheviks.*

Hoover, Calvin B. *The Economic Life of Soviet Russia.*

Iaroslavsky, E. M. (ed.) *Kak Provodit Chistkii Partii* ("How to Carry on the Cleansing of the Party").

Ignatiev, V. I. *Sovet Natsionalnostei, C. I. K. S. S. S. R.* ("The Council of Nationalities, Central Executive Committee of the U. S. S. R.")

Ignatiev, V. K. *Sovetskii Stroi* ("The Soviet Régime").

Instruktsiya o Vyborach v Sovety i na S'ezdy Sovetov R. S. F. S. R., 1930 ("Instruction for Elections of Soviets and Congresses of Soviets, 1930").

Itogi XVI Vsesoyuznoi Konferentsii V. K. P. (b) ("Attainments of the XVI All-Union Conference of the All-Union Communist Party").

Kadry Gosularstvennovo i Kooperativnovo Apparata S. S. S. R. 1930 ("Cadres of the State and Coöperative Apparatus of the U. S. S. R.").

Kaganovitch, L. M. *Mestnoye Sovetskoye Samoupravleniye* ("Local Soviet Self-Government").

Kaganovitch, L. M. *Kak Postroyena V. K. P.* (b) ("The Structure of the All-Union Communist Party").

Kalendar-Ezhegodnik Kommunista na 1931 god ("Almanac-Year- Book of the Communist for 1931").

Kodeks Zakonov o Trude ("Labor Code").

Kolesnikov, *Sovetskoe Stroitelstvo* ("Soviet Construction").

Kotlyarevsky, S. A. *S. S. S. R. i Soyuznye Respubliki* ("The U. S. S. R. and the Union Republics").

Krylenko, *Sud i Pravo v S. S. S. R.* Two Volumes ("Courts and Law in the U. S. S. R.")

Kulakov, G. B. *Konstitutsia S. S. S. R. v Schemach* ("The Constitution of the U. S. S. R. in Topics").

Lagovier, N. *Kak obzhalovat prigovory i resheniye Suda* ("How to Appeal Sentences and Decisions of the Court").

Luzhin, A. and Rezunov, M. *Nizovoi Sovetsky Apparat 1929* ("The Lower Soviet Aparatus").

Mestnye Organy Vlasti, 1929, 1930 ("The Local Organs of Authority").

Mirkine-Guetzevitch, *La Theorie Genéral De L'etat Sovetique.*

Michailov, G. S. *Mestnoye Sovetskoye Upravleniye* ("Local Soviet Administration").

Mokeev, V. *Novy Zakon o Vyborach v Sovetach* ("The New Laws on Elections to Soviets").

Nemtsenko, M. *Natsionalnoye Razmezhevaniye Srednei Asii, 1925* ("The National Division of Middle Asia").

Nizovye Organy Vlasti, 1929 ("The Lower Organs of Authority").

Obolensky-Ossinsky, V. V. (et al.) *Social Economic Planning in the U. S. S. R.*

Pashukanis, E. B. (ed.) *Chrestomatiya po Gosudarstvennomu Ustroitstvu S. S. S. R.* ("Readings in State Organization of the U. S. S. R.")

Polozheniye o Selskich Sovetach ("The Decree in Regard to Village Soviets").

Prava Trudyatshei Zhentshiny ("The Rights of the Working Woman").

R. K. I. v Sovetskom Stroitelstve, Sovetsky Vostok, 1930 ("The R. K. I. in the Soviet Construction").

Robinson, G. T. *Rural Russia Under the Old Régime.*

Shabad-Zalgaller. T. *Prava Trudyatsheisya Zhentshiny v Brake i Pri Razvode* ("The Rights of the Working Woman in Marriage and Divorce").

Shirvindt, E. G. (ed.) *Administrativnye Organy v Novych Usloviyach* ("Administrative Organs Under New Conditions").

Shirvindt, E. G. (ed.) *Osnovy i Zadachi Sovetskoi Ugolovnoi Politiki* ("The Principles and Problems of Soviet Criminal Policy").

Shiryev, *Diszinplinarnaya Otvetsvennost Sluzhatschich* ("The Disciplinary Responsibility of Employees").

Sizonov, K. P. *Voprosy Sovetskovo Prava v Rekonstruktiony Period, 1931* ("Problems of Soviet Law in the Reconstruction Period").

Sobraniye Uzakonenii i rasporazhenii 1918-1932 ("Collection of Operative Laws and Decrees").

Sobraniye Zakonov ("Collection of Laws").

Soveshtaniye po voprosam Sovetskovo Stroitelsta, January 1925, ("Conferences on problems of Soviet Construction").

Sovety v Epoche Voennavo Kommunisma, Two Volumes, 1928 ("The Soviets in the Period of Military Communism").

Spravochnik Selskovo Soveta, 1930 ("Reference Book of the Village Soviet").

Stuchka, *Kurs Sovetskovo Grazhdankavo Prava* ("Course of Soviet Civil Law").

Stuchka, *Utseniye Gosudarstva,* 1926 ("The Science of the State").

Ugolovny Kodeks S. S. S. R. ("The Criminal Code of the U. S. S. R.").

Vilov, A. *Nizovoi Sovetsky Apparat,* 1930 ("The Lower Soviet Apparatus").

Vladimirovitch, *Chistka Gosapparata* ("The Cleansing of the State Apparatus").

Volispolkomy i Selsovety, 1924 ("Cantonal Executive Committees and Village Soviets").

Vsesoyuznoe Soveshtaniye po perevyboram Sovetov v 1929 god ("All-Union Conferences on Reëlection of Soviets in 1929").

Zelitch, Judah, *Soviet Administration of Criminal Law.*

Woody, Thomas, *New Minds: New Men?*

XVII Konferentsia Vsesoyuznoi Kommunistitseskoi Partii (b); Stenografitseski Ottchet ("The XVII Conference of the All - Union Communist Party [Bolshevik]; Stenographic Report").

PERIODICALS AND NEWSPAPERS

Administrativny Vestnik ("Administrative Messenger").

Sovetskoye Pravo ("Soviet Law").

Sovetskoye Stroitelstvo ("Soviet Construction").

Soviet Union Review.

Vlast Sovetov ("The Power of the Soviets").

Izvestiya ("Organ of the Central Executive Committee of the U. S. S. R. and of the All-Russian Central Executive Committee").

Pravda ("Organ of the Central Committee of the Communist Party").

INDEX